Louis Rose:
San Diego's First Jewish Settler and Entrepreneur

18 July 2005
For Karen + Gordon,
Whose love of art,
San Diego and Community
are inspirational,
with appreciation
Donald H. Harrison

Louis Rose:

San Diego's First Jewish Settler and Entrepreneur

by
Donald H. Harrison

Sunbelt Publications
San Diego, California

Louis Rose
Sunbelt Publications, Inc
Copyright © 2005 by the author
All rights reserved. First edition 2005

Edited by Laurie Gibson
Cover and book design by Leah Cooper
Project management by Jennifer Redmond
Published in cooperation with the Agency for Jewish Education.
Printed in the United States of America

Sunbelt Publications, Inc.
P.O. Box 191126
San Diego, CA 92159-1126
(619) 258-4911, fax: (619) 258-4916
www.sunbeltbooks.com

08 07 06 05 04   5 4 3 2 1

"Adventures in the Natural History and Cultural Heritage
of the Californias"
A Series Edited by Lowell Lindsay

Library of Congress Cataloging-in-Publication Data

Harrison, Donald H.
  Louis Rose, San Diego's first Jewish settler and entrepreneur / by Donald H.
Harrison.— 1st ed.
       p. cm. — (Adventures in the natural history and cultural heritage of the
Californias)
  Includes bibliographical references and index.
  ISBN 0-932653-68-5
  1. Rose, Louis, 1807-1888. 2. Jewish businesspeople—California—San
Diego—Biography. 3. Jews—California—San Diego—Social conditions—
19th century. 4. San Diego (Calif.)—Biography. I. Title. II. Series.
F869.S22H37 2004
979.4'985004924'0922—dc22
                                                                    2004019774

Cover Illustration "Louis Rose" courtesy of the San Diego Historical Society.
Background illustration from "Old Town Mural" courtesy Wells Fargo, Inc.

All photos by author unless otherwise credited

What People are Saying about Louis Rose:

A thoroughly researched and highly detailed look at San Diego's early development through the eyes of prominent Jewish merchant and settler Louis Rose (of Roseville and Rose Canyon fame). A partner of James Robinson in Old Town's Robinson-Rose building, Rose became an active member of the Jewish community, participated in the city council, the county board of supervisors, and a number of civic and business enterprises. A must-read for anyone wanting an in-depth picture of San Diego from 1850 through 1880.

— Iris Engstrand, pre-eminent San Diego Historian, Professor of History, the University of San Diego, author of *San Diego: Gateway to the Pacific.*

American Jewish History has been viewed primarily from the perspective of what happened on the East Coast with West Coast Jewish history being discussed primarily in relation to the post World War II migration. As we commemorate the 350th Anniversary of the Jewish arrival in the United States, how timely it is have Don Harrison chronicle the life of Louis Rose and remind us of the major role Rose played in the development of San Diego.

— Professor Lawrence Baron, Director, Lipinsky Institute for Judaic Studies, San Diego State University

Don Harrison has written an informative book about San Diego's early years as part of the United States. Superbly researched, the book focuses on the entrepreneur Louis Rose and the development of the Jewish community in that era. Harrison's book is a tour de force of this remarkable contributor to San Diego's early development. For the Jewish community, it is important to know that Jews are not late-comers here, but were among the earliest movers and shakers in San Diego. Through this book Louis Rose and the Jewish community claim their rightful place in the history of our city. This is a book for anyone who cares about early San Diego or about the history of the Jewish community in our city.

— Howard Wayne, Former Member of the California State Assembly Representing San Diego County

Two themes in **Louis Rose** *were of particular interest to me. The first was that ever since San Diego's beginning as an American city, Jews have been actively involved in its civic life — a tradition I have been honored to follow in. The second is that law enforcement has come a long way, both in its techniques and its sense of ethics, since those early days!*

— Bill Kolender, San Diego County Sheriff

Looking through the eyes of Louis Rose, Don Harrison paints a wonderful picture of the first days of the City of San Diego (population 650). As a former Member of the San Diego City Council, I guess I wasn't surprised that the very first meetings of that body dealt with — member salaries! The early nepotism and shady contract-awarding process also seemed amazingly modern. And it was less than two years after initial incorporation that all the shoddy financial practices led to city bankruptcy and state takeover! Louis Rose figured out right away (again, how modern!) that land acquisition, furthered by good deals from the City Council, was the quickest path to wealth and influence. But live by the bubble and government action, die by the bursting bubble and the next government action — and it was Louis Rose who set the roller-coaster pattern of economics and politics in San Diego's history.

— Representative Bob Filner

 A Beneficiary of the
United Jewish Federation
of San Diego County

This book was published in partnership with the Agency for Jewish Education of San Diego County.

Sales of this book benefit the Agency for Jewish Education (AJE) of San Diego County. The AJE is the central resource for Jewish education in San Diego County, serving children, their parents and educators since 1968. More than 40 schools, 5,700 students and 500 educators have benefited from AJE programs. The AJE is a beneficiary of the United Jewish Federation of San Diego County.

Publication of *Louis Rose: San Diego's First Jewish Settler and Entrepreneur* was made possible through generous grants offered by the following foundations and individuals:

PATRONS
Gary & Jerri-Ann Jacobs
Lipinsky Family Foundation

DONORS
Anonymous
Robert & Lillie Brietbard Foundation
Morey & Jeanne Feldman
Murray & Elaine Galinson
Lucy Goldman Fund
Richard & Ann Jaffe
Jerome & Miriam Katzin
Price-Brodie Foundation
Irving & Edith Taylor
Jackie & Bertie Woolf

For my wife Nancy,
whose patience made this book possible,

I love you.

TABLE OF CONTENTS

ACKNOWLEDGEMENTS

This was a project researched and written over a decade. Its origins extend back even longer, to 1989, when I helped to write the San Diego tour script for Old Town Trolley Tours. As I researched San Diego's early history, I encountered the name of Louis Rose. Affiliated with the *San Diego Jewish Press-Heritage*, I was particularly interested in learning more about San Diego's first Jewish settler. An article coauthored by Rabbi William Kramer (who was a longtime columnist for *Heritage*) and historian Norton Stern called "The Rose of San Diego" appearing in a wonderful collection of essays on San Diego Jewish history, *Old Town, New Town*, further fueled my interest, and I'd like to acknowledge a debt to this seminal work on Rose.

My own research took me to Neuhaus-an-der-Oste, Germany, where Louis Rose was born, to New Orleans, where he became a U.S. citizen, across Texas and the New Mexico territories, and finally back to my home in San Diego, California, where he made his mark.

So many, many people helped me along the way that I fear that I will omit inadvertently some names from this recitation. If so, I want to apologize here and now.

In Neuhaus-an-der-Oste, Olaf Rennebeck and Peter Rondthaler aided me immeasurably in assembling the details and comprehending Rose's early life. Doctoral students Avi Masori and E. Hollister Mathis-Masori took time from their studies at the University of Tuebingen to guide me through Germany. In New Orleans, Carol O. Kaplan, Rita Odenheimer and Merl Huntsinger, family friends of longstanding, hosted and encouraged me as I plowed through a variety of research collections trying to learn more about Rose. I am indebted as well to Mary Lou Eichorn of the Williams Research Center Historic New Orleans Collection, Wayne M. Everard, Colin B. Hamer Jr. and Irene Wainwright of the New Orleans Public Library, Sevilla Finley and Richard Landry of the German American Cultural Center, Virgie Ott of the Gretna Convention & Visitors Bureau, Kenneth E. Owen of the Louisiana Collection at Tulane, and also to Vicki Karno and Gloria Maurin.

In Texas, innumerable researchers and historians shared their knowledge and expertise with me, and I'm so pleased to be able to acknowledge them. An alphabetical roll call of cities brings to mind these honorees: Austin—Ned Brierley. Castroville—Connie Balmos, president of the historical society; Carole Trisler, director, Castroville public library, and Kevin Young, historian, Texas Parks & Wildlife. El Paso—Barbara J. Angus, El Paso Museum of History; Floyd M. "Twister" Geery, Ft. Bliss Museum; Bonnie Renegar, front desk clerk, Sleep Inn; Claudia Rivers, head, special collections, UTEP library, and Roberta

(Bobbi) Sago, UTEP manuscripts librarian-archivist. Marshall—Ruth Briggs, volunteer librarian, Harrison County Historical Museum; Audrey Kariel, then mayor; Louis Kariel. Palestine—Brenda Ladd, Palestine Library. San Antonio— Frank Faulkner and Jo Myler of the San Antonio Public Library, and Jill Jackson and Dennis Medina.

In California, Zina Schiff and Ron, Avlana and Cherina Eisenberg provided hospitality and encouragement for San Francisco Bay area research. Mark Evans of Evans & Brown provided access to photographs of a historic San Diego mural used as an element in the cover; Kim Klausner of the Western Jewish History Center provided ideas and help. In San Diego, there were so many who rendered aid, including Hebrew speakers Sandi and Shahar Masori (my daughter and son-in-law) I. Gerry Burstain and Rabbi Chaim Hollander; Prof. Lawrence Baron of San Diego State University's Lipinsky Institute for Judaic Studies: Chuck Bencik, staff librarian of the San Diego Maritime Museum; David Berg of the San Diego County map department; Malin Burnham and Christopher D. Reutz of Burnham Real Estate; Lynne E. Christenson and Ellen Sweet of the San Diego County Department of Parks and Recreation; Rick Crawford of the California Room of the downtown San Diego Public Library; Jackie Gmach and Leslie Caspi of the Lawrence Family Jewish Community Center; Eldonna Lay of the El Cajon Historical Society; Tom Leach of San Diego Lodge 35, F. A. & M., Betty McMillen, Lakeside Historical Society; Carol Myers, John Panter, Dennis Sharp and Sally West of the San Diego Historical Society; Alan Peterson of the Wells Fargo Museum in Old Town San Diego State Park; Jessica Poole of the staff of U.S. Sen. Barbara Boxer; Judy Schulman and Steve Westbrook of the Rose Canyon Advisory Committee; San Diego County Assessor Greg Smith and his very public-minded staff, Stan and Laurel Schwartz of the Jewish Historical Society of San Diego; Marsha Snelling of Old Town Descendants; Sam Sokolove, Greg Stein and Marc Wolfsheimer of the American Jewish Committee; Lorin Stewart of Old Town Trolley Tours of San Diego; Angelika Villagrana of the Greater San Diego Chamber of Commerce; Victor Walsh and Bob Wohl of Old Town San Diego State Historic Park. In Washington, D.C., Melody Savage of the U.S. Postal Service located records pertaining to Louis Rose's service as a postmaster.

Encouragement was offered as well by the late Herb Brin and his son Dan Brin of the Jewish Heritage newspapers; Norman Greene, co-publisher, Gail Umeham, assistant editor of the *San Diego Jewish Press-Heritage*, and Murray Galinson, chairman of that newspaper's advisory board. Additionally, my wife Nancy (to whom this book is dedicated), her late mother, Sydel, and her father, Sam Zeiden, my son David Harrison and daughter-in-law Hui-Wen all were generous in their encouragement and suggestions, especially as the project moved from the realm of research and writing to that of publishing and marketing. Grandson Shor never failed to provide a welcome break from tension and concerns.

My thanks to Dr. Cecile Jordan and Noah Hadas of the San Diego Agency for Jewish Education, and to Marjory Kaplan and Charlene Seidle of the Jewish Community Foundation of San Diego. No acknowledgments would be complete without a salute to a top-flight production team including Jennifer Redmond of Sunbelt Publications, Laurie Gibson of Word Association, Leah Cooper of Armadillo Creative, and Paul Hartsuyker of Hartworks. Ken Kramer, whose able "About San Diego" commentaries on San Diego's NBC 7/39 have popularized the history of our city, shall forever have my gratitude for his kind foreword. Similarly, I am grateful to the pre-eminent historian of San Diego, Iris Engstrand, for her helpful suggestions.

Lastly, my thanks to the distinguished panelists whose capsule reviews appear elsewhere in this book. They include historians Lawrence Baron of San Diego State University and Iris Engstrand of the University of San Diego, and three remarkable public servants drawn from the Jewish community, Sheriff Bill Kolender, former Assemblyman Howard Wayne, and Congressman Bob Filner.

— Donald H. Harrison
San Diego, Aug. 4, 2004

FOREWORD

At the west end of Old Town State Park in San Diego is a two-story building that serves as the Park's Visitor Center. Every year, hundreds of thousands of visitors shuffle through the place, perhaps pausing to admire the featured display, a miniature model of Old Town as it might have appeared in the 1870s. There, in tiny scale, is the San Diego that Louis Rose helped build.

To most San Diegans, the name Louis Rose is only vaguely familiar. "Yes," a friend told me, he knew the name. "Rose Canyon," he guessed correctly. "The Rose Canyon fault," he added. School kids learn that the Old Town building with the small city inside is actually called the Robinson-Rose House. Each man lived there for a time, and for that fact alone the place must be filled with stories we can scarcely imagine.

Louis Rose was the first permanent Jewish settler in San Diego. He was a tireless entrepreneur, at times served informally as the town's banker, was a dreamer of big dreams, a champion of women's rights, an animal lover, and at times unsensibly generous. He was also given to falling into debt and suffered from what today would probably be called Adult Attention Deficit Disorder. Great chunks of his life remain a mystery. But that only adds to the story.

What follows on these pages is a work of colossal scholarship. Donald Harrison has set out to research and document the life of this San Diegan as never before. And in the process, he has given literary illustration to so many parts of the history of our nation and our city. His work fills in a gap in what is known about the days of Old Town San Diego. We now have an account of what was a sweepingly racist Grand Jury; a newspaper, that, in not too subtle ways echoed that attitude; and a thorough account of how Jews were treated at that time.

This book reflects the kind of work that takes years, and draws upon scholarly discipline and powers of concentration and focus that I have to admire. In truth, I didn't feel worthy of penning a foreword to such a noble effort. I am, after all, just a broadcast storyteller who has a fondness for local history. But here was a very human drama of what drove this ambitious, proud, forward-thinking and flawed man. In coming to San Diego, he could put the broken past behind him and begin anew. That is the stuff of stories, and this book is full of them.

There are historical descriptions of Louis Rose, on the westbound trek from San Antonio to El Paso. By some disagreement, he had been banished from the wagon train; he must ride and camp beside it, but alone and out of sight. At night, alone under a starry sky, he surely both anticipated and dreaded the future. His friend and partner, James Robinson, drawn west by the excitement of the Gold Rush, was also occasionally tormented by the thought that his choice to head here was a ghastly mistake. Their lives would become inter-twined as San Diego endured its painful adolescence.

Beyond their story, here is the most complete history of the other person-alities of Old Town that I have yet seen. There's a description of a City Jail so poorly built that it held nobody and barely held together, of a town so dread-fully run that we lost the right to call ourselves a "city," and of what Rose and Robinson did to try to bring order to the barnyard.

Rose and Robinson wanted to see a railroad come to San Diego from the east. Wanted it so badly they could taste it. James Robinson presided over the effort, Rose was the treasurer. The saga of its ups and downs, victories and defeats, joy and heartbreak must, in private moments, have made them weep.

Could Rose have imagined that San Diego would end up as a cul-de-sac spur off the transcontinental line? That the trains they worked so hard to bring here from the east would end up running north and south through Rose Canyon?

Similarly, the community of "Roseville" never bloomed as Rose had hoped it might. Had the fates been more kind, we might all be familiar with his dreamed-of bayside town. Even today, it appears on some city maps, but no bus or taxi driver would know the way there by that name.

History has not given Louis Rose the same attention other pioneers have received. But his role in the formative period of San Diego's history should not be overlooked. He was a crucial figure in a time when our city was healing from the missteps of his predecessors. He served as a member of the city's Board of Trustees, as a member of the Free and Accepted Masons, and as a businessman who did what he could to provide for himself, his family, and his community.

This book honors Rose, but with fairness and honesty. He made mistakes. He overreached and sometimes miscalculated. He wasn't perfect in his personal life. It's all here.

Noting that Alonzo Horton is often referred to as the "Father" of the modern City of San Diego, Harrison believes that Louis Rose should be called "Uncle." I like that.

One day Louis Rose may be a name as familiar as Alonzo Horton. In that time, this work will be the standard reference on his life. It is that complete and that thorough and that worthwhile.

— Ken Kramer
"About San Diego"
NBC-TV Channel 7/39

CHAPTER 1

The Immigrant

The Purim Baby

Louis Rose was born March 24, 1807, in Neuhaus-an-de-Oste, Germany. Although his name would evolve into "Louis Rose," he began life with two sets of names: one secular, the other religious, and neither of them "Louis Rose."

While family names or surnames were quite common in Germany among Gentiles, in 1807 Jews still followed the ancient practice of simply giving the child one name and identifying him or her as the child of the father. In the Bible, for example, Isaac was known as the son of Abraham. If Hebrew-speakers wanted to identify him formally, they might call him "Yitzhak ben Avraham"— Isaac, son of Abraham.

Louis Rose was given both a secular name and a religious name, with both names following this ancient naming practice.

For secular purposes, he was known as Leffman, the son of Levi Nathan. Leffman was a name that alternated through the generations. (His grandfather had the name as did his great-great-grandfather.) Similarly, Levi Nathan was the name of his father as well as that of his great-grandfather.

Sometimes Louis was called by variants of the name "Leffman"—"Lipman" or "Libman"—by people who did not speak the Plattdeutsch dialect used in this area of Germany near where the Elbe River empties into the North Sea.

The family had migrated downriver to Neuhaus-an-der-Oste from Hamburg, Germany, incrementally over five generations. The great-great grandfather Leffman had lived in Hamburg's Jewish ghetto, but in 1704 he was allowed to leave, having been issued a *schutzbrief*—or letter of protection—by Nils Carlsson Gyllenstierna af Fogelvik, a member of the Swedish nobility who in 1698 had become the governor-general of the Bremen-Verden area of Germany. Great-great grandfather Leffman served as a "court Jew" until 1712 when he and his wife died of the plague. That was the same year that Sweden turned the Bremen-Verden area over to Denmark, which promptly yielded sovereignty over the area to the Kingdom of Hanover.

Great-grandfather Levi Nathan lived briefly in Neuhaus before settling in nearby Ottendorf, where grandfather Leffman later also lived and died. At the time of the grandfather's death, Louis's father, Levi Nathan, was still a minor.

Arrangements therefore were made for him to move to Neuhaus, where he served as an apprentice to his uncle Moses Nathan. The uncle was a dealer in secondhand items made of gold such as candlesticks and jewelry.[1]

Under German law, the items had to be secondhand because artisan guilds, from which Jews were then excluded, reserved to themselves the right to deal in original gold items.

Louis was given a ceremonial Hebrew name on the eighth day of his life. First pronounced at the time of his circumcision (*brit milah*), the name was Yomtov bar Yehuda.[2]

"Bar" is a variant of "Ben," imported into Hebrew from the Aramaic language. Both mean "son of." From this we learn that Louis was the son of Yehuda, which was Levi Nathan's ceremonial Hebrew name. The name "Yom Tov" means "Good Day," indicating that Louis was born on a holiday. March 24, 1807, corresponded with the Hebrew date of 14 Adar II 5567, which was the Jewish festival day of Purim.[3]

In a land where Jews were required to obtain *schutzbriefs* to move from one town to another, and where they were barred from entering the guilds, it can be understood why Levi Nathan would have considered Purim an excellent day for his first son to be born.

The holiday celebrates the triumph of the Jews over an ancient oppressor, Haman, whom the Bible identifies as the vizier in Persia to King Ahashuerus. As told in the Book of Esther, Haman took a distinct dislike to a Jew, Mordechai, who, apparently alone among Ahashuerus' subjects, refused to bow before the symbols of secular authority, believing that to do so would violate the commandment from God to put no other gods before Him. Haman decided by lottery on a day that Mordechai and all the other Jews should be put to death.

What Haman didn't count on was that Queen Esther, whom King Ahashuerus recently had married after banishing Queen Vashti, secretly was a Jew herself as well as a relative of Mordechai's. She persuaded King Ahashuerus to sentence Haman with the same penalty he had planned for the Jews, death on the gallows.

One can imagine that while growing up, young Leffman's favorite holiday might have been Purim, as it is today for many Jewish children. It's an open question how deeply Leffman pondered the meanings of the underlying story, but there would be times in his life when rather than being a Mordechai who asserted his Jewish beliefs openly, he was more like Esther, first winning the affection of powerful non-Jews and later being in a position to help his fellow Jews.

Napoleonic Reforms

In 1810, when Louis was 3, his younger brother Simon was born. They were living during a momentous time in European history. Napoleon Bonaparte and his Grande Armee were winning military victory after victory. After defeating the forces of Hanover and other nearby German states, Napoleon decided that a new kingdom should be created for his brother Jerome. Taking pieces of various German states, Napoleon literally redrew the map of Europe. Neuhaus-an-der-Oste became part of the Kingdom of Westphalia, ruled by Jerome Bonaparte.

For the little town of Neuhaus-an-der-Oste, this perhaps was the biggest change since the legendary day during the Middle Ages when citizens staged a tax revolt by burning down the house of a hated tax collector. Determined to defy the mob, authorities promptly constructed for their agent a "new house," at the confluence of the Oste and Elbe Rivers. According to the legend, the town thereafter was known as Neuhaus-an-der-Oste. It might have identified itself as being on the more important Elbe River except for the fact that there already was a Neuhaus located upstream on the Elbe.[4]

Jerome Bonaparte implemented the reforms in Westphalia that Napoleon earlier had ordered throughout the rest of his empire. For Jews, none was more important than their official emancipation. Thanks to Napoleon, they no longer would be required to obtain a *schutzbrief* to live outside the ghetto. Nor would they be restricted as to the professions they might enter. According to twentieth century historian H.I. Bach, the emancipation formula, reduced to its essentials, was "The Jew as an individual is to be given every right, but Jews as a nation—the word is taken in the limited eighteenth century meaning of 'corporation' or 'community'—are to be denied any right." [5]

In cities like Hamburg, where there were sizeable Jewish populations, such a formula weakened the *kehillah*, a traditional Jewish community that was semi-autonomous so long as its leaders kept order and made certain that taxes were collected. Under the emancipation decree, Jews need not live under the *kehillah's* authority; they might instead mingle with the larger population and live directly under the rules of the general government. In smaller towns like Neuhaus, where the Jewish population was insufficient to support a *kehillah*, one major effect of emancipation was to relieve Jews of the fear that some official might revoke their "protection letters" and send them packing.

Emancipation was not automatic, however. Jews needed to accept emancipation by enrolling as citizens. Part of the process was to take a family name, making work easier for authorities in charge of collecting taxes, enumerating the census, and conscripting people into the military.

Levi Nathan paid for an important notice that appeared on Wednesday, June 12, 1811, in the *Intelligenz Blatt* ("Intelligence Sheet"), the local newspaper: "The public is hereby notified that the inhabitant of this community, Levi

Nathan, who is of the Jewish faith, will take the family name Rose for himself and his offspring. From now on, he will call himself Levi Nathan Rose." [6]

All over Europe, Jews like Levi Nathan were taking family names. Some named themselves after their professions like "Schneider" (tailor); others like "Breslauer" or "Hamburger" named themselves after the city or towns where they lived. Still others picked patronyms like Abramson or Jacobson, or names from nature, such as Berg (mountain), Hirsch (deer), or in this family's case, "Rose"— a flower grown in the Neuhaus area.[7] Once Levi Nathan complied with Jerome's edict, his young sons became known as Leffman Rose and Simon Rose.

Childhood in Neuhaus

Napoleon's army was defeated in 1814 by the combined forces of Prussia, Russia, Austria, and England, ending the French empire as well as Jerome's kingdom. The victorious allies, meeting in 1814 and 1815 at the Congress of Vienna, reconstituted the Kingdom of Hanover and reincorporated Neuhaus-an-der-Oste as a Hanoverian municipality. At the time, the King of Hanover occupied the British throne. The king to whom the Roses again became subject was the same George III from whom the American colonies declared their independence in 1776. George III ruled Britain from 1760 to 1820.

Political gains made by Jews were consolidated in some states of the German Confederation, but rolled back in others. Uneven treatment of the Jews was presaged at the Congress of Vienna after Prussia's delegate and education minister, Wilhelm von Humboldt, attempted to provide that Jews should retain all privileges granted to them "in" the various German states. Reactionary delegates rewrote the provision to say "by" the various German states, thereby permitting each state to retain or repeal those privileges at will.[8]

In Neuhaus, the Jews were too few to be of much political concern, and the Rose family was allowed to live unmolested. The village then had far more regional importance than it does now. It was a county seat where bewigged advocates litigated numerous legal cases and where bureaucrats of various types filled out myriads of forms. With a population of 1,700,[9] Neuhaus supplied manpower to its shipyards and customers to its Ulex Liqueur factory, which was founded in 1796 and has remained renowned in the region to this day.[10]

During Rose's boyhood, life in Neuhaus had its attractions. He could go down to the Elbe River and watch the many ships pass. He could walk about 4 kilometers east to Graf Bremer Park in the neighboring village of Cadenberge, a popular venue for romping and for picnics.[11] He also could be of help as his father attempted to expand his business. In 1815, when Leffman was 8, Levi Nathan Rose put up all his possessions as collateral to secure loans of $1,700 and $500 from a Jewish tradesman in Rotenburg, about 50 miles distant from Neuhaus.[12] The risky strategy must have made an impression on his son; later in his life Leffman would borrow money on similar terms, sometimes with disastrous results.

However relaxed life might be in Neuhaus, elsewhere the post-Napoleonic era was a time of ferment for Jews and non-Jews alike. In the wake of emancipation, some Jews all but abandoned Jewish ways in their eagerness to become "German." Many embraced a concept called "bildung"—as endorsed by such philosophers as Goethe, Humboldt, Schiller and Herder—which essentially combined "rationality" and "refinement."[13] In the name of rationality, many Jews jettisoned all but a perfunctory belief in an unknowable God, and put their faith instead into demonstrable codes of ethics. "It's not what you believe, but what you do," was a typical formulation. In the cause of "refinement," they scorned their rich Yiddish language as inferior to literary German.

Although bildung won some advocates among German Christians, a powerful competitor for their allegiance was the revival of the medieval past, which painted a picture for Germans of a time, according to twentieth century historian Jacob Rader Marcus, "when history was glorious. Germanism was exalted; the medieval German Christian state, a state in which the Jew was a stranger, was looked upon as the ideal." The philosophy was a forerunner of twentieth-century Nazism.[14]

One manifestation of this movement was the so-called "Hep! Hep!" street riots of 1819, when antagonists marched in various parts of Germany chanting a taunting Latin acronym that dated back to the Crusades—"Heiroslyma est perdita"—"Jerusalem is lost." [15]

The ugly mood on the street was reflected in the halls of government. Prompted by Austria's Prince Clements Lothar von Metternich, member states of the German Confederation adopted the Carlsbad Decrees in 1819, imposing censorship and other measures intended to suppress the trend toward liberalization. The Age of Metternich became synonymous with political repression.

Such was the climate in 1820, when Leffman Rose turned 13, the traditional time when a Jewish boy becomes a bar mitzvah (literally a "son of the commandment"). Traditionally on such an occasion, a boy reads from the Torah (first five books of the Bible) and chants a Haftarah. This latter reading is a selection from a later portion of the Bible that relates to the Torah portion.

There is no direct evidence that Rose had a bar mitzvah, but we may infer that he did from two pieces of evidence. The first is his Hebrew name, "Yom Tov," indicating his family had a high level of religious awareness. The second is the fact that later in life, Rose was sufficiently familiar with Jewish ritual to officiate at Jewish wedding ceremonies.

As a boy commits to memory certain passages of the Bible, he may or may not develop an attachment to those passages, depending upon the seriousness with which he addresses the task. We don't know if Rose had a bar mitzvah, and if he did, we don't know when that ceremony occurred. Briefly departing the arena of history for the realm of speculation, we can guess that if Rose did have a bar mitzvah ceremony, it most likely would have occurred on the Sabbath immediately following his thirteenth birthday. What portions would he have read?

Typically, the weekly Torah portion would have been Ki Tisa, the Hebrew name for the story told in Exodus 30:11-34:35.[16] As the son of a man who had dealt in secondhand gold, Leffman in such circumstances might have pondered how angered God and Moses became after the Israelites encamped at the base of Mount Sinai and fashioned the Golden Calf. The Haftarah portion assigned to Ki Tisa is I Kings 18:1-39, describing the fire-lighting contest atop Mount Carmel between the Prophet Elijah and the priests of Baal—a reading that further illustrates the senselessness of worshiping false gods.

But our speculation doesn't end there. Because Rose grew up in Germany, it is likely that he followed the Ashkenazic rite, as opposed to the Sephardic one. Ashkenazim are Jews who lived in the northern and central portions of western and Eastern Europe. Sephardim are Jews who were expelled from Spain and settled in diverse parts of the world, especially along the Mediterranean, in the Middle East and in the Americas.

Some Ashkenazic Jews have a *minhag* (custom) on the Sabbath after Purim of reading Ki Tisa from one Torah, but then when the bar mitzvah boy comes to read the *maftir* (last reading of the Torah service) to switch to another Torah scroll. From this second scroll, the boy will read the commandments concerning the red heifer, related in Numbers 19:1–22:17. In this section, God instructs the Israelites to cremate an unblemished red heifer, and then utilize the ashes in a mixture intended for the ceremonial purification of people who have been ritually contaminated by contact with dead people.

The Haftarah that goes with this Torah reading is Ezekiel 36:16-38, in which God says even though he has scattered Jews among the nations for their iniquities, nevertheless because they are His people, He will return them to their land, and they will worship Him with purified hearts.[17]

The scattering of Jews among the nations had led Rose's family to Neuhaus, where they did not have a formal synagogue, but instead probably met in each other's homes, keeping few records if any. However tempting it is to speculate on the lessons of Rose's presumed bar mitzvah, we simply don't have enough evidence to make the case that he ever gave more than passing thought to any of these Bible passages.

Louis Rose Immigrates to America

The lack of records also leaves an astonishingly big hole in our knowledge of Louis Rose's life over the next twenty years. How the European political ferment from 1820 to 1840 affected him is a matter only of conjecture. We have a few tantalizing hints. We know that Rose found his way in the mixed society of Jew and Gentile, at some point becoming a member of the Masonic order. We know that he had some knowledge of the jewelry business, which he probably learned from his father, Levi Nathan. We know that he was fond of liquor, both as a consumer and as a tradesman. And, we know from later testimonies that he had a lifelong love for both gardens and animals.

Also we know that during this period, Leffman's brother Simon received his medical degree at the University of Goettingen in 1835.[18] Sadly, Simon also placed a notice in the December 5, 1838 edition of the *Intelligenz Blatt*: "During the night of Saturday to Sunday, my beloved father, the merchant L.N. Rose, died in Neuhaus a.d. Oste at the age of 76 due to complications of old age. We ask by this announcement that people remember the grieving relatives and the distressed son in their thoughts and prayers. Stade, Dec. 4, 1838, Dr. Rose." [19]

As the notice was signed by "Dr. Rose," but made no mention of Simon's older brother, one speculates that Louis already might have left the district of Stade before their father's death, or that the two brothers were estranged. Leffman may still have been in Germany at the time, perhaps either in Hamburg or Bremen, or he may have been living in some other part of Europe. We know from later documents that Leffman read several languages besides German, among them French, English, and Spanish.

In the latter part of 1840, Rose boarded the American ship *Wales*, perhaps in Hamburg, perhaps in Bremen, or perhaps when the ship made an unreported stop at Neuhaus-an-der-Oste, located in river waters between the two major ports. The ship's manifest did not distinguish between passengers who boarded in Hamburg and Bremen, and made no mention of any intermediate stops.[20] However, we know that ships often made quick stops at Neuhaus-an-der-Oste to pick up passengers and freight.[21] In addition to his personal baggage, Rose loaded aboard the ship five dozen bottles of cherry brandy, perhaps from the Ulex Liqueur factory.[22]

The square-stern ship on which Rose made a winter crossing of the Atlantic had only two decks. It had three square-rigged masts and a billet head. It weighed slightly more than 446 tons and measured 28 feet wide, 14 feet deep and an inch shy of 125 feet long. It had been built in Topham, Maine, only the year before.[23]

The *Daily Picayune* reported on December 25, 1840, that the ship *Wales* had arrived in the Port of New Orleans; yet, according to U.S. Customs records, Louis Rose and his fellow passengers were not processed until the following day. Most U.S. Customs officials, apparently, took Christmas Day off. *Wales* was not alone in arriving at New Orleans in time for the holiday; eight other ships in addition to one barque, four brigs, eight steamers, and four towboats also were listed in the newspaper's daily summary.[24]

The list compiled by U.S. Customs showed that Rose was one of thirty-six passengers traveling individually aboard the American ship. Additionally, there were five families among the passengers, but the records did not divulge how many members were included in each family unit. The families simply were identified by the names of the heads of household. Lawson L. Watts was the captain, or master, of the vessel.[25]

That the arrival of the *Wales* rated only a line in small type of the *Daily Picayune* was an indication of how busy a port New Orleans had become during the era when cotton was its most sought and principal export. Much like the River Elbe, familiar to Rose from the time of his youth, the Mississippi River witnessed too much commerce on a daily basis for any but the most unusual ship to create much attention. In 1840, New Orleans was considered the fourth busiest port in the world. The very volume of its commerce probably accounted for why Rose immigrated to New Orleans rather than to an American port closer to Germany. Steamboats and side-wheelers brought cotton from southern plantations down the Mississippi River to New Orleans where it was baled and transferred to ships like the *Wales*, which then took the product to mills in England and other countries in Europe. Rather than return with empty holds to New Orleans, the ships went to Germany or Ireland and took on immigrants as human cargo. Such ships offered passage at highly competitive fares.

Rose was 33 when he disembarked in New Orleans.

New Orleans

When Louis Rose arrived in 1840, Louisiana had been a state for 28 years and New Orleans a municipality for 35 years, although the area had been settled by the French, occupied by the Spanish, returned to the French, and sold to the United States in a history that stretched back to 1718.

Rose found his home among New Orleans' Jewish community, whose most famous personage was Judah Touro, son of the cantor in Newport, R.I., for whom one of America's oldest synagogues is named. In 1845, a split occurred in New Orleans' Jewish community with German immigrants like Rose continuing to worship at the 17-year-old Shanarai Chasad (Gates of Mercy) Synagogue, and those preferring the Sephardic rite establishing a new congregation, Kehilath Nodesh Nefatzoth Yehudah (the Holy Congregation of the Dispersed of Judah). Touro became a benefactor to the latter, which became known as the Portuguese congregation. Rose identified with the former con-gregation, which eventually became known as the Deutsche Shul.

Business, not religion, was Rose's main focus during his first years in America. Typically, Jewish immigrants of that era would become peddlers and, after acquiring enough capital, they might open stalls on the levee that restrained the waters of the Mississippi River. If business proved successful enough, the stall might be made more permanent. If really successful, the businessman might move a block from the river to a storefront on Chartres Street, perhaps taking sleeping quarters above it or nearby.[26]

In a doctoral dissertation, "Creoles of Jerusalem: Jewish Businessmen of Louisiana, 1840-1875," Elliott Ashkenazi reported: "Of the approximately 245 business firms I identified in New Orleans between 1841 and the Civil War, more than 50 percent earned their living from the sale of clothing or dry goods. Jews also sold jewelry, tobacco and fancy, imported goods. Some of the more successful businessmen became cotton merchants or general commission merchants trading in several items."[27]

Although Rose was not listed in the various city directories for the period, nor does his name appear in extant records of business licenses issued by the City of New Orleans, there are two pieces of evidence that suggest that while he was in New Orleans, Rose somehow disposed of his sixty bottles of cherry brandy and took up the jewelry trade.

First, as we have already seen, his father, Levi Nathan Rose, earned his living in Neuhaus-an-der-Oste dealing in secondhand gold items. It is not too great a stretch to think that Louis learned his father's trade. Second, one later news article about Rose said, without attribution, that "after a peculiar habit of his race, he became engaged in the sale of diamonds and jewelry."[28]

On March 26, 1844, two days after he turned 37, Rose attended the first meeting (after organization) of a German-language Masonic lodge in New Orleans, later known as the Germania Lodge No. 46.[29] Records of that organization indicate that he was elected as junior warden, a position somewhat akin to second vice president. Typically, though not always, a junior warden will advance to the position of senior warden, and then to the position of master of the lodge. We can draw at least two conclusions from this information: first, because he was found qualified to serve as junior warden, he probably had been a Mason prior to the founding of the Germania Lodge. One suspects that he affiliated in Germany. Second, he had a good reputation among his brother Masons, or they would not have elected him to such a high office. Lodge members held a special meeting April 16 to hear an address by the Deputy Grand Master for Louisiana, voting on that occasion to keep all records in both French and German. In ceremonies on May 4, the lodge officially received its charter, which had been dated April 18.[30]

On January 2, 1846, Rose became a naturalized citizen of the United States. Listing him in this record as "Liebman" Rose, the First District Court of New Orleans reported that "the applicant having presented his petition for naturalization and the deposition of James D. Kamper and C. Probst being duly taken and the formalities of law having been complied with and the oath of naturalization as prescribed by law having been administered to him, the court ordered that said applicant Liebman Rose be admitted a citizen of the United States of America."[31] Kamper was the founding treasurer of Rose's Germania Lodge.[32]

Rose obviously considered it a momentous occasion because January 2, 1846, was probably the very first day he could have become a citizen after a five-year waiting period. His date of immigration was December 26, 1840 so five years would have elapsed on December 26, 1845. Given the American custom of closing down businesses and government offices in the week between Christmas and New Year's Day, January 2 would have been the first day the court would have been opened for such business.

An Ill-Fated Marriage

The next major event in Rose's life came on Sunday, June 20, 1847, when Caroline Marks of New Orleans became his bride in a ceremony officiated at the German congregation. Caroline's Hebrew name was Karas Bat Mordechai. It was an interesting coincidence that a man born on Purim was marrying the daughter of a man named for the hero of the Purim story.

A Jewish marriage contract known as a "ketubah" was pre-printed in Hebrew script, with places for the bride's and groom's names to be filled in, as well as for the male witnesses to sign. The contract was drawn on "Sunday, 6th day of Tammuz 5607 since the creation of the world, according to the count that we are accustomed to employ here in the City of New Orleans on the Mississippi River in the State of Louisiana."

The *ketubah* went on to state that the bridegroom, Yomtov bar Yehuda, "said to the virgin Kaila (bride) known as Karas daughter of Mordechai the Levite 'be my wife according to the law of Moses and Israel and I will cherish, honor, support and maintain you in accordance with the laws of Jewish husbands who cherish, honor, support and maintain their wives honestly. I will set aside for you the portion of a virgin's 200 silver pieces that accrues to you according to Torah law together with your food, clothing and needs and live with you as husband and wife according to universal custom.' And the virgin Kaila known as Karas the daughter of Mordechai pledged her troth to Yomtov, in affection and sincerity, and she thereby took upon herself the fulfillment of all the duties incumbent upon a Jewish wife. And so said Mr. Yomtov, the son of Yehudah, the groom, 'the responsibility of this marriage contract, this wedding dowry and this additional sum I take upon myself and my heirs after me as a responsibility and according to the content of all *ketubah* contracts made in accordance with the institution of our sages of blessed memory."

The groom also acknowledged that, before the wedding took place he had verified that the bride was indeed Karas Bat Mordechai Havili, in a ceremony that harkens back to the biblical story of when Jacob was fooled into marrying Leah instead of her younger sister Rachel. (Genesis 29:22-27) The *ketubah* added: "It is not to be regarded as an indecisive contractual obligation or as a stereotyped form. We have affected the legal formality of binding agreement from Mr. Yomtov, the son of Yehudah, the groom and Kaila, known as Karas, the daughter of Mordechai, the virgin, according to all that is written and explained above that is legally appropriate for establishing a transaction and everything is valid and confirmed."

The *ba'al kiddushim* (wedding official) was listed as Tzvi Bia'a Yehuda Halevy. The witnesses to the contract, who attested that the groom had properly signed the document, were Benyamin l'ben Pesya Avraham (Benjamin, the son of Pesya and Abraham of blessed memory), Yaacov ben Avigdor and Mna (Menachem) bar Ladi. None was further identified.[33]

Either before his marriage, or possibly as a result of it, Rose acquired a building in the heart of the Vieux Carre, at the T-intersection of Chartres and Jefferson Streets. It was a historic neighborhood. At the top of the T, Bartholome Bosque, a native of Palma, Majorca, had built a well-known structure. His daughter, Suzette Bosque, was the third wife of Louisiana's first American governor, W.C.Z. Claiborne. Before the Bosque house had been built, another structure stood on the property, a home owned by Don Bernardo de Galvez, who was the Spanish governor of Louisiana from 1777 to 1785. Galvez sold his home in 1787 to the treasurer of the province, Don Vincente Nunez. But on Good Friday, March 21, 1788, fire burned the structure to the ground.[34]

However well 1847 began for the Roses, it was not a good year—not for New Orleans generally, nor for its Jewish community, and especially not for the newlyweds.

The year was marred by one of the worst outbreaks of yellow fever in the city's history. The benevolent organization known as the Howard Association alone reported attending to approximately 1,200 cases of the disease[35] which science had not yet identified as being borne by mosquitoes. Similarly, the Hebrew Benevolent Association, which had been established March 17, 1844, under the presidency of Gershom Kursheedt, came to the aid of the families of 44 Jews who had died of the fever. The association also ministered generally to the sick and poor of the city. Such was the need for charitable works that the Ladies Hebrew Benevolent Society also began separate fundraising operations.[36]

Cash evidently was short in such circumstances, and Rose, perhaps remembering how his father had borrowed money for his business, took out a series of loans. On October 25, 1847, he borrowed $250 from a man named Phillip Willman.[37] A week later he rented to a man named Adam Reuth the store and upstairs apartment at 172 Chartres Street[38] and apparently moved with Caroline to a less desirable address just outside the old city at 256 St. Claude Street.[39]

The new year of 1848 failed to bring financial relief. On February 28, Rose indebted himself in the amount of $285 to the firm of Voigts Teauremand[40];

on April 1, he borrowed $307.68 from Francis Brichta[41]; on April 5, he borrowed $250 from Theophilus Cohen, and on May 12 he made out a check for $100 to himself, then endorsed it to Henry Courdjou, who subsequently signed it over to Claus Droge.[42]

Thus, Rose had at least $1,192.68 in obligations when, on May 16, a sheriff's deputy knocked at his door and handed him a court summons. He was directed to pay the Voigts Teauremand firm the $285 owing them, plus interest, or to appear in court. As the note had been due since March 20, and Voigts Teauremand had reported in its complaint having on several occasions asked Rose to pay the debt, one can conclude that the sheriff's deputy's knock was not the first unwelcome appearance at the newlyweds' door.[43]

On June 2, 1848, hoping to do something about his mounting cash flow problem, Rose filed suit in the Second District Court against Adam Reuth. He complained that Reuth and his wife were behind in the apartment rent, behind in the store rent, and still owed him the money they had borrowed to purchase apartment furnishings. The total debt was reckoned at $142.35. But, according to documents filed in the case, Reuth and his wife subsequently abandoned the property, leaving the furniture and some groceries behind. At Rose's request, the court ordered the seizure of the furniture, consisting of a bed, armoire, bedding, and other effects, pending resolution of the court case.[44] But that did not bring any money to the newlyweds' nest, and the creditors were at the door.

On June 23, just three days after Caroline's and Louis's first wedding anniversary, another sheriff's deputy presented him with a summons. This one directed Rose either to pay $250 to Willman, plus the interest that had accumulated since the note had come due in January, or to answer in court. Making the case even more embarrassing for Rose was that Willman, in the interim, had transferred Rose's note of indebtedness to Stanislaus Weber,[45] who, with Rose, had been an early member of Germania Lodge No. 46, F. & A.M.

Financial troubles mounted. In the June 30 court proceedings, which Rose did not attend, Judge A. Buchanan of the Fifth District Court of New Orleans entered a default judgment against Rose for the debt owed to Voigts Teauremand plus interest.

Some revenue came to Rose on July 2. William Thomas, who apparently had owed Rose some money, wrote him a promissory note for $335, to be paid on November 2. Rose gave the note to Droge as security for the $100 he previously had borrowed. Droge in turn sold the Thomas note to J. H. Sturchen. On July 7, Charles Peckelin turned over to Rose a note for $210 made out to him by a man named J. Hoist. He also gave to Rose another $325 note, due October 7, in his own name. As he had with the Thomas note, Rose turned over to Droge both these notes as collateral.

There was no getting out from under the burden of debt. On July 10, Ouesiphose Drouet, a notary public, stopped at the Rose home on St. Claude Street and told Caroline he was there to collect on the $250 note her husband had made out on April 5 to Theophilus Cohen. The exasperated wife told the collector that her husband was not at home, and furthermore that he had left her no money with which to pay the debt.[46] Eventually Frederic Engel, who had purchased the note, also brought suit against Rose.

Rose or his wife apparently told the increasingly insistent creditors that Droge and Sturchen were holding in securities far more money than Rose owed to any of them individually. This prompted various creditors to ask the courts to seize those securities pending settlement of their case. The creditors fell to arguing among themselves over which debt should take precedence.

Desperately seeking money, Rose on July 29 sold to John M'Donough the right to whatever proceeds he eventually would recover as a result of his suit against the vanished renter, Adam Reuth. But there was no reprieve. On August 2, a sheriff's deputy served Rose with yet another demand note, this one for the $307.68 plus interest he owed Francis Brichta.

Obviously, the nightmare was not going to end. Rose heard that in San Antonio, Texas, a man might make some money selling real estate. Taking leave of Caroline in August 1848, he told his wife that he expected to return in no more than three months.

After her husband left New Orleans, Caroline moved again, but a process server was able to find her at home at the corner of St. Asise and Treme Streets. This was possibly the residence of Henry and Eliza Thal, her brother-in-law and sister, to whom later court records made reference.[47] The couple subsequently moved with Caroline to Montgomery, Ala.

On August 11, 1848, Brichta filed a supplemental petition in the Second District Court of Judge E.A. Cannon: "Since the filing of the original petition and since the service of the citation said Liebman Rose has left the State of Louisiana permanently," the petition stated.

As had occurred previously in the case brought by Voigts Teauremand, default judgments against Rose eventually were issued by the courts in the cases stemming from the notes written to Phillip Willman, Francis Brichta, and Theophilus Cohen. Most of the holders of Rose's notes had purchased them at discount from the original lenders.

Except for what the court distributed from the securities held by Sturchen, it is not known whether any of the plaintiffs ever collected any money from Rose. However, based on the reputation Rose developed later in life for always paying his debts, there was a possibility that they did.[48] In March of 1849, default judgment finally was entered against Adam Reuth. Court records do not indicate whether M'Donough ever was successful in collecting the debt once owed to Rose.

In his doctoral dissertation, Ashkenazi reported that many of the businesses started in New Orleans by Jewish immigrants were so transitory that the term "birds of passage" came to characterize many of the Jewish settlers. "In a sample of 125 businesses in existence between 1840 and 1866, thirty eight or

30 percent are known to have ended in bankruptcy," he wrote. "The larger firms went through formal court proceedings; the smaller ones simply closed up while owing money."[49]

Although Rose may not have been aware of it at the time, there was another casualty: his marriage to Caroline would never recover from the financial stress.

San Antonio

Rose moved west to Texas, a state that at the time had been the 28th state of the United States for only three years. There are historical parallels between San Antonio, the city where Rose settled temporarily, and San Diego, where he eventually would make his mark. A brief early history of San Antonio therefore is worth noting.

San Antonio traced its origins to 1691, when Father Damian Massanet named a river in Texas after Saint Anthony of Padua, using the Spanish variant of his name, "San Antonio." Settlement began in 1718 when Father Antonio de Buenaventura y Olivares founded a mission church, which he named "San Antonio de Valero." That name honored both St. Anthony and the duke of Valero, who recently had been appointed as viceroy of New Spain, a vast geographic area that included all of latter-day Mexico and the southwestern United States.

The mission later became famous as the Alamo, taking its name from the Spanish word for cottonwood trees, "alamo." These trees grew along the river. A presidio, or fort, also was founded in 1718 and was named "San Antonio de Bexar" [50] In 1724, six years after its founding, Mission San Antonio de Valero was relocated to Alamo Plaza, its current site.

Similarly, a Spanish missionary, Father Junipero Serra, founded San Diego. He celebrated a mass in 1769 at a site that became the location of the Presidio. A mission church was built at that Presidio, but like the Alamo, it was relocated just a few years after its founding.

Jewish Land Barons

The 1840s were both a time of intensive real estate development and considerable German settlement in Texas, accounting perhaps for the German-speaking Rose's hope that he could ease his financial problems if he were to "sell some lands" in Texas.[51]

His business activities in San Antonio are a mystery in the absence of records, but it is possible that Rose connected with either or both of two

Jewish land developers who were active in Texas at that time. One was Jacob Raphael de Cordova; the other was Henri Castro.

De Cordova, co-founder and publisher in 1834 of the *Daily Gleaner* in Kingston, Jamaica, visited New Orleans early in 1836 and later that year went to Texas. A Grand Master of the Odd Fellows fraternal and service organization, he helped to establish lodges in Texas and was so taken with the new Republic that he decided to live there. Hoping to sell land to settlers, he acquired up to 1,000,000 acres, including what would become the town of Waco. He platted the town in 1848 and 1849.[52]

Castro also was an entrepreneur who thought on a grand scale. Born in 1785 in France, he was from a family that claimed descent from a fifteenth century Portuguese nobleman. Biographer Julia Nott Waugh turned up this revealing passage in Castro's diary: "In the fifteenth century, Jean de Castro, viceroy of the Indies, founded towns for the glory of the kings of Portugal. In the nineteenth century, H. Castro, descendant in direct line from that same Jean de Castro, founded towns in Texas for the glory of Liberty. Strange coincidence. Would it not be enlightening to think that the designs of God reveal themselves in certain families and become their appanage in the same manner as their inheritance of nobility and fortune?"[53]

If the two ever had the opportunity to discuss the details of Castro's life, Rose surely would have been interested to learn that Castro had been appointed by the governor of Landes, France, to greet Napoleon on his visit there[54] and even more intrigued by reports that Castro attended the Sanhedrin[55] convened by Napoleon in 1806, because this body of Jewish leaders was associated with Napoleon's decision to emancipate the Jews, provided that families like Rose's adopt surnames.

Like Judah Touro in New Orleans, Henri Castro was an example for Rose of a fellow Jew who, after becoming successful in business, was both a philanthropist and a city builder.

After receiving a charter from the Texas government to create settlements, Castro brought to Texas 485 families and 457 single men in twenty-seven chartered ships. Most of the settlers were German-speaking residents of the Alsace region. During that period, he founded the towns of Castroville, Quihi, Vandenburg, and D'Hanis.[56]

Rose neither had a claim to noble descent nor to a family fortune, but there was much about Castro that the future San Diego land developer could use as a model. Castro's polished manners always set him apart on the rough frontier, and the Rose remembered by San Diegans—as later noted by his daughter Henrietta—was "singularly modest and singularly proud in a way; I never heard him swear." He also was a "good talker" who "never boasted"; "an honest man" and a "man of great honor."[57]

As yellow fever played havoc with New Orleans' economy the year before, an outbreak of cholera wreaked similar results in San Antonio in 1848.

Contemporary newspaper accounts estimated that the cholera took the lives of 500 people, including that of U.S. Army Major General William Jenkins Worth (for whom Fort Worth later would be named). The general died on May 7, only a short time after being given command of the U.S. military's Department of Texas, known also as the Eighth Department of the Army. Another cholera victim, a German immigrant named Conrad Silk, "committed suicide by cutting his throat...he had been attacked by cholera and destroyed himself to escape the horrors of the disease."[58]

There is evidence that Rose had made considerable financial progress in San Antonio, because shortly after his arrival in San Diego he was able to place a sizeable sum of money in a special account with the city government. In 1848, however, the cholera outbreak caused him concern over his future financial prospects in San Antonio.

When he had left New Orleans, Rose told Caroline that he planned to return in three months, but he decided against returning home. Reports of the discovery of gold in California excited his imagination as it did those of so many others. In June of 1849, Rose joined a party of civilians accompanying a large military contingent bound for El Paso, in what would be the first leg of an overland trip to California. He later testified that he wrote to Caroline about his plans, but the letter apparently never reached her.

The Van Horne Expedition

On February 3, 1849, General Worth had issued an order to six companies and headquarters of the Third Infantry Division to depart San Antonio by April 10 and proceed to a point opposite El Paso del Norte (today known as Juarez, Mexico) "and there establish a fort."[59] The cholera, as well as flooding, forced a delay in the implementation of that order.

Worth's successor—Brigadier General William S. Harney—directed the leader of the expedition, Brevet Major Jefferson Van Horne, to follow a newly discovered route that would take the travelers northwest from San Antonio to the San Pedro River, nicknamed the "Devil's River" and from there across a canyon-studded stretch to the Pecos River. The travelers would follow the river's northerly course for about 60 miles, then head west across open country to the Rio Grande River, which they would follow about 100 miles up to El Paso.

The expedition included 275 military wagons, 2,500 animals, and a small contingent of civilians, including Rose. Van Horne later contended that the cholera, bad weather, lack of supplies, and lack of good transportation should have persuaded Harney to postpone the "ill-considered" expedition.[60]

If Van Horne was sour on the expedition's prospects, local newspapers were almost giddy in their excitement. The *Galveston Weekly News* of June 18, 1849, reported somewhat breathlessly that "several ladies accompany their husbands, voluntarily becoming almost exiles from society."[61] The brave souls included the wives, and in some cases, children, of Brevet Major W.S. Henry, and Lieutenants J.G. McFerran, J.N.S. Whistler, and John D. Wilkins. Thirteen unaccompanied officers, including Van Horne, also participated in the expedition.

Not mentioned in the newspaper article, but generally traveling in advance of the main contingent, was a group of topographical engineers commanded by Lieutenant Colonel J. E. Johnston and Captain S.G. French, and including surveyor R.A. Howard. A company from the First Infantry Division, commanded by Captain King, escorted the engineers.[62]

A celebrity of the expedition, who typically traveled with the scouting party ahead, but was a frequent visitor up and down the line of march, was Jack Hays, one of the founders of Texas' official and highly regarded contingent of Indian fighters known as the Texas Rangers. Hays, who knew the Texas landscape perhaps better than any other Anglo, was headed to territory that later became Arizona. The federal government had appointed him to be its agent to the Indians living in the Gila River area.

The various contingents of the expedition stayed within a day or two's travel of each other. They kept in communication and were generally coordinated by Van Horne's headquarters company. At any given time, a scouting party might be days ahead of the rest; an engineering or fatigue party might be widening and smoothing the road; a well-armed main contingent of the Army, impressive enough to discourage attacks by Indians, might be assembled not too far behind, and civilians, arrayed in various traveling groups, might be traveling semi-independently or to the rear of the main line of march.

One of the civilians accompanying the expedition was Thomas B. Eastland, a Tennessee native who had moved to New Orleans in 1840, the same year as Rose, and had become a cotton broker regarded well enough to win election in 1846 to the Louisiana Legislature. Traveling with his son, Joseph, and a slave named Dow, as well as with other associates, Eastland kept a diary of the journey, nicknaming himself and others who wanted to go all the way to the West Coast "the Californians."

He supplemented our knowledge of the events that occurred en route to El Paso with letters home to his wife, Josephine. In one of his earliest letters, he noted that severe rains had hampered the beginning of the expedition, but that the travelers were using the time to acclimate themselves to a new lifestyle. Writing on June 3, he added: "Our mode of living is very simple. We eat twice a day, cook our provisions on a brush fire. Our coffee is very good, so is our fried bacon and beef, as well as our corn and wheat bread. We are never troubled with changes of dishes and scorn anything in the shape of dessert... I have only five persons in my mess, and will not increase the number knowing that the fewer we have, the less will be the trouble and the expense…"[63]

Castroville

One of the first places where the expedition "laid by" was the town of Castroville, situated about 30 miles west of San Antonio, on the bank of the Medina River. Although Rose, who one day would lay out "Roseville" on the shores of San Diego Bay, left no written comment on the new American settlement created by a fellow European Jew, other travelers on the same expedition did record their impressions.

Captain S.G. French of the topographical engineers arrived there on Monday, June 4, 1849, and noted in his diary that it had "about 500 inhabitants, mostly German emigrants." He could not resist adding, disapprovingly: "The place presents but a few signs of improvement and idleness and poverty are more visible than industry and wealth; houses are falling to decay and the rich lands lie uncultivated."[64]

The town made a far better impression on Eastland, who recorded in his diary after arrival there on June 8: "This camp was on the Rio Medina, near Castroville (a settlement of Germans who appear to be industrious and very clever). The river is a beautiful stream and abounds in fish. Got my wagon tongue mended, or rather got a new one made, the old one having taken the liberty of separating on the prairie, 7 miles from town." [65]

By the time Rose and the other travelers saw the small new town, numerous buildings had been erected, some of which still survive.

An early curiosity of Castroville was a home built by Peter Pingenot, which had two chimneys instead of the usual three favored by Alsatians. It also had the steepest roof in town, and timbers marked with Roman numerals just in case re-assembly were required. Like his neighbors, Pingenot used a single oak beam to center his roof; and to this 60-foot pole he attached crossbeams. Fachwerk, reminiscent of many a cottage in Alsace, was used for the interior walls.[66]

Castro had built several other towns in the area, providing Rose and the other emigrants more impressions of life on the frontier. Captain French, poetic at times about scenery but typically quite critical about people, said in his official topographical report that from Castroville the southern road to El Paso "leads over some gentle hills and thence through a tract of land pretty well timbered until it opens out into what here is known as a 'hog wallow' prairie.

> We found the road owing to the rains as bad as can be imagined. Beyond this prairie is a slightly elevated ridge from the

top of which, spread out before him, the traveler sees the beautiful valleys of the Quihi and the Hondo, pent in by the blue hills in the distance…The village of Quihi is a German settlement, being a branch of the main one at Castroville and consists of only a few miserably rude huts—distance from Castroville 10 miles. Six miles further on the road is the town of Vandenburg, third settlement made by the same colony. It consists of some 21 houses or huts. The country around is beautiful and productive and nothing but industry is required to make it teem with all the productions of agriculture.[67]

Life on the Wagon Trail

After leaving the Castro group of settlements, the Army and the emigrants had months of wilderness ahead of them. Where they would find good water and grazing for their animals, and whether there might be hostile Indians ahead, were their principal preoccupations as they trudged across Texas.

The Eastland party spent June 13 camping and "cleaning up our arms, moulding bullets and getting our harness fitted for any emergency...Some Indian signs in the neighborhood; all we fear is that the rascals (like snakes) will creep upon us in the night and steal our animals. Woe be to the man who loses any, for no more are able to be had outside the settlements. The troops being encamped near us, we are treated with the music of a find band every evening which puts one in mind of 'sweet home.'"[68]

Their fears appeared justified two days later when Eastland's party "heard today of the murder of four Mexican teamsters by Indians, at our Camp No. 7 on the Sabinal"—the same place where his own party had camped ahead of the troops. "These poor creatures had been employed at San Antonio to hawl (sic) public property to the Leona, on their return to San Antonio they were encamped at the place above named, where they were found next morning dead and stripped of every vestige of clothing, their cattle driven off and nothing living in the camp save a spaniel dog."

Voicing prevailing sentiment among Anglo emigrants, Eastland thundered to his diary, "it would be doing but justice to exterminate these heartless murderers." Returning to his diary later, Eastland became more stoical: "This affair caused a momentary excitement in the camp, but when night came, we lay down upon our hard beds and slept as soundly as though we were at home in our comfortable beds. Men become used to anything, even to having a snake or other venomous reptile for a bed fellow."[69]

The party pushed on. In a journal entry on June 24, a Sunday, Eastland remarked: "This is the Sabbath and although we have hardly anything to remind us of it, yet I believe not one of our party…would openly or know-ingly violate the Holy Day. We trust in God for our future welfare." It is fair to conclude from this comment that Rose neither said nor did anything to cause Eastland to realize that Jews celebrate the Sabbath not on Sundays, but on Saturdays. Ironically, in his journal for the same day, Eastland went on to speculate in most un-Sabbath-like fashion about a possible new commercial enterprise. "Here," at the thirteenth camping place utilized by the settlers since leaving San Antonio, at a distance of about 130 miles from that city, "we found the plant called rosea, the seed of which is very pungent and used as snuff, produce(s) the same effect as tobacco, but without the smarting sensation of the latter," he observed. "At some future time it will become an article much sought after by those in this life who are effected (sic) by slight colds and can afford the luxury."[70]

Captain French and the engineers meanwhile were approaching the San Pedro River, nicknamed the "Devil's River" by previous travelers. The military officer reported: "The descent to the river is made through crooked ravines that required much labor to make them passable. This is perhaps the only point at which it is possible to gain the opposite bank for several miles, either up or down the river."[71]

When Eastland arrived at the same point on Friday, June 29, he facetiously pretended to be disappointed in how well the engineers had done their job: "Here we expected to find his satanic majesty in the shape of rugged moun-tains and impassible ravines, for rumor had connected everything horrible in the way of difficulties in passing this river. Quite different did we find it. The Engineers (with whom we caught up at this point) had made a good road…to the stream (about 100 yards wide) which we crossed without difficulty except that my pony slipt down and gave me a good wetting." [72]

Notwithstanding the rains, fear of Indians, and heat, the first month of the three-month expedition from San Antonio to El Paso passed fairly smoothly. Testifying to this was José Policarpo Rodríguez, a well-regarded guide who was nicknamed "Polly" by Lieutenant Colonel Johnston and the engineers with whom he traveled in advance of the main party. In a reminiscence published in 1897, nearly a half-century after the event, he wrote with perhaps only slight exaggeration:

"Where the prairie was smooth and open the colonel gave the teamsters orders to follow me and not turn to their right or left, and I led them in a per-fectly straight line. When you looked back from the front, you could see but one wagon—the one in front. The road we made was beautiful. You could see the white trail through the clay soil for miles and miles as straight as an arrow. The troops followed on behind us."[73]

The first week or so of July 1849 was equally pleasant. But later the party's luck began to change. For Rose, who was singled out to bear the brunt of the general frustration, July would prove disastrous.

On July 1, Eastland and other civilians left their camp at the San Pedro/Devil's River, pausing briefly to admire a cave found on the left of the wagon road. Using the symbol "&c" in his journal to indicate "etcetera," Eastland wrote of finding paintings of "various figures of men, women, buffalos &c no doubt the work of Indians, and intended to commemorate some event, or as a sign to others."[74] As was typical, French had only scorn for the works of other men. The area was known as "Painted Caves," he commented, as a result of "some rude Indian paintings on the rocks."[75]

Two days later, Eastland and company made camp at a place called "Cherry Springs." The name was derived "from the fact that a man of that name in the company had discovered them," Eastland explained.[76] (Within a decade, Rose, who also passed Cherry Springs, would have a canyon in San Diego named for him. Just as travelers were misled by the name to search fruitlessly for the cherries at Cherry Springs, so too in the future would they search in vain for roses in San Diego's Rose Canyon.)

American Independence Day, July 4, was cause for a prairie ceremonial. "A salute was fired at sunrise," but "there being no higher elevation in this wilderness of the prairie," the celebrants decided to improvise. "The Stars & Stripes (was) hoisted to the end of a wagon," Eastland wrote. "No doubt this is the first time such things have been known hereabouts...We celebrate the day as best as we can and drink (to) the health of our country, wives, sweethearts, children & friends..."[77]

While the celebrants drank and ate heartily, they were careful not to waste anything, a lesson which for Rose would prove instructive for his later life in San Diego, where businesses as both a tanner and a butcher would be among his many enterprises. Eastland related that "what is considered worthless in beef in civilized society is in camp proven to be the best. The head roasted as it comes off the beef (except the horns) can't be beat—a pit is dug, the head put in, covered up, and a good fire kept over it from some 6 to 8 hours, take it out, season to suit and epicures would start with wonder at its richness. The marrow gut is also delicious, and the bloodpuddings very good, so are the feet and shin bones. If I live to get home again, these fixins will not be forgotten."[78]

Eastland's last expression of worry was not without its cause. Even amidst the drinking and hollering of July 4, he noted troubling signs that seemed omens of things to come. Here the expedition was only a third completed, yet "all are out of fresh provisions and we are getting out of the deer range. I much fear our staple supplies will become much reduced." Additionally, he noted, during the celebration, 'there was a fight or two between some outsiders, and the stealing of a horse at night, which however was recovered and the thief was driven from the camp."[79]

Alcohol had brought the tensions among some of the travelers out into the open; it would not be long until various forms of adversity brought other tensions and frustrations to the surface. Eastland's diary provides a barometer of the growing restiveness. On Monday, July 9, he reported, "fire broke out in the prairie not far distant from the camp which at one time seriously threatened us, but by active exertions it was subdued. This fire was caused by the main body who unexpectedly came up and encamped in our neighborhood (at Big Drunk Camp)...At night Dow was on guard with his old musket, which accidentally went off, alarming the whole camp, which was soon under arms ready for action. Dow's explanation made all quiet again..."

His July 10 entry noted "the main body came up and encamped near us, much to our annoyance as they pretty soon consumed nearly all the water from our springs and threw on our grazing ground more than a thousand animals—however we believe there is enough for all."

Eastland's attempt at optimism didn't quell his disquieting thoughts. On the next day, a month-old newspaper brought by dispatch rider from New Orleans told of the death on June 15 of former U.S. President James K. Polk, who had been the nation's eleventh chief executive, as well as the death of General Edmund Pendleton Gaines, who had served a half century in the U.S. military. Gaines perhaps was remembered best as the man who captured and later brought to trial for treason America's third vice president, Aaron Burr, who later was acquitted on charges of attempting to create a breakaway nation in America's Louisiana Territory. Of greater immediacy to the emigrants was the news that reportedly had been received by General Harney that there appeared to be "a rising among the Indians to cut off parties passing through the country."

On Thursday, July 12, Eastland complained to his diary that Van Horne, the expedition's commander, "permitted his horses, mules &c to use our springs, which, to say the least, was contrary to the usual practice among travelers in the wilderness. I fear this course will be the means of driving us on, before we are prepared to go..."[80]

Eastland did not confide to his diary whether he was a superstitious man, so there is no way of knowing whether he considered "Friday, the 13th" to be especially unlucky. But, as a search party looked for an artillery officer and a wagon master (who later turned up safe), his mood on that day was gloomy: "We are now in the heart of Indian country, and small parties are going out daily; until some of them are cut off, I fear the vigilance that ought to be exercised will not be."

Rose is Banished

That Sunday, the emigrants were alarmed by a near stampede among their animals. Eastland's sense of humor returned to him as he wrote that the animals in the stampede found it "was no go, and they concluded it was best to behave themselves according to the Rules & Regulations made and provided in such cases."

The following Thursday, Eastland's worries again dominated his mood. "I much fear we have been too sanguine in our anticipation of more speedy traveling. There appears to be great difficulty in finding a passageway to and over the Pecos (River); the guide is now out reconnoitering and we hope he will be successful in finding a good route."[81]

A route finally found, the expedition set out on Sunday, July 22. Eastland's Holy Day was spent marching "over a very rough road, and ... the heat of the sun made hard work for our animals." That evening "our horses were stolen from Major Van Horne's command, one of which was found." The following day there was found "some distance from a camp killed by an arrow, the poor animal having no doubt given out. This will at least have the effect to make the night guard more vigilant and more care taken of the animals."[82] Two days later, on July 25, for reasons never further explained by Eastland:

> ...one of our party (a Jew named Rose) was (by order of Maj[o]r Van Horn[e]) drummed out of camp. He was condemned without a hearing, and thus disgracefully punished. A little brief authority in the hands of a damned fool, is ever exercised injudiciously, and therefore (except by accident) allways (sic) injuriously. The 'Californians' feel the insult, but like good citizens bear it for the sake of their country's good. Perhaps the time is not far distant, when this officer will be made to know, that a citizen traveling through his own country in a time of peace cannot be thus arbitrarily dealt with, no odds what the offence. Poor Rose cannot return to camp except at night, or when the troops are out of sight. We have determined that he shall not be driven entirely away.[83]

The only other time Eastland mentioned Rose in his diary was the very next day, leaving us mystified both as to what caused the falling out with Van Horne, and whether the situation returned to normal at some point before the party reached El Paso at the beginning of September.

"Last night, the government horses and mules stampeded, the cry was Indians, every man sprang to his arms, and was ready to fight, but the animals were stopped and safely herded to camp," Eastland wrote on July 26. "It is uncertain what caused the stampede but as Indians had stolen horses a few nights before, it is reasonable to suppose they did it. This morning after the troops had marched, Rose returned to camp to see his property which had been taken care of. He was advised to keep out of sight for the present."[84]

The theft of the horses on the night of July 22, preceded Rose's expulsion, but care should be taken when inferring any cause and effect. Although civilians did have responsibilities to stand guard during the trip—as we know the hapless Dow did—we have no way of ascertaining whether Rose stood guard the night of the horse's disappearance or if Van Horne's ire with Rose had anything to do with that. None of Van Horne's official reports for the period mentioned either the incident or Rose. If Rose ever spoke about the incident later in San Diego, no one wrote it down.

Coward of the Alamo

One gets the sense, but again it can't be proven, that Rose's Judaism might have had something to do with Van Horne's anger. Or perhaps Van Horne might have mistaken the Louis Rose on his wagon train for the Louis "Moses" Rose who became known in Texas lore as the "Coward of the Alamo."

Born in 1775 in Laferee, Ardennes, France, Louis "Moses" Rose was serving in Napoleon's 101st Regiment in 1807, the year that Leffman "Louis" Rose was born in Neuhaus-an-der-Oste. The order of the French Legion of Honor was conferred upon "Moses" in 1814 for his role as an aide-de-camp to General Jacques Montfort. After emigrating to Texas, he lived in Nacogdoches and became a friend of hunting knife inventor James Bowie, whom he accompanied in 1836 to the Alamo.

"Moses" Rose later related the famous story of how, inside the surrounded fortress, Colonel William Travis drew a line on the ground with his sword, and urged those willing to make a last stand for freedom to step over the line. Bowie, who was ill, ordered his cot carried over the line, and all but one man similarly pledged their very lives to Texas' freedom. The lone holdout was Moses Rose who slipped out of the Alamo and dashed for freedom on March 3, three days before the forces of Mexican General Antonio Lopez de Santa Anna mounted their final assault. Repeatedly asked why he hadn't fought with the others, Moses Rose was said to have invariably replied, "By God, I wasn't ready to die."[85]

Ironically, although the story of Travis drawing the line in the sand was elevated by Texans nearly to the level of a Bible story, many of the state's residents and commentators refused to believe that Moses Rose was the man who had witnessed the event. Nor did they believe his tale of escaping on the afternoon of March 3 and scrambling through the brush to the Zuber family ranch house in Grimes County, where bruised, lame and exhausted from his flight he was nursed back to health. W.P. Zuber, who was a child at the time but who heard the details of the incident from his parents, felt compelled in 1901 to issue a point-by-point refutation of those who called Moses Rose a liar. If Moses Rose wasn't the one who told the story, and everyone else died, then where else could the tale about Travis drawing the line with his sword have come from? [86]

Passions against Moses Rose ran pretty strong. Back in Nacogdoches, and even in Logansport, La., where he died in 1851, he was taunted for his alleged cowardice. Children called him "Louisa" instead of "Louis," in derogation of his manhood.[87] As many members of the Jewish community who wince at the role played by Moses Rose are quick to tell you, there were two Jews who died along with the other martyred Alamo defenders: Anton Wolfe, a native of England, and Gabia Fuqua, a native of Gonzales, Texas.[88]

There were strategists over the years who argued that Moses Rose's course was far more prudent than that of Travis; had the latter endeavored to slip his forces out of the Alamo, instead of dying, they might have lived to fight another day.[89] Maybe so, Travis's partisans counter, but were it not for the selfless actions of the Alamo's defenders, the cause of Texas might have been left devoid of the passion necessary to defeat Santa Anna's superior numbers.

It can't be proven, but perhaps someone with a similar name as the "Coward of the Alamo" could have been a convenient scapegoat on whom Brevet Major Van Horne took out his mounting frustrations. It must have been comforting for Rose to know that the feeling against him was not universal; that, in fact, his fellow emigrants felt that he had been treated unfairly and decided to render him important aid, including looking after his personal effects, while he traveled alone, out of sight of the army.

What must have made Rose burn with the injustice of it was that the punishment for his "offense"—whatever it may have been—was the same meted out to the unnamed person on July 4th who tried to steal horses. Thieving horses in the Old West was a serious offense, often dealt with by what sardonically was called a "necktie party"—that is, a lynching. Forcing a person to travel alone in hostile Indian country could very well come to the same result as a lynching; stragglers were subject to ambush. The murder of the four Mexicans at the Sabinal, reported by Eastland on June 15, illustrates how dangerous unprotected travel could be. For however long he was banished from the wagon train, Rose must have been in constant fear for his life.

As one reads Eastland's trip diary, one tries to imagine the subsequent events from Rose's perspective, as he walked or camped somewhere off in the distance, kept from his companions and his personal effects, all the while knowing that he was a tempting target for any enemies who might see him.

Wagon Train Religion

Among those traveling with the wagon train was a group of California-bound New Yorkers, who styled themselves "The Fremont Association." Eastland went to their camp on Saturday, July 28, to hear preaching by a member of a sect then known as "Millerites" and today called "Adventists." Inasmuch as the sect's leader, William Miller, had predicted earlier in the decade that the world would end in 1843, the emigrants listened in 1849 with some skepticism to the acolyte. Eastland wrote humorously: "He did not touch on the peculiar tenets of his creed, that he promised to do tomorrow... Whether he intends to fix the day and the hour for 'ascension' is uncertain, but if he does I hope he will postpone it until we have journeyed out of this uncivilized wilderness, and let us all join our friends and go up with them."

The revival meeting, in Eastland's view, provided "a fine scene for a painter: at night in the midst of a camp, surrounded by wagons, tents, fires, horses, mules and all the paraphernalia of emigrants bound for a far distant land and through an unknown wilderness, suddenly to hear many voices joining in songs in praise to God, then the effective prayer, and then the word of God proudly and fully defended by one who pretended to no learning, and who no doubt sought according to his own understanding to teach the truth—such must have been the scenes when the Apostles preached in the wilderness, and taught the truths of the Gospel. I will not soon forget 'the sermon in the valley' preached in the 'stilly night,' the dark hills shutting out all save the starry heavens above and the bright moon."[90]

The meeting also was mentioned in a journal kept by a member of the Fremont Association, Robert Eccleston: "Mr. Brown," he wrote, "preached a sermon after supper from the words, 'if a man hate not his father and mother, brethren and sisters, yea and his own life, he cannot be my disciple.' After the sermon it was late enough to go to bed." [91] What were Rose's thoughts as the sound of the Christian worshippers, safe together, were carried to the lonely camping place of the Jew? One can only speculate.

On Sunday, July 29, the lay preacher Brown spoke again, attempting to persuade his listeners that although Miller had miscalculated the date of the end of the world, due "to the incorrectness of ancient history as to the record of time," the error could not have been of great magnitude.[92] A greater impression was made on the part of twenty-five emigrants by the sudden appearance at sundown of a bear in the camp. "We ran to meet him," Eastland wrote. "He walked within 40 yards of us. I waived my shot for Jo. He fired and missed. Another fired with as little success. The third brought him down, thus supplying us with fresh meat and no doubt preventing a stampede among our animals as they had been brought in for the night."[93]

Eastland's irritation with Van Horne continued to mount on the first day of August. A rider came bearing mail from New Orleans. He brought letters dated as recently as July 9. "Some of us wrote our family letters to be sent back, but the express was sent off, without even notifying us of it," he complained. "This shows a want of civility on the part of the officers of the Army toward citizens that is unpardonable."[94]

Saturday evening, August 4, one of the emigrants, Mrs. Ridgeway, gave birth to a son while the party was camped near the confluence of Live Oak

Creek and the Pecos River. Eastland thought that for the "little stranger" the name "Hard Times" would be appropriate—just the opposite from "Yom Tov," the name given at birth to Rose. On the day of the birth, Eastland worriedly noted, there were "fresh Indian camps here," adding that "a party that had been gone some six weeks into Mexico for mules for the Army and for whom we felt great anxiety returned today. They report the Indians very troublesome..."[95]

Crossing the Pecos River on August 7 was a complicated affair, with wagons taken over by government flatboat; animals, meanwhile, were prompted to swim to the other shore. Three days after this was accomplished, a Mr. Beaman died because of "old age and a complication of maladies," Eastland wrote. He had been sickly for the previous month or so. The party "buried him near the road (right side) and marked his grave with a cross bearing his name. The burial service was read by Dr. Cook...The ceremony, though in a wilderness, was very impressive. To see many hardy emigrants bent on their knees around the grave of a comrade in the wild wilderness, engaged in a prayer to God, was to my mind one of the most solemn scenes I ever witnessed. We left our poor fellow traveler with sorrowful hearts."[96]

A birth on August 4, a death on August 10. How transitory life was, especially for transients. All the emigrants may well have shared such an emotion. If Rose still was under Van Horne's ban, he may have felt the sorrowful news all the more acutely.

Nearing El Paso

On August 11, Eccleston recorded an act of cruelty by Brevet Major Henry, the Company K commanding officer traveling with his wife and family.

> Our notice was attracted this morning by a young colored woman who came near our camp, crying and imploring aid. She said her mother had been beaten and she said she was afraid they would tie her up. She said that the offender was Major Henry. On going up the road we found the old dame. I will now describe our heroine. She was about 18 years old, of middle stature and fine figure. Her features were not African in the least. She was neatly dressed, her low neck dress showing a breast which in form would eclipse many a belle, whose might have been whiter. Her waist was small and exquisite, her color was a shade darker than a mulatta and but for the prejudice of color, she would be a charmer. Her mother was different, being darker and bearing all the marks of the African race. She said that she had talked sassy to Major Henry but that

she could not help it, as she had been used to decent treatment. She said she was as free as Major Henry was... Her traps
were all thrown out in a heap on the campground, and the
Army train went on, leaving her and her daughter without
provision, to the mercy either of Californians or the savages. I
wished it was in my power to relieve them, but it was not. Mr.
Ridgeway... offered to take one, but they would not separate.
I afterwards heard that Mr. Stanmore took them under his
protection. Major Henry bears a poor name and indeed I
think he richly deserves it, when he would leave even his
worst enemy under such circumstances.[97]

The parallel in the treatment meted out by Major Henry to the two
African-American women and that inflicted upon Rose by Major Van Horne
is remarkable. Even though one wonders whether Eccleston was more moved
by the injustice of the situation or by his obviously libidinous feelings toward
the 18-year-old girl, one cannot disagree with his negative assessment of
Henry, and by extension of Van Horne. Coupled with Eastland's earlier denun-
ciation of Van Horne's treatment of Rose, Eccleston's account deepens one's
suspicion that both officers were bigots whose actions were motivated by racial
and religious hatred.

The party camped for several days along the River Limpia, waiting for the
engineers to confirm a good road with sufficient water for the trip from the
Pecos River to the Rio Grande. Except for constant grumbling about the heat
and the length of the wait for the engineers, this was a period of quiet. About
the most exciting incident occurred on Friday, August 23, when the wagon
train rumbled over a "prairie dog village." Eccleston reported that people from
another mess shot three of the rodents so as to vary their supper, adding the
heart-breaking information that the prairie dogs "are very hard to get even
after you shot them as they will crawl down into their holes, and if unable to
do this another will pull them in."[98] Eastland was far less anthropomorphic in
his assessment. Prairie dogs, he said, "are nothing more than ground squirrels,
resembling very much the fox squirrel and in taste precisely similar. They make
an excellent stew."[99]

On Monday, August 27, the emigrant party seemed at a loss of direction.
Instead of following the main road, the ox train was instructed to turn "at
nearly right angles to the road...Not knowing how far it was to water or anything else," fumed Eccleston. "Such work is indeed a disgrace, not only to the
Army but to the United States." He said there were rumors that Major Van
Horne of the main body and Lieutenant Colonel Johnston of the engineers felt
"considerable enmity" for each other. "The former is closing in upon the latter before the road is redy (sic) and thus the fruits (results), traveling out of the

way, hunting water here and there, dividing the train and putting us to a considerable inconvenience who they have invited to accompany them."[100]

There was worse news two days later, when the party still was about 170 miles from El Paso. Reported Eastland: "Some of the Californians are entirely out of provisions, what the poor fellows will do I know not. None of us have any to spare, but will of course help them all we can. Last night, the beef contractor lost all his cattle. If he should not find them again, there will be great suffering. I much fear the Indians stole them, as many fresh signs are seen in the neighborhood."[101]

On August 30, Eccleston and other members of the Fremont Association decided to change their position in the wagon train and made plans to "slip, if possible, after the Engineer train... When about ready to start, Lieutenants Whistler and Mason (came) with orders from Major Van Horn(e) for all Californians to fall in the rear of the ox train. This was a damper... Upon expostulation, we got permission on condition that we could help and open the road. We consented and again made an attempt to start, in which we were successful, notwithstanding the wind and rain which the animals did not care about facing. The road was only tolerable..."[102]

Eastland reported killing "a very large rattlesnake while out hunting" on August 31[103] and so ended the third month on the long road to El Paso. For Rose, the conclusion of a tortuous and humiliating journey was near.

A welcome sight greeted the emigrants on September 3 as they followed the Rio Grande north toward El Paso. They "met two Mexican carts from the El Paso Valley loaded with grapes, peaches, apples, onions &c.," Eastland enthused. "After upwards of 3 months living on meats altogether, we greedily devoured these luxuries without fearing cholera or any other malady." Two days later, the group met several more fruit carts and the emigrants "again feasted to our hearts content."[104]

The party reached the village of Isleta on Thursday, September 6, where rooms to rent and expensive provisions were available. Eastland decided this was a place to rest and make ready for the next leg of his journey. One assumes that Rose, having little or no motivation to continue in the wake of Van Horne's expedition, also decided to stop here or nearby. Thereafter, the paths of Eastland, Eccleston and Rose diverged. Eastland decided to go south to Chihuahua, Mexico, and then across to Mazatlan, where he planned to catch a ship north to California.[105] Eccleston continued by wagon to California in the company of 100 other emigrants and Jack Hays, the former Texas Ranger. They arrived in December of 1849.[106] Rose rested some months before setting out overland for San Diego. As for Van Horne, he established an Army post across the border from the Mexican town of El Paso del Norte.[107] Eventually the American settlement that grew up around the post became known as El Paso; the Mexican town that had bore that name was renamed as Juarez in 1888 in honor of the former Mexican President Benito Juarez.[108]

While resting for the trip ahead, Eastland, drawing on his diary and other observations, wrote a long letter to his wife summarizing the trip. Without specifying a date or a place, he related:

> On one occasion after a hard day's march, night overtook us, and not a drop of water could be found, the hole we depended upon having dried up. Our poor animals cried piteously for it, indeed our whole party were suffering, most of them not having enough to make a cup of coffee, and the worst of it was, we knew of no water for many miles ahead, and all began to be seriously alarmed for our animals. While standing around our camp fires talking about our situation, it became cloudy and in less than half an hour (and for the first time in many days), the rain poured down, giving us a full supply and filling up the water holes all along the road until we reached a fine spring. Thus kind Providence supplied our wants, and I doubt not, that every individual in the camp looked upon it as a special dispensation of God's goodness to his children in the wilderness. This was not the only time we escaped suffering by being supplied by the same inexhaustible fountain. [109]

This analogy to the biblical Exodus, if applied to Rose's situation, would have been quite ironic. For Rose, "liberation" came not with the journey but in finally being freed from its leaders.

Rose and His Mentor

After recuperating for a while in the El Paso area, Rose joined a wagon train bound for California that had among its passengers James W. Robinson, his wife, Sarah, and their son, William. An interesting and close friendship developed between these two men, one a Jew, the other a Christian; one born in Europe; the other born in the United States; one with developing business acumen, the other with political savvy. Eventually Robinson and Rose would combine their backgrounds and talents to nudge their adopted city of San Diego toward its destiny.

Theirs were tales of the nineteenth century, a restless time of startling social changes and amazing technological advances. Millions of people were on the move during the nineteenth century, typically westward. Men like Louis Rose voyaged from Europe to the United States, where they met men like James W. Robinson bound for America's far frontier. As they headed west, they could reflect on their lives, on their past mistakes, and could resolve to do better. Sometimes, in the process, the men tried to reinvent themselves.

Rivers influenced both their lives. Rose grew up near the confluence of the River Elbe and the River Oste in what is today northern Germany and what was in his time the Kingdom of Hanover. Robinson settled on a farm near the Little Miami River in Ohio.

When Rose looked out on the River Elbe—the busiest river in Europe, connecting the industrial city of Hamburg to the North Sea—he saw the possibilities that come with commerce. When Robinson, a school teacher, looked across the Little Miami, he saw the temptation of a better life with Sarah, who was considerably younger than his wife, Mary, then pregnant with their third child. Robinson deserted his first family and fled with Sarah to Canada. They later worked their way to Arkansas, and eventually to Texas.[110]

In Nacogdoches, Robinson built a new life for himself as an attorney. When President Santa Anna suspended the liberal Mexican constitution, Robinson was among those who protested. He was elected a delegate to the Consultation of 1835, where delegates were divided between those who favored immediate independence for Texas and those who sought to condition future acceptance of Mexico's sovereignty on the restoration of the Constitution. The Consultation set up a provisional government in which Henry Smith, who was pro-independence, was elected as governor over Stephen Austin, a land baron who preferred a go-slow approach. Robinson, who had helped draft the Organic Law governing the affairs of the provisional government, was elected lieutenant governor. The position was to last but four months—Texans planned to hold a Constitutional convention on March 1, 1836.[111]

Smith and the leadership of the Legislative Council, each jealous of their prerogatives, fell to bitter quarreling. It got so bad between them that at one point the Legislative Council voted Smith out of office while Smith, simultaneously, dissolved the Legislative Council. In a time of military danger from Mexican military forces, Texas, for all practical purposes, had two governments that did not recognize each other's authority. One was headed by Smith, the other by Robinson, who had been elevated by the Legislative Council to the position of acting governor.

While members of the Texas government carried out their quarrel, Texas revolutionary forces suffered major defeats at the hands of the Mexican troops, culminating a few days after the Constitutional Convention convened with the fall of the Alamo.[112]

As soon as his term of office expired, Robinson joined the Texas Army (led by General Sam Houston) as a private soldier and participated in the Battle of San Jacinto.[113] Later, the government of the new Republic of Texas appointed him a district court judge, but some of his rulings were so questionable that he eventually was persuaded in a closed-door session of judges to resign from the bench. In one famous case, Judge Robinson ordered a defendant whipped before his lawyer could appeal the verdict. In another case, the judge heard that friends of a defendant in a capital case were planning to break him out of jail the morning he was to be executed. Robinson ordered the sheriff to hang the man that very night.[114]

After he left the bench, he practiced law, and was at the courthouse in San Antonio for two famous incidents. One, in 1842, was a meeting between representatives of the new Texas government and the Comanche Indians concerning hostages for whom the Indians wanted ransom. Robinson was outside the courthouse amusing himself by throwing up quarters for young Indians to shoot with their arrows. Suddenly there was a war whoop from inside the courthouse, indicating a bloody battle had commenced between the Texans and the Indians, and the youngsters promptly started firing their arrows at the other bystanders outside the courthouse. Robinson was wounded.[115]

Two years later, Robinson was among those at the courthouse who were captured in a raid staged by Mexican General Adrian Woll and later marched to Perote Prison in Vera Cruz, Mexico. Robinson wrote a letter to Santa Anna requesting a meeting. When the audience was granted, he proposed to carry back to Texas President Sam Houston a proposal from Santa Anna that Texas give up its independence and instead become an autonomous region of Mexico. Santa Anna agreed to the plan, and arrangements were made for Robinson to travel to the neutral American port of New Orleans, and from thence to Galveston, Tex. On arrival, Robinson published details of the plan, ahead of a meeting with Sam Houston.[116]

Not in the least bit interested in Texas again becoming part of Mexico, Houston nevertheless saw the communication as a way to open negotiations with Mexico and thereby to put pressure on the United States to annex Texas as a state. Subtly playing one country against the other, Houston thereby was able to overcome objections from anti-slavery forces in the Congress to admitting another slave-holding state. The admission of Texas as the twenty-eighth state of the Union was one of the factors leading to the Mexican–American War, which resulted in Mexico ceding tremendous tracts of territory, including California, to the United States.[117]

Those Texans whom Robinson had left behind at Perote denounced him as a traitor and turncoat. No explanations about the subtlety of diplomacy could erase that image.[118] Thereafter, Robinson never was able to reestablish a successful law practice. After news of the California gold rush reached Texas, Robinson realized that California soon would become a state, and that there would be plenty of work for a lawyer familiar with the carryover effects of Spanish land grants and Mexican land law. With Sarah and William in tow, Robinson decided to head west.[119] That he and Rose would wind up together on the same wagon train was for San Diego an important coincidence.

As tributaries to a river arise in locations separated by great distances and dissimilar geography, so too did Rose and Robinson travel long ways to meet each other and aggregate their forces. Their combined force helped carve the downstream landscape.

Robinson and Rose Join Forces

We do not know the details of how or when Robinson and Rose made each other's acquaintance in the El Paso area, nor the exact nature of the chemistry that transformed two men, seemingly opposites in background and temperaments, into business and political partners who would help to change the face of San Diego. What we do know is that Robinson was the obviously senior member of the partnership, not only by virtue of his being 9 years older than Rose but also because he was a man of much wider public experience. Yet, no genuine friendship is one-sided. Robinson learned much from Rose who, unlike him, had lived and traveled in Europe and who had absorbed some of the Old World's lessons.

The two men also may have recognized in each other similarities based on their own regrets. Gold and an energized economy were the primary magnets drawing the emigrants to California, but they were not the only reasons. California represented a place where a person could start one's life over, where one could get out from under the yoke of a damaged reputation. In California, Rose could leave behind the New Orleans' shame of bill collectors pounding at his door. Robinson could put distance between himself and the charges of "traitor" generated by the proposals he brought to Houston from Santa Anna. Instead of resigning himself to the deterioration in Texas of his once-booming law practice, he might with his superior knowledge of Spanish and Mexican land grant law build his practice anew in California.

Both men knew that starting over was indeed possible. Robinson had left a life in Ohio and had been welcomed in Texas. Rose had immigrated from Germany to New Orleans and initially did well enough in business to feel marriage to Caroline was warranted. Another possible bond between the two men probably was never expressed, especially given the presence of Robinson's wife, Sarah, and son, William, in the wagon train. Both men had corners of their lives that they preferred to keep secret. For Robinson, it was the fact that he had abandoned his pregnant first wife and their two children—a fact that only became generally known in San Diego many years after his death when his will was probated.[120] We don't know what Rose wanted to bury with the past, but we do know that he was extremely reticent to discuss the portion of his life that occurred before his arrival in the United States.[121] Finally, there was another bond between Robinson and Rose: one which has brought together Jews and Protestants for centuries in fraternity and fellowship. Both had become members of the Masons; Robinson in Texas and Rose somewhere in Europe.

The trail that the Robinson-Rose party followed in the spring of 1850 along the Gila River to California, and thence through the desert and mountains to San Diego, was fraught with constant danger. The elements were harsh enough, yet sometimes they were overshadowed by the cruelty of human predators—both Indian and Anglo—who often laid in wait for emigrants. Whatever the initial chemistry was between the two men, their friendship was catalyzed by shared apprehension and adventure. No doubt it also was solidified by many hours of discussions that unfolded along a trail that seemed to stretch endlessly before them. Robinson was a talker and in Rose he found an attentive listener.

From Robinson, we have all-too-brief, yet direct testimony about the journey. From Rose, we have a story remembered eighty-one years after the event by a daughter born in the autumn of his life. "I came here broken in fortune, not a cent in pocket," Robinson confided in a letter to his friend Amasa Turner, written about ten months after the party's arrival in San Diego in May 1850. "Our suffering on the road here cannot be credited. Those that had means of comfort were compelled to divide until all was exhausted. I only got in with 2 mules, two waggon (sic) and nearly dead. Many died on the road, some from disease, some from exposure and others from starvation and a combination of all these causes. On mules back and very light pack on mules, is the only way and then the suffering is great. The best route is by way of Texas, start from Indianola to El Passo (sic), down the Gila to San Diego, California. There is a ferry and military post at the mouth of the Gila." [122]

From Rose, we have second-hand testimony. His daughter, Henrietta, recollected in a 1931 interview with San Diego historian Winifred Davidson that her "father had come with Judge Robinson. He told about Mrs. Robinson being captured by the Indians en route...Father said that his party came in by way of the Cuyamacas. They were all starving. The men were glad to chew their belts, they were so hungry." [123] Further details of Sarah Robinson's abduction remarkably are missing from this account. Inasmuch as she arrived safely in San Diego with her husband, obviously Mrs. Robinson had been liberated somehow from her captors, but whether by force of arms or by ransom is left to our imagination. So, too, is the place where the incident occurred and the identity of the Indians. At least two groups were greatly feared along their route. If Mrs. Robinson's capture occurred near the beginning of the trip, it might have been by Apaches; if near the Colorado River, by Yumas.

Taken together, the two accounts tell us that the party either underestimated the amount of time it would take to get to California, and thus began their journey with insufficient supplies, or that they encountered some mishap—perhaps at the time of Sarah Robinson's abduction—which left them in dire need of food. Apparently the party particularly was unprepared for the heat of the Arizona and California deserts, thus Robinson's reference to death by exposure. Although they did not travel in the height of the summer, the party probably encountered temperatures in excess of 100 degrees, which are common in the desert in the months of April and May. Robinson's comment about the advisability of going with a light pack on a mule is telling: Trying to get the wagons through the desert and up and over the mountains consumed valuable time and required the consumption of more and more rations. That there was a necessity "to divide until all was exhausted" is reassuring testimony to the generous character of the emigrants: although their own lives were at risk, the party did not selfishly withhold aid from each other. Yet even so, some emigrants died from starvation. There must have been some form of rationing which, for some, simply was insufficient to their physical needs.

Historian John Henry Brown, who chronicled the life of Henry Smith, informs us that the man who contested Robinson for the Texas provisional governorship, met up with him en route to El Paso. However, Robinson preceded Smith to California. Smith's route took him "through the mining town of Corralitos, Hannas, Santa Cruz, San Gabriel, the Pima and Maricopa villages on the Gila, across the Colorado and the desert beyond, into California."[124] This is a variant of the routes followed to San Diego in 1846 by the Army of General Stephen Watts Kearny and later that year by the Mormon Battalion. It is likely that the Robinson-Rose party followed a similar course.

Trouble at the Colorado River Crossing

Robinson made specific reference in the letter to Turner to the "ferry and military post at the mouth of the Gila." From the earliest times of the Gold Rush, the spot where the Gila River flows into the Colorado River became an important crossing for the emigrants heading for California. At first, Quechan Indians—part of the group today known as Yuma Indians—helped to swim animals and supplies across the Colorado River, which today forms the boundary line between Arizona and California. A more formal ferry was established late in 1849 by the U.S. Boundary Commission while mapping the exact border between Mexico and the United States in this area.

When the Boundary Commission departed, a man named Able Lincoln started a commercial ferry, which, though expensive to operate, was quite profitable. In April of 1850, he wrote to his parents:

> I have been here some three months, during which time I have crossed over 20,000 Mexicans, all bound for the mines and I am still carrying some 100 per day. During the three months I have been here, I have taken in over $60,000. My price, $1 per man, horse or mule $2, the pack $1, pack saddle 50 cents, saddle 25 cents. But my expenses are high. I have 12 Americans, deserters of the army, that I am paying $100 a month, also 10 Americans that I pay $40 a month each. These men I have all armed with Colt revolvers for which I paid $75 each. I have also 16 U.S. rifles and a small piece of artillery

which I purchased of the American consul at Guaymas. In addition to this I have to pay $20 a bushel for corn meal, 75 cents a pound for flour, unsifted, and for dried beef (the only meat I can get) I pay $1.90 per pound. For coffee I paid $4 a pound and all things according. [125]

Lincoln's fortune was too good to last. The notorious John Glanton and his gang arrived on the scene and informed Lincoln that henceforth they would be his partners. Appreciating the fact that he was outgunned, Lincoln had no option but to agree to this "business arrangement." After serving in the Texas Rangers, Glanton had been commissioned as a junior cavalry officer in the U.S. Army during the Mexican–American War. After chasing one Mexican man, gunning him down, and taking his horse, Glanton was ordered imprisoned by his commanding general, Zachary Taylor, who would go on to become the twelfth president of the United States. Glanton, hearing of the order for his arrest, escaped to San Antonio and somehow managed to be mustered out of the service without further discipline. Had Taylor insisted upon a court-martial for Glanton, the killer might have been in prison in the years following the war instead of on the loose.

As a civilian, Glanton and a colleague, Michael H. Chevallie, persuaded the Legislature of Chihuahua that he and his band of gunmen could protect citizens of that Mexican state from the Apache Indians, who had been raiding settlements and terrorizing the frontier. A deal was struck: Glanton's band would receive payment for each Apache scalp brought back to the government.

For a time, government officials believed they had solved his problem, but then Glanton started turning in scalps that were not necessarily those of Indians. When the bodies of scalped Mexican villagers were discovered, a warrant was issued for the arrest of Glanton and his gang. In the Mexican village of Jesús María, Glanton and his gang showed their contempt for Mexican authority by tying the national flag to the tail of a donkey and dragging it through the streets. From windows and doorways, the outraged villagers opened fire on the gang, killing some and wounding others, but Glanton and most of his cohorts got away.[126] Unfortunately for Lincoln, they soon came to the junction of the Gila and Colorado Rivers.

About the time the band of murderers was muscling its way into Lincoln's business, the Quechan Indians were attempting to establish a rival ferry operation with boats bequeathed to them by travelers who had built their own means for crossing the river. Santiago, a Quechan chieftain, attempted to negotiate with Glanton. He suggested that the white men ferry people and supplies while the Quechans would concentrate on swimming animals across the river. Glanton's reply was typically brutal. He beat Santiago senseless. In so doing, he sealed his own doom. The Quechans bided their time, waiting for Glanton to return from buying supplies in San Diego to effect their plot. On April 21,

1850, after Glanton and his men became sleepy from drinking too much of the liquor they had so carefully transported east from San Diego, the Quechans attacked, clubbing not only Glanton to death, but also Lincoln and a number of Glanton's men.[127]

In all likelihood, the Robinson-Rose party arrived at the ferry crossing weeks after the bloodshed. Unless this was the time of Sarah's abduction, the party apparently was not mistreated by the Quechans. The Indians, by that time, perhaps assumed that with Glanton gone things would return to normal. But when Rose arrived in San Diego on May 30, he found California citizens up in arms about the incident. So great was the outcry that the American military commander in California, General Persifor Smith, issued Special Order No. 23 on July 4, instructing Major Samuel P. Heintzelman to establish a military post at the river crossing.[128] Heintzelman did not actually arrive at the river until November 1850 and then formed a commercial partnership with entrepreneurs who had started a new ferry operation in the interim. Heintzelman named his new military post "Yuma" after the Indian grouping to which the Quechans belonged. This was the "military post" to which Robinson alluded in his March 2, 1851, letter to Turner.

The Last Leg

As they made their way to San Diego, Robinson and Rose would have passed a site that is located today in Imperial County, but then was part of sprawling San Diego County. "Fort Salvation" had been constructed as a military installation in 1849 under the direction of Lieut. Cave J. Couts, military escort officer for the U.S. Boundary Commission.

During the three months that the commission and escort troops had worked in that desert area, the camp served as a welcome oasis for emigrants on the California trail. Although it was already abandoned by the time Robinson and Rose came through, it was a recognizable landmark that no doubt occasioned some comment—lightening the discussion as they looked forward to finally arriving in San Diego.[129] In their destination city, Robinson and Rose would get to know Couts quite well.

The travelers might have commented on the similarity in names between "San Antonio," a city where they both had spent time, and "San Diego," the city of their destination. It is tempting to imagine Rose, a Jew, and Robinson, a Protestant, comparing notes on these two cities named for Catholic saints.

Like San Antonio, the city of San Diego had been named in accordance with the Catholic custom of honoring the saint whose feast day fell closest to the day of discovery. In San Diego's case, there was a twist. The bay on which the city sits was claimed September 28, 1542, by Juan Rodríguez Cabrillo, in

command of two ships in the service of Spain, and named according to the custom, as "San Miguel." The name is the equivalent of "St. Michael," who is
known to both Christians and Jews as "Michael the Archangel."

On November 12, 1602, another Spanish explorer, Sebastian Vizcáino,
arrived at the bay, but either decided not to acknowledge it as the body of water
that Cabrillo had discovered, or failed to recognize it as such. Accordingly, he
named it after the saint whose feast day was closest—St. Didacus, who in
Spanish is known as San Diego. This saint was credited for performing medical
miracles aiding the Spanish royal family. Although the bay utilizes the name
given the area by Vizcáino, its discovery officially is dated back to Cabrillo.

Notwithstanding Cabrillo's and Vizcáino's "discoveries," the lives of the
Kumeyaay Indians, who had occupied the land since the days prior to written
history, proceeded according to the rhythms of the seasons without interruption. In the winter months, the Kumeyaay lived near the coast, where it was
warm. In the summer months, they migrated back to the mountains, where it
was cool.

It was not until 1769 that the Spanish—concerned lest Russians or British
attempt to colonize the area—decided to send an expedition northward from
New Spain (latter-day Mexico). The Franciscan Father Junipero Serra and the
Baja California Governor, Gaspar de Portola, established a military camp and
founded a mission and presidio on July 16, which they named in accordance
with the name given to the area by Vizcáino.

To Henrietta Rose's recollection of stories of her father coming to San
Diego "by way of the Cuyamacas"—a mountain chain lying to the east of San
Diego—we can add an observation set down in 1873 by a San Diego diarist
and jurist, Benjamin Hayes, in a eulogy for María Victoria Dominguez de Estudillo.

"In the mining days, during the rush of 1849, Mrs. Estudillo had many
opportunities of showing the native goodness of her heart," Hayes wrote.
"Large bodies of immigrants crossed the Colorado Desert and came down
through the Cajon, where her husband owned a large ranch. She was always
ready to succor those footsore and often destitute people. Among the rest, Mr.
Louis Rose, of Old Town, came to the Estudillo mansion with precisely ten
cents in his pocket, tired and hungry. The deceased Good Samaritan fed him,
lodged him and sent him on his way rejoicing, with a lunch prepared for the
journey. So unremitting and exquisite was her kindness that she received from
these people the affectionate appellation of 'mother.'"[130]

We have to take this story with a grain of salt. Rose arrived in 1850, not
in 1849, and if he had only a dime in his pocket apparently he had many dollars
in his saddlebags, with which he soon was able to acquire property. Furthermore,
it was not Mrs. Estudillo's husband, but her daughter and son-in-law, who
owned the ranch. Nevertheless, we must thank Hayes for the information that
Rose came down through the Cajon.

There were two routes by which travelers crossed the mountains separating the desert from the coastal plain. According to historian Arthur Woodward, the more popular route involved traveling northwest from Ocotillo in present Imperial County to Warner Springs and then southwest to Santa Ysabel, Ballena, Santa Maria, "to the hill leading down into San Pascual Valley and thence by way of Los Penasquitos and (modern day) Rose Canyon into San Diego." The less well-known alternative trail "traversed the Santa Maria Valley, angling southeast and crossing the old Mussey Grade, now partly under the waters of San Vicente Dam, and thence through the area now occupied by Lakeside, on across Rancho Santa Monica or El Cajon, down Mission Canon and into San Diego."[131] In order to arrive at the Estudillo Rancho en route to San Diego, Rose would have had to travel on the latter route.

What about Robinson? Apparently his family and Rose separated near the end of the journey, Rose perhaps deciding to rest at Warner's Ranch before making the last leg of the trek to San Diego. Another possibility is that the two friends decided to try different ways to San Diego from Warner's, with Robinson taking the more traditional route and Rose choosing the meandering path that passed by the rancho where he encountered Mrs. Estudillo. At any rate, the Robinsons arrived on May 20, 1850; Rose reached San Diego on May 30.[132]

Louis Rose, circa 1854
©San Diego Historical Society

Casa de Estudillo, Old Town

CHAPTER 2

San Diego

The Family Estudillo

As Louis Rose made his way to San Diego, he visited the 48,799-acre Cajon Rancho, where he enjoyed the hospitality of María Victoria Dominguez de Estudillo, affectionately known as "mother" by kin and non-kin alike. The rancho covered more than 11 leagues and was surrounded by mountains, hence its name cajon or "box." The large rancho enveloped the area now occupied by the modern-day cities and communities of El Cajon, Santee, Lakeside, Bostonia and Flinn Springs.[1]

Rose could not have chosen anyone better than Doña María Victoria to introduce him to San Diego society. Through marriage, her large and influential family was related to many of the major figures of San Diego. She was the daughter of María Reyes-Ybanes de Dominguez and Cristobal Dominguez, who during the Spanish times had been a sergeant serving at the San Diego Presidio.

Doña María Victoria's husband, José Antonio Estudillo, similarly had come from a military family. His father, José María Estudillo, had been assigned by Spain in 1806 to the presidio at Monterey. With the coming of independence in 1821, he transferred his allegiance to Mexico and served as a lieutenant until 1827. That year he was promoted to a captaincy and was transferred to San Diego, where he remained until his death.[2]

Almost from the time of the Estudillo family's arrival in San Diego, José Antonio had been active in civic affairs. In 1828, he served as San Diego's revenue collector and treasurer. Over the next thirteen years, he was granted various tracts of land at Otay (near the present Mexican border), Temecula (just north of the present San Diego County-Riverside County line), San Luis Rey (in northern San Diego County), and San Juan Capistrano (in southern Orange County). The large landowner was able to remain neutral in the Mexican-American War of 1846. On April 1, 1850, voters in San Diego County elected him as their tax assessor.

The Estudillos had five sons: José María, Salvador, José Guadalupe, José Antonio, and Francisco. They also had four daughters: Francisca, María del Rosario, María Antonia, and Concepción. Through these children, the family made alliances with many other important families in the San Diego area.

For example, the son, José María Estudillo, married Luz Marron. She was the daughter of Juan María Marron, who had been elected as a councilman of San Diego in 1834, during the town's Mexican period, and as alcalde or mayor, in 1848 during the period between the American conquest and California's statehood. Marron was the owner of Rancho Agua Hedionda north of San Diego.

Daughter María Antonia Estudillo de Pedrorena was a favorite of Pio Pico, the last Mexican governor of California. In 1845, he granted to her the Cajon Rancho,[3] which, according to custom, was thereafter controlled by her husband, Miguel de Pedrorena, until his death in March 1850. When Rose arrived at the rancho, he was entertained by the widow's mother.

Pedrorena was a native of Spain who had resided in Peru before immigrating to California. He had backed the American cause in the Mexican–American war, serving as a cavalry captain. He became San Diego's customs collector in 1847, serving through 1848. Pedrorena had embarked with San Francisco businessman William Heath Davis early in 1850 on a premature project to build "New Town" on the part of San Diego Bay where modern downtown San Diego now stands.[4]

Another daughter of José Antonio and Doña María Victoria was María Francisca Estudillo de Aguirre, the first wife of José Antonio Aguirre. The couple lived briefly in Santa Barbara, but in 1842, at age 17, Francisca died. Four years later, Aguirre married her sister, María del Rosario Estudillo, in the chapel of the large home that her parents maintained on the southeast end of the Plaza in Old Town San Diego. In 1850, Aguirre built a house for his new bride about a block east of his in-laws' home.

Born in Spain, Aguirre had remained loyal to his native country during the Mexican Revolution. Politically unpopular as a result, he moved to the United States and was naturalized in New Orleans, nine years before Louis Rose went through a similar rite in the same city. Subsequently Aguirre settled in Upper California, where he became the owner of the brigs *Leonidas* and *Joven Guipuzcoana*, the latter of which was interesting in a tangential way to the story of Louis Rose.

Although Rose was the "first permanent Jewish settler"[5] in San Diego, he was not the first Jew to come to San Diego. A full decade before Rose arrived, Lewis Polock had been arrested as an illegal immigrant by Mexican authorities in Yerba Buena (now San Francisco) and put aboard the *Joven Guipuzcoana* (Maid of Guipuzcoa) with other prisoners bound for San Blas, Mexico. They stopped in San Diego en route. Polock later returned to San Francisco, where in 1851, he was interrupted during a union with a prostitute. Her former lover shot Polock through the head.[6]

Aguirre, a gentleman, would have shuddered at such a tawdry association with his name. The home he had built in Santa Barbara was one of the finest residences of that city, and his Spanish-style home in San Diego likewise was widely admired for its tasteful furnishings. Like Pedrorena, with whom he had a business partnership, Aguirre had an interest in the William Heath Davis project to create New Town on the bay.

Davis himself was married to a niece of José Antonio and Doña María Victoria. José Joaquin Estudillo, a brother of José Antonio, established a ranch in San Leandro after their father had been transferred from the presidio at Monterey to the one at San Diego. Davis traveled frequently on business to San Francisco from his native Hawaii. On one of his trips, he met María de Jesus Estudillo, a daughter of José Joaquin's. Several members of the family into which Davis married became original investors in his New Town project.

In his memoirs, published in 1929, Davis wrote:

> Of the new town of San Diego, now the city of San Diego, I can say that I was the founder. In 1850, the American and Mexican commissions, appointed to establish the boundary line, were at Old Town. Andrew B. Gray, the chief engineer and surveyor for the United States, who was with the commission, introduced himself to me one day at Old Town. In February, 1850, he explained to me the advantages of the locality known as Punta de los Muertos (Point of the Dead), where a Spanish squadron anchored within a stone's throw.... (S)everal sailors and marines died and were interred on a sand split adjacent to where my wharf stood, and was named as above... Messrs. José Antonio Aguirre, Miguel Pedrorena, Andrew B. Gray, T.D. Johns and myself were the projectors and original proprietors of what is now known as the City of San Diego. All my co-proprietors have since died, and I remain alone of the party... The first building in new San Diego was put up by myself as a private residence—the building still stands, being known as the San Diego Hotel. I also put up a number of other houses... Under the conditions of our deed, we were to build a substantial wharf and warehouse. The other proprietors of the town deeded to me Block 20, where the wharf was completed in six months after getting our title in March, 1850, at a cost of $60,000... At the time I predicted that San Diego would become a great commercial seaport from its fine geographical position and from the fact that it was the only good harbor south of San Francisco...[7]

Whether Doña María Victoria mentioned this project to Rose during his brief visit with her is conjecturable. Exhausted after his long cross-country trek, Rose probably was not in any condition to assess the prospects of Davis' New Town. Within a short time after New Town began to falter, Rose would begin the process of accumulating land on another side of the bay, apparently believing Davis might have had the right idea, only in the wrong location.

Historic San Diego

For the present, however, Rose wanted only to reach Old Town and begin the process of starting his life anew. The San Diego River route along which Mother Estudillo sent him from Cajon Rancho was historically quite interesting. As he trudged westward to the Presidio, he passed a pair of landmarks of the Spanish era in San Diego. First, Rose passed the ruins of an adobe dam built across the San Diego River by Kumeyaay laborers supervised by Franciscan padres during the years 1813 to 1816. A tile flume on the upstream side of the dam siphoned water from the river system and by gravity flow brought it to San Diego Mission.[8] The mission, established in 1774 as the second mission building in the area, was the second site of interest that Rose would have passed. The original mission, in the opinion of the padres, had been built too close to the military Presidio and its resident Spanish soldiers who lusted after the Indian women acolytes.

A few miles beyond the mission, Rose reached the Presidio site itself, where Father Serra in 1769 had celebrated a mass marking the founding of the settlement. Following the base of the hill of the Presidio in a counter-clockwise direction, Rose next reached the tiny town of San Diego, today known as Old Town. We can assume that he subsequently located the Robinsons, and that his wagon train companions shared with him the benefit of their ten-day seniority in San Diego.

It is likely that the trail mates compared notes on rebuilding their lives, and, so they fervently hoped, on making their fortunes. In that latter respect, they were like numerous travelers, past and present, who have anticipated gathering or earning remarkable riches in California.

The very name of the state bespoke the fantastic expectations of those who had traveled over great distances to reach California. In the early sixteenth century, Garcia Ordoñez de Montalvo wrote an adventure story about a fictional Queen Caláfia and her realm. "(A)t the right hand of the Indies very near the location of the Garden of Eden, there once was an island called California, which was inhabited by black women without any man being among them, so that their way of life was almost Amazon like," the famous tale began. "They had strong bodies and valiant, fervent hearts and had great courage. The island itself was the most impregnable to be found in the world, due to crags and bold rocks. Their arms were all of gold, as were also the harnesses of the wild beasts on which, after having tamed them, they rode; for in all the island there was no other metal."[9]

The tale, which captured the imagination of its Spanish readers, made its appearance within two decades after Christopher Columbus' voyage in 1492 to the New World. From the Iberian peninsula, the troops of Spanish Conquistador Hernán Cortés brought to New Spain (later to be called Mexico) the belief that there actually was an island filled with gold, if not necessarily populated by warrior women. The rugged land separated from the Mexican mainland by the long narrow body of water dubbed "The Sea of Cortés" seemed to fit the description of Caláfia's mystical queendom. Although Francisco de Ullea sailed in 1539 to the northernmost reaches of the Sea of Cortés and proved that this California was a peninsula, not an island, the name already had taken hold.

Three years later, the explorer Juan Rodríguez Cabrillo sailed up the Pacific Coast of that peninsula and marveled at the natural harbor lying one league north of the modern-day border between Mexico and the United States.

When Spain sent Father Serra and Gaspar de Portolá north to colonize "Alta" or Upper California, the joint military-religious expedition went by ship and by foot. From La Paz, at the bottom of Baja, or Lower, California, went forth the *San Antonio* and the *San Carlos*, filled with supplies and sailors, many of whom unfortunately came down with scurvy and other illnesses.

The ships named for the two saints arrived in San Diego Bay on May 4 and 5, 1769, and the sailors recuperated at a place known today as Spanish Landing. There they awaited the arrival of the overland expedition, which came in segments on May 14 and July 1.

The Spanish had three practical rules guiding where new settlements should be established. First, settlements needed to be defensible, so construction on high ground was favored. Second, they had to be near a source of fresh water. Third, they ought to be located within the vicinity of Indians to whom the message of Christianity might be preached. The area known today as Presidio Hill met all three criteria. It had an unobstructed view of any enemy who might approach. The San Diego River, in the days before it was diverted, flowed by the base of the Presidio. Also, there were small settlements of Kumeyaay Indians nearby in the areas known today as Mission Valley and Mission Hills.

So the Spanish marched away from the bay, inland to Presidio Hill, to establish their fort and their mission. Through 1821, when Mexico won its independence from Spain, the soldiers generally remained quartered inside the Presidio, except those who were detailed to the mission or the bay.

After independence was gained, however, the soldiers were permitted to build houses close to the fort. The soldiers accordingly made their homes in the area that we know today as Old Town. A satellite settlement also was begun at La Playa, a flatland area on the Point Loma Peninsula, slightly north of the spot on San Diego Bay where Cabrillo had landed. La Playa subsequently became a depot for cattle hides, known to leather manufacturers as "California dollars."

In 1846, during the Mexican-American War, American forces raised the U.S. flag over the Plaza in Old Town, effectively bringing to a close San Diego's Mexican period. Soon, more and more American settlers came to San Diego, blending their culture with the Spanish/Mexican heritage of the original settlers. After gold was discovered in Northern California in 1848, the flood of immigrants quickly led to calls for statehood.

A New City and County Take Shape

As California awaited formal entry into the union, the state began organizing lower levels of government. On February 18, 1850, the state legislature divided California into twenty-eight counties and assigned to San Diego County the area that covers present-day San Diego, Riverside, Imperial, and Inyo Counties—a land mass larger than those of some small states on the East Coast of the United States.[10] On March 27, 1850, the Legislature adopted an act incorporating San Diego as a self-governing city.

The elections for county officials were held on April 1, and besides picking José Antonio Estudillo as assessor, the voters chose William Ferrell, another investor with William Heath Davis in the New Town venture, as district attorney.[11] They also chose John Hays as county judge (no relation to the Indian agent in the Gila River area); Richard Rust as county clerk; H.C. Matsell, county recorder; Juan Bandini, county treasurer; Henry Clayton, surveyor; Thomas W. Sutherland, county attorney, and John Brown, coroner. Agoston Haraszthy, who was Sutherland's stepbrother, defeated Philip Crosthwaite for the office of sheriff by a vote of 107 to 47 but after Bandini declined the office of treasurer, Crosthwaite was appointed in his stead.[12]

The Legislature decided in 1850 that a county judge in San Diego should be paid $1,500 per year (compared to $6,000 for the same position in San Francisco, $5,000 in Sacramento, and $2,500 in Los Angeles)[13] but was unable until the following year to establish a fee schedule for sheriffs and other officials.

The next round of elections, for city offices, was scheduled on June 16— less than a month after the arrivals in San Diego of Robinson and Rose. It can be assumed that the old Texas politician and the Jewish immigrant who had become naturalized as a citizen at his earliest opportunity both followed the election with considerable interest. Residents of Old Town cast 88 votes in that contest, while La Playa residents accounted for 69.[14]

Joshua Bean, the major general of California's militia who also had been serving as alcalde of San Diego, was elected as mayor. Estudillo, meanwhile, added another public office to his portfolio: that of city treasurer. Also elected with Bean, and taking office the very next day, were the five members of the first San Diego Common Council: Atkins S. Wright, who was elected by his colleagues as the council's first president; Charles Haraszthy; Charles P. Noell; Charles P. Johnson; and William Leamy.[15] Haraszthy's son, Agoston, the county sheriff, was named city marshal. His stepson, Thomas Sutherland, already serving as county attorney, became the city attorney.

Rose Settles In

The first task for Rose, meanwhile, was to find a place to live and to begin earning a livelihood in the town of 650 residents. "Mother" Estudillo helped him solve his problem. At the southeast corner of Juan and Washington Streets, she owned a single-story adobe with a plank-roofed porch on two sides known as the Casa de Reyes-Ybanez.[16] Captain Francisco María Ruiz, the commander of the Presidio, built the structure in 1823, not long after the newly independent nation of Mexico permitted Presidio soldiers to move out of the fort. The commander deeded the property two years later to María Reyes-Ybanez, the wife of Sergeant Cristobal Dominguez. When she died in 1833, the property was bequeathed to her daughter, Doña María Victoria. Leasing the property from Mrs. Estudillo, Rose converted it into a boarding house and saloon complex. He renamed it as the Commercial House.

As mentioned, we know the story recounted by Benjamin Hayes about Louis Rose arriving at the Cajon Rancho with "precisely ten cents in his pocket" either was apocryphal or that the immigrant immediately did a booming business at his boarding house and saloon. The list of first taxpayers in the County of San Diego showed Rose being assessed $2,580 for personal property and real estate. His holdings included two buildings valued together at $2,000.[17]

In addition to the Commercial House, Rose had acquired a two-story adobe building on Juan Street from Lorenzo Soto.[18] It was the first known of many real estate acquisitions in Rose's career.

Robinson meanwhile acquired property nearby to build his first home in Old Town, a house measuring 23 feet by 41 feet.[19] It was one of two Robinson properties worth a total of $600 listed on San Diego County's property tax inventory of 1850. Robinson's total taxable property was listed at $1,125.

Plundering the New City

Although Robinson and Rose could not have known it then, the profligate ways of the San Diego Common Council would lead within a short time to the bankrupting of the city, and to their own subsequent elevation to the political leadership of San Diego. Members of the Common Council almost immediately clashed over three issues in which they put self-interest first: salaries, the construction of a jail, and the distribution of land titles.

On a 3–2 vote, the council decided to pay an annual salary of $1,200 to the mayor, $600 to each councilman, $1,000 to the marshal, and $1,000 to the city attorney. Given that Councilman Haraszthy was the father of Sheriff Haraszthy (who simultaneously served as the marshal) and stepfather of City Attorney Sutherland, that meant $2,600 for family members. One of the dissenting council members, Charles Noell, entered a strong protest on the record. During the election to decide whether San Diego should become a city, he said, Sutherland had assured him that he and others would work without pay. "What my surprise then! At the very first meeting at which the Board was organized, the subject of conferring salaries upon the city officers was brought up and the matter urged at every subsequent meeting until its final passage into an ordinance at the last regular meeting."[20]

That was enough for Mayor Bean, who vetoed the ordinance. Thereafter Councilman Haraszthy tried another approach. The mayor's salary would be lowered to $1,000, that of his son the marshal to $900, and council members would work without salary. However, a new position of land commissioner would be created, to which Councilman Haraszthy would be appointed. He would be empowered to receive a commission on every parcel sold by the city. Noell, sensing Haraszthy would win this exchange, successfully moved to reduce the city attorney's proposed salary to $500.[21] This time, Mayor Bean signed the ordinance. The embarrassed Sutherland declined to accept a salary for his services as city attorney.

Councilman Haraszthy later put through an ordinance assigning to himself a 5 percent commission on land sales, with prices for lots ranging from $25 for those of 100 vara (vara being a Spanish measure equaling 33 inches) to $320 for those of 160 acres. In addition Haraszthy persuaded his colleagues on the council that he should be permitted to charge fees for recording the deeds, ranging from $1.50 for a house to $20 for recording ownership of 160 acres.

If the council members who approved Haraszthy's proposal did the math, they knew that their avaricious colleague would realize $8 for selling a $160 parcel and another $20 for recording it.[22]

Even with such a potential income stream, the Haraszthy family was unsatisfied with the salary Agoston drew as a marshal and father Charles earned as a land commissioner. They conspired to become city contractors as well.

The Jail Debacle

Councilman Noell had suggested on June 29 that City Marshal (and Sheriff) Haraszthy be directed to "rent a good and secure room, and to procure the necessary stocks, irons and chains to keep securely such provisions (prisoners) as may be given into his charge; and also to procure a good and suitable person as a policeman..."[23] However, on July 6, City Marshal Agoston Haraszthy reported, according to the official minutes, that "he had been unable to hire any other place for such purpose and could not comply with the provisions of Ordinance No. 15 relative to a city jail."[24] The next week, the council's minutes reported that "the following resolution moved and carried: 1) resolved that the marshal under the provisions of Ordinance No. 15 be fully authorized to repair the present jail for the purpose mentioned therein..."[25]

Councilman Haraszthy offered a resolution on July 29 that a jail of three or more rooms, including one room for the jailor, be built as soon as possible on land reserved for public use near the Plaza. At this point neither his salary ordinance nor his compensation scheme for comptroller commissioner had been adopted. Haraszthy's resolution also directed that "a member of the Common Council shall be appointed for a reasonable consideration or daily allowance, the amount of which is to be previously decided by the Common Council in compensation of his trouble and time lost."

The council member so appointed would have the duties, under Haraszthy's proposal,

> ...to superintend the whole work; ...to contract with mechanics and hands necessary for that purpose; ...to provide for the necessary materials by purchase or otherwise; ...to keep a correct amount of all expenses, to be laid before the Common Council at the end of the work or whenever required by the same; ...to file the duplicates of the agreements together with all receipts and other vouchers for amounts paid, in order to account for the same with the Common Council and act afterwards as advised by the same; ...to asurtain (sic) at the earliest possible time of what material the building could be most properly constructed, viz-of stone, adobe, or logs, and if possible the difference of price among the three kinds, and report the same to the Common Council.[26]

Ever suspicious of his adversary, Noell demanded that Haraszthy's resolution be tabled until the next meeting and that, meanwhile, "a committee of three be appointed who in connection with the marshal shall take the subject into consideration and report at the next regular meeting, in relation to the building of a jail with a plan thereof, and estimates of the cost." Upon the motion's approval, Noell, Haraszthy and Noell's ally, Leamy, were appointed to the committee. On Aug. 5, the committee returned with estimates that a brick jail would cost $9,813, cement $5,074, and adobe $3,055. The Common

Council decided that a cement jail should be built not by the old Plaza, but instead "on the reserve near the new plaza fronting on Arista Street and adjoining San Diego Avenue." Furthermore, "Lot No. 2 of Block 88 is hereby appropriated for that purpose."

After some skirmishing, Noell was able to eliminate the idea of a single council member receiving pay to serve as the contractor for the work. Noell, who was a partner in a general store with County Judge John Hays,[27] persuaded the Common Council that the procedure to be followed, instead, should be

> that a committee consisting of three members be appointed to advertise in three of the most public places, in both English and the Spanish languages until the 20th day of August for sealed proposals to build said jail, and that a minute description of the character of the building and also of the materials of which it is to be composed shall be fully set forth in said advertisement, which proposals shall be opened by the committee, and the lowest bidder shall upon giving bond in the sum of $5,000 for the faithful performance of his contract (which contract shall be filed in the office of the clerk) with two or more sureties to be approved by the council, shall receive the contract. Within ten days after signing the contract the work shall commence and be completed in ninety days thereafter. The whole work shall be under the superintendence of the committee, whose duty it shall be in connection with his honor the mayor to inspect the work from time to time at least once each week, and report to the council at each regular meeting the progress of the work and all other necessary matters connected therewith and to see that it is performed according to contract. [28]

Haraszthy, Leamy, and Wright were appointed to the committee. On August 21, Haraszthy reported on the committee's behalf that his son, Agoston, the city marshal (and sheriff) "had offered the lowest bid, and had been declared by the committee entitled to the contract."[29] This was not precisely true, however. As reported by twentieth-century historian James R. Mills (who later would become the powerful President pro tempore of the California State Senate): "The low bidders were the Israel brothers, who wanted to erect it for $3,000. However, the county's first sheriff, Hungarian Count Agoston Haraszthy, was the son of Councilman Charles Haraszthy and a bid of $5,000 which he submitted was accepted. The council explained to the public that the members wanted a good job, not a cheap one." [30]

According to a biographical sketch of the Haraszthy family prepared during the late twentieth century for San Diego's House of Hungary, Agoston

Haraszthy had been an associate of Hungarian reformers Baron Wesselenyi and Louis Kossuth during the 1830s, but after his friends' arrest in 1837 he decided to travel to other parts of Europe and the United States. During 1840–41, he was entertained in Washington, D.C., by U.S. President John Tyler, and by Daniel Webster, with whom he discussed improving U.S.-Hungarian trade relations. He returned to Hungary in 1842 and persuaded his nobleman father "to liquidate the ancestral estate and have the entire family emigrate to America." They first went to Wisconsin, where they founded the town of Szeptaj (Beautiful View), which later became Sauk City. In Wisconsin, Charles Haraszthy married the mother of Thomas Sutherland, who had served as U.S. Attorney for the Wisconsin territory. The extended family arrived in San Diego County in 1849. [31]

With Charles Haraszthy's ally George Hooper by then having replaced Johnson on the council, and with Leamy seemingly warming up to Haraszthy, Noell could "count" how in future controversies the votes were certain to line up. His resignation came five days later, on August 26. Historian William Ellsworth Smythe, writing about Noell more than a half century later, opined that the merchant "did everything in his power to prevent the looting of the city treasury by the ring which were then in the majority." [32]

The drama of the jail did not end with the awarding of the contract and Noell's departure from the council—far from it. On November 7, Sheriff Haraszthy came before the Common Council and, according to the minutes, admitted that, following the heavy rains, "the walls of the cement jail he was building by contract with the city had fallen down in consequence of the bad quality of the lime used, which lime he stated was as good as could be procured in this part of the country. He wished the council to examine the matter and if they were convinced of the impossibility of making said jail as contracted for he asked to be relieved from the contract."

His father, Councilman Haraszthy, promptly moved that the Council should form itself into a committee to inspect the jail.[33] On the next day, the council reconvened and Sheriff Haraszthy, according to the minutes, "made a statement to the council that in the prosecution of his contract for building a cement jail he had incurred a heavy loss and prayed the council that as they had rejected his petition to be relieved from the contract they would add $2,000 to the amount to be paid to him and substituting stone in place of the building material."

Leamy, now as compliant as the rest of the council, offered a resolution that the younger Haraszthy's "petition be granted and that contractor should be allowed to draw from city treasurer from time to time as he may require." [34]

If there yet remained any question of the Haraszthy family's determination to appropriate as much public funds as possible to their own use, Councilman Haraszthy's next action should have settled the issue once and for all. Although prices for public land and fees for recording deeds had been set less than three months before, the councilman persuaded his colleagues that prices and fees needed to be much higher. Whereas $25 was sufficient to purchase a 100-vara lot three months before, now it would buy only a 50-vara lot. The price of the 100-vara lot was doubled to $50 and some of the larger lots went up by an even greater percentage. The 5-acre parcel climbed from $30 to $75; 10 acres from $50 to $120; 20 acres from $80 to $200; 40 acres from $140 to $320; 80 acres from $240 to $480, and 160 acres from $320 to $800. Haraszthy also resolved that the fees paid to him for land purchases should also increase, but by even larger percentage amounts. Whereas three months before, he was to be paid $1.50 to record a 5-acre deed, now the fee jumped to $15. For a 10-acre deed, he extracted $20; 20 acres, $25; 40 acres, $25; 80 acres, $40, and 160 acres, $50.[35]

Before 1850 closed there were two more developments in the jail debacle. On December 26, Agoston Haraszthy informed his father and other members of the Common Council "he was in want of money to prosecute his works on the city jail and desired a full council at the next meeting to furnish the same."[36] When all-too-cooperative council members assembled on December 30, the city marshal informed them that he was willing to accept in payment state bonds at "70 cents on the dollar of their face." The minutes recorded that "being motioned and seconded, it was resolved: that all the state bonds in the city treasury excepting such amount as the city may need for the purchase of paying the state tax, be given to A. Haraszthy at 70 cents on the dollar on their face." [37]

Robinson and Rose in Civic Affairs

There were two public events during 1850 in which Robinson and Rose were likely to have participated. Learning of the death in office of U.S. President Zachary Taylor, on July 9, 1850, the council on August 26 declared that the following day should be set aside "for purpose of observing the solemnities of the occasion." The resolution asserted "it becomes the duty of every American citizen to pay a fitting tribute to the memory of the illustrious dead." Taylor and a variety of other generals from both sides of the Mexican-American War already had been honored with streets named for them by Old Town surveyor Cave J. Couts. [38]

Robinson and Rose also were drawn into other types of civic affairs during their first year in San Diego. Robinson, who had vast experience in Texas with Spanish and Mexican land grants, was called in by the Common Council to serve as a consultant in the dispute between the council and the mayor over the ownership of City Hall. Mayor Bean said the city building had been built on a 50-vara plot of land that he and Cave Couts owned. Robinson thereafter examined documents relating to the claim of Bean and Couts, the Army officer who had laid out Fort Salvation in the California desert and who had platted many San Diego streets. For this task, Robinson submitted to the city in August a bill for $150, perhaps figuring this inflated amount was in keeping with the fees and commissions Councilman Haraszthy was receiving.

The Common Council accepted the charge apparently without complaint, but Mayor Bean wrote back on September 28 that he was vetoing the "appropriation to one Jas. W. Robinson of the one hundred and fifty dollars in part for services rend(ered). I object to it as being too much, and more than his services are worth for the whole of the service rend., much less for part. I therefore hope the council will reconsider the matter well before they make such reckless appropriation of money confided to their care." [39]

The council sustained Bean's veto, but an attempted compromise to pay Robinson $100 also was vetoed and sustained. Finally, a $75 payment—half what Robinson asked—was permitted provided that he furnish "a full receipt."[40] Meanwhile Council President A.S. Wright sat down with Bean and worked out a trade, whereby Bean relinquished his right to the land on which City Hall sat, and the Common Council, in turn, transferred to Bean and Couts an adjoining piece of land.

Rose was selected in September to serve on San Diego County's first Grand Jury. After the humiliation he had suffered en route to El Paso at the hands of Major Van Horne, this must have been a gratifying assurance to him that he would be accepted into the ranks of San Diego County residents.

Sworn in to the Grand Jury by Presiding Judge Oliver S. Witherby with Rose were Aguirre, Couts, Holden Alara, Loreto Amador, Seth B. Blake, J. Emers, Councilman Haraszthy, Bonifacio Lopez, Cristobal Lopez, William H. Moon, José de Jesus Moreno, Ramon Osuna, Manuel Rocha, and James Wall.[41] The first case brought to the Grand Jury by Sheriff Haraszthy involved the death of a Mexican man from Sonora who was shot by Indians near San Luis Rey, after he took from them more meat than they had agreed to sell. Although the Indians contended the man had shot first in the ensuing confrontation, the Grand Jury voted its finding that a murder had been committed and ordered the sheriff to bring the Indians to trial.[42]

Councilman Leamy and a citizen named John Capman testified in the next case that Santiago Ortiz and Philip Keating had become involved in an argument during which Keating accused Ortiz of having ravaged women and robbed churches in Mexico. Ortiz brandished a pistol and Keating ran for his life. The Grand Jury recommended that Ortiz forfeit a bond he previously had posted for disturbing the peace and also be prosecuted on a charge of assault.[43]

Roseville Genesis

Robinson and Rose believed a potentially profitable real estate development could link Old Town with the other established settlement at La Playa, while bringing the boundaries of commercial San Diego right to the bay. By October, the two friends were sufficiently well-financed to apply to the city for adjoining 80-acre lots "on the northwest side of San Diego Bay between the Playa and Old San Diego."[44] Under Councilman Haraszthy's price and fee schedule, the two friends were required to pay $480 each for their parcels, and an additional $40 to register their deeds. The overall land acquisition costs for prime real estate on San Diego Bay therefore worked out to $6.50 an acre.

Beginning to acquire sufficient land for a development was the first step in a long process that would culminate many years later with Rose laying out the townsite of Roseville. From the standpoint of competition, Robinson's and Rose's timing seemed propitious. William Heath Davis's "New Town" was at that time faltering; the proprietors of the 32-square-block development were embarrassed by having to send water trains to Old Town to secure potable water. Sheriff Haraszthy, Judge Witherby, Couts, Councilman Noell, José María Estudillo and Juan Bandini since May had been developing "Middletown," a 687-acre land parcel connecting Old Town and New Town, but sales had lagged. The 1850 assessment rolls for the City of San Diego valued taxable property at $374,260 for the entire city. Old Town and La Playa accounted for $264,210 of this; New Town $80,050, and Middletown just $30,000.[45]

With his knowledge of the commerce of the river ports of Neuhaus-an-der-Oste and New Orleans, Rose had concluded that however appropriate the Presidio area had been for the location of San Diego's fort in 1769, the historic site made no sense as the commercial hub of a city. As a merchant, Rose knew that convenience was an important criterion for attracting trade, whereas the distance separating Old Town from San Diego Bay made the town far from convenient. Ephraim W. Morse, a businessman who also had arrived in San Diego in 1850, remembered in a speech fifty years later that: "The regular landing place in the harbor at that time was at La Playa near where the United States quarantine station is now located. There were no wharves, and both passengers and freight were taken ashore in ship's boats and landed on the beach by the sailors. The freight, destined for Old Town, five miles away, was hauled up in Mexican carts, drawn by oxen."[46]

As one of the most experienced land lawyers in the Southwest, Robinson understood the process by which land could be amassed to meet overseas commerce at the water's edge. Together, he and Rose, who had accumulated far more money, purchased the bayside land without trumpeting their plans about someday developing the waterfront. Robinson's wife, Sarah, also was enlisted in the cause. On October 21, 1850, she applied to Councilman Haraszthy for a parcel of land "commencing at the termination towards old San Diego of an entry made by James W. Robinson of eighty acres on the bay of San Diego...running towards old San Diego as far as there is vacant land."While she was at it, she also applied for slightly more than 15 acres in Old Town near the land where William Leamy operated a slaughterhouse.[47]

The joy of owning land—no easy accomplishment for a Jew in Europe— soon transformed Rose into a speculator of the first order. With the profits earned from his Commercial House, or possibly with funds brought from Texas or received from family members overseas, Rose invested in more and more real estate. Legal documents listed him not as Leffman Rose, but by the more Americanized "Louis Rose," alternatively spelled as "Lewis Rose." By year's end, Rose had leased an adobe house in Old Town from his Grand Jury colleague Manuel Rocha, and together with Robinson had purchased two parcels from Ramona and William Curley. He also bought a few parcels of varying sizes from the City of San Diego.[48]

So enamored with land did Rose become, and so lacking was San Diego in having any kind of reputable banking institution, that Rose deposited with the cash-hungry city on December 19, 1850, the sum of $6,650, thereafter drawing down his account with wide-ranging land purchases. The receipt, which was "subscribed and dated at San Diego AD One Thousand Eight Hundred and Fifty, the Nineteenth of December" was signed by Mayor Bean, Council President Wright, Councilman and Land Commissioner Haraszthy, and City Clerk William E. Rust. It read: "Know all men by these presents that we the mayor and Common Council of the city of San Diego in the State of California are jointly and severally held and bound unto Lewis Rose and his heirs and assigns in the sum of six thousands six hundred and fifty dollars lawful money in the U.S. to the payment of which will and truly to be made, we do bind ourselves and each of our successors in office jointly and severally by these presents." [49]

Perhaps one can obtain a fuller appreciation of what a deposit of $6,650 meant to the city by comparing the figure to the amounts mentioned by E.W. Morse in a story that has become part of the cherished lore of early San Diego:

> Philip Crosthwaite was county treasurer in 1850, and the law then required each county treasurer to appear in person in Sacramento and pay over money due to the state and settle with the state treasurer, so he proceeded to Sacramento at the required time, paid over the funds due to the state—somewhat less than $200. His traveling fees amounting to $300, he returned with more money than he took up, having made his annual and very satisfactory settlement. But it is said the state treasurer suggested to him that, under similar conditions, it would be more satisfactory to the state if he should play the

role of embezzler and run away with the state funds before settlement day.[50]

Another way of understanding the amount is by a chart that was devised by the Federal Reserve Bank of Minneapolis for converting dollar amounts of 1850 into dollar amounts of 2004. Using the bank's formula, $6,650 in 1850 would have been worth $149,093 in 2004.[51]

Rose was in no hurry to use up his land credits, instead making his purchases over the years with the deliberation of a poker player trying to decide whether to draw for a flush or a straight. Rose hoped to one day create a string of developments all along the Point Loma side of San Diego Bay. Early on, he combined five 160-acre parcels into a J-shaped holding that had its base at the tip of Point Loma, where Cabrillo National Monument now stands. He also purchased properties a little further up the peninsula as well as in La Playa. Some parcels, like Lot No. 1 at the very point of Point Loma, he purchased in full. But others such as Lots 2 and 3, immediately northwest and northeast of Lot No. 1, he cautiously decided to buy on the installment plan.[52] Purchases on the Point Loma peninsula, at best, were highly speculative because the United States Army and the City of San Diego had conflicting claims over the territory. A few weeks before the first Common Council was elected, Joshua Bean, in his capacity as alcalde or mayor, on May 27, 1850, had sold 637 acres in the La Playa area to a combine of powerful San Diego citizens including José María Estudillo, Agoston Haraszthy, Bandini, Couts, Noell, Sutherland, Witherby, Wright, Henry Clayton, and William H. Emory.

At its first meeting on June 17, 1850, the Council joined with Mayor Bean in reaffirming the Playa grant, notwithstanding a notice from California's pre-state military governor, Brigadier General Bennett Riley, that the land in question previously had been reserved by the government of Mexico, and that therefore the government of the United States, not the City of San Diego, was the proper successor-in-interest to the lands. Riley stated that any sales made by the City of San Diego in the area claimed by the military would be "null and void."[53] The council attempted to specify at its June 18 meeting that the acreage in question "may not be included in the reserve hereafter to be made by the government," [54] but that was not a stipulation that was within its power to make. Nevertheless, Sutherland, in his capacity as city attorney, subsequently was dispatched to Monterey to try to persuade Riley to withdraw the claim. With Riley already departed for the East Coast, Sutherland instead presented the case to General Persifor Smith at Benicia.

About the same time that Smith ordered Major Heintzelman to establish a fort at the junction of the Colorado and Gila Rivers, he also instructed the San Diego-based Army officer to reserve in La Playa the parcel on which the quartermaster's building stood, as well as a rectangle of land three blocks deep and approximately 100 yards wide fronting on San Diego Bay. Other land in

La Playa should be relinquished for use by the city, Smith instructed.[55] Such was sufficient to establish the City of San Diego's claim so far as the Common Council was concerned, notwithstanding the fact that Smith's word was far from the final one in the U.S. military chain of command.

New Council, Same Troubles

As a result of the elections held late in 1850, Robinson replaced Estudillo on January 9, 1851, as the city treasurer. Even though he had been Agoston Haraszthy's obviously incompetent contractor for the city jail, David B. Kurtz was elected mayor, succeeding Bean.[56] Haraszthy, himself, continued as city marshal as well as the county sheriff, while his stepbrother Sutherland remained as city attorney. Their father and stepfather, Charles Haraszthy, and the rest of the first Common Council were replaced. The new council, comprised of A. Blackburn, John Brown, John Jordan, George Parris Tebbets, and Enos Wall, soon had to grapple with some familiar issues.

Tebbetts and Jordan, serving as a committee to review José Antonio Estudillo's accounts as city treasurer for the year 1850, reported on January 21 that "they believed drafts had been drawn on him without being in the form required by the charter and ordinances of the city." Therefore they recommended that a committee consisting of Kurtz, Sutherland, Agoston Haraszthy, Jordan, and Tebbetts be "appointed to investigate" Estudillo's accounts.[57] The matter remained muddled throughout 1851 and through the first quarter of 1852 when a successor committee reported that "they used every endeavor upon their part, to ascertain the financial condition of the city, but owing to the unsettled accounts of the treasurer of the year AD 1850 and the manner in which the accounts of the city have been kept, that they are at an utter loss to give any report on the assets or debts of the city."[58]

The issue of salaries resurfaced on January 23, 1851, when the council adopted Blackburn's proposal, in light of the city's precarious finances, that Mayor Kurtz's salary be reduced from $1,000 per year to $700; that City Marshal Haraszthy's be trimmed from $900 to $700; that Robinson be paid $500 instead of the $700 that Estudillo had earned as treasurer, and that the authorized salary of the city attorney—which Sutherland had refused—remain at the $500 level.[59]

Mayor Kurtz promptly vetoed the measure, and the council decided on January 30 to take no immediate action on what course to follow next— perhaps because of the surprise that former Council member Charles Haraszthy brought to City Hall. Haraszthy contended that Jordan was ineligible to hold the council office, a contention which Tebbetts, Brown, and Wall supported following a lengthy hearing. The official minutes of the meeting provided no indication of the nature of Haraszthy's objections to Jordan, but they did record that, as a result of the hearing, the seat was declared vacant.[60] In a subsequent election, Jordan's seat was won by Thomas J. Wrightington. Seated February 20, the new councilman was an old-time San Diegan. In 1833, Wrightington had become one of the first native-born Americans to settle in Mexican-ruled San Diego.

Robinson's duties as city treasurer included serving as a member of the city school board. Based on his recommendation, the financially wary council on January 30 adopted an ordinance authorizing construction of a schoolhouse in San Diego—provided that the low bidder would take payment in the form of city land. Later that day, the council turned to the continuing problem of the jail. It appointed a committee of five to examine the jail and "to ascertain whether said building has been erected in accordance with the contract." The committee had three public members—Mayor Kurtz and Councilmen Wall and Brown—and two private members, Mr. Campbell representing New Town and Dr. Tremain representing La Playa.[61] The committee returned on March 25 with a favorable report, so the jail was accepted. Sheriff Haraszthy then suggested that half the jail be rented by the County of San Diego for its prisoners, a suggestion that eventually led to an agreement that the county government would pay $75 a month in rent to the city. That was good news, but not good enough to offset the large balance still owing to Haraszthy for the jail's construction.

In response, the council unanimously adopted Ordinance No. 14, which would prove to be an important milestone en route to the City of San Diego's financial demise:

> Be it ordained, Sec. 1st, that Agoston Haraszthy, jail contractor, should be paid three thousand four hundred and ninety five dollars ($3,495), being the balance due to said Haraszthy on the contract for building the jail, in city scrip signed by the president and the clerk of the Common Council. Sec 2nd, Said scrip to bear interest of 8 percent per month until advertised for payment, and be given in amounts of one hundred dollars and one for $95 and the said scrip to be numbered. Sec 3rd, the treasurer and marshal are hereby directed to receive said scrip for any indebtedness to the city either for payment of lots and lands or licensing and fines. Sec 4th, All lands sold by the Land Commissioner on terms, if the installments should be paid at once, within a month from this date, will be reduced 50 percent of the purchase price. Sect. 5th, It shall be the duty of the treasurer whenever he has in the treasury sufficient funds to redeem one or more of the above scrip to give notice thereof and the payments to be made according to their

numbers, and no interest shall be paid after such notice on the scrip so advertised. [62]

Although eight percent a month was the "ordinary interest at the time," it was ruinous for a city already badly in debt.[63] In a year's time, if nothing were paid on the loan, the amount due would more than double to $8,800.93—a figure well in excess of the cost of the original jail plus the rain-required renovation. There is a tremendous irony in the fact that Haraszthy was the chief law enforcement officer for the city and county of San Diego. In a manner that a modern-day confidence man would have to admire, Haraszthy first had suggested that a jail be built. Next, his father persuaded fellow councilmembers to give his son the contract, despite the fact that there had been a lower bid. When rains caused the jail to collapse, instead of being censured, Haraszthy was able to persuade the council to give him more money. Finally, when the city was financially distressed, he insisted that the council accept terms that would drive the city deeper and deeper into a financial hole. He "squeezed" the Common Council like the grapes for which he later would become famous as "the father of California's wine industry" after moving to Northern California.[64]

Now that Haraszthy's father no longer served on the Common Council, its members felt free to repeal the ordinances by which fees for recording property deeds went as high as $50 for 160-acre parcels. Ordinance No. 13, also adopted on March 25, stated that henceforth, "the land commissioner shall be entitled to receive from the person or persons who apply for city lands the sum of five dollars for each grant of land of whatever size sold by said commissioner, as a compensation or fee for drawing the bond, deed, or other necessary papers issued after this date." [65]

Robinson brought some personal matters to the March 25 meeting of the council. Block 21 in Old Town, which he and Rose had purchased from the Curley family, apparently had been sold to the Curleys without the city having clear title to the land. Robinson and Rose reconveyed the land to the city, and sought Block 12 of Old Town in its stead. Wrightington, appointed as a committee of one, affirmed that Block 12 was indeed in city hands, and accordingly it was conveyed to Rose and Robinson.

More City Financial Woes

Worried about the mounting interest accruing to Haraszthy, Tebbetts on April 19 persuaded the council that it should permit Haraszthy to try to sell approximately $725 in state bonds at no less than 75 percent of their value. Proceeds of such sale were "hereby appropriated to the payment of city drafts bearing interest, according to their numbers." [66]

On April 24, the council once again addressed the issue of city salaries, but not unlike many later political bodies, decided to hide the issue from the view of city voters. Rather than voting specific dollar amounts for salaries, the council, on Blackburn's recommendation, tied the salaries of various city officers to those of county officials, whose salaries and fees were set by the state legislature.

Henceforth, "the mayor shall be entitled to receive the same fees as allowed by law to justices of the peace. The marshal or deputy marshal the same fees as the sheriff of the county is entitled to receive, the city treasurer, the same fees as the treasurer of the county." For positions lower down the political scale, the council became more specific: "The city assessor ten dollars per diem, but he shall not be allowed a deputy or interpreter unless by special permission of the Common Council. The clerk of the Common Council $50 per month. The jailor, $30 per month." [67]

Tying the marshal's fees to the sheriff's meant that Haraszthy would have to engage in similar accounting for both positions. The state legislature in 1851 had been quite specific in listing fees to which a sheriff was entitled. For example, for serving a summons, he could get $3; for travel from the court house, 50 cents per mile; for taking bonds $2; for certifying a copy of a bond, $1; for serving a subpoena $1, for travel in serving that subpoena, 50 cents per mile to the most distant location in the same direction; for executing an arrest, $5; for advertising property for sale, $2; for drawing a deed pursuant to a sale of a property for taxes, $8; for putting a person into possession of a property, or removing the occupants $5; for summoning a jury, $5; for attending that jury $2; for bringing prisoners to habeas corpus hearings or to testify, $2, and so on.[68]

Adding to the city's financial obligations, W. P. Toler was hired by Robinson and other members of the school board to teach in temporary quarters at City Hall. It was not until May 1, when the council voted to pay him $100 for the month of April that Toler's monthly salary was fixed. Evidently it was an amount far less than Toler desired, because on June 5, Robinson notified the Common Council that Toler had resigned.

Mayor Kurtz, meanwhile, announced he had business in San Francisco that would take him away from the city, so Council President Tebbetts was vested on May 15 with authority as acting mayor. Wrightington in turn became president pro tempore of the Common Council.[69]

Demonstration that the city government was none too popular during the economic hard times came in the high turnover at the Common Council— both Blackburn and Wall resigned—and from a petition presented by several citizens in June urging that salaries for city officials be abolished. The council thereupon decided to reduce the salary for its clerk from $50 a month to a rate of $5 per meeting. Except in special circumstances, meetings thereafter would take place only on Monday nights, meaning that normally the clerk would draw pay for no more than four or five meetings per month. The salary of the city attorney was abolished, but this was merely symbolic, as Sutherland had not been collecting a salary. John Dillon, a 21-year-old dentist from New York, and J. Judson Ames, publisher of the new *San Diego Herald*, subsequently won an election called to fill the two vacant seats on the City Council. On July 8, the same day they took their seats, Matsell resigned as city clerk. Fred Painter succeeded him.[70]

San Diego's Jewish Population Grows

Another office filled in that special election was that of city assessor. A. Jacob Marks, who had Americanized his name from Marks Jacobs, but later changed it back, was the winner. Marks and his partner in a general store, Charles Fletcher, were Jews, as was another merchant who recently had arrived in San Diego, Lewis Franklin. Rose no longer was the only Jew in town.

The United States Census of 1850, which was not completed until 1851, showed Rose residing in census dwelling No. 89—apparently the Commercial House—with five members of the Fisher family and two brothers of the Schruck family. Although all the men, including Rose, were listed as "laborers" in the census report, Rose was the only one among the dwelling's eight residents whose net worth was recorded, which by then had grown to $4,000. This figure did not include the unspent portion of more than $6,000 that Rose had on deposit with the City of San Diego.

Brothers William and Nathan Schruck, both in their 20s, soon would leave Rose's life, but he would enjoy a lifelong friendship with the Fisher family, whom the census report listed as including Gustav, 46; Sophia, 29; Frederick, 15; Louisa, 12, and Louisiana, 3. We must be somewhat careful about relying on the ages listed in the census reports, as Rose was listed as being 40 years old, whereas in 1850 he already was 43. Suffice it to say that he and Gustav were approximately the same age, and both spoke German.[71] The Fishers were a Christian family, evidence of the ease with which San Diego's first Jewish settler mingled with non-Jews. In subsequent records, Fisher was often spelled "Fischer" and Gustav spelled "Gustave."

The census documented the growing internationalization of San Diego. For example, it listed Marks, 35, a merchant from Poland, sharing dwelling No. 39 with Fletcher, 22, a merchant from Bohemia. Franklin, 30, a merchant from England, meanwhile lodged at a boarding house designated as dwelling No. 56 with Councilman Dillon; shipmaster Samuel Naghel, 32, from Maryland; his wife, Emilia Naghel, 18, from Portugal; George S. Wapen, 26, from New York; and John Galbraith, 33, from Scotland.

Rose contracted for some business from the city, which, though it brought him payment, probably did little to increase the popularity of his Commercial House. When a Mr. McWilliams, sick and destitute, turned up in San Diego, the Common Council paid Rose $17.15 to lodge the unfortunate man prior to his death. The city jail still not up to its task, Rose was paid $54 on June 5 for having lodged some prisoners, while Hiram Goodlander was paid $32 for having accommodated others.[72]

Manuel Rocha, owner of the private residence on Juan Street that Rose was leasing, lost $22 in a court suit brought against him by Philip Garcia but the award together with interest and court costs was more than Rocha at first was able or willing to pay. Accordingly, plans for a June 10 auction of the house to pay the expenses was announced by Sheriff Haraszthy in the inaugural issue of the *San Diego Herald*.[73] Rocha apparently decided to pay his taxes after all, and Rose was able to continue his three-year lease of the building without interruption.

Secessionist Sentiment in San Diego

Tension between the "cow counties" of Southern California and the more densely populated areas around San Francisco surfaced in the August 28 issue of the *San Diego Herald* in a petition offered by twenty-six San Diegans urging that a convention be held in Santa Barbara to sever the state in half. Robinson was among the signers, as were Sheriff Haraszthy, William Heath Davis, Juan Bandini, José Antonio Estudillo, Judge John Hays, District Attorney W.C. Ferrell, surveyor Cave Couts, such past and present members of the Common Council as J. Judson Ames, John Brown, George Hooper, Charles Johnson and Charles Noell, and mercantile partners E. W. Morse and Levi Slack.[74] A week later the newspaper reported that Robinson had chaired an August 30 meeting at which a committee was appointed to petition the U.S. Congress to create a new territory. Members were Ferrell, Haraszthy, Noell, Hooper, Couts, Joaquin Ortega, and Pedro Carrillo.[75]

Left unreported was the fact that a new state at the continent's southern border with the Pacific Ocean might get to decide whether it wished to be a "slave" or "free" state. Many, but by no means all, San Diego's residents hailed from southern slave states.

Tempers were flaring at the Common Council, meanwhile, over the city's mounting indebtedness to Haraszthy. By resolution, council members said "if the city marshal shall fail to present a report of his collections before the next meeting of this council, the mayor shall, and is hereby instructed to commence legal proceedings against his securities." The anger apparently was not mitigated by the fact that Haraszthy was able to get better than 75 percent of face value of the state bonds. The same minutes reported that "after deducting the percentage and brokerage there remained $612 which is paid into the city treasury" and thereafter, per agreement, was paid out to Haraszthy.[76]

Although council members were upset with Haraszthy, the political aristocrat charmed other San Diegans. They chose to elect him to the next term of the state assembly. Simultaneously, former Councilman George Hooper was elected to succeed Haraszthy as sheriff, while Estudillo was elected as county treasurer, Couts as county clerk, and Noell as public administrator. To this familiar cast were added the names of Santiago Arguello as county assessor and Francisco María Alvarado as coroner. Ames, Dillon, Toler, and John Blecker were elected justices of the peace, while Goodlander and Joseph Reiner were chosen as constables. [77]

Robinson, who already had been serving as county attorney in an acting capacity, won election to the post in his own right. One of Robinson's earliest undertakings on behalf of the people had been to bring suit against five men who operated the ferry across the Colorado River "without having a license therefore...to the evil example of all other persons..." [78]

Editor Ames editorialized in the *Herald* on September 11 that the interests and the wants of the residents of Southern and Northern California "are entirely dissimilar, and the sooner the state is sundered the better for both portions." In Haraszthy, San Diegans had elected to the state assembly a man with "the ability and energy to push the matter ahead," in Ames' estimate. In a prognostication that turned out to be 180 degrees from what really would happen, Ames added: "We have elected a man to the Assembly—Colonel Haraszthy— whose whole soul is wrapt up in this movement and moreover he is a man who has an interest at stake amongst us and will not be pulling up stakes and putting out as soon as his term of office expires." Taking their cue, Ames' colleagues on the Common Council decided four days later to put their quarrel with Haraszthy behind them. They voted to expunge from the record their previous resolution on the subject.[79]

Ames ran on about the public case for an independent Southern California in the *Herald's* next issue, again leaving unmentioned the slavery issue which was gripping the rest of the United States:

> The north, with her noble and beautiful rivers, with sufficient depth of water for steamers, acting as so many arteries sending at every pulsation into every portion life, luxury and wealth of commerce and bringing back in return the richest deposits of earth in millions, while the south is entirely dependent upon agriculture, and the grazing of cattle and without a sufficient market amongst themselves for their products and the difficulties and cost of transportation to the north being so great that all profits are consumed, and the labor and capital of the people in the south rendered non-productive beyond a bare subsistence; thus creating a greater difference in the value of a dollar in the south, and the value of the same dollar in the

north—consequently any revenue law which levies the same percent upon the dollar must fall heavier upon the lower than the upper country.[80]

At the beginning of October, Ames, W. W. Jackson, and three members of the Fisher family all applied to the Common Council to purchase acreage in the Canada de las Lleguas (Canyon of the Mares), the beginning of settlers' interest in the area that later would become known as Rose Canyon. However, occasional land sales could not arrest the downward slide of San Diego's fiscal condition. Wrightington resigned from the council on October 6. Five days later, the remainder of the council, eyeing the financial potential of land sales in La Playa, joined Acting Mayor Tebbetts in a petition to federal officials to "raise the military reserve at the beach."

With no fiscal relief in sight and Haraszthy's interest clock still ticking, the council on November 10 ordained that a tax of one-half of 1 percent should be levied on all property within the city. When the city's own property tax bill of $286.37 from the State of California came due, the embarrassed council looked all over the city for someone to lend them the money. Tebbetts reported that Haraszthy provided the "lowest bid offered at eight percent per month" for a period of three months. Ordinance No. 33 of 1851 directed Robinson, as city treasurer, "to retain in his hands out of any money that may come into the city treasury a sufficient sum to liquidate such note." Only the $30 per month salary paid to the city jailor was deemed to have greater priority for payment by the city.[81] Dillon on November 21 persuaded the council to offer discounts of 25 percent to any person then in the process of purchasing city land on installments if they would pay instead for the land in full.[82]

Masons and Jews

Amid these state and local political developments, there also were some important fraternal and religious occurrences that would prove important to the small, yet soon-to-grow, community of Jews in San Diego: the creation of a Masonic organization in San Diego and the first observance of the Jewish High Holy Days.

The story is told that at a picnic seven men discovered that they had been members of the Masonic fraternity in other cities. A notice was placed in the *San Diego Herald* on June 19, 1851, reading, "All Masons in good standing with their respective lodges are requested to assemble at the Exchange Hotel, in the City of San Diego, on Friday evening the 20th ... to make arrangements for the celebrating of our patron Saint, John the Baptist."[83]

Although no records were kept of the meeting, apparently it was on this occasion that a petition was drawn up to the Grand Lodge of California, located in the San Francisco area, for dispensation to form a lodge in San Diego. Deputy Grand Master Benjamin D. Hyam, who had authority to issue such dispensations between meetings known as "Communications" of the Grand Lodge, granted San Diego's request on August 1. He instructed the organizers to fulfill various requirements before the Grand Lodge's next Communication in November.[84]

The *Herald* noted on September 11 that officers for the San Diego Lodge, U.D. (under dispensation) were William C. Ferrell, master (and county district attorney); John Judson Ames, senior warden (and editor of the *Herald*), and John Cook, junior warden (and member of the state assembly). A meeting of the lodge was held October 10 at the home of Sheriff Haraszthy, one of its members.[85] Ames took the steamer from San Diego to San Francisco to attend the November 6 session of the Grand Lodge's Communication. He won approval for his request for more time for the San Diego Lodge to meet various requirements for a charter.[86] After Ames' return to San Diego, Robinson recorded the proceedings of the November 21 lodge meeting, including the results of the elections of officers. Ferrell was chosen as the lodge's worshipful master, Ames as senior warden, Daniel Barbee as junior warden, R.E. Raimond as treasurer, Sheriff Haraszthy as secretary and W.H. Moon as tyler (similar to sergeant-at-arms). Also attending as lodge members were William Heath Davis and Assemblyman John Cook.

Rose also was present, but was listed as a "visiting member" rather than as a regular member of the lodge. We only can speculate why Rose, alone among the people who had been Masons in other cities, was listed as "visiting" rather than simply being accepted as a regular member of the lodge. One possibility is that because Rose likely had joined the organization in Germany, and continued his affiliation at a German-speaking lodge in New Orleans, the English-speaking Masons simply were unfamiliar with his particular nomenclature. Another possibility was the religious issue: while Masonry today, in the twenty-first century, prides itself as a fraternal order that embraces members of every religion, so long as they believe in God, that attitude has evolved over centuries. Masonry's origins are shrouded in mystery and legend, but the organization clearly was rooted in Christian doctrine as attested to by the notice Ames had inserted into the *Herald* calling for Masons to plan a celebration for "our patron Saint, John the Baptist." Some Masonic brothers considered their organization an adjunct of the Christian religion; others, attempting to rationalize how Jews and other non-Christians could affiliate with an organization paying deference to John and other Christian saints, de-emphasized theology. Yes, they said, Masons paid deference to St. John, but likewise they extolled King Solomon, whose Temple architects are considered by Masons to be the archetypes of their fraternity. Not for their divergent theological teachings are Solomon and John so venerated, but for their core beliefs and practices, which all Masons can respect, no matter what their specific religious leanings. Whatever the issue that made the Masons hesitate to accept Rose as their lodge's own member, it was soon resolved. Rose went on to hold a variety of offices in the local lodge.[87]

Meanwhile, the Jewish Day of Atonement, Yom Kippur, fell in 1851 on October 6. Although they were in the process of dissolving their mercantile partnership,[88] Marks and Fletcher joined Lewis Franklin at his residence to observe the occasion. This tiny assemblage is remembered in local Jewish history as San Diego's first High Holiday service, even though the gathering was seven people short of the ten people, or *minyan*, required for certain prayers. On October 9, the *Herald* wrote: "The Israelites of San Diego, faithful to the religion of their forefathers, observed their New Year's Day and Days of Atonement with due solemnity. The day of atonement—one of the most solemn and sacred days of the Jewish calendar—was observed by Messrs. Lewis Franklin, Jacob Marks and Chas. A. Fletcher (the only three Hebrews in town) by their assembling in the house of the former gentleman and passing the entire day in fasting and prayers. (We are glad to record such an act of religious faith under circumstances the most unfavorable.)"[89]

The prayer service attracted the attention of Isaac Leeser, the Orthodox editor of the Philadelphia-based *Occident*, who wrote in April 1852 that the gathering "proves conclusively what has been often advanced, that give the Jew of right feeling an opportunity and he will show his attachment to his faith by joining with others to honor his God after the ancestral rites."[90]

For Franklin, it was the third such trailblazing High Holiday—the two earlier ones having been observed in San Francisco. Fellow Jews had gathered in his tent on Jackson Street to mark the Days of Awe in 1849.[91] A year later, before an *ad hoc* assemblage that styled itself the Kearny Street Jewish Congregation, he delivered a sermon that showed him to be well-versed in Ashkenazic liturgy for the High Holidays, as well as with writings of the Torah, later Hebrew Scriptures, and the Talmud.[92]

After issuing a traditional call for repentance, Franklin exhorted his listeners to help build Judaism in California.

> Brethren you cannot be insensible to the benefits you enjoy, in this blessed land of religious freedom," he said. "The Jew is as unfettered in this Republican country as though he were again in the Land of Promise. No restraint is he under, neither in the precept, or practice of the religion of his fathers. Rather does America invite Israel to become a people in her midst. California, in her infant state, asks you to build her cities, and will you not erect such edifices as your children and your children's children, from generation to generation, shall delight in? And I ask you, shall there be no temple built to Israel's God?

Shall there be no watchtower to guide the traveler on his journey through the thorny paths of life, and direct him in the way
he should go? Will you not provide for the wants of hunger-
ing thousands, who will crave for the food of religion? Shall
their lips be parched and utterance denied them when the
heart is bursting with gratitude to all-bountiful Providence?
You, yourselves, have reaped an harvest, forget not a tithe for
the gleaners—give them food from the dainties of the Law,
and drink from the fountains of Divine Inspiration. You yourselves, be their example, and teach them how to live. Yes, bid
the mason hew the stone, and the artisan cast the molding, and
raise a new house, worthy [of] the handicraft of God's chosen
people.[93]

Why Rose did not attend the 1851 Yom Kippur services with his three fellow Jewish San Diegans has been a source of modern-day speculation. Some
have suggested that he did not identify with the Jewish community; that he was
more an assimilationist. Others have suggested that Ames' parenthetical comment about "the only three Hebrews in town" meant that Rose simply was
away from San Diego at that time. It is one of those riddles for which there
seems to be no solution still. But, as the Jewish community grew over the following years, so too did Rose's level of involvement with his co-religionists.

The Garra Uprising

Meanwhile, relations between San Diego's Native American population
and the Mexican and Anglo settlers were coming to a boil, with Sheriff
Haraszthy once again right in the middle of the controversy. The county government, like that of the city, was financially hard-pressed as a result of the general economic slowdown and a scarcity of currency with which to operate. The
county's economic straits were eased only slightly by the decision of the
Legislature earlier in the year to transfer the administration of the San
Bernardino area from San Diego County to Los Angeles County.[94]

Although Native Americans living throughout the county were denied the
same rights as Anglos—and in fact were constantly harassed by squatters on
their traditional lands—some San Diegans nevertheless believed that
"Christianized Indians" should pay property taxes, especially on their herds of
cattle that grazed in the public domain. The opinion was far from unanimous
among San Diego's leadership, with no less a figure than former Major General
Bean having publicly advised the Indians that they were exempt from such payments. Haraszthy, on the other hand, took a hard line, telling Indians through-

out the county that they had a stark choice. They could pay their taxes, or have their cattle seized and then sold for payment.[95]

Juan J. Warner, born in Connecticut as Jonathan Trumbull Warner, had lived in California since 1831 as a Mexican citizen. Warner's Rancho San José del Valle (later to become known as Warner's Ranch) was located near Agua Caliente, a hot water spring, in a lush valley that emigrants, likely including Robinson and Rose, reached after climbing a mountain trail that rose from the harsh California desert. From Warner's Ranch the emigrant's road forked northwest to Los Angeles or southwest to San Diego.

Close to Agua Caliente was a village of Native Americans whose headman, Antonio Garra, had been befriended by Bill Marshall, a former crewmember on a whaling ship. Marshall had married a Luiseño Indian woman and worked as a storekeeper at Warner's Ranch. When Garra complained to Marshall about Haraszthy's tax collections and other ill treatment that Cupeños and other Native American groups received, Marshall lent a sympathetic ear.

Violence erupted initially near the Gila and Colorado Rivers, where four Americans tending a large flock of sheep were slain by a joint raiding party of Cupeños and Yumas, who thereafter quarreled over a division of the livestock. On return to Agua Caliente on Friday evening, November 21, the Cupeños murdered four more Americans who, ironically, were visiting the hot springs to improve their health. These victims were Levi Slack, the partner of E.W. Morse; Joseph Manning; and two others known simply as Ridgely and Fiddler.[96]

According to the *Herald's* account, approximately 100 Indians surrounded Warner's house early on the morning of November 22. Thanks to a warning two days before from Fannie, his Indian housekeeper, Warner had sent his wife and family away, and had saddled some horses and tied them to his door. After running off Warner's cattle, the Indians attacked. Warner's hired man was killed, while four of the attackers were wounded, two of them fatally. Warner and an Indian boy jumped on the already-saddled horse and fled to San Diego.

On Monday morning, November 24, San Diego citizens "assembled in town meeting and proclaimed "martial law." With U.S. Army Major Heintzelman's assistance, they formed two companies of "Fitzgerald's Volunteers," named for Major G. B. Fitzgerald, who led about forty volunteers, including Rose, out of town in pursuit of the Indians. A slightly smaller contingent constituted a home guard, who remained behind to secure the main approaches to the city, just in case rumors of an impending Indian attack on San Diego should prove correct.

Only single men were permitted to join the traveling group; thus Rose was among the company that left on Thursday, November 27, while Robinson was among those who remained in San Diego.

Cave Couts, named as the captain and adjutant, was second-in-command of Fitzgerald's Volunteers, while Sheriff Haraszthy was third in line as a first lieutenant. Then came Franklin, as quartermaster; George P. Tebbetts as an ensign;

Robert D. Israel, as first sergeant; Philip Crosthwaite third sergeant; and Henry Clayton fourth sergeant. Jack Hinton, who was the second sergeant, meanwhile was ordered to remain in San Diego in command of the home guard.[97]

The first night out Rose and the other volunteers camped at Mt. Soledad, overlooking the canyon that someday would be known as "Rose Canyon." Although they were on horseback, members of the party did not reach Agua Caliente until December 2. Finding the village abandoned by its Indian residents, the volunteers put Agua Caliente to the torch.

Haraszthy, leading a detachment, meanwhile, "captured the notorious Bill Marshall who is said to have ordered the murder of Mr. Slack and three others at Agua Caliente," the *San Diego Herald* reported. "He is now undergoing a court martial in Old Town, which is not yet concluded. ...We learn through (Thomas) Tilghman who went with the volunteers that a friendly Indian by the name of Juan Antonio, and a Frenchman have succeeded in capturing the chief (Garra), and have taken him to Los Angeles..."[98]

Although Rose saw no action, except the burning down of a deserted village, his brief experience as an American Army volunteer must have been a bittersweet moment. The last time he rode in association with a military party had been with Brevet Major Van Horne, who had humiliated him by ordering him to follow behind the wagon train. Now Rose was a member of the team; with Franklin, one of two Jews who had been accepted into the voluntary military ranks.

Back in town, Thomas Whaley wrote to his mother and sister: "There are only thirty-five of us left to protect the town... My turn to stand guard comes rather frequently...I am well armed with a brace of six shooters and have a horse ready to saddle at any moment."[99]

After two weeks on the trail, the Fitzgerald Volunteers returned to San Diego on December 8 with the captured Marshall and accomplices in tow. Expressing a desire to be baptized a Catholic before his trial, Marshall accordingly was initiated into the Church. Notwithstanding the outraged popular sentiment against Marshall, Crosthwaite, who had known the accused in his whaling days, agreed to serve as his sponsor or godfather, while Lugarda Dionisia Osuna de Machado similarly accepted the role of godmother.[100] Marshall and an accomplice, Juan Verdugo, on December 13 were found guilty of treason and sentenced to death.

Volunteers escorted the two condemned men later the same day to the scaffold that, for the sake of convenience, had been erected near the Catholic cemetery. After receiving absolution from Father Juan Holbein, the condemned men were permitted to speak their last words. "Marshall was the first to speak," the *Herald* reported. "He said that he was prepared to die... that he trusted in God's mercy and hoped to be pardoned for his many transgressions. He still insisted that he was innocent of the crime for which he was about to die." Verdugo, speaking in Spanish, "acknowledged his guilt and admitted the justice of the sentence passed upon him, and was ready and willing to yield up his life as a forfeit for his crimes and wickedness," the newspaper account continued.

> The ropes were then adjusted—the priest approached them for the last time—said some consoling words to them—repeated a final prayer—extended the crucifix, which each kissed several times. Then he descended from the wagon, which immediately moved on, which left the poor unfortunate wretches suspended about five feet from the ground. The fall could not have been more than a foot, at the most, for their necks were not dislocated. Marshall struggled considerably, but the Sonoran scarcely moved a muscle... After being suspended for about an hour and a half, the bodies were cut down and interred in the Catholic burying ground.[101]

Writing to his fiancee, Anna Lannay, on December 17, Whaley told the story dispassionately: "Marshall and one of the chiefs were found guilty of high treason and suffered the penalty of death by hanging Saturday last... Martial law has been abolished. The company of the Fitzgerald Volunteers is not yet disbanded, though we are no longer compelled to keep guard at night."[102]

Lieutenant Thomas Sweeney led a detachment of the regular Army into San Diego on December 21, where, according to his journal, he and his men were "hailed with enthusiasm by the entire population and particularly the fair portion of it, who looked upon me as their deliverer from the tender mercies of the savages..."[103]

Another danger meanwhile had arrived in San Diego in the form of a company of volunteer rangers who had been recruited in San Francisco, and who decided to take the steamer to San Diego even after being informed on December 11 by Ferrell that the danger had since passed. Although the San Francisco volunteers were welcomed to San Diego, there was little in the way of provisions to feed them. They offered their services to Sweeney, who declined, saying they weren't needed. With nothing to do, the men frequented San Diego's saloons, which were all too plentiful, and soon became involved in various kinds of mischief. Before long, the men who nominally served under a Captain Haig came to be called "The Hounds" after street gangs that had terrorized San Francisco in 1849.

Finding no Indians to fight, the San Franciscans seemed "determined to have a row of some description before they returned home," Sweeney wrote in his journal. On January 4, 1852, Robinson and Sweeney were having a discussion with Crosthwaite, who had been serving as acting sheriff since December 23, the date when Haraszthy resigned as sheriff to take up his duties in Sacramento as a state assemblyman. The discussion was interrupted when Lieutenant Watkins of the San Francisco volunteers approached Crosthwaite. Moving away to let the men talk, Robinson and Sweeney watched as Watkins protested the New Year's Eve arrest of a Sergeant Thomas on a charge of attempting to steal Juan Bandini's mule. Watkins threw a punch at Crosthwaite, which the acting sheriff eluded. Next, Watkins pulled out a pistol, put it next to Crosthwaite's chest and fired—only the pistol was jammed. Nearly as astonished as Crosthwaite, Watkins turned tail and started running, whereupon Crosthwaite pulled out his gun and shot Watkins in the thigh. Other San Francisco volunteers opened fire on Crosthwaite, whom a bullet penetrated through the pelvis into the abdomen. George Ogden then dragged Crosthwaite into a store and as the San Francisco volunteers began to rush forward, Sweeney ordered his nineteen soldiers to intervene. The San Franciscans threw down their weapons and subsequently left the town on a ship chartered by the San Diegans.[104] Crosthwaite recovered from his wounds, but Watkins' leg had to be amputated as a result of an infection. The limb was wrapped up by San Diegans and presented to Crosthwaite.

A military escort brought Garra to San Diego on January 8. He was promptly tried by a military court headed by General Bean, and including Major M. Norton, Major Santiago Arguello, Lieutenant Hooper and Lieutenant Tilghman, with Cave Couts serving as judge advocate.[105] Garra agreed during the trial that he had participated in the killing of the sheepherders near the Colorado River, but said he was not involved in either the killings at Agua Caliente, nor the attack on Warner's Ranch. Instead of Marshall and Verdugo being instigators of the violence, Garra maintained that Estudillo and Ortega were behind the uprising in the hope of ridding San Diego County of Anglos. These charges were denied both by Estudillo and Ortega, and not given any credence by the court.

Garra was sentenced on January 10 to die at 4:30 p.m., just an hour and a half after the verdict was returned. Sweeney, as a member of the U.S. Army, had declined to sit on the court martial because the state militia had convened it. He similarly declined to have his men carry out the execution, "but lent General Bean my musketoons and ammunition to carry the sentence into effect."[106]

Sergeant Israel, Whaley, and others in a 12-man squad of Fitzgerald's Volunteers escorted Garra to a site next to an open grave. Garra accepted the opportunity to say a few words. "Gentlemen," he proudly intoned according to the *San Diego Herald* version, 'I ask your pardon for all my offenses, and expect yours in return." The newspaper may have jumbled the quote. It seems more likely he might have said, "I ask your pardon for all my offenses, and grant you mine in return," but we are left only with the one version. The newspaper account continued: "Then suffering his eyes to be bandaged, he kneeled at the head of his grave." Sergeant Israel, serving as provost marshal, turned to his troops and commanded "Ready! Aim! Fire!" Garra's bullet-ridden body toppled into a grave in the same Catholic cemetery where Marshall and Verdugo were already buried. "He died like a man," Sweeney wrote approvingly in his journal. "Peace and quietness now reign and the social relations of life have resumed their accustomed sway," Whaley wrote to his fiancee.[107]

Last Days of the Common Council

The Garra Uprising was over. But the city's fiscal emergency was not to be ended so easily. On the first Monday of January, in an election in which Robinson served as a poll inspector, and Franklin and Estudillo served as judges at the polling places in Old Town, the San Diego electorate chose a new slate of city officials. Tebbetts, who had served as acting mayor in Kurtz's absence, now became mayor in his own right. Robinson—the former Texas politician—returned to his old career. He advanced a rung on the political ladder from city treasurer to city attorney. Combined with results from the previous elections for county offices, Robinson was now the lawyer for both the city government and the county government. Additionally, he was sworn in January 10 as the city's land commissioner. In the wake of Haraszthy's relocation to Sacramento, Robinson also became the secretary of the Masonic Lodge.

José Antonio Estudillo, previously elected county treasurer, succeeded Robinson as city treasurer—so he too occupied a pair of similar offices. Joseph Reiner succeeded Agoston Haraszthy as city marshal. Two members of the first Common Council, William Leamy and Charles Johnson, were returned to serve on the third. They were joined by R.E. Raimond; the former teacher William P. Toler; and Charles Fletcher, one of the three members of the Jewish community who had attended Franklin's Yom Kippur gathering. Also sworn in were Santiago Arguello as city assessor and Fred Painter as clerk of the council.[108]

The tenure of these city worthies proved to be brief indeed. With Haraszthy now a member of the Assembly and in a position to influence such legislation, the state government on January 30 repealed the law of 1850 that had incorporated San Diego as a self-governing city. The governor and state legislature decreed that at the beginning of March, the Common Council should pass out of existence and that it should be replaced by a three-member Board of Trustees, charged with a very precise mission: "To adjust, settle and pay all debts due from the Mayor and Common Council of the city of San Diego, and collect all debts due said Mayor and Common Council, by suit or otherwise." For the purpose of settling the debts, the trustees "shall have the power to sell the public property of said city, for cash or city liabilities: Provided, however that said Trustees shall make no difference in said sales or in payment of any kind of city property between cash and any kind of city liabilities; and further Provided, that said Trustees shall have no authority whatever to create any further debt on the part of said city." Should the sale of property prove insufficient to pay off the debts, the Trustees "shall have the power to levy and collect a reasonable and moderate tax, to aid in paying such debt," the Haraszthy-inspired legislation said. "They shall also have power to grant licenses in said city permitted by the laws of the state..." Once the debts were paid off, however, "no more of the city property shall be sold, except by a vote of the inhabitants of said city...nor shall any taxes be collected, nor licenses paid, unless by a vote as aforesaid." The compensation for the Board of Trustees was fixed at "one-fourth of one percent of all moneys received by them, and no more."[109]

Pending the seating of the new Board of Trustees in March, the old regime struggled impotently. Underscoring what a fiasco the Haraszthy family's jail had been, the *San Diego Herald* reported on February 6 that some Indians who had been incarcerated in the structure recently had made their escape by climbing through a broken window. [110]

Council members Toler and Fletcher were authorized on February 17 to find a contractor who would erect a fence around a cave-in on the road between Old Town and New Town. They were given a budget of $30 to get the job done. At the same meeting, Treasurer Estudillo was directed to retain sufficient funds in the city's account to pay $68.52 in interest on the Haraszthy notes. Three days later, Toler and Fletcher reported to their colleagues that they "found it impossible to get the work done for the amount appropriated."[111] The following day, Mayor pro tem Raimond received formal notification from the state legislature of the revocation of the City's charter and the requirement that elections for a Board of Trustees be held on March 1.[112]

Meanwhile members of the city government began making new arrangements for their careers. On February 28, Robinson, with his strong background in Mexican land law, announced a new affiliation in the *San Diego Herald*: "James W. Robinson, attorney and counselor at law, and notary public, San Diego, California, has formed a law partnership with Messrs. Wm. Carey Jones, P.W. Tomkins and C.B. Strode, Esquires, of the City of San Francisco, for the purpose of presenting for adjudication and confirmation, California private lands claims by the Board of U.S. Land Commissioners, and also for prosecuting the same before the U.S. District Court and in the Supreme Court of the U.S. where Colonel Benton, and other eminent lawyers will attend to the same. He will also practice in the first District and in the Supreme Court of the state and in the U.S. District Court for the Southern District of California."[113]

An illustration of the importance of such a career came February 24, 1852, when the military formally recommended to U.S. President Millard Fillmore that he reserve for American defense purposes all the land between the tip of Point Loma and a line stretching across the peninsula approximately one and a half miles north of Fort Guijarros—a recommendation the thirteenth President officially adopted two days later.[114] This was a particularly tough break for Rose. He could neither own the vast acreage on Point Loma that he had purchased at the end of 1850, nor was he likely to get a refund in the very near future: the city that had sold the land to him now was officially bankrupt.

The Common Council voted on its last day of existence, February 28, to put all the city's property temporarily under the jurisdiction of the county's Court of Sessions until the Board of Trustees could be seated. The *San Diego Herald* wrote a sarcastic adieu to the charter city of San Diego, which would not again become a fully self-governing municipality for another thirty-seven years:

> From and after Monday next, our hitherto busy, bustling city, dwindles into a quiet village. A little less than two years ago, with some twelve or thirteen thousand dollars in the treasury and when land speculation was rife throughout the state, our precious city showed itself in a wonderful manna, splendid fortunes from wonderful rises in real estate, were thought of and aldermanic fees and soup dinners were feasted on with most voracious appetite. Our virgin village made her debut and took her place among her sister cites of the state. But alas like everything else abortive, she soon drooped and withered as a newly planted flower. With an empty treasury, and in debt deeply—with nothing to show for it but the half finished skeleton of a house, which stands alone, on a gloomy spot by a gloomy roadside, to frighten the solitary traveler at night, with its naked ribs and ghostly appearance, we return to the 'first principles,' redeemed, regenerated and disenthralled. An election will be held on Monday at the Playa, Old Town and New Town for the election of three trustees. Let every man vote for those whom he knows are capable and responsible.[115]

The disincorporation of their city marked a low period for San Diegans. Robinson wrote dejectedly on March 12, 1852 to his friend Amasa Turner in Texas:

> The rush of emigration to California is still astonishing. Many of them will lay their bones here, cut down by disease, contracted by extreme exposure incident to an emigrant's life in California. Many will return broken in health & spirit, penniless, and in some instances, what is worse, ruined in morals. If I was back in Texas, situated as I was when I removed here, I would think it madness to remove here and unwise to remove anywhere. But the die is cast, that cannot be recalled, when it is too late. Coming here I lost my property by the way & what was more serious my health, but the latter is now nearly

restored, but it has impaired my constitution. I have made a
living but have not accumulated money or property. It was my
intention to send my wife & son back to Texas this Spring, but
cannot do it now, for want of money. But I have placed my
son at school at San José, a good institution, now. This however makes it imperative on me to exert my utmost to raise
the money to meet this new demand and I must beg of you
the favor to transmit me the amount owing from you... Time
wears on with me rapidly & I feel my days are not numerous
under any circumstances. My means (are) small & therefore
must gather them speedily together... I intend coming to Texas
to die & lay my bones, but cannot say when, not until the
means will warrant me in doing so...

However, there was a note of hope at the end of this sad letter: "A wide
field of land litigation is opening to me here in the old California titles & I am
commencing a career in them before the U.S. Board of Land Commissioners
to investigate California private land claims, but I must take land or wait for
fees & must subsist in the meantime on other resources."[116]

Robinson began a series of articles in the *San Diego Herald* under the title
of "California Land Laws" on March 6, 1852. The purpose of the series was to
better acquaint San Diegans with Robinson's capabilities as a land attorney and
also to denounce President Fillmore, a Whig, in an effort to lay the ground-
work for the election to the U.S. presidency later in the year of a fellow
Democrat.

The attorney quoted the Treaty of Guadalupe Hidalgo as saying that citizens in areas ceded by Mexico to the United States shall "be maintained and
protected in the free enjoyment of their liberty and property." He argued that
this meant that the Land Commission must not require more proof or docu-
mentation from former Mexican citizens regarding their land titles than the
Mexican government would have required of them. By requiring these citizens
to pay between $200 and $2,000 for a new survey of their lands, the Commission was violating the treaty and imposing an unfair tax on the former
Mexican citizens, Robinson argued.

He then suggested that whereas neither the treaty nor the U.S. Congress
intended to impose such a hardship on the former Mexican citizens, such
indeed was "the wicked and oppressive act of Mr. Millard Fillmore, and his
Whig associates, an oppression and injustice to the people of California. And as
if our cup of sorrow was not yet full to overflowing, another wrong is added,
and the present administration lifts the poisoned chalice to the quivering lip,
and requires us to drink it to the dregs." Not only were the former Mexican
citizens being asked to pay for a survey but also to provide translations for all
relevant Spanish documents in their possession. This requirement was notwith-

standing the fact that "there is a translator appointed and paid by the United States for this purpose and the discharge of other duties."[117]

In the next installment, written in the same florid style, Robinson continued to inveigh against the "baleful influence of Whig policy in California." Among his arguments were that a "Whig administration forced upon us prematurely a state government when a territorial government would have saved us millions"; that the Fillmore administration "has neglected to protect us against the incursions of ten thousand hostile Indians on our border, and thereby compelled the citizens of the state to protect themselves" and, that each claimant of a Spanish or Mexican land grant has been forced to incur the cost of a "plat and survey and copy and translation of his grant." Furthermore, he wrote, "these acts of national robbery under color of law... these acts for the purpose of confiscation, by operation of law, the property of a harmless, ignorant and comparatively friendless portion of our citizens... emanate from the same foul source, the Whig policy... and they operate like a vampire draining the last dollar from the impoverished inhabitants of our state..."

Robinson charged that members of the Land Commission were planning to cause even more unwarranted expense for his potential clients by restricting the location of commission meetings to San Francisco, a decision, in effect, "to drag our citizens seven hundred miles to appear in suits." His conclusion was filled with oratorical flourishes. "Is there no remedy for these evils? Will the President grant no relief? Will the members of our Legislature take no action to remedy the evil? We shall see. It is doubtful if they ever see their constituents in peace if they do not. There is little hope but a change of rulers in the general government, and in the establishment of a territorial government in the Southern portion of California. Both of these are within reach of the people. The remedy is at the ballot box."[118]

However much citizens agreed with Robinson's rhetoric, it did little to allay fears that San Diego was no longer a good place for business. Marks and Fletcher announced that they were selling their entire inventory of liquors and dry goods in order that Fletcher might relocate to the East Coast.[119] Marks stayed in San Diego, but in Fletcher the town lost a man who had been a city councilman, and a devout member of the Jewish community.

First Board of Trustees

The city voters chose for the new Board of Trustees, Charles Noell, who had been Haraszthy's opponent on the first Common Council; Cave Couts, and G.B. Tebbetts, who didn't have the opportunity to finish his term as mayor.[120] The board was sworn in March 25, with Noell becoming president; Couts, treasurer and Tebbetts, secretary. On the following day, the trustees decided to meet every evening (except Sunday) at 7 p.m., and also to trade office space for the legal services of the cash-pressed Robinson. The trustees resolved "that as J.W. Robinson has tendered his services as legal adviser and also to furnish other assistance to this board to facilitate its operations, that the vacant room in the rear of City Hall formerly occupied by the mayor be and is appropriated to his use as an office."[121] On March 27, the trustees called upon the citizenry to pay any unpaid taxes or license fees, and also decided to schedule land auctions on April 17 and May 15. They also decided to advertise that 100 lots owned by the city would be available for purchase on each of those Saturdays.[122]

Whatever momentum the trustees were building toward solving the fiscal problems was soon lost when they failed to produce a quorum at any of the next five meetings. When they did reassemble on April 3, they decided to authorize Tebbetts to run an advertisement about the land auctions in the San Francisco newspaper *Alta California* for two weeks. Additionally, they resolved that the past and present district attorneys, "Wm. C. Ferrell and J.W. Robinson be requested to examine the papers of the late city of San Diego and ascertain as far as possible the assets and liabilities of said city and such other information as may be of use and advantage to the Board of Trustees for which the thanks of the board will be most sincerely tendered. The secretary for this purpose is hereby authorized to furnish such books and papers to them as may be in his possession."[123]

Franklin's Grand Jury

The Court of Sessions served as the governing body of the County of San Diego prior to the creation of the County Board of Supervisors in 1853. On April 6, 1852, the court—consisting of Judge John Hays and associate members J. Judson Ames and William Toler—impaneled a new county Grand Jury, which Robinson, in his capacity as county attorney instructed as to its duties. Besides hearing presentations involving the facts of specific cases, and deciding whether the facts warranted the cases going to trial, the Grand Jury also was empowered to inquire into the operation of governmental bodies of San Diego and to make recommendations. Jury members selected Lewis Franklin to serve as their foreman.

Under Franklin's leadership, the Grand Jury of 1852 proved to be particularly memorable. On being presented evidence that Phantly Roy Bean and John Collins had arranged to settle an argument by dueling, a practice which was illegal in California, the Grand Jury indicted both of them on charges of sending and accepting a challenge. Bean, a younger brother of former Mayor Joshua Bean, was thrown into the famous Haraszthy jail and promptly dug his way out—some say with a spoon, others say with a pocketknife.[124] He was not heard of again in San Diego, but in the post–Civil War period he became a legend in the town of Langtry, Texas, where, as "Judge Roy Bean" he operated a saloon and served as a colorful but arbitrary justice of the peace who became known throughout the world for his claim to be "the Law west of the Pecos."[125]

Franklin's Grand Jury report regarding government operations urged "prompt and efficient action for the suppression of vice, which has so grown up and fattened in our midst, all its enormity has become a reproach to each and all of us." The report then inveighed against intemperance of the alcoholic variety, while being the very picture of intemperance in the sense of bigotry when discussing Native Americans and African Americans.

Saying the Grand Jury was distressed by heavy drinking both among leaders of San Diego's society, who "oft times rend the air with their wild shouts of drunkenness" and among ordinary citizens who frequent bars "where too frequently Indians become their companions in the wine cup," Franklin recommended that saloon licenses be restricted to those proprietors who put up a bond to guarantee that they maintain an "orderly house." The report named several barkeepers who maintained "low groggeries where at any hour of day and night the lazy and indolent Indians congregate" and also pointed a finger at two stores believed to be selling liquor to the Indians.

Having expressed contempt for Native Americans, the racist report next turned to African Americans, contending that a "den of sable animals who have come into our midst, and aping the way of their betters, freely use spirituous liquors and indulge their brutal appetites by dragging the Indian women who infest our town. They seemingly have no vocation. We your Grand Jury recommend that these colored men be compelled to leave our town, unless they be employed in some useful labor."

Further, "we, the Grand Jury, suggest that a removal of the numerous rancheros (Indian settlements) should be ordered, as they are not only an eyesore, but the hiding place of idle pilfering Indians. None of these remnants of a degenerate age should be allowed on this side of the river and as the lots upon which these rancheros are now built, or being built, belong to us and our late city, we your Grand Jury would respectfully ask your honorable court to direct their removal at the same time directing the trustees to grant the Indians the occupancy of vacant lots across the river."

Expressions of contempt for people who were neither Anglo nor Mexican were not the Grand Jury's only complaints about life in early San Diego. "Filth is thrown down within the limits of the town, the stench of its decay being sufficient to breed distemper in our midst," Franklin wrote. "In the public streets, pools of putrid matter are formed by offal, slops and other garbage being heaped up. The pure stream of water which would otherwise flow in our river is muddied and made obnoxious by the habit of washing clothing at the foot of every street. Cattle are allowed to run at large and annoy and obstruct us in the paths of our every day walk, and endanger our lives when darkness closes in. These animals should be disposed of that our citizens could enjoy unmolested the privilege of going wither their own choice might direct them..."

As for operations of county government itself, the Grand Jury said inasmuch as the county auditor and treasurer were still in the process of "disentangling the confused mass of irregularities of their predecessors, we leave to some future Grand Jury the duty of such investigation." Complaining that official record keeping was sloppy, even among members of the judiciary, the report closed with the admonition that "in the present and future operations of our magisterial officers such loose and slovenly conduct will not occur." Ending the report with a self-righteous and self-important flourish that seemed to characterize Franklin throughout his tenure in San Diego, he added: "laws and institutions are after all in themselves but the dead skeleton of society and can only derive their life and efficiency by the spirit breathed into them by the character and moral condition of the people. They are the body; this is the animating soul."[126]

Previously the people of San Diego were so taken with Haraszthy's continental charm that they turned a blind eye to the family's ruinous avarice. Now the same people appeared spellbound by Franklin's vocabulary and earnestness. The *Herald* enthused: "We will venture to say that there never was a body of men convened for similar purpose in this country who, so ably, faithfully and fearlessly performed their duties as the present Grand Jury, and although every member of that body deserves and has received the thanks of both the court and the people, yet we cannot forbear to mention particularly Mr. Lewis Franklin, the foreman, for the zeal with which he entered into the great work of correcting abuses and suppressing crime in our midst."[127]

Franklin's report was the talk of the town for some period after its publication, but it would be hard to point to a single reform adopted either by the Court of Sessions or the Board of Trustees resulting from his finger-pointing. Within a month, the report's currency as a topic of conversation faded. The *San Diego Herald* had more exciting news in its May 8, 1852, edition, although like many similar articles that would follow in its columns about other mines, the report proved to be mainly wishful thinking: "Gold mine in San Diego!!" the headline proclaimed. "Our town of San Diego was put into a furor last Wednesday by the exhibition of some fine specimens of the gold-bearing quartz, full of the 'real stuff,' which was brought in by two Indians, who declared they found it in one of the gulches between Old Town and the Mission. Should this report prove true, that there does exist such a mine in our immediate vicinity, we may expect to see San Diego, with its superior natural advantages, soon rivaling our famed sister, San Francisco. The specimens may be seen at the bar of Mr. George P. Tebbetts, Old Town."[128] One could imagine editor Ames adding, in between silent parentheses, "and once you are in Tebbett's bar, don't worry too much about all that intemperance stuff."

On the same day that this report appeared, the Masonic Grand Lodge of California was holding another of its Communications. Noting that no representative of the San Diego Lodge, U.D., was in attendance, L. Stowell offered the following successful resolution:"Whereas San Diego Lodge, U.D., has been prevented, from accident, or otherwise from attending this Communication— Therefore: Resolved: that if said Lodge applies for a charter, or an extension of its dispensation, the same may be granted upon the presentation to, and approval of their work by the Grand Master, or Grand Secretary, and the payment of requisite fees."[129]

Demise of the First Board of Trustees

Meanwhile, the San Diego Board of Trustees, which once so resolutely had decided to meet six evenings a week, did not reassemble after April 3 until May 20. With great embarrassment, as a first order of business, the trustees ordered the secretary not to include in the minute books separate entries for the missed meetings, and then, they repealed the resolution committing them to meetings of such frequency. Had the land sales meanwhile been advertised in the San Francisco newspaper? Tebbetts replied that inasmuch as there had been no meetings since April 3, there had been no opportunity for anyone to approve the minutes of that meeting. Therefore, he had felt powerless to proceed. So the resolution authorizing the auction of the lots also was repealed. The state legislature, meanwhile, had authorized the trustees to represent the city's interests before the U.S. Lands Commission in Los Angeles in the dispute over ownership of various lands, including those at Point Loma.[130]

The trustees voted to ask the former city attorney T.W. Sutherland, who was residing in Los Angeles at the time, to serve as their attorney there. But that resolution was the last substantive action taken by the trustees. Couts resigned at the farcical May 20 meeting, explaining that out-of-town business would make attending meetings impossible.[131] On June 9, Noell followed suit, writing for the record that "finding it impossible to attend to the duties required of me as one of the trustees of the city, I herewith tender my resignation of the same."[132] On June 10, Tebbetts as the last remaining trustee, wrote to Judge John Hays, head of the Court of Sessions, which then functioned as the government for the County of San Diego. "Circumstances beyond my control compel me to tender you this resignation as one of the trustees of the late city of San Diego."[133]

Ferrell and Robinson, who had been charged with examining the city's books and financial records, now decided to step forward as candidates for a new board of trustees, to be chosen in an election on June 21. Louis Rose was persuaded to run also, no doubt upon the urging of Robinson, with whom he had arrived in San Diego only slightly more than two years before.[134]

Ferrell, Robinson and Rose all were members of the recently formed San Diego Lodge of the Free and Accepted Masons. Three days after their success at the polls came the annual Masonic parade around the Plaza, followed by a dinner. The priest who had administered last rites to the men condemned in the Garra uprising took quite literally Pope Clement XII's Bull of 1738 forbidding Catholics from joining the Masons. The Masonic parade honored St. John the Baptist and St. John the Evangelist, but Father Holbein not only forbade his parishioners from participating in the festivities, but on pain of excommunication, he also ordered them to stay inside to avoid giving any indication to the Masons that their activities were welcomed. The priest's hard-line attitude towards an organization involving the very leaders of the city was at the least quite impolitic. In retaliation, members of the Masons, as individuals, declined to give financial support for construction of a new Catholic church. It was not long before Holbein was transferred to another post.[135]

Court House, Old Town

James W. Robinson, circa 1856
©San Diego Historical Society

CHAPTER 3

San Diego's Robinson–Rose Era

An Instant Majority

*B*ecause they worked for the common good, rather than for narrow self-interests, Robinson and Rose gradually were able to lift the spirits of San Diegans, persuading them that far from having no future, the city and bay had a destiny to fulfill. This new era began July 31, 1852 with the organization of the second Board of Trustees with Robinson as its president, Ferrell as its secretary and Rose as its treasurer.[1] Although Ferrell often voted the same way as his two fellow Masons, Robinson knew that he could always rely on the man with whom he had braved travel over deserts and mountains to a new life in California. Together, Robinson and Rose formed an instant majority.

The time that Robinson and Ferrell had invested in studying the records and finances of the City of San Diego came quickly into evidence at the next meeting, August 25. Noting that Sutherland had never responded to the previous Board of Trustees about whether he would represent them before the U.S. Board of Land Commissioners, the trustees directed that a new letter be sent to the attorney to inquire whether he was interested in rendering such service and inquiring how much he might charge. Next, on Ferrell's motion and Rose's second, they adopted a policy statement that it was their intention to follow the Legislature's directive to pay off the city's debts by holding an auction of public land. They decided to run an advertisement for two weeks in the *San Diego Herald* urging anyone to whom the City of San Diego was in debt to come forward and to specify exactly what form that debt took—scrip, bond or open account.[2]

Having thus attended to the debts, the trustees on the next night addressed revenues. They authorized Joseph Reiner, who had served as city marshal under the Common Council, to serve as the board's agent in collecting unpaid city license fees. Additionally, they instructed him to collect those taxes that had been assessed in 1851 by Marks Jacobs, but which had gone uncollected in the political turmoil thereafter. Responding to an April 16 act of the state legislature, which had set aside funds for the indigent sick, they also voted 2-1, with

Ferrell in the minority, to ask for $2,000 in state funds to attend to people who arrive ill at the Port of San Diego.[3]

The Sad Saga of "Yankee Jim" Robinson

Robinson meanwhile continued to serve as the district attorney for the County of San Diego—a role that in August of 1852 found him prosecuting a case that was to become part of the lore of San Diego's legal system. The defendant, accused of stealing a boat, was a man who had the same name as James Robinson. To differentiate the accused thief from the man who then was both the president of the city Board of Trustees as well as the district attorney, the defendant was called "Yankee Jim" Robinson.

It had been widely rumored that "Yankee Jim" was a desperado of the worst sort—the kind of man who used to wait in ambush for miners to murder them for their gold. After arriving in San Diego, Yankee Jim and two companions—James A. Loring and William Harney—were accused of stealing a boat from J.C. Stewart and Enos Wall for an excursion to the harbor. Subsequently, they set the boat adrift in the ocean, just beyond the harbor, and it washed up on a beach a few miles down the coast. Robinson brought charges of grand larceny against the three men and they were arraigned before the county Court of Sessions, consisting of Judge John Hays and Justices of the Peace William T. Conlon and J. Judson Ames.

Yankee Jim, who was tried first, should have sensed that something was amiss when both Stewart and Wall—the very men from whom he stole the boat—were impaneled as part of the jury. Perhaps he believed that since they had recovered their property, they would go easy on him. To the contrary, the jury likened the stealing of a boat to the stealing of a horse—a crime that in frontier towns was a "hanging offense." That is what the jury recommended for "Yankee Jim"—that he be hanged until dead on September 18. The gallows were set up on a spot in Old Town that later became the site of the Whaley House. Legend has it that up to the time his neck was stretched, Yankee Jim didn't believe that he actually would be executed for stealing a boat.

On the day of the execution, Yankee Jim was standing in a cart with a noose around his neck. He spoke to the large crowd on hand to witness the event, saying that he had been misjudged, that he was a good man, who had given money to the poor. Undersheriff Philip Crosthwaite checked his watch. Even though Yankee Jim was still orating, the time for execution was at hand. Crosthwaite gave the signal to Gustave Fischer, who was driving the cart; Fischer cracked the whip, and Yankee Jim was hung in mid-sentence. The incident was reminiscent of the way District Attorney Robinson dispensed frontier justice when he served as a judge in Texas. (Today the story of "Yankee

Jim's" hanging is popular fare at the Whaley House, which—according to legend—is haunted by the ghost of "Yankee Jim" who still is angered by this miscarriage of justice.[4]) As for the accomplices Harney and Loring, they subsequently were sentenced to a year each in state prison.

Rose Sets Down Roots

Rose's career was not so colorful as Robinson's, although it was, in a way, bloodier. While maintaining his ownership of the Commercial Hotel, he decided to also become a butcher. He purchased from former Common Council member William Leamy and his partner M. Sexton the slaughterhouse that, in the style of the times, was marked with a red pennant outside its entrance.

"Attention," wrote Rose in a newspaper advertisement: "Captains and owners of vessels will take particular notice that the subscriber has purchased the interest of Messrs. Leamy and Sexton in the butchering establishment at Old Town and that his arrangements are now complete for supplying at a few hours notice fresh beef, pork, mutton, veal, poultry and vegetables of every description, and all kinds of livestock at the lowest rates and in quantities. The advantage afforded to Panama Steamers by this arrangement whereby they can get fresh provisions and vegetables here in any quantity and at short notice, will be apparent to anyone and when it is known that such supplies can be had here at much less price than in San Francisco, masters and owners of vessels, will, if they consult their best interests, make arrangements for the subscriber for a regular supply." This advertising notice was signed "Louis Rose."[5]

The notice gives us a good a sketch of how Rose analyzed a situation, and then, in entrepreneurial fashion, tried to develop it into a business opportunity. San Diego lay many days sailing south of San Francisco and many more north of Panama, where emigrants, after crossing the isthmus from the Atlantic Ocean, still boarded San Francisco-bound sailing vessels. By the time these ships reached San Diego from either direction, their passengers and crews would welcome fresh supplies of meats and vegetables. Rose saw opportunities that, like San Diego's own future, depended on the sea. He knew he also could count on local customers starting, of course, with his own Commercial House, to buy his products.

About this time, Rose purchased for $250 a small piece of property on Fitch Street from Maria Russell.[6] Perhaps feeling he was now positioned well enough in both a financial and civic sense to make his wife proud, Rose wrote to Nisan J. Alexander, a nephew then residing in New Orleans, to attempt to locate his wife, Caroline. He urged Alexander to plead his case to Caroline, to tell her that he was now in San Diego and that he had prospered in the four years since they had parted company in 1848. He desired for her to join him in San Diego. Alexander dutifully communicated this information by letter in October 1852 to Caroline's sister and brother-in-law, Eliza and Henry J. Thal of Montgomery, Alabama, with whom Rose's wife then was staying. The Thals later testified that Caroline had not heard from her husband since the time he had left New Orleans for San Antonio and had assumed he was dead.

The records do not indicate whether Caroline felt relief that her husband was alive, or anger that he had, up to then, left her without knowledge of his whereabouts, or perhaps both emotions. Of one thing, however, Caroline Marks Rose was quite certain: she had no intention whatsoever of rejoining her husband, success or not. At a later date, she would demonstrate that conclusively. [7]

Meanwhile, with distance and communication being what they were, Rose had no immediate way of knowing Caroline's intentions. In later divorce proceedings, Robinson, serving as Rose's lawyer, would contend that in the years since Rose had left New Orleans, he had used "all the industry and economy in his power to provide a comfortable home for himself and his said wife—to enjoy his property with him."[8]

As he waited for Caroline's response, Rose and other city trustees convened on November 29 to discuss with Reiner his progress in collecting debts owed to the city.[9] They decided on December 7 to proceed with the auctions of various city-owned lots, instructing Ferrell to publish in the *Alta California* of San Francisco, the *San Francisco Herald*, the *Los Angeles Star* and the *San Diego Herald* the following advertisement:

> Sale of real estate—the trustees of the town of San Diego will expose to public sale on the 23rd & 24th... a large number of valuable fifty-vara lots located at the Playa and at Old Town as surveyed and platted by Cave J. Couts, some of them having shipping privileges, also other valuable lots or parcels of land ranging in size from 5 to 160 acres as surveyed and platted by Henry Clayton Esq., lying immediately outside of Couts' survey in the adjacent valleys of the town of San Diego. Conditions cash or city liabilities at par. A list of the lots to be offered for sale with the maps giving their locations can be seen at the office of the president of the Board in the courthouse.[10]

This time, under the new administration, the instructions to place advertisements were carried out promptly. Robinson would have many visitors at his office at the court house/town hall.

The trustees also decided to require that the minimum bid for any parcel of land be one-half the price established by the Common Council on August 26, 1850. Thus the minimum bid on a 5-acre lot, which the old Council would have sold for $30, was set at $15. Minimum bid for the largest parcel of 160 acres was set at $160, or $1 per acre. Robinson, beset on December 10 with health problems, did not feel well enough to walk two blocks from his home to the courthouse, so a Board of Trustees meeting was held at his home on Juan Street. With the auction two weeks away, the trustees debated what should be done about land that had been sold on the installment plan by the old Council, but for which payments had not been made by the purchasers. They decided that the price of such land should be reduced by one-third, and that the purchasers should be required to pay the outstanding balance by the end of February 1853. It was noted that some people had applied to the old Common Council to purchase certain lands, but that the transactions were not completed because the city's charter had been revoked. Should these lands be auctioned? The trustees decided, in fairness, that people who had made such applications should be given until February to complete the purchases.[11]

The great land auction was held December 23 and 24. Auctioneer Philip H. Hooff reported confirmed sales of $1,225.76. Rose decided to forego receiving interest on his two-year-old city scrip that dated from the time he had opened a land account with the city, and used those notes to purchase seven lots in the Playa and 23 more lots in Old Town. Blocks generally contained four lots each, and Rose paid as little as $5 for some lots and as much as $27 for a choice lot at the Playa. His average expenditure was $18.62 per lot. His aggregate $559 payment represented a little more than 45 percent of the total revenue raised.[12]

Another $781 had been offered by people who wanted to pay with scrip that had been accruing at 8 percent interest per month. The trustees met on December 28 on the call of Robinson. After directing Sheriff Reiner to seize and sell all properties on which taxes still had not been paid, the trustees turned to the issue of the 8 percent bonds that originally had been issued to pay Sheriff Haraszthy for the jail that stood unfinished. Robinson told his colleagues "he had not been able to satisfy his mind that the Common Council had authority to create such a liability and impose such a burden of interest upon the property of the city." Ferrell disagreed with his fellow attorney Robinson.[13]

Unable to win each other over to their respective points of view, the two attorneys put the issue off until the December 30 meeting. At that point, Robinson offered his colleagues a resolution on the matter: "Resolved that the trustees of the city of San Diego, in order speedily to settle and pay the debts of the same, that in the payment of property purchased from the city that they will receive all kinds of city liabilities; but they will in no case pay interest on said liabilities—believing that the large portion of the so-called debts of the city were contracted without authority of law. And especially the interest stipulated in the eight percent bond for which we believe no consideration was received by the city authorities and this and other debts were contracted by the Common Council contrary to the charter of said city."[14]

After Rose seconded Robinson's resolution, the issue was all but settled. The formal vote resulted in the resolution's adoption by a margin of 2-1, with Ferrell in the minority. Accordingly, at their meeting on January 6, 1853, the trustees issued deeds only to those people who were willing to accept face value for their 8 percent bonds.[15]

Bitten hard by the land speculation bug, Rose coupled the purchases he made during the city's auction with an acquisition on January 3, 1853, of another 76 undeveloped lots spread over 14 blocks of Middletown, for which he paid Oliver S. Witherby $900—or slightly more than $11.84 per block.[16] He purchased another five lots in Old Town on March 31 from Bonifacio Lopez.[17]

Meanwhile, Robinson announced at the trustees meeting on January 8 that business would require him to travel to the state capital of Sacramento and that he did not expect to return to San Diego until February.[18] On his return, he, Rose and Ferrell temporarily set aside the matters of city government in order to organize the affairs of the County of San Diego. The state legislature had decided to replace the county Court of Sessions with a county Board of Supervisors. The three trustees for the City of San Diego were joined on the initial board by J. J. Warner, who had represented San Diego as a state senator; Ephraim W. Morse; George Lyons and Eugene Pendleton, whom Rose soon invited to become his partner in diverse business interests. At the February 3 organizing meeting, Ferrell was elected president of the county Board of Supervisors with the support of his two fellow trustees.[19] This perhaps alleviated any resentment Ferrell felt at the likelihood of being regularly outvoted by Robinson and Rose on city matters.

At the suggestion of Warner on March 14, the supervisors formed themselves into a committee to take a field trip to Temecula for the purpose of laying out the route of a public highway between the two towns.[20] As they were empowered under law to require citizens to either donate labor or money for the construction of a public highway, this was not just a sightseeing trip. On their return two weeks later, they put on the public record their itinerary and impressions: "The first point of examination was the hill at Soledad Valley, and the committee felt satisfied that the present difficulty of the Soledad hill can be easily overcome without any great labor," they said. "From Soledad they proceeded to San Digito (sic), where they also discovered a practicable road from San Digito to the Encinitas. There is no serious obstacle from Encinitas by the Ranch of Buena Vista into the valley of the San Luis Rey River; a good practicable road may be made. Then they passed up the valley of this river to where the present road to Temecula leaves it, then followed this road. The next difficulty presenting itself was found at Temecula Mountain. Your committee are of opinion however that the difficulty of this mountain may be overcome and the valley of Temecula reached, thus opening a good wagon road from San Diego into the valley of Temecula, over which loaded wagons can pass without any serious obstacle."[21]

Robinson, Warner, and Pendleton were formed into a committee on March 28 to develop a financial plan for the construction of the road. They were instructed to consult with members of the Army Corps of Engineers, who at that time were billeted in New Town, to determine what help, if any, the military might offer in the road's construction. On April 4, the Board of Supervisors decided to extend the road from Temecula to the northern limits of San Diego County, thereby bringing the terminus of the highway closer to the growing town of San Bernardino, which then was a part of Los Angeles County.[22] Members of the Mormon Church, at the time, were settling San Bernardino. San Diegans recognized that construction of this new public highway could foster a new pattern of trade, by which San Diego could serve as San Bernardino's port of choice.[23] Warner, whose ranch was a lot closer to the northern sections of the proposed public highway than the properties of the other supervisors, was designated as "superintendent of highways." Upon his motion, the Board of Supervisors then allocated for the project "three-fifths of the poll tax," and ordered every able-bodied man between the ages of 18 and 45 in the county either to perform manual labor on the road or pay an in lieu fee of $2 per construction day.[24] On April 13, Robinson offered the motion, with Warner's second, that the board again travel to Soledad to determine the public road's exact route.[25]

Creating transportation links to and from their region, located literally in the southwest corner of the United States, was a preoccupation, even a passion, during the Robinson-Rose era. Robinson also had become active in efforts to have a railroad built to San Diego. Colonel J. Bankhead Magruder spearheaded the drive following his election as president of the Pacific and Atlantic Railroad, a company that existed as yet only on paper. John Hays, William Moon, and Frank Ames were elected as vice presidents, and J. Judson Ames as secretary. Based largely on Robinson's recollections of his trip with Rose across the country, Magruder issued a report in May 1853 suggesting that the railroad follow a west-bound course along the 32nd Parallel through Robinson's old stamping grounds of Texas and also along the Gila River route that he and Rose had followed to San Diego. J. J. Warner, Cave Couts, E.B. Pendleton, Charles Poole, and O.S. Witherby joined Robinson on a committee to promote the route.[26]

The Making of Rose Canyon

The city Board of Trustees, which had been on hiatus since January to permit its members to focus on county issues, reconvened on June 6, 1853, and spent an entire meeting determining which citizens still had claims pending to purchase city lands from the days of the Common Council.[27] Once satisfied that they understood the situation, the trustees began on July 12 to sell lands to people who previously had applied for them. Witherby was permitted to purchase 50 acres in the area lying between Old Town and the Playa. Rose, who still was owed money by the city from the time in 1850 when he had deposited more than $6,000 into a special account, was authorized to buy 800 acres in La Cañada de las Lleguas for $1,066 or slightly more than $1.22 an acre.[28] This area, which later became known as "Rose Canyon," not only lay along the route to Los Angeles, it was also along the proposed path of the public highway to Temecula. Unknown to Rose, it also lay along a major geologic fault line, which subsequently would bear his name.

Additionally, Rose purchased 231½ acres near the Playa for $308.66, or also about $1.33 per acre.[29] Some of the land fronting on San Diego Bay would be incorporated years later into the development that would be called "Roseville."

On July 13, Rose was permitted to acquire three more parcels all lying between Old Town and False Bay, as Mission Bay then was called.[30] Additionally, the Fischer family, which according to the 1852 census, was living in the same Old Town dwelling as Rose, was authorized to purchase three 160-acre parcels in La Cañada de las Lleguas.[31]

Rose's fellow trustees presented their own longstanding land claims. Robinson sought and received permission to acquire Block 12 in Old Town after trustees reviewed the minutes of the March 25, 1851, Common Council meeting at which that property had been traded pending clarification of title. In addition, he was permitted to purchase a 160-acre parcel in Mission Valley, a 73½-acre lot adjoining one of the same dimensions owned by Rose near La Playa, and six other parcels of varying sizes. Ferrell opted to purchase 35 acres in two parcels. Former Sheriff Haraszthy was allowed to purchase 50 acres, while his father, the former councilman, acquired 160 acres.[32]

On July 21, Robinson paid $1,000 to Joseph Reiner for property on the northwest side of Old Town Plaza. It was here that he constructed a two-story house that offered a cultural contrast to the Casa de Estudillo located across the plaza. Whereas the Estudillo house had walls around it to insure privacy, and was built looking inward around a central courtyard; Robinson's home had windows and a balcony suitable for viewing and being viewed by people in the Plaza. Besides being the residence for the Robinsons—who lived upstairs—the structure would also house numerous businesses.[33]

Acquiring all that land had tax consequences, as Robinson, Rose, and Ferrell would realize perhaps better than anyone when the time came on July 28 to set the county's tax rate. Perhaps gulping as they voted, members of the Board of Supervisors decided upon a rate of 50-cents per $100 assessed valuation for real estate and personal property. Possibly sympathizing with themselves as much as with their constituents, the supervisors next adopted a resolution declining to levy a special tax authorized by the Legislature for the construction of a county jail—needed because the city's was still useless—"because we deem the taxes already assessed for state and county sufficiently burdensome upon the taxpayers for the present year."[34]

Rose by far was the wealthiest of the three city trustees. His properties were assessed at $18,500, meaning that at 50 cents per $100 assessed valuation, he was liable to a tax bill of $92.50. Rose might have calculated sadly that with the same amount of money he could have purchased another 60-70 acres of land at prevailing prices. On top of that, the business in which he and fellow County Supervisor Eugene Pendleton were partners, now known formally as Rose & Pendleton, was assessed at $8,000 value—another $40 tax bite.

The property assessment listed 152 parcels of land in Rose's ownership, ranging from tiny town lots in Old Town and the Playa, to large tracts of acreage in La Cañada de las Lleguas. Missing from the inventory was the large acreage on Point Loma, leading one to speculate that, because of the cloud put over its title by the military, perhaps Rose turned the lots back to the city in return for other property. The assessment roll also noted that he owned two houses in San Diego, that he had constructed a tannery and buildings on Lot 4 in La Cañada de las Lleguas, and that he owned 98 horses, mares, and mules.[35]

In Yiddish, there is a word "sachel" (say-kh'l), denoting excellent judgment or "native good sense."[36] It perfectly describes Rose's thinking in relation to the tannery and his previously established butcher business. Until then, hides from the cattle that roamed Southern California were brought to "hide houses" at La Playa, from which they were transported to San Francisco or to East Coast cities by ships that had to make long, arduous, and expensive trips around South America's Cape Horn. After being tanned and fashioned into shoes, belts, jackets and other leather goods, everything had to be shipped back to San Diego. The expense of the round-trip transportation added considerably to the cost of the finished goods. Rose had the *sachel* to realize there was an opportunity for someone to make a lot of money if the hides could be tanned in San Diego, right where they came from, and the middlemen and expensive costs of transportation eliminated. So, he invited his nephew Nisan Alexander—who had experience in the tanning business—to come to California and help him set up a tannery in La Cañada de las Lleguas, which was situated along the route of the new public highway. Inasmuch as Rose also operated a butcher shop in Old Town, full use could be made of the cows. There was profit to be made on both their hides and their meat.

When Alexander arrived in San Diego and was gifted some property by Rose[37], he told his uncle that he had corresponded with the family of Rose's wife, Caroline. Alexander probably was unaware at that point that Caroline had no desire to join her husband, nor that she had taken up company with a Frenchman by the name of Depanier.[38] With a nephew at his side and his wife possibly coming to join him, Rose perhaps allowed himself to dream about starting a family. Prior to his nephew's arrival, Rose had found companionship in a menagerie of animals that he had been assembling since his arrival in San Diego. His many pets could roam free in Rose Canyon, or keep him company at his home in Old Town. Since approximately 1851, one of his favorite pets was Chili, a terrapin, which it was indulgently claimed "was so strong it could move a man on its back." He also had a pet dog, Pat, and a large variety of farm animals.[39] Now, at least for a brief while, the lonely bachelor also had a human family member.

San Diego County Bookkeeping Woes

Rose and Robinson were among the county supervisors who listened to a committee report on July 30, 1853, that chronicled how haphazard and mismanaged public finances had been in the San Diego County government. Committee members Ferrell, Pendleton, and Warner had examined Auditor Santiago Arguello's records as well as the county treasury accounts first kept by Crosthwaite and later by Estudillo. As Crosthwaite, who now was serving as county clerk, was present in the room, the committee members needed to be most tactful in the way they presented their criticisms. The committee reported that "difficulties of no ordinary character, arising partly from the fact that no settlement or adjustment of county affairs had ever been made from her organization (in 1850) up to present times, but more particularly from the incorrect and confused (not to say incomprehensible) manner in which the books of the county and auditor and treasurer have been kept... It is true the auditor's book informs us of the number, for what purpose, and the amount of county warrants that have been issued from the organization of the county to the 1st of April 1852 inclusive, but it has been so interlined, pencil-marked and blotted as to reflect but little credit upon these officers who have had it under their control." The report went on to say, "But the treasurer's book defies comprehension or description. It is worse than confusion confused. It is a botch of blotches, scraps incomplete, incomprehensible and in several instances incorrect entries thrown together in one confused mass without system or order and neither your committee nor any other that might have been appointed or any that may hereafter be appointed can ever ascertain from it the amount of county funds received and disbursed by this officer."

The committee consulted a variety of other sources, including records of payments to the state treasurer. As a result, it reported, it arrived at a "satisfactory adjustment of the receipts and disbursements of Philip Crosthwaite, the first county treasurer, up to the end of his official term, the 1st of March 1852, and while it is to be regretted that he has been so negligent in keeping his accounts, your committee feel they would be doing him great injustice were they not to state that in their opinion the county has not had a more honest and trustworthy officer as to the proper use of all monies, coming into his hands."

Nor did the committee question the integrity of Estudillo, who had recently died, but pointed out that he had made a few bookkeeping mistakes. They recommended that the Board of Supervisors "purchase a new set of books" and "employ some person having knowledge of book keeping to take the books of these officers from the organization of the county to the present time and to transcribe their accounts as far as they can be ascertained from the present books and explanation which these officers can give..." It is essential, they suggested, that "it may be ascertained in a moment, not only the number, date, to whom and for what purpose each county warrant is drawn, but when presented for payment, when paid, and the amount of interest (if any) paid theron, the amount of money received from what source and for what purpose received when disbursed and for what purpose..."[40]

Attitudes toward Jews in San Diego

One assumes that a local convention of Democrats was mindful of the report when J. Judson Ames nominated Rose for county treasurer and Charles P. Noell nominated former county judge John Hays for the same office. Rose defeated Hays in subsequent convention balloting. By voice vote the convention proceeded to make Rose's nomination unanimous. The same county convention sent Robinson and J.J. Ames to Los Angeles for the state convention. The local Democrats also put up Warner for county judge, and William Cole and Marks Jacobs (who had changed his name back from Jacobs Marks) as justices of the peace.[41]

Twelve days after that nomination, Rose ascended to another important office: he became junior warden of the San Diego Lodge No. 35 F.A.M., the same Masonic office that he once had held in the Germania Lodge of New Orleans. His selection to the office was reaffirmation of the acceptance, albeit with some ambivalence, that San Diego's Anglo population accorded to the Jews among them.[42]

Although accorded positions of public trust, Jews still were subject to stereotyping, and the Jewish religion was resented as a departure from Christian norms. In August 1853, *Herald* editor Ames editorialized, "it gives us sincere pleasure to state that Messrs. Franklin (Lewis and his brother Maurice) the only 'observing Jews' among a large number in our midst, have signified their willingness to close their place of business, not only on the Jewish Sabbath, which has always been their custom, but also on the Christian Sunday. It is so seldom that we witness such liberality on the part of religionists of any denomination, that it gives us sincere pleasure to record instances of this kind when they transpire."[43]

Notwithstanding the fact that the Commercial House, the butcher shop, and the tannery did business on Sundays, Rose was reelected as a member of the city Board of Trustees on August 23, 1853. Ferrell and Robinson, meanwhile, were replaced by George Lyons and E.W. Morse.[44]

Lieutenant George Derby, a topographical engineer with the U.S. Army and a humorist who wrote under the pseudonyms "Squibob" and "John Phoenix," had arrived in San Diego in January 1853. The San Diego River, at that time, followed an uncertain course, some seasons emptying into San Diego Bay, in other seasons into False Bay. Wanting to regulate the flow of the river, and to protect the settlement of Old Town from flooding, Derby studied building a dike near Presidio Hill and forcing the San Diego River to empty permanently into False Bay. Members of the Masons were pleased to learn on March 7 that Derby previously had served as the first master of Temple Lodge No. 14 in Sonoma, Calif.[45] He had acquaintances who might be of help when the Communication considered San Diego Lodge, U.D.'s long-delayed application for a charter. Accordingly, Derby was prevailed upon to attend the May meeting of the Grand Lodge in San Francisco, where, according to the official *Journal of Proceedings*, "the committee on Dispensations and Charters reported on the books and work of San Diego Lodge, and recommended that a Charter be granted; which report was concurred in; a Charter was ordered, and Bro. Geo. H. Derby was admitted as the representative of that lodge."[46]

While in San Francisco, Derby wrote a letter to Ames at the *Herald*. The fictional "news" report would become part of his pattern of writing satiric articles about Jews and Judaism: "The sympathies of the community have been strongly excited within the last few days in favor of an unfortunate gentleman of the Hebrew persuasion, on whom the officers of the *Golden Gate* perpetrated a most inhuman atrocity, during her late trip from Panama. I gather from the information of the indignant passengers, and by contemplation of an affecting appeal by the public, posted in the form of a handbill at the corner of the streets, that this gentleman was forced by threats and entreaties, to do violence to his feelings and constitution, by eating his way through a barrel (not a half barrel, as has been stated by interested individuals, anxious to palliate the atrocious deed) but through a barrel of clear pork!" Derby went on, "The handbill alluded to is headed by a graphic and well-executed sketch by Solomon Ben David, a distinguished artist of this city, and represents the unhappy sufferer as he emerged from the barrel after his oleaginous repast, in the act of asking, very naturally, for a drink of water. The offense alleged, I find from a hasty perusal of the resolution in the handbill, was simply that this gentleman, whose name appears to have been Oliver, was heard inquiring for Colonel Moore, our well-known and respected Ex-Postmaster. My friend Saul Isaacs, who keeps the 'anything on this table for a quarter' stand tells me that on 'doffing his cask,' the miserable Oliver was found completely bunged up, and that he is now engaged in composing a pathetic ode, describing his sufferings to be called 'The Barrel,' with a few staves of which he favored me on the spot. It was truly touching..."[47]

When Derby returned to San Diego, he was authorized to serve as the installing officer for the now chartered Masonic Lodge. Robinson had been elected to succeed Ferrell as worshipful master, but he surprised his brother Masons by declining the position, explaining that he was not sufficiently familiar with the rituals. Derby therefore became the master through the balance of 1853, and was succeeded in 1854 by Crosthwaite.[48]

Editor Ames subsequently enlisted Derby to substitute for several weeks as editor of the *San Diego Herald* while Ames attended to business in San Francisco. In the newspaper's August 24 edition, Derby drew this picture of the town: "San Diego has been usually dull during the past week, and a summary of the news may be summarily disposed of—there have been no births, no marriages, no arrivals, no departures, no earthquakes, nothing but the usual number of drinks taken, and an occasional small chunk of a fight (in which no lives have been lost) to vary the monotony of our existence. Placidly sat our village worthies in their arm chairs in front of the 'Exchange,' puffing their short clay pipes and enjoying their *otium cum dignitage* a week ago, and placidly they sit there still."[49]

Perhaps because there was nothing else to write, or perhaps because Derby decided to show just how independent of the Democrat Ames he could be, he published what he described as the "Phoenix Independent Ticket," urging read-ers to "make such alterations therein as they may deem proper, and then cut it from the paper, and deposit it in some secure place, in readiness, for the day of the election" in September. His choices for statewide offices included some Whigs while at the local level he recommended Hays over Warner for county judge, and urged in the races for justices of the peace substitution of P. H. Hooff and D. H. Rodgers for Cole and Jacobs. Robinson and Rose were included on the Phoenix slate for district attorney and county treasurer respectively.[50]

In the September 3 issue of the *Herald* however, Derby had a change of heart about his recommendation of Rose for county treasurer. Concerning Rose's election as a city trustee along with Lyons and Morse, Derby said: "We congratulate the citizens of San Diego on the election of these gentlemen. They are all trustworthy and estimable men in private life and we doubt not will fulfill their public duties in a satisfactory manner." In a nearby article appearing in the same issue, Derby also wrote: "We regret to announce that Judge Hayes (sic) positively declines to become a candidate for reelection as county judge under any circumstances. The judge states that there is but one office which he would accept if elected. This is the treasureship of the county, a position to which he does not aspire for either honor or profit, but simply with a view to the welfare and prosperity of the county. We accordingly place his name before the people as a candidate for that office and doubt not that the simple announcement that he will serve if elected will be sufficient to insure his election. The present Democratic candidate, Lewis (sic) Rose, is in every respect worthy the esteem and confidence of the public, but he now fills the office of trustee, and we presume that he does not care to hold a multiplicity of public situations. We present to the people as our candidate for county judge the Hon. J. J. Warner, who we believe to be perfectly unexceptionable and who, next to the present incumbent, is undoubtedly the best man in the county to fill the office."[51] In Derby's rush to find some justification for dumping Rose, he neglected to point out that George Lyons, his candidate for county assessor, also had just been elected a city trustee.

Rose took Derby's advice seriously and withdrew from the race for county treasurer. Hays defeated the only remaining candidate, P. H. Hooff, 81 votes to 9 for the position. Warner easily won election as county judge, garnering 98 votes compared to 41 for former Mayor G. B. Tebbetts and 41 for Lewis Franklin, the former Grand Jury foreman who subsequently had served as a justice of the peace. Elected as coroner was Louis Strauss who, along with H. Kohn, recently had opened a general store in San Diego.[52]

If Rose felt badly about having to withdraw from the county treasurer's race, he could take pride in being selected on September 10 by his colleagues on the city Board of Trustees to serve as their president.[53]

On the surface, San Diego was a town that was quite friendly to its Jewish residents. Rose now was president of the trustees; Franklin a justice of the peace, Strauss the coroner. Previously, Jacobs had been an assessor; Fletcher a member of the Common Council. But under the surface, something else, subtle, seemed to be going on. The *Herald*, which generally rewarded advertisers with a little bit of editorial space, introduced another member of the growing Jewish community in its September 18 issue: "J. A. Goldman—this clever little merchant has removed from his old stand to the building owned by José Antonio Pico (near Rose's) where his establishment, like a cocoa nut, will be found rough outside but within full of the richest kinds of drinks, and to carry out the simile, well-supplied with the 'milk of human kindness.' We hope to see this little man well patronized. He has everything for sale, from a horse rake to a fine tooth comb, and at reasonable prices. His advertisement will be found in another column."[54] Why, in an advertising "puff" piece, did acting editor Derby describe Goldman as a "clever little merchant"? Notwithstanding the compliments about Goldman's "kindness and reasonable prices," was there a tendency to stereotype Jewish merchants as "clever"?

The October 1 issue was the last that Derby edited before Ames' return from San Francisco. On page 2, he offered "a syllogism—David was a Jew; hence the harp of David was a Jew's harp. Question: how the deuce did he sing his psalms and play on it at the same time?"[55] It was, of course, a joke based on word play. King David played a full-sized instrument; not on the twanging piece of metal called in derogatory fashion "a Jew's harp." Why this particular piece of filler? The subject of Jews obviously was on Derby's mind, and when he had the chance, he kept returning to it. Ames also seemed fascinated by Jews.

To fill its many news columns, the *Herald* regularly reprinted items its editor found in newspapers from around the world. The system of "exchange newspapers" provided readers with a diet of interesting feature stories from locales that otherwise might have no connection to San Diego. As Ames was religiously inclined, he regularly selected articles having to do with Scriptures. One headlined "The Hebrews—Their Fasts and Feasts" read as follows:

> We find in a foreign journal a letter written by M. Victor Place, the French consul at Mosul, in which he provides an entertaining description of the fast in that Moslem city in commemoration of the penance imposed on Ninevah by Jonah. He says the fast has been kept from time immemorial not only by a few Christians there, but by the Moslem population. Mosul is but a short distance from Ninevah, and nearby is a tomb traditionally assigned to Jonah. It is a striking confirmation of the truth of Mosaic writings that a...commemoration of an important event recorded in them is observed after the lapse of so many years in the spot where it is said to have happened. The plains of Ninevah are now a dreary waste. The Hebrews have been scattered throughout the world nearly two thousand years, and yet the ancient penance is enforced.[56]

Another Jail Escape

The September 3 issue of the *Herald* also reported that William Jones, who had been arrested for stealing, and Joaquin Carrillo, who went by the alias of John Hewitt and had been arrested for attempted rape, somehow managed to pull their shackles loose from the walls of the "temporary jail" and had escaped—the city's jail problems apparently never ending. Another item in that issue was that Leah Marks, daughter of Jacobs Marks (his old name) had been married on August 24 to Marcus Katz in a ceremony officiated by H. Kohn—evidence that San Diego's Jewish community was growing.[57]

The jailbreakers were captured before crossing into Mexico, and the hearing into the Hewitt case was held September 5. Martina Bareles had complained that she often would find Hewitt standing naked in her room, and said she was in such fear of being raped that she had on occasion tied her legs together. Apparently Hewitt did not actually attempt the rape, so the charges were reduced to assault and battery, and breaking jail. Jones meanwhile was committed to trial for battery. On September 9, Hewitt came back to court, this time to accuse William Evans of having been the mastermind behind his and Jones' escape. Justice of the Peace Lewis Franklin questioned Hewitt closely and his testimony was so confused and contradictory, it was concluded that he had fabricated the story. Evans was exonerated. As Hewitt emerged from the courtroom, an indignant and threatening crowd surrounded him. Franklin, coming outside, was able to restore calm momentarily, but when he left the scene, the mob surged toward Hewitt, pulling off all his clothes and beating him nearly senseless. Juan Bandini tried to intervene in Hewitt's behalf, but to no avail. Breaking himself free, Hewitt ran completely naked towards New Town with nearly one hundred people in pursuit. As night had fallen, Hewitt eventually was able to safely hide himself. His brother also decided to sneak out of town. The *San Diego Herald* was moved to editorialize: "Though by no means advocates of lynch law generally, we cannot regret in this instance such prompt and energetic action was adopted. Neither life or property can be considered safe while such scamps are suffered to infest a community and as we have no place of security to be used as a jail in this county, the course of our citizens in this matter was not only excusable but to our way of thinking worthy of commendation. Hewitt will never return to this village, and we hope the sudden manner in which he was compelled to leave will prove a solemn warning to any other worthless beachcombers who may think of making San Diego their place of residence."[58]

The Entrepreneurial Rose

After Ames' return to San Diego, the editor placed two promotional items about Rose in the October 29 issue of the *Herald*. On page 3, Rose informed his customers that as costs to him had gone up, he was now obliged to "charge twelve and a half cents for beef cut up at the city market. While regretting the necessity for this advance, the subscriber hopes that his customers will acknowledge its justness and continue their patronage which he has striven so hard to deserve."[59]

On the same page, editor Ames also placed a news item: "Our enterprising friend Rose has commenced a tannery at his ranch on quite a large scale, so that the immense quantity of hides that are yearly thrown away in this part of the state will be turned to some account. The same gentleman is also erecting a fine mansion for the accommodation of his family which are soon expected out from the Atlantic states."[60]

Historians have reason to be thankful for the above-mentioned item. Circuit Court Judge Benjamin Hayes copied the information about Rose's tannery into one of his extensive sets of notebooks that he kept on life in

California. At that time, Hayes apparently decided to pay a visit to Rose's tannery in the future, which would result in one of the best descriptions left to us of Rose and his businesses.[61]

The reference to Rose's family provides us with some insight into his state of mind after finally writing to Caroline via his nephew Nisan J. Alexander. By that time, Caroline was in South Carolina, sent there by her sister and brother-in-law after they learned that, nearly a year after receiving her husband's invitation to come to California, Caroline had become pregnant by a French man named Depanier, who promptly returned to Europe. As Rose went about building a home for his wife, he apparently still was unaware that he had been cuckolded. Eventually, Caroline would miscarry the baby that her family desired to be born away from the wagging society tongues of Montgomery, Alabama.[62]

Robinson, still district attorney but no longer a member of either the San Diego Board of Trustees or the county Board of Supervisors, went before each of the bodies respectively October 29 and November 9 to attend to the financial side of his affairs. In trade for his services as a legal advisor, Robinson again obtained from the city "the use of a room in the rear of the City Hall as an office." The County Board of Supervisors fixed his yearly salary as district attorney at $500. Rose, still serving on both boards, voted for both propositions.[63]

Although not having Robinson to guide him was an adjustment for Rose, the entrepreneur quickly had grasped the concepts of government. Along with his fellow supervisors, Rose voted on November 7 to elect Eugene Pendleton as the new president of the Board of Supervisors.[64] Ever so briefly, the firm of Rose & Pendleton—although formed as a business partnership—appeared to be a political powerhouse as well. Rose, the senior partner, served as president of the city Board of Trustees. Pendleton, the junior partner, served as president of the county Board of Supervisors, or did, until he decided, for unannounced reasons, to resign his position in December.

At the end of 1853 and the beginning of 1854, Rose refurbished the Commercial House property he originally had leased from "Mother Estudillo." He also purchased the property he had leased from Manuel Rocha a few days before the latter's death from tuberculosis.[65] Additionally, he built up his holdings in La Cañada de las Lleguas (the future Rose Canyon) and continued to acquire land along San Diego Bay in the area that in 1869 would become known as Roseville.

In two articles in the December 24 edition of the *San Diego Herald*, editor Ames commented on the Commercial House's improvements. In one brief, he noted, "Mr. Rose has fitted a new roof to his old establishment, besides painting, plastering and otherwise decorating it." In another, titled "Reopening the Commercial House," Ames reported: "This excellent establishment, temporarily closed for repairs, is to be reopened 1st Jan. by Mr. Rose, its enterprising proprietor, whose hospitable doors are never shut to anybody. It is not necessary for us to say a good word for one so well known and deserving as Mr. Rose, who is emphatically the man of business of this place, and whose improvements both in town and country do honor and credit to his enterprise and industry."[66]

Rose elaborated somewhat on his new enterprise on January 28, saying in an advertisement for the Commercial House: "The proprietor respectfully informs his friends and the public that he has thoroughly repaired and refitted the above establishment, and it is now open to visitors. The bar contains the choicest of wines, the best of liquors, and the finest cigars, and he hopes to merit a continuance of the favors already bestowed upon him."[67] One can imagine the Ulex Liqueur factory in Rose's native Neuhaus-an-der-Oste possibly having similarly touted its liquors.

Herald editor Ames gave another example of the industry of Rose, his fellow Mason, when he published the first description of the tannery that Rose had set up in La Cañada de las Lleguas with the help of his nephew Nisan Alexander: "We inspected a specimen of home manufacture a day or two since from the tanning and leather manufactory of Lewis Rose, esq., which is situated (as everyone knows, or ought to know, and pay it a visit too) about five miles from town, on the road to Los Angeles. This leather is tanned and finished in the most thorough and complete manner and equals the best articles in the markets of Philadelphia and Boston. The establishment is now being increased in its capacity for production by the enterprise of its proprietor, and when fully expanded, will give employment to a large number of men who, with their families, cannot fail to create a large settlement at the place now known as Rose's Ranch, but destined to bear the title Roseville whenever it shall reach the dignity of townhood."[68]

Ames' crystal ball was a little clouded. Whereas a townsite called "Roseville" would one day arise in San Diego, it would be located on San Diego Bay. The area he called "Rose's Ranch" in La Cañada de las Lleguas became known first as "Rose's Canyon" and later simply as "Rose Canyon."

Rose ran an enthusiastic advertisement on February 25 about the tannery. "Leather! Leather!" screamed the headline: "The subscriber having at great pains and expense perfected one of the most extensive tanneries in California, is now prepared to furnish the people of the southern counties with sole, harness and saddle leathers in the best description and at reasonable prices. These leathers are tanned in the best manner (without use of hot liquids) and will be sold, for the present, for the following prices for cash only. Saddle and harness leather, according to thickness, from 60 to 65 cents. Sole leather 50 cents—Lewis Rose." In a postscript, he added: "Particular attention will be paid to the filling of orders, as it is determined if possible to give perfect satisfaction—L.R."[69]

Settlement of the Jail Controversy

The Oct. 29, 1853, issue of the *San Diego Herald* reported that Jones, who had been captured after escaping with the notorious Hewitt, had escaped again on October 9 "from his temporary place of confinement by filing off his irons."[70] It was Jones' third getaway. San Diego's Swiss cheese jail system was the laughing stock of the west.

The lingering city issue of what to do about the 8 percent bonds came to a head in November, after some of the bondholders told the Board of Trustees that they were unwilling to accept only face value on their investments. Robinson, who had been the prime architect of the policy to declare the 8 percent interest to be without effect, now came back to the board in his role as legal adviser. On November 2, he answered arguments made by Ferrell against the policy. Two days later, he parried objections raised by Witherby. The trustees spent their entire meeting of November 5 discussing the controversy and returned to the subject during their meeting of November 10. Finally on November 12, they unanimously reaffirmed the decision not to pay the interest.[71] As one might have expected, the unhappy bondholders decided to sue. The case was set for hearing before District Court Judge Benjamin Hayes in December. In the meantime, the trustees set about replenishing the city treasury. Ratcheting up the pressure on the recalcitrant bondholders, they ordered the resale of properties that had been the subject of bids during the auction the previous December, but that had not been paid for. At the same time they ordered the insertion of advertisements in the San Diego and San Francisco newspapers announcing another land auction would be held January 25, 1854.

In December, Hayes presided over the hearing in *D.B. Kurtz vs. Rose, Lyons and Morse, Trustees of the City of San Diego*. Robinson, arguing for the trustees, contended that the city shouldn't have to pay any interest on the bonds because the jail was "wholly worthless" and because plaintiff Kurtz, had been the contractor, he, especially, had no reason to complain. Robinson argued that prior to obtaining the bonds from Haraszthy, Kurtz certainly knew the true situation—having been mayor of the city, a workman on the jail, as well as a member of one of the committees that investigated whether the city should accept the jail. Furthermore, Robinson argued, the trustees had provided a reasonable compromise when they offered to accept the bonds at face value. To require the city to pay the full 8 percent interest compounded monthly would saddle the city with a debt exceeding the total revenues of the city and was contrary to the charter.

Before the case could be decided, however, two members of the jury took sick. Neither side was willing to have the case tried with only ten jurors, so Hayes declared a mistrial and set a date in February 1854, for the case to be retried.[72] However, for various reasons, the case was delayed well beyond February. While the case still was pending in August of 1854, Kurtz and the trustees negotiated an out-of-court settlement, in which the trustees agreed to pay 4 percent interest instead of the original 8 percent. They also agreed to apply the aggregated amount to the purchase of city land. Other creditors of the city like O.S. Witherby and Captain E.F. Hardcastle quickly agreed to also accept 4 percent interest payments. A long lingering controversy was at last settled under the leadership of Rose and Robinson.[73]

Seeking to gain a foothold in his new city of residence, Alexander—apparently acting both on his own behalf and as an agent for Rose—accounted for more than 23 percent of the $7,962 in sales at the January 25 land auction. He paid a total of $1,652 for four parcels adjoining his uncle Louis's holdings in La Cañada de las Lleguas as well as for six lots in the Playa area. Rose himself kept an uncustomary low profile at the auction, buying only two lots, one of them Lot 1 of Block 25 in the Playa area. This adjoined Lot 2 of Block 25, which Alexander purchased the same day.[74] While the purchases occasioned little comment at the time, the Block 25 purchases eventually were to prove quite controversial because the U.S. military would claim the same land for Fort Rosecrans.

Unshackling San Diego

With the burdensome jail debt of San Diego at last disposed of, the city could turn its full attention to the development of important infrastructure, in particular highways and a school.

Rose, Morse, and Lyons were reelected as city trustees on March 6, 1854. Rose's colleagues again chose him as their president. By their re-election, the three men also were entitled to remain as members of the county Board of Supervisors, which since Pendleton's resignation had selected J. L. Blecker as its chairman. Rounding out the seven member county board were G. P. Tebbetts, George McKinstry and George F. Hooper.[75]

At J.J. Warner's urging the year before, the county Board of Supervisors had designated the proposed road to Temecula "a public highway," but the shortage of county revenues enabled little work to be accomplished. The former president of the Board of Supervisors, W.C. Ferrell, inquired at a town meeting in March about the amount of money necessary to complete the road. Told it would require $10,000, citizens in attendance decided to organize themselves into a formal committee to raise the requisite amount. Rose's business partner, E.B. Pendleton, was elected as chairman. On Robinson's suggestion, Pendleton then named a sub-committee to determine exactly what must be done to finish the road. He named Robinson, Rose, Witherby, Morse, Jacobs, Bandini and Maurice A. Franklin, and then by resolution from the floor was himself added to the committee. By April 1, the committee had raised $800 toward cutting of the road.[76]

In an April 8 editorial, Ames expressed hope that a road to Temecula could cement a relationship among the Mormon headquarters in Salt Lake City, the Mormon colony in San Bernardino, and the port of San Diego.[77] Acting on the same optimistic impulse, the Board of Supervisors during June and July designated a system of roads that should also become public highways; on June 19, a date that Rose was absent, his colleagues decided that one public highway should run from Soledad via Penasquitos, San Pasqual, San Ysabel, Warners, San Phillipe, and Vallecito to Fort Yuma on the Colorado River. Additionally they declared that the road from Old San Diego via La Punta to the Iron Monument (marking the U.S-Mexico border) be a public highway." A month later, with Rose in attendance, the board declared the routes of two other public highways. One was "the road from Encinitos (sic) to Marron's Ranch thence to San Luis Rey, Pueblito, Las Flores and San Mateo"; the other "the road from San Diego to Mission San Diego, Cajon, Santa Maria and to junction with the road leading to San Ysabel." The latter was the route that Rose had traveled in the opposite direction when he came to San Diego in 1850.[78]

The school system and securing San Diego's title to Point Loma lands against the claims of the military were other civic issues commanding the attention of the optimists during 1854. Morse, who was a colleague of Rose's on both the city Board of Trustees and the county Board of Supervisors, later remembered 1854 as the year in which San Diego finally got a public school. Telling the story in the third person forty-six years later, he recollected that "up to July 1854, there had been no public school in San Diego County, but on that day, the county court being in session, Cave J. Couts, judge, appointed W.C. Ferrell, county superintendent of common schools, who at once appointed E.W. Shelby, census marshal, and J.W. Robinson, Louis Rose and E.W Morse school trustees for the whole county. Within a few hours the trustees had received the marshal's report, had hired a room for the school, and employed a teacher, so that before night a public school was in full operation under the school law of the state... This unusual expenditure was found necessary to entitle the school to its *pro rata* at the next apportionment of the school funds."[79] Sarah Robinson, whose son William then was 14, was one of the principal advocates in behalf of establishing a school.[80]

During this period, Sarah's husband also was kept busy representing the city before the United States Land Commission in Los Angeles, his old rival Sutherland evidently failing to respond positively to the trustees' invitation to represent San Diego. Sending a delegation to Los Angeles was an expensive proposition, as shown by the August 24, 1854, minutes of the Board of Trustees, which noted the payment of the following invoices: $500 for former County Auditor Santiago Arguello for passage to the hearing of the Board of Land Commissioners in Los Angeles; $250 to J.W. Robinson for professional service in going to Los Angeles and eliciting Arguello's testimony in the case of the *United States vs. The City of San Diego*; $140 to George Lyons, for use of wagon and horses in taking Arguello and Robinson to Los Angeles; $170.33 to Lyons for cash paid out to law agent, board for witness, etc., in Los Angeles and expenses on the road; yet another $29.14 to Lyons for provisions supplied for the road; $18 to E. W. Morse for provisions, and $110 to Floyd & Kerr for the use of two horses to Los Angeles and back. The total cost for the trip was $1,117.47.[81]

Attitudes toward Jews in San Diego, Part II

San Diegans in 1854 fluctuated between hope and despair as they consid-ered the future of their city, so pleasantly situated near a deep-water bay, yet overshadowed by San Francisco. The town was so small that coastal steamers often bypassed it while plying the waters between Panama and the rest of California. Money was tight. But surely, thought the optimists like Rose, all that could be changed. Roadways could be built to foster trade, maybe even a rail-road. Such was the message of hope. But despair also had its message for San Diegans. Nationally, this sentiment was expressed in the emergence of the nativist American party—nicknamed the "Know Nothing" party—which began in reaction to bloc voting among Catholics, Jews, and other non-Protestant "foreigners" who crowded into eastern seaboard cities. In San Diego, the movement attracted people who distrusted everyone but white Protestants. In the view of such bigots, native *Californios* and the Jews represented forces that prevented progress. The bigots held not only the Catholicism of the *Californios* against them; they stereotyped these San Diego natives as naturally indolent. As for the Jews, the bigots seized upon all the usual canards: Jews, they said, were more interested in their own profits than the general welfare.

Protestant suspicions about Jewish neighbors found voice in several satiric articles published by the *San Diego Herald*. The first, innocuous in itself, appeared in the May 27 issue under the quite accurate title, "A Wretched Pun": "Whilst out amongst some squatters, a short time since, we passed by a tent where our friend Cohen was stretched out, smoking a pipe. We remarked to our companion, 'There is a happy man.' 'Yes,' he replied, 'he seems to be Cohen-tented.'"[82] But on June 17, the humor took a more vicious turn. The *Herald* claimed to have received a letter from a Moses Bendigo—which appeared to be a made-up name meaning "Moses son of (ben) San Diego (digo)." Titled "The new Jerusalem," this so-called letter was written in what was supposed to be a Jewish-sounding dialect. It suggested that with so many Jews in San Diego, the name of the town ought to be changed.

Mishter Editursh: It dish time dat old shuprstitions of dish place vos done away vith. De alterations dat ave taken place in dish town in de last few years in point of society, calls for corresponding alterations in manners, customs and names. Every vare in dish happy litte blace, all der cornersh, in all de shtores, in all de offiches, you shee da beautiful curvilinear nosesh, de arching lips and lovely black air of de shildren of Zion. Ve are de population of dish place. Our harps are no longer any by der riversh banks, but de little boysh blays onem mit der fishsh in all de bupblic blacesh. De Brothers Jonathan (a ship) that comes today from New York brings much more of our beoples, and a large invoice of Jew-harps fer dem to blay upon. I have some to see myself at a dollar naif a dozen and shelp me Chrised I don't make a dollar on em. Mishter Editursh I porpose dat vee cal dish town now Jerusalem, in accordance vith de vishes of de bopulation, and nexth sdeamer, I dinks myshelf dat de Mesiah himzelf vill come here and vill make him County Shudge. San Diego is to old and superstitious a name for dish little Zion, and it is time it was shanged.[83]

Both the Cohen pun and the Bendigo letter had the hallmarks of being the productions of George Derby, but if there were any doubt on this score, it should have been removed on June 24 when the *Herald* printed a satiric poem from a "stranger" which later was attributed to Derby, a.k.a John Phoenix, a.k.a. Squibob. The poem included allegations of rampant sodomy, while denigrating Mexicans as "greasers" and castigating Jewish merchants.

> SANDAYGO-OH-MY!
> What a trying thing it is for a feller
> To git kooped up in this ere little plais
> Where males don't run regular nohow
> Nor the females nuther cos there ain't none
> But by the mails I mean the post orifices...
> The natives is all sorts complected
> Sum white sum black and sum kinder speckled
> And about fourteen rowdy vagabonds that
> Gits drunk and goes about licken everybody.
> And four stores for every white human
> Which are kept by the children of Zion
> Where they sell their goods bort at auction
> At seven times more than they costed
> With a grand jury's that sittin' forever
> But don't never seem to indite nuthin

And if they do what comes of it
The petty ones find them not guilty
And then go off in much licker
And hit the fust fellow they come to.
All nite long in this swet little village
You hear the soft noe of the pistol
And the pleasant scicak of the victim
Whose been shot, perhaps in the gizzard
And all day hosses is running
with drunken greasers astraddle
A hollerin and hoopin like demons
And playin at billards and monte
Till they've nary a red cent to ante
Having busted up all the money
Which they borrowed at awful percentage
On ranches which they haint no title
And persons fite duels on paper
Oh its awful this here little plais is
And quick as my business is finished
I shall leave here you may depend on it
By the very first leky stembote
Or (if they are all of them busted)
I'll hire a mule from some feller
And just put out to Santy Clara. [84]

In November, there was a fanciful story about the large grouper called a "Jew Fish" in which Jews were made the butt of the joke. Under the headline, "A Big Fish," the item read: "A party of gentlemen went over the island on a fishing excursion last week, and among their 'hauls' was a strapping 'Jew Fish' weighing about 400 lbs. We will venture there is not an Israelite in this whole country of half that weight. We have fin-ished this scaly paragraph and it just fills the column." Evidently needing to fill a hole elsewhere, another item, "Lucky Escape," likened the supposed fishing expedition to the experience of the biblical Jonah: "The fishing party of whom mention is made in another place, as having captured that large 'Jew-fish' came near being shipwrecked in the gale of wind while upon their excursion. They affirm that a few rods from their vessel the sea was perfectly calm, but in their immediate vicinity consid-erable blow. They only escaped destruction by throwing the fish overboard as an additional anchor—the vessel dragging both bowers."[85]

Some considered Derby to be a true frontier humorist, but among the city's Jewish residents there was no doubt another opinion. Here was a differ-ent type of anti-Semite, but an anti-Semite all the same. The Jewish commu-nity suffered his "humor" in silence. Franklin, who had offered blatantly racist language in his famous Grand Jury report to describe Native Americans and African Americans, in any event would have been unable to offer any compelling ethical arguments in objection.

From both sides of the divide, it was recognized that the city was too small, and residents too dependent on each other, to suffer an open breach. Even Derby put aside his prejudices long enough to enlist Rose's help in funding the ongoing work on the San Diego River dike project. He subsequently signed a receipt stating: "I hereby certify that there is due to Mr. Louis Rose of San Diego... on account of the improvement of the San Diego River two hundred and ninety two dollars for beef, beans and bale wire for the use of the workmen on the river, during the month of November 1853, which sum I, as officer in charge of the work, was unable to pay owing to the failure of Congress to (make) the appropriation..." Derby urged that Rose be reimbursed "out of the first appropriation," but in fact seventeen years later, after which records disappear, the government still had not repaid Rose for his generosity.[86] The loan to Derby was not the only example of Rose serving informally as the town's banker. A well-known tale concerned another time that Rose was visited at his home in Old Town by E. W. Morse, and some army officers, who needed to pay the soldiers stationed at New Town. Rose excused himself, went somewhere in his back yard, and returned with a moneybag still covered in dirt. Rose quite literally "dug up" the funds.[87]

Plenty of Tsuris

Although he was a success in business, Rose had more than his share of *tsuris* (Yiddish, for "troubles") in his family life. The reason Rose had been absent at the June meeting at which the county Board of Supervisors considered the routes of public highways was that a settlement was then in the process of being negotiated in his divorce suit against his wife, Caroline. Robinson served as Rose's attorney in the suit. The irony of the fact that the lawyer once had abandoned his own wife was probably not expressed to the client. In a complaint prepared for District Court Judge Benjamin Hayes, Robinson wrote: "Plaintiff was informed that his said wife has been guilty of the offense of adultery with one man to plaintiff unknown, and so plaintiff so expressly charges that his said wife is guilty of adultery, wherefore plaintiff prays that you will decree a dissolution of the bonds of matrimony, and both himself and his said wife shall be free and at liberty to enter into other contracts of marriage and all other contracts as single unmarried persons." Additionally, the petition asked "plaintiff be decreed to have the sole rights of property and possession of all property both real and personal that he has now acquired or may hereafter acquire."

Henry H. Thal traveled to San Diego to represent Caroline, who was his wife's sister. Not wanting to remain in the city until the next district court session, he negotiated the settlement with Robinson, and gave a sworn deposition in the matter to D.H. Rodgers, a justice of the peace. He swore under oath that Rose had left Caroline about five and a half years before while a "poor man" with the intent "to go back to Texas and sell some lands." Although Rose had said "he will be back in three months," Caroline did not hear from him and was under the impression that he was dead.

The interrogatory continued:

> Q. Had she to your knowledge a connection or intercourse with another man?
>
> A. Not that I was aware of at the time. I had a friend by name of Depanier who visited my house continuously and paid her attentions more than I should have approved of had I been aware of it at the time.
>
> Q. Do you know that she was in a family way by him in the absence of Rose?
>
> A. I do.
>
> Q. And how do you know it?
>
> A. By my wife (Eliza Thal) and by the doctor who attended her.

Thal identified the doctor as a Dr. Bobyn of Montgomery, Ala. He said Depanier had left the United States, presumably for Europe. Caroline traveled to Charleston, S.C., where she had a miscarriage approximately six months prior to Thal's deposition. The fetus was buried in Charleston, S.C. "under the name of the mother Caroline Rose."

> Q. Did you ever receive a letter of N. Alexander from New Orleans in which he stated his uncle wishes to know the whereabouts of his wife Caroline?
>
> A: I did
>
> Q. How long since you received the letter?
>
> A. About 21 months in October 1852.
>
> Q. Did you or not inform the defendant Caroline Rose of the contents of the above mentioned letter. If yea, at what time?
>
> A: I did tell her directly when I read it.

Caroline's sister, Eliza, also was questioned. After reiterating that Rose had left as a poor man and that Caroline never expected to hear from him again, she provided these details about Caroline's pregnancy.

> Q. Did you know she was in a family way?
>
> A. She was sick, and I was so informed of it by her attending physician.
>
> Q. What physician attended her?
>
> A. Dr. Baylor of Montgomery, Ala.

No attention was paid to the discrepancy in the couple's testimony about the name of Caroline's attending physician—leading to the supposition that there was an error in transcription. The adultery having been established as legal grounds for divorce, there remained the issue of settlement. Choosing a number that corresponded to the "200 silver pieces" mentioned in the *ketuba* that Rose had given Caroline in 1847, the couple agreed that Rose would pay Caroline "each year two hundred dollars for her support and maintenance as long as she should not marry another man, and it is further agreed that Mr. L. Rose agrees to pay that amount at the option of his wife either at the end of each twelve months from this date, or in installments of $50 at the expiration of each three months as Mrs. Caroline Rose or her attorneys may deem. In consideration of which, Mrs. Caroline Rose with the consent of her attorney Henry H. Thal bind themselves to be satisfied with the mentioned amount and renounce all and each claim or claims of said Rose of whatever nature they may be or under, whatever name they could be enumerated, they being entirely satisfied with, and agree to this of their own free will and after mature reflection. In testimony of which both parties subscribe to thee with their own hands and seal." The document was signed by Louis Rose and Henry H. Thal, serving as Caroline's proxy. H.L. Kohn witnessed their signatures. Rose paid $82 in fees, including $5 a day for Rodgers' time.[88]

Kohn, who served as a lay rabbi in San Diego, may also have issued a formal Jewish divorce decree, known as a "get," according to latter-day historians, Norton B. Stern and Rabbi William Kramer.[89]

Other commentators have suggested that Rose got off quite easily in the settlement, given the extent of the fortune that he had acquired.[90] If this be the case, Rose was not one to gloat. The year 1854 from the standpoint of family was one of Rose's saddest. Not only did his separation from Caroline become final and irrevocable, but in that year his nephew and partner in the tannery, Nisan Alexander, also died. As the date, location, and cause of his death are not recorded in San Diego's registry of vital statistics, one is led to the conclusion that whatever happened, it occurred somewhere other than San Diego County. Yes, Rose had accumulated wealth, but except for his many pets, he was quite alone. Involvement in public life and acquisition of land must have been for him a kind of tonic. The assessment rolls for 1854-1855 estimated Rose's personal property and real estate holdings as worth $18,090.

In the summer of 1854, Rose continued to develop La Cañada de las Lleguas. In July he conveyed a 160-acre lot to Gustave Fisher, whose family had stayed with him at the Commercial House back in 1850. Now these friends stayed with him again, at his canyon ranch house, while they built their home on what would become the Fisher ranch adjoining Rose's own spread.[91] Rose also had the sad duty in September of taking possession of the lands both in the canyon and the playa that his late nephew Nisan had purchased for him.

Law and Order

Cave Couts was walking toward his residence at 2 a.m. one morning when he saw a man attempting to force entry into Rose's Commercial House. The would-be thief fled, leaving a crowbar behind.[92] Other Jewish merchants were less lucky as San Diego suffered a series of robberies. In August, a store owned by Hyman Mannasse was entered at night while a guard lay asleep on the counter. The intruder or intruders removed belongings from a trunk, including clothing, a pistol, and $50.[93]

In September, someone dug under the fence of a corral near the Goldman store. "The noise awakened Mr. H.L. Kohn, who ascertaining the cause, aroused Mr. Mannasse and the two proceeded together to secure him," the *Herald* reported. "Mr. M. entered the corral and startled him, while Mr. Kohn stationed himself with a pistol outside the gate. The robber came out upon being discovered and notwithstanding Mr. K snapped several percussion caps, and finally succeeded in discharging the pistol, the thief is still at large."[94]

Marks Jacobs hosted High Holiday services at his house in September and October, advising the citizenry of San Diego via the *Herald* that Jewish-owned stores would be closed over the two days of Rosh Hashanah and the single day of Yom Kippur.[95] One assumes that the merchants took the precaution of continuing to post guards. Two months later, on December 12, thieves stole a roan horse, along with a saddle blanket, bridle and saddle from the coral of Franklin & Company.[96]

In the public arena, there were both negative and positive news developments as 1854 waned. On the negative side was a long simmering dispute between the county Board of Supervisors and two other officials, Sheriff William Conroy and county Treasurer Hays—the man whose election Rose had assured by his withdrawal from the race. Both Conroy and Hays were instructed to present their books for customary inspection by the Board of Supervisors. Even though Conroy did so, the dissatisfied Board of Supervisors asked Robinson, as district attorney, to explore bringing charges against the sheriff for failing to turn over various revenues to the treasurer—a course of action made unnecessary in October when Conroy made up some deficits in the account.

Hays meanwhile kept delaying providing his books for inspection. After giving him repeated deadlines, only to extend them, board members were galvanized into action after their fellow board member, Rose, joined by Philip Crosthwaite, presented a petition on October 21. "The undersigned Louis Rose and Philip Crosthwaite respectfully represent to your Hon. Body that they are securities on the bond of the present treasurer John Hayes (sic) and that they are desirous of being relieved from all liabilities arising thereon after this date and they assign as a reason thereof the failure of said treasurer to comply with the requirements of law in his office, the failure of said officer to make monthly settlements required by statute." The board promptly voted to send a copy of the Rose-Crosthwaite communication to Hays, in effect telling him it was now up to him to provide the funds to back his bond.[97] When Hays still did not comply, Morse moved, Lyons seconded, and the board on November 15 unanimously adopted a motion to declare the office of county treasurer vacant. Hays presented his books at the December 4 meeting and tried unsuccessfully to get the board to rescind its action. But the board said the deadline had long since passed. Robinson, Warner, and James Baldwin were appointed on December 30 to examine Hays' books, and they came back on January 4, 1855, with the recommendation that suit be commenced against Hays to recover an amount, not specified, believed to be missing.[98]

The Hays matter dragged on until June 15, 1855, by which time a new Board of Supervisors was serving—on which Rose no longer was a member. Hays agreed to pay in August $367 owed to the county building fund, $81.26 owed to the state treasurer, and $18 owed to the Indian fund—a total of $466.26. Additionally, he agreed to pay the still outstanding balance of $1,671.23, but no interest on his delinquent accounts prior to June 15. Hays also agreed to reimburse the county government its court costs—provided the board would drop its suit against him. The board accepted the settlement with the proviso that the suit would be dropped only after the money was in hand.[99]

The San Diego & Gila Southern Pacific and Atlantic Railroad Company

Uniting many San Diegans in a far-reaching enterprise was the drawing up on November 1, 1854, of articles of association for the San Diego & Gila Southern Pacific and Atlantic Railroad Company. Robinson and Rose—the old friends who had come together by wagon train over much of the route under consideration—were in the forefront of this enterprise to create a railroad stretching from San Diego to the Yuma crossing of the Colorado River. The San Diego & Gila, as it was called, superseded the proposed Pacific and Atlantic Railroad Company, which had been formed on paper by Magruder, Hays, Moon, and the two Ameses, but which never had obtained a state charter.

National developments encouraged San Diegans in their railroad aspirations. In the final year of the administration of America's thirteenth president, Millard Fillmore, Congress had authorized surveys for a transcontinental route. These were duly carried out by the administration of the fourteenth president, Franklin Pierce, under the auspices of his Secretary of War (and future President of the Confederacy) Jefferson Davis. Pierce removed a major obstacle to the southern transcontinental railroad route when he completed the $10 million Gadsden Purchase by which the United States acquired from Mexico an area of 45,535 square miles south of the Gila River—a territory midway in size between the states of Pennsylvania and Mississippi. A route completely over American territory thereby assured, a southern transcontinental railroad was recommended with two more northerly routes as meriting the serious attention of the federal government. This southern route, strongly favored by the states that later would join the Confederacy, could link with railroad lines that stretched from the Atlantic Ocean to Louisiana, and then head west through Texas to California.

Rather than wait for East Coast interests to determine their future, San Diegans organized so they could have a hand in deciding where the last leg of such a railroad, from the Colorado River to San Diego, would be laid. Joseph R. Gitchell, an attorney, was sent to Sacramento with the proposed articles of association and returned to San Diego with a state charter for the railroad. Robinson and Rose, meanwhile, went on a trip of their own: retracing the San Diego River route that had Rose had followed en route to San Diego.[100] They were joined by Anson Sutton, who hoped the aid he rendered in surveying the route could lead to a permanent job with the railroad.[101]

Under terms of the articles of association, the corporation was formed to build a 150-mile railroad from San Diego to the Colorado River, near the mouth of the Gila; such railroad "to be of the same scale and gauge as the Mississippi and Pacific Railroad now being constructed through the state of Texas." Capitalization of $4 million was authorized. Before the company could begin operations, a minimum of $150,000 needed to be subscribed. Initially, 1,895 shares were issued, with Robinson and Rose the largest investors, with 300 shares each, followed by Hays with 250, Ferrell 200 and Captain H.S. Burton 100. [102]

Morse, Pendleton, J.C. Bogart, Crosthwaite, and Moon were authorized to act as sales agents for the railroad's stock, and by the time elections were held under the charter, other prominent San Diegans also had purchased shares. Robinson was chosen to serve as president of the railroad. The San Diego & Gila's office was set up in Robinson's house on the Plaza, resulting in the structure often being called "The Railroad Building."[103] Witherby, who had come to San Diego as a quartermaster for the U.S. Boundary Commission, then served as a judge and later was appointed by President Pierce as collector of customs for the Port of San Diego, was elected vice president of the railroad.[104] Rose became the treasurer, and Tebbetts, the secretary. The four officers served on a board of directors on which other founding members were Burton, Morse, Reiner, Hays, Sexton, Strauss, Gitchell, Lyons, and Ferrell.

On November 24, Rose paused for a social occasion. Louisa Fisher, daughter of his friend Gustave, was married at his neighbor's home to Edward Schneider, with D.B. Kurtz, now a county judge, performing the ceremony. Soon afterward, Schneider opened a store opposite Rose's Commercial House. Unfortunately on New Year's Eve, the roof of the store collapsed, destroying most of the shelf goods and several casks of liquors. Far worse, on April 25, 1855, Gustave died of stomach cancer. In his old friend's will, Rose was named executor of the estate, but after a brief period this responsibility was turned over to Schneider.[105]

The Entrepreneurial Rose, Part II

At the beginning of 1855, Rose and Pendleton decided on a trial basis to expand their business partnership to include a general store located in a space that Rose previously had leased to cousins Hyman and Moses Mannasse. Pendleton traveled to San Francisco to purchase inventory, returning aboard the steamer *Goliah* with dry goods, groceries, clothing, hardware, liquor, "segars," and tobacco. In an advertisement to announce their January 29, 1855, opening, the partners expressed their "hope to receive a liberal share of the public patronage." Judging from the advertisements that followed in subsequent issues of the *Herald*, there was spirited competition among the various general stores. Moses Mannasse, having ended his partnership with his cousin Hyman, opened a store on February 6 in Robinson's Railroad Building. His stock included "dry goods, fancy goods, clothing, furnishing tools, hosiery, groceries, tobacco, hardware..."Indirectly taking aim at Rose & Pendleton and other establishments, Mannasse's ad stated: "Having no partner with whom to divide my profits, I can afford to sell my goods much lower than any other establishment."[106]

Probably enjoying the prospect of continued competition in its advertising columns, the *San Diego Herald* noted in the February 10 issue: "Among the arrivals by the *America* last Monday we notice our old friend Strauss. He has been absent some time and returns with a new and fresh stock of goods, which he says can't be beat in San Diego."[107]

The Franklin Brothers, calling the attention of newspaper readers to their various wares, bragged that they were chosen by L.A. Franklin, "whose judicious selections for this market, in point of taste, are well known."[108] Rose & Pendleton in May amended their standard advertisement to say that, in addition to everything else available, the store also carried "a first rate article of butter. Also a lot of fine hams." About this time Ephraim Morse purchased the store formerly owned by J.A. Goldman, and began competing to sell such items as "groceries and provisions, dry goods and clothing, crockery, tin and hardware, boots and shoes, powder and shot, farming and mining tools, school books, stationery, tobacco, cigars, fresh flour."[109]

Newspaper advertisements were not the only way these stores competed. In the mid-nineteenth century, going to the store was a social occasion, offering buyer and vendor the opportunity (while bargaining over prices) to discuss city affairs, books, or neighborhood gossip.[110] Rose, so well informed about the affairs of the city and county governments and the railroad, enjoyed holding forth with his neighbors. In early 1855, however, Rose's terms on the Board of Trustees and the Board of Supervisors expired.[111] He could take a great deal of satisfaction that, under his leadership, the trustees finally had been able to liquidate most of the city debts created by the 8 percent bonds. However, stepping down from those official positions left Rose with unaccustomed time on his hands.

It is possible that the bachelor believed that simply owning and operating a hotel, slaughterhouse, tannery, and general store, plus being an active member of the Masons, treasurer of the railroad, and one of three school board members couldn't suffice to keep him busy. Or perhaps a man who speculated in real estate couldn't resist another kind of speculation. Whatever the reason, Rose decided to embark on yet another venture. Undeterred by the lack of profitability that others had experienced in such ventures, Rose outfitted two men "with all the paraphernalia necessary for a gold hunt and three months' provisions, and dispatched them for the mountains where gold has already been discovered in small quantities, with instructions not to return till they have found good paying diggings," the *Herald* reported on April 28. "He says he will send them supplies for a year whenever they order them, but in no case to return or give up the search—so confident is he that there are rich deposits through the whole region of country between here and the desert."[112]

In June, Rose & Pendleton successfully defended themselves against a charge that their store had illegally encroached upon the public right of way on Juan Street. Represented by Gitchell in the court proceedings, Rose was able to show that he, not the city, owned the property in question.[113] But the firm's victory, in a sense, was short-lived. Just as Rose's attention was diverted by the prospect of finding gold, so too was Pendleton's distracted by the prospect of collecting the people's money. In August he became a candidate for the position of county treasurer, the office for which Rose once had been a candidate until he withdrew in favor of Hays. In September, Pendleton defeated Morse by a vote of 150-80.[114] In his new official capacity, Pendleton placed a notice in the *Herald* that "unless the licenses due the county are immediately paid...they will be collected according to law."[115] With the two partners worrying about other concerns, nobody seemed to be minding the store. On November 1, they announced: "Our partnership expiring by limitation on the first of January next (1856), and not intending to extend it, a rare opportunity is offered to those desirous of purchasing dry goods, clothing, groceries, etc, etc. Our stock is large and well assorted and we will sell cheap for cash and cash only."[116]

As Rose & Pendleton had to do before him, Robinson was required to defend against a charge that the grounds of a building he had constructed on the south side of his Railroad Building had encroached on city land. Charles Poole and Cave Couts, the surveyor, told the court that there was in fact a small encroachment, whereupon D. B. Kurtz, serving as judge, decreed that "the said Jas. W. Robinson be fined the sum of one dollar and he remove the obstruction of said street within sixty days."[117] The building in question, which had impinged upon what then was known as Garden Street, housed the classroom of San Diego School District 1, which Robinson—himself a school board trustee—had rented to the district for $15 a month on the approval of Rose and Morse, his board colleagues.[118] Being a landlord apparently was an important income supplement for Robinson, who never was able to amass the kind of fortune in real estate or money that his friend Rose did. Besides Mannasse's store, tenants in Robinson's combination home and commercial building included at various times the *San Diego Herald*, the Masonic Lodge, and the San Diego & Gila Railroad.

Rose meanwhile continued to speculate in real estate, with his 1855 tax assessment indicating a preoccupation with developing the tannery. He owned 105 "mools," horses and mares; a buggy and carriage, four wagons, and $2,500 worth of commercial improvements for the tannery, among other holdings. In La Cañada de las Lleguas he owned 11 lots of 160 acres each, and another 160-acre lot in the Rincon Valley. He also had smaller holdings in Old Town, the Playa, and Middletown.[119] His Old Town holdings were enlarged by a foreclosure suit brought against Magdalena Estudillo in District Court in August. As a result of a sheriff's sale conducted to satisfy Rose's claims against the property, Rose acquired two blocks intersected by Mason and Jefferson Streets containing dwellings, outhouses, and a corral.[120]

Rose also began building up a debt at Strauss's store for a variety of equipment, supplies and consumables needed by his gold prospectors and other associates and friends. "Sugar, candles, lumber, flour, milk, barley, rawhide, coffee, hat, shoes, yoke of oxen, candles, tobacco, broom, children shoes, perfumes, powder, writing papers, beans and brandy," said the initial order in July of 1855.[121]

Indians and Mormons

Moved by the nearly destitute condition of Indians, the Masonic Lodge took upon itself in July 1855 the obligation of creating a fund to feed the unfortunates. In this, they may have been influenced by the exhortations of the Reverend John Reynolds, an energetic U.S. Army chaplain and brother Mason who was credited with delivering the first Protestant sermon in San Diego.[122] Meanwhile, outreach by San Diegans to another minority group—the Mormons in San Bernardino—was motivated by the reverse impulse. San Diegans realized that in many ways the Mormons could help them. In February, G.B. Tebbetts and H.C. Ladd advocated bypassing the hill at Temecula to San Bernardino to encourage trade between the two cities. The *Herald* editorialized:

> It is important to the merchants and businessmen in this city that the road should be immediately opened. By so doing, we would open the advantage of our harbor to the merchants of San Bernardino and they would be able to supply us with flour, butter, lumber and all kinds of vegetables, at a much lower rate than we can possibly get them from San Francisco. During the past week some two or three wagon loads of flour, butter and eggs were consigned to Mr. (Marcus) Katz from San Bernardino, and we are assured that if the road is opened so as to avoid the Temecula hill, much, if not the entire business of that place will be done through this city. Merchants who put money into this improvement are sure to make a good investment.[123]

The *Herald* returned to the subject in May, telling readers that because of Indian wars in U.S. territory "all along the route from Missouri," the Mormon headquarters at Salt Lake City faced interruption of immigration and trade. It was, of course, a misfortune for the Mormons but "a God-send to the people of San Diego, if the businessmen here have sense to turn the thing to advantage," editor Ames wrote.

> In absence of supplies from the east overland, the Mormons, who are large consumers of general merchandise, and are the best class of customers probably in the United States, because they have plenty of money and always pay cash, must look to the Pacific Coast for relief...The question of the most vital moment in this connection to the citizens of San Diego is shall we make an effort, by improving the road between here and San Bernardino, to secure the present and perhaps the future trade of the great country around Salt Lake which is so rapidly filling up with settlers, or shall we lay supinely on our backs and let the rich treasure slip through our fingers?

Warning that Los Angeles merchants already were seizing the opportunity, the newspaper complimented Katz for continuing to pursue a San Diego connection. "One of Mr. Katz's teams arrived here on Monday with a load of produce, including eggs, butter, beans &c. Eggs are selling here for 50 cents per dozen, butter for 50 cents per pound and other things in proportion. Before Mr. Katz commenced this trade it was difficult to procure eggs here even for one dollar. The best flour for sale in our market comes from San Bernardino..."

At this point, the newspaper editor decided to scold San Diegans: "There is a lack of enterprise among the men of capital in San Diego or we should have a first class flouring mill instead of depending on San Francisco and other places for that important article of consumption—bread. There is but one flouring mill in this whole county, and there is a manifest lack of energy in conducting that, for a good-sized family can eat the flour as fast as the mill can grind it."[124]

San Diego's "men of enterprise" were not idle when it came to the issue of the railroad, for which they conducted another survey—this time all the way to Fort Yuma on the Colorado River—and concluded that the route was quite practicable. The stockholders balloted on October 1, choosing J.C. Bogart, D.B. Kurtz and E.B. Pendleton to replace Tebbetts, Hays and Strauss on their board. The stockholders also discussed the details of submitting an important question to the city electorate on October 19: should nearly two leagues, or approximately 8,850 acres, of public land be conferred to the San Diego & Gila for the purpose of building such a railroad to the Colorado River?[125]

Ten days before the citizens of San Diego answered that question affirmatively, Robinson wrote one of his rare letters to his brother in Ohio. After pleading to him to forward some money owed to his wife from her father's estate, so it could be used for their son's education, he turned to the state of affairs in San Diego:

> We have grown potatoes, barley, corn and vegetables enough for home consumption. The mines are as good as ever, that is the quartz mines, requiring expensive machinery for working—but the placers, or surface digging is not too good. Many placers are exhausted, but new ones are discovered. Vice and immorality abounds and there is not much pleasure for a good man here. But a man must get books & a few friends & avoid immoral company. That is the only remedy that I have. We have formed a Railroad Co. at this place, with a capital of $5,000,000 to construct a R-Road from the city to the Colorado of the West opposite the mouth of the Gila River, the boundary of our state, to serve as so much of the grand track of the Great Pacific & Atlantic Railway, by way of El Passo (sic)... to the Mississippi River. Of this company I am president and we have surveyed the route, which is 180 miles— made maps, profiles and engineers' report etc & expect the same will be published next winter as part of the report of Lieut. Park, U.S. Topg. Engineers. We are very sanguine that this place will be the terminus of this great road. If this takes place, my property will be valuable. If not, then it will not...

Robinson also indulged himself in memories of Ohio, which he had abandoned to run off with Sarah more than 20 years before.

> Though far, way far away, in memory I am very often at our Father & Mother's old stone house, well, barn and grave yard, the walnut tree that stood in the lane, the locust trees. ...The copper stones of our father's house, that I carried 2 months before I left home and the 'old oaken bucket that hung on the wall' but all them I shall see no more, forever but solitary and alone. I must lay my bones on the shore of this mighty ocean and leave my son as I left all my kindred, solitary & alone. How deeply melancholy is the thought. But these things I whisper not here only to my God and you do I unreservedly pour out my feelings for both understand and know me and it is a relief to do so and I thank God that he permits me to enjoy this privilege while I tarry on Earth.[126]

Attitudes toward Jews in San Diego. III

The *Herald's* attitude toward the Jewish community seemed to moderate in 1855. Instead of satirical articles in which Jews were often made to look ridiculous, now the newspaper took delight in running articles about circumstances, real or imaginary, in which the Jews got the better of their persecutors—who typically were foreigners or northern Yankees. Even so, the articles had an undertext of intolerance against the Jews as well as other "outsiders." Again and again the articles emphasized how different and how "cunning" the Jews were. On September 28, for example, the newspaper related that "a beautiful Jewess attended a party in Philadelphia where she was annoyed by a vulgar impertinent fellow. 'And you never eat pork, Miss M?' asked he tauntingly. 'Never, sir.' 'Nor eat lard lumps?' he continued. 'No sir, our religion teaches us to avoid everything swinish, physically and morally; therefore you will excuse me for declining to have any more words with you.'"[127]

Quite a long tale of a similar vein ran November 17, in which Christian travelers in Germany tried to outwit a Jew in a game of "curious questions." Someone asked "How many soft boiled eggs could the giant Goliath eat upon an empty stomach?" Only the Jew knew the trick answer: "One, for once he had eaten one egg, he cannot eat a second one on an empty stomach. "The second question came from Christian Scriptures: "Why did Paul write the second Epistle to the Corinthians?" but again the Jew was not stumped. "He was not in Corinth, otherwise he would have spoken to them." The story ended with the Jew asking a question that no one could answer—"How can a man fry two trouts in three pans so that a trout may lay in each pan?" After eight men admitted to not knowing the answer and paying their bets, a ninth man asked the Jew for the answer. He responded he did not know either. When the others protested that this was not fair; the Jew pointed out that they had agreed that anyone who could not answer a question should pay the questioner. Thereupon he paid one of the eight pieces he collected to the ninth man. "They all being rich merchants and grateful for the amusement which had passed an hour or two pleasantly for them, laughed heartily at their loss and at the Jew's cunning."[128]

Yet another story was published on January 19, 1856. "'Do you know,' said a cunning Yankee to a Jew, 'that they hang Jews and jackasses together in Poland?' 'Indeed! Then it is well that you and I are not there,' retorted the Jew."[129] The fact that the buffoon this time was a "Yankee" was a telling indication of San Diego's political sentiment in the pre-Civil War era. Many of its settlers came from states south of the Mason-Dixon line. Although California was admitted at its own government's request as a "free state," most San Diegans favored the cause of the slaveholding states. Editor Ames, in fact, had settled in San Diego with the idea of building up political sentiment for a north-south division of California—with the southern portion to be readmitted to the United States as a slave state. So the jackass "joke" had a political undercurrent to it. However friendly the newspaper was in its columns to the Jewish merchants of San Diego, such "friendship" came with a price. San Diego's Jews were expected to support the cause of the "South," or at the very least to keep contrary opinions to themselves. Rose, believed by many to be a "unionist" at heart, kept his own counsel.[130]

As a Christian, a native-born American and a former acting governor of Texas—a slaveholding state whose citizens, in fact, had defied Mexico's anti-slavery laws—Robinson was a man whose political views never were in doubt and were greatly admired, at least in so far as they applied to the growing North vs. South conflict. But in local politics, Robinson proved to be as subject to the voters' caprice as any elected official, losing his position as district attorney to J.R. Gitchell in September 1855. Robinson could take some solace in his advancement to the top position in the local Masonic fraternity at the beginning of 1856. Whereas three years before he felt he was insufficiently conversant with Masonic ritual to be the "worshipful master," he now accepted the top position.[131]

Tight Economic Times

On February 2, 1856, someone stole through the window of Moses Mannasse's store in Robinson's Railroad Building, and took between $60 and $70 from the cash drawer. A store owned by T. R. Darnall was struck the same night. According to the *Herald*, a Mexican employee of Mannasse and an Indian employee of Darnall had not been seen since the night of the robbery, and suspicion therefore was directed at them.[132]

With or without robberies, money was tight in San Diego, yet the economy was viable enough to encourage brisk competition, expansion, and new entries into the market. After Rose and Pendleton shut down their business, the building that housed their store was taken over by Louis Strauss, who desired a second location for his business. "Mr. Gerson, who has charge of the business here in San Diego, has been some time amongst us—has married and settled here—and is thereby justly entitled to our support and patronage," Ames editorialized. "Mr. Louis Strauss, the founder of the house here, unlike many others, commenced by a permanent investment in real estate, and avowed his intention of making San Diego his future home. This course created him friends among the old residents—contributed much towards establishing a solid credit in San Francisco and has been the chief cause of his success. He will continue for the present to reside in 'the great metropolis' and attend to purchasing for the house here. Mr. Gerson, with his assistant, will be happy to attend to the calls of their friends, at either store..." The *Herald* described the store as being located in "Rose's Block," which fronted on Juan Street.[133]

Jacob Elias meanwhile took over a store previously operated by Bandini and Reiner in the Casa de Bandini, facing the eastern corner of the Plaza. He employed Hyman Mannasse—whose partnership with his cousin, Moses, had been dissolved. Another merchant competing for the favor of San Diego residents was Maurice Franklin, brother of Lewis Franklin, who opened premises on the southwestern side of the Plaza in what was the Exchange Hotel and which soon would be renamed the Franklin House.[134]

Rose had twin sad duties in 1856 of settling the estate of his nephew, Nisan Alexander, as well as that of his friend and neighbor, Gustave Fisher. On March 24, 1856, Gustave's widow, Sophia, was bitten fatally by a rattlesnake en route to a family picnic on the shore of False Bay.[135] Once Lucy Anna "Louisiana" Fisher, 8, may have considered her greatest worries to be the orthography, reading, writing, geography, arithmetic, and English grammar courses taught to her in the school room adjoining Robinson's Railroad Building by teacher Joshua Sloane.[136] Now, in just a year's time, both her parents had died. Greatly affected, Rose decided he would do everything he could to help Louisiana and the other orphaned children of his friends. Gustave and Sophia were buried side by side on a knoll overlooking their ranch. Louisa's husband, Edward Schneider, was named executor of Sophia's estate, adding to the worries of the young man. Schneider asked any person having claims against Sophia "to exhibit them with the necessary vouchers within ten months..." Rose in a nearby notice in the *Herald*, announced that an auction would be held June 12 to dispose of Gustave's property, which included: "Carriage and harness, large two-horse carriage, a lot of tinware and crockery, a lot of furniture, 3 mules, 3 mares, 3 colts, 20 hens, 2 yoke of oxen and 10 two-year-old steers."[137]

Ironically, while settling financial affairs for others, Rose was beginning to repeat the pattern of borrowing that got him into financial trouble in New Orleans. Besides running up his account at L. Strauss Company, for what seemed an inordinate volume of alcoholic products, he also in June 1856, began borrowing more money at interest. The records kept by L. Strauss Company in 1856 showed Rose purchasing bottles of brandy on 11 occasions between March 2 and June 24. The same inventory also showed Rose purchasing whisky, apparently favored by his workers, six times during the same time span.[138] On June 10, Rose, with Joseph Reiner serving as a co-signer, borrowed $500 at 4 percent interest per month from Witherby. A week later, Rose borrowed an additional $650 from him on the same terms.[139]

Know–Nothing Movement

Herald editor Ames, on June 7, 1856, passed over both the Democratic nominee for President, James Buchanan of Pennsylvania, and the newly formed Republican party's nominee, California's own John C. Fremont, to endorse the third-party candidacy of former President Millard Fillmore, now running on the ticket of the American party, better known as the "Know Nothings." One of the major planks of this nativist party's platform was "Americans must rule America, and to this end, native-born citizens should be selected for all state, federal and municipal offices of government employment in preference to naturalized citizens." Rose and all other Jewish adults then in San Diego, in Ames view, should be precluded by their foreign birth from holding office again. While Rose and the others might retain their naturalized citizenship, any other foreigners coming to American shores should be required to hold "continual residence of 21 years" before they could become citizens.[140]

The Know Nothings had built their party on anti–Catholic sentiment, so one can imagine the glee with which Ames may have reprinted a story on June 28 from the *Cincinnati Times*. Dependent on the good will of all his readers for advertisements, Ames could neither openly attack the local Catholic Church nor the Jewish religion. But he could print out-of-state stories, mirroring his party's prejudice against foreigners in general, Catholics in particular, and if anyone complained, he could simply shrug and say, "It's news." That such a news item once again could warn Jews that it was in their best interests to stick with their "friends" decidedly was an additional benefit. "Singular persecution of a boy," announced the headline. The article continued:

> One of the most remarkable cases of alleged persecution of a boy on account of his religious professions was brought...on Saturday 26 April. The defendants were a pair of Germans

consisting of the proprietor of a lager beer house, in Front Street above Coates, and thirteen other persons. The complainant was a boy about 14 years of age. According to the story of the boy, it appears that he and his father boarded at the beer house. On the 22nd of April, it was alleged that the defendant and a number of other Germans beat the boy severely, and then carried him up stairs and threw him upon a bed, where they stretched out his limbs and pricked him with pins, in the meantime covering his mouth with a pillow to smother his cries. They then locked him up in the room until his father came to the rescue. The reason assigned for the outrage was that the perpetrators were Catholics and the boy a Jew, and they were practicing a mock crucifixion upon him. The proprietor of the house and another of the party were held on $800 bail each...[141]

Ames sent another veiled warning to the Jewish community on July 26 when he wrote "Our friend Joe Mannasse is rebuilding his store, on Judea Street, and is going to enlarge his business. We are pleased to see this indication of prosperity, for Joe is a clever fellow, and will probably vote the American ticket at the coming Presidential election."[142] Judea Street, located on the northeastern or backside of the stores facing the Plaza, paralleled Juan Street, and was so named because so many Jewish merchants had their businesses there. It was doubtful that Mannasse who, like his brother Heyman (also spelled "Hyman"), was born in Prussia, ever would consider voting for the American ticket, which wanted to disqualify him from ever holding a public office. In fact, Joseph Mannasse, following Rose's example, would soon emerge in San Diego as a preeminent man both of business and government.[143]

Meanwhile, Ames and Robinson led the Masons in their annual procession honoring the birthday of St. John the Baptist. Such Jewish members of the fraternity as Solomon Goldman, Marcus Schiller, and Nathaniel Vise were mentioned as participating in the parade, but Rose was missing from the list, possibly off to his mines or working at his tannery. Victoria Jacobs, whose girlish diary provided historians with a peek into everyday life of San Diego, noted in her entry for that date: "Seen the procession of the Masons pass our house. We were invited to a ball the same evening, but did not go."[144]

Ever anxious to demonstrate their patriotism, many members of the Jewish community answered a call for volunteers to create a militia company, the San Diego Guards, which eventually chose George Pendleton—brother of Rose's former partner, Eugene Pendleton—as captain. Ames, politically hostile to foreigners, stressed at the organizing meeting "the importance to the people who live on the frontier of Mexico of bearing arms and ammunition on and in case of emergency."[145] Among members of the Jewish community who organized for such duties as drilling and firing ceremonial salutes were Hyman and Joseph Mannasse, their cousin Moses Mannasse, Marcus Schiller, Charles Gerson and Maurice Franklin.[146] Rose, by now 49, may well have decided this was work for younger men. He gave his backing to a more sedentary pursuit, the creation of the Lyceum and Debating Club which would hold discussions and debates on such topics as capital punishment, "The Mechanical Industry and Inventive Genius of America," and "Is the Use of Spirituous Liquors Beneficial to Mankind?"[147] Perhaps wisely, the Lyceum and Debating Club did not schedule debates on such polarizing issues as slavery or immigrants' rights.

Trade with San Bernardino

Marks Jacobs, like Marcus Katz, believed that San Diego's prospects for the future would improve if ever a good road were built to connect it to the Mormon settlement at San Bernardino. "Sir, having just returned from San Bernardino where I have been some six or seven weeks, I communicate to you a few jottings, which you may publish or not as you may think fit," he wrote to the *San Diego Herald*, continuing: "I shall not refer to religious topics, firstly because it is not in the province of a secular newspaper to occupy its columns with such matters and secondly, inasmuch as I did not go to the Mormon settlement to convert them to Judaism, so neither did I go among them for the purpose of being converted to Mormonism. I extend the same toleration to others which I claim for myself." Having thus made what might be considered a jab at editor Ames, Jacobs went on to say that the Mormons in the few years since arriving in San Bernardino had developed the town "by the sweat of their brow...into one vast hive of industry... Sawmills propelled by one of the 27 streams of water which are found on the ranch, have been erected on mountains which before the advent of the Mormons were thought inaccessible," Jacobs reported. The colony had built roads, sawmills, and now they had flour mills "which can be compared favorably to any in the world." He went on to say:

> To gratify the curious in those matters, I brought a sample of flour ground from new wheat, which was furnished to me by the politeness of General (Charles) Rich, and which may be seen at the store of Franklin & Co. ...The quality of butter and eggs produced on the ranch is almost incredible. I am not sufficient well informed to give you the precise amount of these articles produced weekly, but I may safely put the quantity at two thousand pounds of butter and one hundred dozen eggs weekly, nearly all of which find a ready market among our

neighbors in Los Angeles, and it is only because of a lack of very little enterprise among us in San Diego that we are deprived, or rather are depriving ourselves, of a valuable trade. With comparatively small cost Temecula hill could be cut down and a good wagon road made between here and San Bernardino, the people of which place are desirous of connecting themselves to us by the ties of commerce, and have authorized me to communicate to my fellow citizens that they are willing to complete one half portion of the road if we complete the other half.[148]

Robinson Takes Ill

Robinson, who had been afflicted with dropsy, felt well enough to travel to Los Angeles on business. However, while there he was taken so ill that as a precaution, he made out his will on July 31, 1856. "Being weak and infirm in body, but of sound and perfect mind and memory, blessed be Almighty God for the same," Robinson directed that his funeral expenses and just debts be paid, and that his estate be divided equally between his wife, Sarah, and his son, William, with any residue after Sarah's death also to go to his son. No provisions were made for any members of his first family. He appointed Sarah along with his law partner, Jonathan Scott, to serve as executors of his estate and as guardians of his son. The document called for the settling of his estate without going through probate court. It was witnessed by Kimball Dimmick, Jacob Elias, and James H. Sander in Los Angeles.[149]

Robinson's illness subsequently caused some confusion in a case brought by Maurice A. Franklin against Sheriff Joseph Reiner for what the former contended was an unlawful seizure by the sheriff of his property. Maurice alleged the property in question belonged to him and not to his brother, Lewis, against whom the sheriff had been enforcing a judgment. As Robinson had served as the attorney in an earlier dispute between Maurice and his brother, he had some evidence in his possession affecting Maurice's contention. Robinson gave to his wife, Sarah, a portfolio that he believed included papers pertaining to the case, and she turned them over to Robinson's law partner, Scott, so that the latter might handle the San Diego matter during Robinson's convalescence in Los Angeles. However, when the portfolio was opened, the documents in question were not among the papers inside. Embarrassed, Sarah Robinson and Scott both had to give sworn statements to this effect in the District Court.[150]

The Entrepreneurial Rose, Part III

The county tax assessor valued Louis Rose's personal property in the middle of 1856 at $4,500, exclusive of real estate. The property included 54 horses, 35 mules, 16 cattle, 3 wagons, 2 carriages, furniture, leather and 2 mortgages. When his real estate holdings were added, Rose was liable to taxes on property valued at $20,252.50.[151] These bare figures told only a fraction of the story. A far more meaningful assessment of Rose was provided by District Court Judge Benjamin Hayes, who heard cases throughout Southern California and kept extensive notes on the sights he saw and the people he met within his jurisdiction. While riding on a saddle horse to San Diego, he passed through Rose Canyon on August 23 in the company of J.J. Warner. Suddenly, "the horses jumped from the road," Hayes wrote.

> Coming up I found a large rattlesnake coiled in the sand. Drawing his Damascus blade, Don Juan (Warner) dismounted, stirring the sand near with its blade, then suddenly changing position and striking the enemy twice on the head till it was harmless. Then passing the sword through its neck, he held it up for observation of the trophy. It was about four feet in length. 'Here,' said he, 'is the snake *que mató la vieja,* (that killed the old woman)' referring to the lamented death of Mrs. Fischer, who was supposed to have been struck about this place by a rattlesnake: her little girl said she saw the snake. From the nature of the wounds, I suppose she had wounded her ankle against the cactus. Don Santiago pulled off the eleven rattles; Don Juan fastened them in the band of his hat we proposed this should be his coat of arms. We soon drew rein at Rose's in the City of San Diego. I stopped here; the rest quartered themselves among their Californian acquaintances.[152]

Hayes made do with the quarters at Rose's Commercial House until his wife arrived by steamer from San Francisco on September 2, 1856. Emily made clear her displeasure with the accommodations:

> She had lived for some time in Calhoun Co., Ill., has traveled a good deal in Western Missouri (and so have I); has crossed the isthmus (of Panama) before there was a railroad; and once we spent two weeks traveling on horseback in Los Angeles County and San Bernardino. But, she says, the bed she had to sleep on the first night at San Diego was anything but a bed of roses. A little room about eight feet by seven, containing a bedstand, bureau and washstand, hardly enough room to turn

around. Friend Rose was still talking of making better arrangements when Mr. Blount Couts, county clerk, offered us a sleeping apartment furnished, with a parlor to receive company, at the house of his brother, Colonel Cave J. Couts. Emily soon took possession of these airy and convenient premises, arranging to board with the family of my friend Nat Vise.[153]

When there was a break in his court duties, Hayes was an accomplished tourist. He headed for Rose's tract of property on the road to Los Angeles: "A little over four miles from Old Town, at the foot of the lofty hills that form one of the sides of La Cañada de las Yeguas (sic) and just as you emerge from the Canada, toward False Bay, Mr. Louis Rose has bored 170 feet for an artesian well. The work is now suspended. In boring, they passed through four different strata of stone coal: too thin to pay for workings." [154]

Hayes noted that Rose's ranch consisted of 1,920 acres lying along a creek (which became known as Rose Creek):

He bought it in a separate quarter sections at the city public sales since 1853, paying high, in order to secure a large tract in a compact body. As things now stand upon it, and perhaps counting interest on money and taxes, he thinks every acre has cost him $8.00. The proof of his own appreciation of it, he would accept an offer of $20,000 per acre, including the tannery, garden and other improvements. It has a new frame house, in good order; a garden of four acres, with a stone fence five feet high. The cost of the fence has been, with $325 cash, boarding of two men six months and use of teams to haul rocks, a total of $1,000. He had grape vines growing freely, but they have been neglected. He has raised excellent tobacco. A gardener would cost $30.00 per month. The garden would have to be irrigated from wells. Digging eight feet, water is plenty; but on most parts of the rancho, sufficient water is obtained at the depth of three feet or less. Live creeks flow through it during the rainy seasons, and four months after, many springs make large ponds from two to three feet deep. And there is ample pasturage. At present, he has only 20 head of cattle and 100 horses and mules. There is enough of sycamore and willow to fence ten miles square and very little oak.[155]

The sightseeing judge also inspected Rose's tannery:

> Mr. Rose commenced this establishment in the year 1852. It is only one of the various charming features of Rose's Rancho. There is no other tannery in the county. There are 20 bark vats, six lime and water vats, two capable of containing 500 gallons each; a new bark mill, an adobe house, for curing the leather. Each vat will contain from 80 to 100 sides. There are force pumps and everything else complete. He now makes 3,000 sides per annum, and 1,000 skins of deer, goat, sheep, seal and sea lion. Many goats have been brought to him from Guadalupe Island (where goats abound)... off the coast of Lower California. Seal are abundant off our own coast. Last year, he sold $8,000 worth of leather at San Francisco. It was much praised there. Oak bark is obtained 10 miles from the tannery, in abundance, at from $12 to $15 per ton—delivered. He employs head tanner, at $100 per month; two assistants at $35 each per month; three laborers, each at $10 per month; boarding them. Indian laborers command $8 per month; Mexicans at $10, both classes are easily got here. Hides are readily obtained to keep the tannery always in operation. He trades for them a good deal with shoes, saddles and botas which are made of his own leather. Deer skins, goat & bear the standing price of $3 a piece. Today I found him busy, cutting out soles and uppers, because he had little else to do; the uppers were of deer skin. These are manufactured by a Mexican shoemaker, according to Mexican style. They will do well in dry weather.[156]

Fascinated by Rose, Hayes inquired more deeply into his financial affairs. "Speculation," was the heading he gave this subject in his diary. It was quite clear Hayes thought Rose's hopes were pipe dreams:"Mr. R. owns lots in every part of the city. A map he showed me of only 2,900 of these, in a body, indicated him as a stupendous speculator of the 'make or break' order. I hope he may realize the first character. They lie upon the Bay of San Diego, commencing about half a mile from La Playa; extend along the water's edge, three-fourths of a mile—with deep water in front, he says—nd then back into the hills well on to a half a mile... Of course, though advanced in years, he calculates upon seeing the Pacific Railroad finished to San Diego. This done, his property is just where it should be. Peradventure he puts down the lots at $5,000 each, on the average. Fourteen millions, five hundred thousand dollars! Whew. Then the rancho at $38,400 is hardly worth talking about. But it should be worth more than that to supply the future London of the Pacific with potatoes and milk. Like brilliant calculations, I religiously believe, feed the fancy of this amiable community."[157]

Hayes noted that politicians in Washington would determine the terminus of the transcontinental railroad. He predicted with considerable accuracy that many San Diego speculators would be unable to hold onto their properties for as long as such a debate might take. Much land was purchased with borrowed money, at 3 percent interest compounded per month. "May Rose never have one cent less than he fondly dreams of—in that hour when railroad cars shall roll along this shining bay."[158]

All of Hayes' questions left Rose wondering what the judge's intentions were. "Miscalculations," Hayes labeled a later entry. "Friend Rose appears to think I had some object (so he said) in my inquisitiveness about his rancho. Being on the street this afternoon buying peaches from a Santa Ysabel careta, he called me into his store, saying he had stopped me to tell me had forgotten that the rancho would be a great place for a dairy. Milk could be delivered in the future city, at 6 o'clock in the morning. I answered him, 'yes, I have thought of that.' Having learned that money can be had at San Francisco at low interest, he wishes to borrow $20,000 for two years, within which time he can pay it with leather. But—to my miscalculation, I informed him, I had made him out worth $14,000,000. He declined rating the 2,900 lots so high, but thought eventually they might be worth something, and added, he had a large number besides, scattered over the neighborhood."[159]

At no time, on any county assessment list, did Rose ever have as many as 2,900 parcels of land, leading one to the conclusion that what Hayes saw was a plan that Rose had drawn up showing how his various properties someday might be subdivided.

While Rose spoke openly to Hayes about his business affairs, he became withdrawn when the judge began inquiring into his past life: "He told me that he was now 48 years old, and only wished he could have back twenty years. 'You must have led an eventful life, Mr. Rose,' I said. 'Sit down with me and give me an outline: for I believe, it must be instructive.' 'No, 'tis not the time yet. My brother in Europe has often written for this. Some of these days I will prepare it. I have encountered death, in every form—I will write it after awhile. My father and mother,' he continued, 'were over eighty when they died. With my family—if they do not die very young—they live to a good old age.' Promising to call upon us, we parted. I am not writing for publication but his affairs present many things that attract notice." [160]

"Death in every form"—what an intriguing statement on Rose's part. We know about the yellow fever in New Orleans; the cholera in San Antonio; deaths from exhaustion and exposure on the trip to California; the hanging of Marshall; the firing squad that took Garra's life; the unexplained death of Alexander; the cancer that took his friend Fischer; the rattlesnake (or possibly cactus) that claimed the life of Mrs. Fischer. On a more figurative level, we know of Rose's "mortification" at the hands of Van Horne in Texas, and later, upon learning that his wife had committed adultery rather than move to California to join him. Yet we sense that there is far more to Rose's statement than even this litany; we wonder what horrors Rose might have endured before deciding to quit Europe for America. We also are left wondering whether Rose misspoke or Hayes misheard the information about Rose's father who died at age 76, according to the notice placed by Simon Rose in the *Intelligenz Blatt*.

Hayes made yet another note, about Rose's love of animals. He went "to a stand at Mr. Rose's—to see the turtle. It is six years old, came from the Galapagos Islands; weighed when brought here 35 lbs, now 100 lbs. We presented it a slice of bread; it quietly snapped off a piece. Hens and little chickens gathered around for a share, even picking at the crumbs in its mouth—to all which it paid no attention. Then the cook put a piece of pancake in its mouth. A little pet dog helped himself to part. It merely raised up high on its feet, to let the dog play beneath... Rose has a great fondness for pets. I saw him go up and kiss a mule the other day."[161]

Hayes and Rose became quite friendly. On September 18, 1856, the jurist wrote in his diary: "Friend Louis Rose offers me his best lot if I will come here to reside and put a house upon it. Can't say. I may lose $10,000 by not accepting the proposition. That is his opinion. Time will show."[162]

Carefully observing religious customs, Hayes noted on one Sunday: "The Jewish Sabbath (the day before) was kept by only one person, Mr. L.A. F. (Lewis A. Franklin). On this Christian Sabbath, all goes on as usual through the rest of the week, one store alone being closed, that of Mr. Morse; he and his good lady are from New England." In contrast, the diarist noted on September 30: "This is the Jewish New Year. Their stores are all closed."[163]

Two weeks later, on October 14, Hayes headed back north, his court duties in San Diego concluded. Marks Jacobs' daughter, Victoria, wrote that day in her diary about the Jewish harvest holiday, which is traditionally celebrated by spending time in a booth or tabernacle known as a "succah." "Today is Succoth and we are all busy doing nothing as there is no synagogue here. The only difference (is) that we pass our time at home instead of going to a place of worship. Pa started to San Bernardino today, about eleven o'clock, in company with Judge Hay(e)s and Mr. Gitchell."[164]

Hayes also noted his departure from San Diego, saying he was accompanied by Colonel Kendrick, the Democratic candidate for the Legislature, as well as by "Mr. Marks Jacobs, a prominent Jew and J.R. Gitchell, Esq., district attorney." He then listed the sites he passed as he traveled north: "The Presidio with its solitary date tree. The mission valley and river. Circle around False Bay, a beautiful sheet of water for sailing, rowing, fishing or bathing; too shallow for large vessels to enter. Great abundance of clams on its northern shore... Ornamental bush on the side of the road; pretty foliage, full of clusters of red berries looking at a little distance like masses of gay flowers; might be trimmed for a garden. To Rose's coal mine, 5 miles; to the tannery, one mile farther. The graves of Mr. and Mrs. Fischer on the very top of the hill that overlooks the house he built; a strange idea of burying them there. Over the lofty hills, affording an extensive prospect of the county, on to Soledad Valley. This valley is the boundary of the city in this direction, 12 miles from Old Town. The sea in sight here; little good soil (what is its extent?) Six miles further San Dieguito, formerly an Indian pueblo."[165]

Two days after Hayes left, Rose expanded his holdings in La Cañada de las Lleguas area by 480 acres, as confident as the judge was dubious about the future value of San Diego real estate. The purchase finally closed the large account that Rose had opened with the city six years before. In a receipt made out to city trustees Thomas R. Darnall, Thomas B. Collins, and Joseph Smith, Rose acknowledged having received from them Lots 9, 11, and 13, in a document witnessed by A.S. Ensworth and Henry K. Whaley: "Therefore, I, Louis Rose, of said City of San Diego, hereby release and relinquish all claim, right, title or interest, which before the execution thereof I might have had, to any lands, belonging to the corporations, by virtue of any sale at auction, and which have not heretofore been deeded to me by the trustees of said city, and I hereby relinquish all debts, due & demands, both at law & in equity which I might or may have had against said corporation before the ensealing hereof."[166]

Besides voting for President on November 4, San Diegans also chose candidates for a variety of local offices, including justice of the peace. For editor Ames, it was bad news that James Buchanan triumphed over Fremont and Fillmore to become the nation's fifteenth president. Given Ames' nativist outlook, one supposes that he considered it good news that the foreign-born Marks Jacobs was defeated for justice of the peace by two native-born Americans, George Pendleton and James Nichols. Her father's defeat did little to dampen Victoria Jacobs' spirits: she was at that point deep into her courtship with Maurice A. Franklin. One of their favorite destinations by horseback was Rose's ranch.[167]

Needing for his various enterprises the cash for which he had considered going to San Francisco, Rose on December 1 instead borrowed $650 at 4 percent interest per month from Frank Ames.[168] Apparently in replacement of the slaughterhouse that had been operated under the Rose & Pendleton partnership, Rose opened a meat market December 17. "Go it Rose!" cheered the *Herald*, no doubt anticipating a new source of advertising revenue. At the same time, Rose gave over management of the Commercial House to Edward Schneider, who had been struggling financially ever since the roof of his store had fallen in.[169]

General optimism about the economy could be detected in the facts that "Charley Gerson has just finished his new store... Joe Mannasse & Schiller ditto... Moses Mannasse has remodeled and put a roof on his store on the

Plaza."[170] Mannasse and Schiller celebrated their partnership by hosting a Christmas Eve party for the residents of San Diego. "Yesterday, there was a ball at the Gila House given by Schiller and Joe Mannasse,"Victoria Jacobs penned in her diary on December 25. Her sisters "Fanny and Jane went but I did not."[171] Editor Ames described the Christian-oriented event sponsored by the two foreign-born merchants as "magnificent." [172]

Attitudes toward Jews in San Diego, Part IV

With the advent of 1857 New Year, D.B. Kurtz succeeded the ailing Robinson as worshipful master of the Masonic Lodge. The *Herald*, on January 3, referring obliquely to the heavy drinking that Rose had been doing, reported: "The New Market is, we are happy to say, doing a smashing business and to see our worthy friend issuing forth at daylight in the snow white apron, prepared for his daily avocation, with his smiling face and 'cheek of bloom' is proof of the strength of early associations. We are pleased to see 'Richard's himself again.'" [173]

An earthquake struck San Diego on January 9, which the *Herald* estimated lasted "half a minute and appeared to pass from east to west. Considerable alarm was manifested by a few of our citizens, and many seats around breakfast tables were vacated without a request to leave. At the storehouse of Mr. Gerson, several articles of merchandise were thrown from the shelving." [174]

Marks Jacobs sold periodicals and magazines from his store—possibly the source for the *Voice of Israel*, a San Francisco periodical that the *Herald* quoted approvingly on January 24. "The daughter of Israel we would single out as an example of the world," said the San Francisco newspaper. "We concur," said Ames, "and add that we never saw a Jewess in attendance at criminal court, or at any other bad place." [175]

The article appeared to mark the beginning of a turnaround in editor Ames' public pronouncements concerning foreign-born citizens in general and Jews in particular. Fillmore's political thrashing at the hands of Buchanan perhaps served notice on the editor that his nativist views were out of step with the mainstream. Thus on March 7, he hailed the election of Marcus Schiller, Joseph Smith, and D.B. Kurtz as city trustees, notwithstanding Schiller's Prussian and Jewish birth. "The board is a good one—amen," Ames editorialized. On July 25, he noted: "Our fellow citizen, Mr. Jacobs, who is at present acting as deputy, is a candidate for county clerk at the next election. A long residence in the county, habits of industry and temperance and ample qualifications for the position will render Mr. Jacobs a formidable competitor in the race for the most important and lucrative position in the county."[176] Jacobs opposed two native-born Americans, George Pendleton and Edward Kerr, in a race in which

Pendleton prevailed.[177] After the election, Ames editorialized on September 12: "As will be seen from the returns, the vote at the Colorado Township will ensure the election of Colonel Gitchell as district attorney over Mr. Solomon Goldman. However much we may have desired the election of our promising young legal friend Goldman we are satisfied that Colonel Gitchell will serve the people faithfully as he has heretofore done in that capacity."[178]

Despite his failure as a candidate, Jacobs had reason to remember 1857 fondly. The community celebrated with him and his wife Hannah on March 31 when their daughter, Victoria, the young diarist, married Maurice Franklin at the Jacobs' home in Old Town. "In the new relation of husband and wife, may our friends find their cares lessened by sympathy and their joys multiplied by participation," the *Herald* was moved to comment on the occasion. "May they be spared to each other to a good old age, and in the evening of life, when hanging with fond affection over the records of the past, may they be able to say, as they take a retrospective view of their lives, 'O God! We have endeavored so to serve thee and keep thy commandments, as to entitle us to hope for a place in thy kingdom, when we shall have ended this earthly pilgrimage.'"[179]

Boom and Bust

Competition remained lively among merchants, with Moses Mannasse erecting a piazza in front of Robinson's Railroad Building for his store. His cousin Heyman advertised an assortment of ladies' dresses and fancy goods; a new store was opened by Jacob Newman; another merchant named Stein brought from San Francisco a consignment of clothing, dry goods, groceries, and provisions, and Joseph Mannasse, brother of Heyman, promoted "a large quantity of frijoles, from Los Angeles, and they are superior to those from San Francisco."[180] The merchants also banded together when it was perceived that cooperation would help them all. Goldman and Heyman Mannasse, for example, were active in a campaign to have the road improved over the Cuyamacas, particularly at the Carrizo Gorge.[181]

A major item of news was the accidental death on May 24 of John Hays, who had served at one time as a county judge before his controversial tenure as a county treasurer. At a coroner's inquest, Solomon Goldman testified that he saw Hays riding his horse at about 9 o'clock the previous evening, and later saw him lying on the stoop in front of a store in Old Town. "He was intoxicated," Goldman declared. The coroner's jury found that "deceased came to his death by falling from a steep bank and dislocating his neck while in a state of intoxication."[182]

A few weeks later, Thomas Whaley was foreman and Newman and Gerson were among the members of a grand jury that called upon the court "to instruct its officers (of the need for) the more rigid enforcement of the laws concerning drunkenness, the carrying of deadly weapons and the selling of spirituous liquors to Indians." Turning to the city's long standing embarrassment, the jail, the grand jurors said that so many grand juries had commented on its condition, without avail, "that we deem it altogether wasting our time, and encurring expense to the county useless, to give the subject the attention which it deserves."[183]

In July, twice-monthly mail service was inaugurated between San Antonio and San Diego via a stagecoach line operated by James Birch. Because the route over the Cuyamacas was at some points too steep for a stagecoach, the mail had to be transferred to pack horses and mules, then transferred to another stagecoach waiting on the other side of the mountain. The intermediate service earned the line the derisive name of "the Jackass Mail" from detractors. Nevertheless, the arrival on August 31 of Birch's first mail coach touched off an enthusiastic celebration. "San Diego is rejoicing," Judge Benjamin Hayes wrote in his diary. "As the cannon is unsafe, two anvils were procured and 'Boston' (a nickname for J. Judson Ames), Captain Stevens, an old sailor of this coast, with etc., etc., have been firing for some time in honor of the event."[184]

San Diego hoteliers and merchants alike believed that prosperity was hitched to Birch's team of horses. On the wave of excitement, Strauss opened a new store in September. It took some time before news reached San Diego that on September 12 Birch died when the steamer on which he was a passenger sank off the coast of Cape Hatteras. Birch had been heading to Washington, D.C., to lobby Congress for continued support, but the fortunes of his San Antonio & San Diego sank along with him. The Butterfield Stage Company persuaded Congress that mail for San Diego could be carried overland from the east to Warner's Ranch, then sent on a spur route to San Diego, while the main shipment was routed directly to a terminal in Los Angeles.

Within two months, Strauss realized how San Diego's business prospects had changed. Instead of San Diego being the trans-shipment point for both mail and passengers, it in essence would be a cul-de-sac. Strauss notified customers that if they didn't pay up their accounts by January 1, "the same will be left in the hands of an attorney for collection."[185] Goldman, disheartened both by the demise of the mail route and his defeat in the district attorney's race, also decided to pull up stakes for San Francisco.[186]

Another major topic of conversation in San Diego's business community was the apparently unprovoked knife attack on Henry Whaley and Lewis Franklin by William "Reub" Leroy, who then bolted from Franklin's store, pulled an unidentified man off his horse, and dashed to Presidio Hill, where he unaccountably remained in the saddle until authorities came along and arrested him. Whaley's arm had to be amputated but the wound to Franklin's abdomen was superficial. Somehow the charge concerning the attack on Franklin was heard by the county before it was formally informed of the more serious attack on Whaley. The judge released Leroy on $5,000 bail, prompting someone writing under a pseudonym to protest in a letter to the newspaper. One guesses the writer was Franklin himself. Eventually, Leroy was brought before the court again for the attack against Whaley, and ordered held in the county "jail." As seemed to be routine in San Diego, Leroy soon escaped along with a prisoner named Jesus Castro.[187]

Mine Speculations

For Rose, 1857 was a year of deepening financial commitment to his real estate and mining ventures, but he also hedged his business bets. He took out a mysterious sounding advertisement on February 21 that "persons desiring to purchase permits from the U.S. government for lands finally confirmed, will find it in their interest to apply to the undersigned for further information." The mystery was clarified a week later with an advertisement for H.S. Washburn, U.S. deputy surveyor of public and private land claims, which stated "ranches and all other claims faithfully surveyed on favorable terms. References: Colonel John C. Hayes, Major Ira Munson, Hon. V.E. Howard, San Francisco; Hon. B.D. Wilson, Thomas Foster, Horace Wheeler, Los Angeles; Hon. J.J. Kendrick, E. W. Morse, E. B. Pendleton, San Diego" and signed by "Louis Rose, agent San Diego."[188]

Rose borrowed $1,500 on March 1 from James Donohoe at 2½ percent interest per month and on April 23 he borrowed another $400 from Morse at 4 percent interest. Both men probably were delighted to read the *Herald* on May 2, which reported that Rose "continues indefatigable in his endeavors to develope (sic) the mineral resources of our county, and his mines bid fair to fully compensate him for his energy and labor. During the past week, several tons of ore have been taken from his claim, which we think will yield from twenty five to thirty percent copper, with a small percentage of silver. So far as this vein has been opened, it has continuously increased in thickness and richness until its yield is now more than remunerative with a fair prospect of exceeding richness. The success of Mr. Rose will lead to the formation of companies to open several other veins in our county, which upon the surface presents more flattering appearances than the one being worked..."[189] Two weeks later, in a dispatch from San Francisco, Ames reported, "I brought up some copper ore from Rose's mine, which I am having assayed, and will send you the results by next boat."[190] The *Herald* was uncharacteristically silent on the results, using a double entendre instead to report in its June 20 issue the fact that Rose had purchased a saloon adjoining the Commercial House, "and no doubt when he opens, will create as theatrical characters express it, upon the de-but of a crack actress, quite a sensation."[191]

In the interim, Rose had borrowed another $700 from Morse on May 23 and four days later had a survey done of 320 acres of land in San Diego's interior—possibly land he hoped would prove suitable for mining.[192] He persuaded Morse to lend yet another $1,143.07 on July 10, and two days later, he borrowed $524 at 3 percent interest from Andrew Cassidy.[193] On September 12, the *Herald's* reportage turned again to Rose's mining ventures: "Mr. Louis Rose, who has spent a small fortune in prospecting and working copper and silver mines in San Diego County, with varied success, has at last struck a copper lead that promises richer than any found yet in Lower California. We have in our office a lot of ore, taken from one foot below the surface, which is the best specimen of carbonate of copper that we have seen yet—not excepting the fine ore from the Jesus María mines in Lower California. This afternoon we shall witness an analysis of Mr. Rose's copper ore and report progress before we go to press." However, in a postscript to the article, reminiscent of the unfulfilled hope in May, the *Herald* reported: "Mr. Rose did not call us as agreed upon, to see the assay, so that we are unable to give the result."[194] Nine days after this article appeared, Rose borrowed $425.25 at 3 percent interest from Strauss.[195] There was quiet until November 14, when the *Herald* floated a rumor that Rose's copper mines might even be worth as much as $8 million, and added: "Speaking of Squire Rose's copper mines, reminds us that in connection with his copper vein, he has discovered a vein of gold-bearing quartz, some rich specimens of which have been shown to us, and can now be seen in the squire's office, by all those having doubt on the subject."[196] The newspaper's final word on the matter for 1857 came on December 5, when it reported: "Mr. Lewis Rose brought in on Thursday some fine specimens of gold bearing quartz and copper ore, from his mine at Buena Vista, which we have seen and examined, and from the appearance of the quartz and the acknowledged richness of the copper ore, the prospect of rich remuneration for the large amount of money and labor expended in opening the mine, could not be more favorable. Mr. Rose deserves success, for never did man evince such indomitable energy and perseverance that has been bestowed upon this undertaking."[197]

Three days after this article appeared, Rose borrowed $750 from Donohoe at 2½ percent. On December 8, Rose paid down the initial $1,500 debt owed Donahoe to $209.75.[198] One of the first people to loan Rose money, Frank Ames, brought successful suit on December 11 against Rose for non-payment of the $650 loan he made to him the previous year at 4 percent interest per month. Rose did not contest the suit, in which Gitchell represented Ames. He signed an affidavit to "authorize the clerk of the District Court...to enter judgment against me in favour of said Ames for $650 principal and $322 interest together with the clerk's fees for entry of judgment by confession..." Ames then endorsed the total $979 judgment over to E.W. Morse and Charles Gerson.[199] On December 28, Rose made an additional payment to Donohoe of $109.75, bringing the principal due on his first note to $100.

What was happening? Why would a man whom a newspaper described as having a mine worth possibly $8 million be running up so many debts, which by the end of 1857 exceeded $7,500, exclusive of interest and an ongoing tab at L. Strauss & Co. The answer was that after seven years building up his real estate holdings, Louis Rose was land rich and cash poor. Besides his 1,760-acre holding in La Cañada de las Lleguas, the 1857 assessment rolls showed 151 other properties of various sizes belonging to Rose. In personal property, he had a pair of mortgages worth $8,000 and various animals, wagons, and household furniture worth $200.[200] Like many a gambler, Rose had hoped to pay off his debts with future earnings. If the ore extracted from the mines had proven as rich as expectations, Rose would have had no difficulties. But, in fact, notwithstanding the *Herald's* puffery, the mine pickings thus far had been slim. Every day for Rose meant lost money. Each day the expense of labor, groceries, and supplies, and the interest on various loans added to his debt. Would the next day bring a rich strike? Or would he have to mortgage his property, take out personal loans and risk financial ruin? One can sense the pressure Rose was under. In August, he had attorney A.S. Ensworth send a letter to Tucker & Lloyd, a law firm in Washington, D.C., asking them to do whatever was possible to expedite repayment of the $292 worth of food and equipment he had provided to Lieutenant George Derby's engineers in 1853 while they were constructing the dike on the San Diego River.[201]

Death of Robinson

The health of Rose's mentor, Robinson, continued to deteriorate in 1857. Except for the rents he charged tenants of the Railroad Building, the lawyer could not depend on a steady source of income to support his wife and son. Robinson, 67, simply didn't have the stamina.

District Court Judge Benjamin Hayes, whose rounds brought him back to San Diego in August 1857, paid a courtesy call at Robinson's home, where he found the latter suffering with dropsy, a condition in which fluids build up between the wall of the abdomen and the internal organs. "He put down a book to converse for he is fond of conversation," Hayes recalled. "I had the curiosity to inquire what he was reading. It was (Sir Edward) Coke on (Sir Thomas) Littleton, title *Lapsed Legacies.*"

A discussion of the legal textbook ensued, prompting Robinson to reminisce about his days as a judge and an attorney in Texas. Robinson told the story of a man named Campbell whom he sentenced for murder, perhaps the same man he had ordered hanged lest his friends break him out of jail. He also told Hayes about his time at the Perote prison and the communication from Santa Anna that he had carried back to Sam Houston in Texas. And he talked about his wife, who was among the first Anglo women to settle in San Diego. The end seemed near; Robinson was looking back. [202]

At the annual meeting of the San Diego & Gila Railroad board of directors, however, Robinson felt well enough to accept reelection to the presidency,[203] but death clearly was on his mind. At some point, Robinson told his brothers at the Masonic Lodge of his plans to donate a large piece of property between the Playa and Old Town for use as a Masonic cemetery. Before he could complete the legal paperwork, however, he died.

As a band provided by the First Dragoons played a dirge, the largest procession that anyone in San Diego remembered bore Robinson's remains on October 28, 1857, to the piece of land he had in mind for the Masonic cemetery—near the modern-day intersection of Rosecrans Street and Barnett Avenue. Along the way, the carriage carrying his coffin broke down, marring the solemnity of the occasion. "Judge Robinson," as the ex-acting governor was called, was buried according to the Masonic rite. The *Herald* eulogized him as one of the "most prominent" men to have come to San Diego.

Subsequently, representatives of the Masonic Lodge asked Sarah Robinson to complete the act of transferring the cemetery land, but she took no action. Later litigation brought by members of his first family tied up Robinson's estate for many years, ultimately blocking the transfer.[204] On November 20, 1857, school board trustees had the sad duty of making out a check for $12—reduced from the previous $15—for the rental of the school room, not to James W. Robinson, as was the custom, but to his widow.[205]

Robinson-Rose House, Old Town

Map of Roseville

CHAPTER 4

Rose on His Own

Beset by Creditors

As 1858 dawned, Louis Rose probably never felt more lonely or bereft. His best friend and mentor, James W. Robinson, was dead. Financial problems reminiscent of those that had prompted his departure from New Orleans were mounting. His mining ventures were not paying off. Friends were making pointed demands for repayment of the money they had loaned him. How could he get out from under this situation?

In January, Rose reportedly sold a 50 percent interest in one of his mines for $30,000[1]—enough money to permit shipment of 1,000 tons of ore-bearing material and to carry on operations, but not enough to pay his debts. In February, he told the *San Diego Herald* that he discovered a new vein, for which he had high hopes.[2] But he received news in April that would discourage other men, an assay of a sample from his copper mine indicated that it contained only 9 percent ore, too little to be worth shipping. Relaying this news to Morse, A.J. Chase of San Francisco wrote, "The sooner he is convinced of its worthlessness, the better for all concerned."[3] On May 1, Chase wrote again to report that an assay of another Rose sample came in at 9½ percent copper—still not enough but close enough to make further testing desirable. An assayer would be sent to San Diego to do a test on site, Chase wrote. If a sample were to average "10 to 12 percent" it will pay to ship," he said. "But it would be better if possible to assort it at 15 percent." Then, too, there was the problem and expense of transporting the copper approximately 10 miles from the mines to where it could be loaded on boats on the lagoon known as Agua Hedionda. "We shall want to be assured that Mr. Rose will commence at once to haul it to the beach as soon as the one is assorted."[4]

Recognizing that he was in difficult financial straits, Rose sold six horses and six mules, more than a third of his stock on the hoof, to Henry Marks for $700. Hopeful that he could rescue his financial affairs, Rose wrote a proviso into the agreement: "If I pay the above sum back again in or within 40 days from this date, then this sale is null and void, and otherwise remain in full force."[5]

Rose also proposed to settle with his creditors at 60.5 cents on the dollar. Chase's partner, Daniel Breed, wrote from San Francisco to Morse. "I should like to receive the whole amount but am willing to do as others will."[6] Soon, however, the cash-strapped Rose was asking his creditors to accept 39 cents on the dollar. "I am disappointed," Breed thundered to Morse. Noting that 39 percent of what Rose owed him amounted to $111.50, he instructed Morse to send that amount by the next steamer. "I am in want of money very much," the San Francisco merchant admitted. "All you can send will help me and enable me to keep you well supply (sic) with goods."[7]

When Rose questioned what the likely charges would be for assaying diggings from his mine, Chase expressed irritation in a letter on June 3 to Morse. "Please say to Mr. Rose that we have no means of knowing what an assayer would charge for assorting the ore," he said. "If he don't think it will pay to have the ore assorted, it will certainly not pay to ship it... As to the length of time it will take it will be longer or shorter as the case may be. I think Mr. Rose is 'all things to all men' and not much account anyhow. I am sorry that you did not fully secure yourself for your own sake—for I think that Mr. Rose is just the man that would as soon unintentionally do you an injury as a favor."[8] That San Diegans who personally knew Rose disagreed with this harsh assessment of him was made obvious by a letter that Chase sent two weeks later. "I think that you have been rather too merciful for your own interest in Rose's case but the good book says 'Blessed be the merciful.' We were not aware that a positive proposition was made with regard to the mine. However when you come up, we think we may be able to make an arrangement satisfactory."[9]

An action taken by Rose to settle his debts accounted for the difference in tone of the Chase's two letters. Rose let his creditors know that he was negotiating a large loan from Lorenzo Soto, a wealthy landowner, which would enable him to pay off much of his debts. In the meantime, he suggested, formal suit should be brought against him for the remaining balances—which he would not contest in court. With capital once again at his disposal, Rose began paying down the debts owed to Solomon Goldman, James Donohoe, Andrew Cassidy, L. Strauss & Co., O.S. Witherby, and Daniel Breed. He reserved a larger portion of the loan to pay for the mine operations.

E.W. Morse, Charles Gerson, Solomon Goldman, and W.C. Ferrell agreed to serve as guarantors for the loan that Rose had secured from Soto at an interest rate of 2 percent per month. Additionally, Rose gave Soto mortgages on much of his property holdings as collateral—amounting to 153 land parcels located throughout San Diego County, as well as the Rose Copper Mines themselves "together with all the tools, implements and machinery used in working the same, together with about 300 tons of ore taken out of said mine as well as all the ore to be taken out..." Ores removed from the mine were to be shipped to Soto with the proceeds used to liquidate Rose's debt and interest. The Schneider and Fischer families, who owned the ranch adjoining Rose's holdings in La Cañada de las Lleguas, pledged an additional eight properties as collateral.[10]

Learning of the arrangement, Breed wrote expectantly: "Please see...Rose and get all you can get from him or his lawyer and send by next boat, with as much other funds as possible. I have been short for means to carry on my business, having so much in our hands. It has cramp(ed) me..."[11]

Although Rose was able at last to satisfy some creditors, he was aware that unless the mine produced usable ore, the large mortgage he gave Lorenzo Soto could cause him great financial harm. Much of what he had labored for since arriving in San Diego eight years before with James W. Robinson could be lost. Somewhat bitterly he must have reflected on the fact that his creditors could hound him for payment, even take liens against his property, but when the government was the debtor, as it was to him for the loan made to Lieutenant George Derby for the building of the dike on the San Diego River, all he could do was petition sweetly that his money please be paid to him. On July 13, the Washington, D.C., firm of Tucker & Lloyd wrote to Rose's attorney, A.S. Ensworth, in regard to the debt. "We have to state that there are no means yet available for the payment of those claims, and the settlement must necessarily be deferred until means are provided by Congress. An appropriation has been asked for..."[12]

Asking is not receiving, as Tucker & Lloyd had to concede in an October 19 letter to Ensworth. "The claims are evidently good but there is no money to pay them, the appropriation made for the improvement of the San Diego Harbor being exhausted. An appropriation has been asked of Congress to pay arrearage due on account of this and other public works and we have reason to believe one will be made at the next session..."[13] One could not spend such assurances.

Franklin vs. Franklin

Other familiar San Diego figures were experiencing troubles in 1858, perhaps none more spectacularly than the Franklin brothers. After purchasing the Exchange Hotel from George B. Tebbetts, Lewis and Maurice Franklin had the building extensively refurbished and reopened as the Franklin Hotel. Their February 6 advertisement boasted that the hotel was as fine as any in San Francisco, having such features as baths, livery stable, billiard saloon, and bar, the latter of which "will always be supplied with the choicest wines, liquors and segars."[14] The *Herald*, ever friendly to advertisers, suggested in its editorial columns two weeks later that the Franklin House "is now the best in all Southern California."[15] But the rosy press notices stopped March 13, when Lewis Franklin announced in the paper, "The interest of Maurice A. Franklin in the business of the hotel keeping and conduct of the Franklin House ceased on the 4th instant. The subscriber from this date becoming sole proprietor respectfully solicits a share of the public patronage pledging himself to use his best endeavors to please."

No doubt the public took greater notice of the postscript that Lewis Franklin attached to the advertisement:"I hereby give notice to the public that I will in no way become responsible for any debts contracted by my brother on his behalf and request all demands against himself individually or the Franklin House to be rendered for immediate adjustment."[16] The fight between the brothers took another turn the following week when, right under a repetition of Lewis Franklin's ad, appeared another ad which stated:"I, Maurice A. Franklin, give public notice that the above advertisement inserted by Lewis A. Franklin, purporting to announce a dissolution in the firm of Franklin & Brother, of which firm I am a partner, is without my knowledge or consent."[17]

In a town where litigation substituted for entertainment, the fraternal fracas promised to relieve the boredom. On April 3, the *Herald* reported:"Not an item of news can be scared up in this blessed town. The only thing that has occurred to mar the harmony of our placid existence is a small-sized fight that came off in front of the Franklin House, on Sunday last, between two children of Zion, in which there was no bodily injury to either of the belligerents, though one of them was pretty scared." So amused was the *Herald* that it offered a quatrain of doggerel:

> Children you should never let
> Your angry passions rise;
> Your Jewish hands were never made
> To teach each others' eyes.[18]

Franklin & Brother was put into receivership on May 4. Judge Benjamin Hayes appointed George A. Pendleton as receiver. The responsibility of running the Franklin Hotel was assigned to former Sheriff Joseph Reiner. Attorneys for the brothers worked out an agreement that each could retain his respective sleeping quarters and each should have kitchen privileges in the hotel pending resolution of a lawsuit brought by Lewis against Maurice.

In that lawsuit, Jesus Gonzales, who worked at the hotel, and Hyman Mannasse, who sold it furnishings, both testified that Maurice's young wife, Victoria, felt that Lewis had been so insulting to her that she refused to come down to the common dining room for meals, preferring to eat in her own room.[19] The brothers accused each other of shirking duties and cheating each other. It was an awful spectacle, which, of course, the citizens of San Diego relished.

Ultimately Judge Hayes ordered Maurice to pay $1,111.64¼ owed to Lewis, and dissolved the partnership. The judge found that "about the 4th day of March, 1858, the harmony of said partners was finally broken by and in consequence of their mutual misconduct and there ensued between them a state of wrangling, discord, violence and of an irreconcilable ill will, proving wholly inconsistent with the safe and profitable transaction of said business." Except for a quantity of pharmaceuticals that Maurice had brought to the business, the remainder of the personal effects were declared common property and were ordered sold at auction to meet the hotel's debts. Any proceeds left over were to be divided equally between the feuding brothers.[20]

Louis Strauss and Charles Gerson had a business breakup of another sort. As he long said was his intention, Strauss relocated from San Francisco to San Diego. He then took over the store that Gerson had managed for him. Gerson, whose wife gave birth to a daughter in October 1858, decided after so many years being the manager, he was not cut out to be the second fiddle. So on November 13, he announced he had rented a store once occupied by E. W. Morse. Henceforth, he would sell dry goods, clothing, and provisions "cheaper than anyone in town," especially, one supposes, his former boss, Louis Strauss.[21]

The Great Seaweed Adventure

There were probably a variety of reasons why Louis Rose looked to the ocean for another business in 1859. First, he may have realized that his heavily mortgaged copper mines were requiring more and more capital, which he did not have. Another business requiring labor but not much capital was an investment worth trying, particularly if it generated fresh capital. Additionally, he may have thought that if treasures could be mined from land, why not from the sea, which lay available to anyone's exploitation?

The business he conceived still has people scratching their heads in wonder. He saw the large beds of kelp off San Diego and decided to harvest them. Many decades later, scientists would learn that kelp could provide a rich source of pharmaceuticals as well as a congealing agent that would be used in many processed foods. But Rose saw in the fast-growing sea plant another possibility as was outlined in the *San Diego Herald* on January 29, 1859: "Our public-spirited fellow citizen, Louis Rose, Esq., has commenced the manufacture of mattresses. They are made of seaweed in an exceedingly soft and pliable texture. The weed is subjected to a simple and winnowing process, by which it is divested of its offensive impurities and at once rendered fit for use. The floating whale lair, thus cleansed, is superior to wool, straw or moss, and is nearly as soft and durable as hair. The introduction of manufactures of every description in our state is what is now required to render us prosperous and independent as a people."[22]

Southern Californians were all for independence—in fact, they finally were able to pass legislation calling upon Congress to sever California into two states—but stuffing their mattresses with seaweed was simply an idea before its time. It still is.

Bad timing also bedeviled the campaign to make Southern California a separate state. As the United States came closer and closer to its Civil War, any proposal that could extend the territory where slavery was permitted was unlikely to win the favor of northern, anti-slavery interests.[23] Eventually, the Civil War made the issue moot. Ironically, in the twentieth century, the idea of splitting California was renewed almost on a yearly basis, unsuccessfully, by Northern Californians alarmed over the growth of Southern California and the southern portion of the state's corresponding dominance over state politics and resources, especially water use.

The merchant Strauss apparently didn't fare well in the competition with his former storekeeper, Gerson, because by March 1859 he decided to sell off his stock and move back to San Francisco. Another merchant, Henry S. Burton, defaulted on numerous loans, producing the same flurry of lawsuits to which Rose had been subject the year before. Maurice Franklin, meanwhile, moved with his wife Victoria to the San Bernardino area, while brother Lewis Franklin regained an interest in the Franklin Hotel. However, the Tebbetts family, who owned the structure when it was known as the Exchange Hotel, obtained the controlling interest and ran it again. Eventually, Lewis Franklin quit San Diego for the East Coast.

The San Diego Incident

One factor in Lewis Franklin's departure may have been what has become known in Jewish annals as the "San Diego Incident." Members of the Grand Jury wanted to finish their business on a Saturday, so that they wouldn't have to reassemble on a Monday. Considering a routine assault to which Moses Mannasse had been a witness, the Grand Jury issued a subpoena for him to testify. Unfortunately, Mannasse was seated in a room in the Franklin Hotel, a short distance from the court house, participating in Jewish High Holy Day services. When Deputy Sheriff Joseph Reiner delivered the subpoena, Mannasse declined to accompany him back to the Grand Jury proceedings, explaining that his presence as a tenth man was needed by his fellow Jews in order to have a *minyan* to pray. Furthermore, it was the holiest day of the Jewish year, and the Sabbath to boot. Reiner explained the situation to the Grand Jury, which instructed him to bring Mannasse back by force, if necessary. So Reiner tried to bring Mannasse back, but fellow congregants interceded. Finally, Reiner summoned a posse to physically remove Mannasse and bring him to the Grand Jury room. While seated in the witness chair, Mannasse refused to answer any questions until after sunset when the holiday had ended. Once night fell, Mannasse gave his routine testimony.

The *Herald* complained that the Grand Jury was "overanxious to conclude their labors before sunset, at the expense of the violation of conscience of a good citizen."[24] A much harsher indictment of the Grand Jury boiled from the pen of Lewis Franklin, who years before had been that body's celebrated foreman. In a letter to the *Weekly Gleaner*, a Jewish newspaper in San Francisco, Franklin wrote: "I know not what feeling mostly activates me, in recapitulating to you the occurrences which have disgraced civilization in this our remote little town of San Diego. Were I to say that unmitigated disgust fills my bosom, I would scarcely express myself as a wrong of the nature I shall here recount to you knows no parallel in the annals of the civilized world. An offense has been committed against all decency, and I, in common with my coreligionists, call upon you to give publicity to the matter so that the perpetrators may be marked with the rebuke of scorn by a free and independent press...."[25]

Although no court case actually resulted, the "San Diego Incident" drew national Jewish attention, with Isaac Leeser commenting in the December 22, 1859, edition of *The Occident*: "It is certainly curious that such things should be done under the aegis of liberty and that freedom of conscience should be so singularly offended."[26]

In San Francisco that same year, there was a similar incident. A jury was set to deliver a verdict in a civil suit, but could not because juror Julius Levy had disappeared. Found at a local synagogue, he refused to return to the jury because it was Yom Kippur, the Day of Atonement. A posse was sent to collect him, but he had disappeared. A judge fined him $500 in absentia. When the juror-defendant returned to court the following Monday, the judge said if Christians occasionally were required to deliver verdicts on Sundays, then the holy days of other religions ought not to be sacrosanct either. In a spirit of compromise however, he cut the fine to $250.[27]

Rose Loses His Canyon

Rose's debt to Lorenzo Soto was the subject of a bitterly contested court suit in 1860. Soto said Rose owed him $20,000 principal plus 2 percent interest per month since 1858. Rose responded that he owed only $10,000 plus the 2 percent per month interest. How could there be such a disparity between the two versions? Rose said he signed a $20,000 promissory note to Soto on the understanding that Soto would give him back his previous note of $10,000. He said Soto neither returned the previous note, nor did he advance more money to make up the difference.

Furthermore, Rose told the court, his agreement with Soto was that any ore taken from the copper mine would be shipped to Soto, who in turn would sell it and deduct the proceeds from the note. Soto denied that he had obtained

Rose's notes by fraud, and said the reason he didn't sell any ore Rose had shipped to him was because "it was entirely worthless."

Judge Hayes ruled in Soto's favor, saying Rose legally was in debt to Soto for the sum of $27,416.67. He ordered that as much of the mortgaged property as necessary be sold to satisfy Soto's claim and to cover $156.65 in court costs.[28] In settling his account with Soto, Rose was forced to turn over seventeen properties. These included a dozen parcels which totaled 1,700 acres as well as various city lots and buildings within the Old Town area, including the one at which Rose conducted his principal business as a butcher.[29]

Although he no longer owned all of Rose Canyon, by this time Rose had turned away from his tanning business. He still retained some interest in his mines, and, what would be more important in the future, he also retained his extensive acreage near San Diego Bay in the area that after the Civil War he would develop into Roseville.

Growth of San Diego's Jewish Community

Meanwhile, there was a growing feeling of community among Rose's fellow Jewish settlers in 1860, perhaps fueled by the incident at the previous year's High Holy Day services. Hyman Mannasse, whose cousin Moses had been the focal point of the incident, led a campaign to raise funds on behalf of oppressed Jews in North Africa.

Their plight had been receiving worldwide attention since 1857 when Batto Sfez, a Jew, was executed in Tunisia for having blasphemed Islam. Following the execution, France had attempted to force the Bey of Tunisia to grant equal rights for all religions, prompting insurrections by Muslims that spread through the Sahara.[30] Hyman Mannasse's exertions were in behalf of a group of Moroccan Jews who, in fleeing such persecution, had arrived destitute on Gibraltar. The *Herald* editorialized:

> It gives us great pleasure to observe, as we did by the last number of the *(Weekly) Gleaner*, published at San Francisco, that the Jews of California have been the most liberal of contributors to the fund. We noticed particularly that our little burg contributed its quota, but in enumerating the donations we see that the whole amount is credited to the liberality of Mr. H. Mannasse. The sum total is $61, of which amount we learn he "pungled down" the handsome sum of $10. With a very little trouble and the paper in other hands, we have been assured by a friend of the cause, the amount could easily have been doubled. At any rate it is a praiseworthy and charitable movement,

and reflects credit upon Jew or Gentile who contributed to
the fund.[31]

Apparently, after only a brief interlude, Ames was reverting to form. The
above-quoted "news item" was as snide as numerous *Herald* stories over the
years in which Jews were the subjects. Take for example, an item that appeared
two months earlier about a store owned by J. Meiers: "The universal variety
store of our friend Meiers, on the corner of Washington and Rose Streets, has
just received a large addition to its already extensive stock, so that there is now
scarcely anything, from a cooking stove to a jewsharp, in the hardware line;
from a ten-ton stock of flour to a can of roast turkey, in the way of provisions;
from a barrel of whisky to a bottle of native California wine on the liquor list,
or from a bale of sheeting to a stick of tape on the dry goods side of the house,
that you cannot be accommodated with at the shortest possible notice."[32]

A jewsharp—a small piece of metal that can be held in the mouth and
twanged with the finger—was hardly a major item in Meier's inventory, if he
carried it at all. The editor simply wanted, oh so cleverly, to once again remind
his readers that Meiers was a Jew. In itself, this was hardly cause for major complaint, but, as we have seen, it was part of the pattern of the *Herald's* coverage,
indicating to members of the Jewish community—so soon after the High Holy
Day incident—that although they had gained political and commercial promi-
nence in San Diego, to some eyes they would always be the outsiders, the "others."

Judge Benjamin Hayes recorded in his diary an expression of the growing
Jewish self-awareness. He noted that Louis Rose had borrowed from R.E.
Doyle *A Short History of the Ancient Israelites* by Claude Fleury. The judge said
he planned to read the book after Rose finished.[33]

Later in 1861, under the leadership of Marcus Schiller, the Jews decided
formally to organize their own congregation. On June 20, 1861, the following
letter appeared in the *Weekly Gleaner.* "San Diego—A meeting was held by us,
the few Israelites at the above place. Mr. Marcus Schiller being called to occupy
the chair, he opened the meeting by stating the object of the call: to form ourselves into a congregation. This proposition was unanimously adopted... Since
we could number ten persons only, it was resolved to call our congregation
Adath Yeshurun and resolved also that we solicit the Reverend Dr. Julius
Eckman, the editor of the *Gleaner* to aid us in instructing us by sending us a
form of Rules and Regulations for our guide, and hereby enable us to succeed
in our laudable undertaking."[34] Adath Yeshurun also was spelled "Adath Jeshurun."

However the name is transliterated from Hebrew, it means "Congregation
of the Righteous." The "leading spirits" of Adath Jeshurun "were Marcus
Schiller, J.S. Man(n)asse, Louis Rose, Rudolph Schiller and I.J. Asheim, all men
it was my privilege to know," Samuel I. Fox wrote in 1922. "Services were held
principally on the holidays at one of the residences, very often at the home of
Marcus Schiller, who was president of the congregation."[35]

Not long after Adath Yeshurun's establishment, Rose deeded to it five acres for a cemetery in an area that would adjoin Roseville. Schiller and his business partner, Joseph S. Mannasse—the brother of Heyman—donated sufficient lumber to erect a fence around the cemetery. Approximately fifty pepper trees were planted on the grounds.[36]

Nearly thirty years later, when Schiller and other congregants of Adath Yeshurun decided it was time to build San Diego's first synagogue building, they renamed their association as Beth Israel—or House of Israel.[37]

Neither the formation of Adath Yeshurun nor the conveyance of the cemetery by Rose to the organization was reported in the *Herald* for the simple reason that the newspaper had gone out of business—a victim, it might be said, of the Civil War. Up until 1860, political forces favoring the partition of California into two states—a northern "free" state and a southern "slave" state—had been subsidizing editor Ames to militate for the split. But when it became obvious that the North and the South would go to war against each other, there no longer was any purpose to such advocacy. So the investors pulled the plug, leaving San Diego without a newspaper until the *San Diego Union* published its inaugural edition on October 10, 1868.

Although California sat out the American Civil War, the military conflict shut down much trade while causing money, which always had been tight in Southern California, to become even more difficult to obtain. The demise of the *Herald* did not mean the end of anti-Semitism in San Diego; it simply denied the attitude a public forum. Attorney A.S. Ensworth and Thomas Whaley were partners in a store, which, unlike most other concerns in town, did not accept credit, only cash. People who owed money elsewhere therefore were afraid to be seen shopping in their store as it would be an admission that they had disposable cash. In a letter January 25, 1862, which showed how hard times can bring anti-Semitism to the surface, Ensworth complained to Whaley:

> Nobody has money down here. On yesterday, I gave Witherby $1,000 of Hinton's money, and took a mortgage on his ranch. Couts has been to me to get $1,000 on the same money, on mortgage, but I do not like the security. These have been supposed to be the most money men in the county. I think some of starting a new currency down here—cowries, using abalone shells for the shells they use in the east for that purpose. The fact is, if a man gets money enough to buy a bag of flour, he dare not come to me for fear some of the Jews will find it out and sue him. Many is the time they have come for it after dark, for fear of being seen by some men whom they were owing. As I said to you in my letter, you seem not to have read, you had better hold onto the goods a little until we see what is what, if I don't mistake, some of these Jews will burst up...[38]

If anti-Semitism were not at an end, neither was philo-Semitism. The Masons elected Marcus Schiller as their worshipful master in 1861, and from 1862 to 1867, Rose served again as tyler for the lodge. Meanwhile Rose continued to support himself as a butcher, miner, and retailer during the depression days of the Civil War, often accepting hide and wools in payment. On July 2, 1863, D.N. Breed, whose opinion of Rose had improved since Rose paid his debts, wrote from San Francisco to his agent, E.W. Morse:

> Say to Mr. Rose that we should be pleased to receive his wool and hides and will sell it at the highest market price. Wool and hide buyers come to us in the mail and every steamer. Your box of copper ore was received all right. Some of the specimens look well. Those from Rose's mine the best... Glad you are taking an interest in the mining cause of your county. Keep it before the people and stir them up and San Diego will yet come out all right. I have much faith in it (that is the county).[39]

An engraved invitation to the social event of the year for San Diego's small Jewish community read: "The pleasure of your company is respectfully solicited to attend the nuptial ceremony of Hyman Mannasse and Hannah Schiller at the residence of Marcus Schiller, San Diego, June 26, 1863, ceremony at 3 o'clock p.m." Rose officiated at the wedding that united the siblings of the two principals of the firm of J.S. Mannasse & Co., which was growing in strength and prestige in San Diego. That he was sufficiently versed to perform the ceremony was one more confirmation of Rose's deepening commitment to Jewish religious life.

Almost immediately after the marriage, Hyman set out on a cattle drive to Arizona, leaving Hannah practically destitute and forcing her to take shelter in the home of her brother Marcus[40]—a situation that may have caused Rose considerable remorse as it was very similar to the way he had left Caroline on her own. The Mannasse-Schiller marriage ended three years later in divorce. On February 13, 1867, Hannah married Hyman's brother, Joseph, in a ceremony officiated by a visiting rabbi from San Francisco, Abraham Galland.[41] It is possible that Rose was the intermediary who introduced the couple to the rabbi, as the rabbi and Rose's nephew, L.S. Rose, had business offices in the same San Francisco building.[42]

Rose Recovers Financially

The year 1864 began on a bright note for Rose. On New Year's Day, he was among eight San Diegans who participated in an excursion near Joseph S. Mannasse's ranch in the Encinitas area. The group located a mine they hoped would prove to be rich in silver and copper ore. Rose filed a claim for 200 feet of mine, "with all the dips, spurs and angles" and adjacent claims were filed by Mannasse, Marcus Schiller, E.W. Morse, Joshua A. Sloan, A. Adams, A.W. Luckett, and I. Rent. The group also claimed an additional 200 feet "by right of discovery" bringing the aggregate claim to 1,800 feet. Located about 300 feet north of the Encinitas Silver and Copper Lode, the new claim was named the Saint David Silver & Copper Lode by the hopeful and happy New Year's group.[43]

Rose had recovered financially sufficiently enough on February 4, 1864, to purchase back from Lorenzo Soto for $600 both the two-story adobe building in which his butchering business was located as well as another parcel of land in Old Town.[44] Evidence of the continuing regard in which he was held by his fellows came on March 1, 1864, when George A. Pendleton, school superintendent, appointed him as a trustee of School District No. 1, filling a vacancy caused when incumbent E. Van Vackenburgh moved out of the county.[45]

In 1864, Rose was elected anew to the three-member county Board of Supervisors, and, in deference to his service on that board a decade before, his colleagues Cave Couts and Joseph Smith elected him as chairman. He was reelected as chairman the next two years before finally leaving the board.[46] Despite the general scarcity of cash, a San Diegan was able to report in September 1864: "The merchants here are all doing well, or rather very busy. Tebbetts in the plaza sells beef at 4 cents per pound, feeds his beef cattle on hay at $40 per ton, and is doing a thriving business... Rose sells beef by the quantity, a bit will buy any quantity. He is also doing well."[47]

It is possible that Rose's financial recovery was on the strength of his butcher business and mining interests. There are no surviving records indicating just how successful those enterprises were. According to a remembrance years later by a family member, Rose made a point of never writing down the details of his business dealings, preferring to keep track of such matters in his head.[48] There was a strong possibility that Rose had financial backing from his brother Simon's son, Ludwig S. Rose. The nephew—who later Americanized his name to "Louis"—had migrated from Germany to the San Francisco area in time to establish himself and take out an advertisement in *The San Francisco Directory* for the year commencing December 1865. The advertisement introduced him to the community as "L.S. Rose, Stock and Exchange Broker, 617 Montgomery Street, west side between Washington and Merchant, San Francisco. Legal tender notes, California and United States bonds bought and sold, mining stock bought and sold on commission, loans negotiated."[49]

With the U.S. Civil War concluded and his nephew living in San Francisco, Rose, the eternal optimist, again was embarking upon the acquisition of land. On January 9, 1866, he purchased property on Juan Street in the Old Town area from the estate of María Clayton for $235.[50] One month after that, he purchased a nearby parcel on Juan Street from the estate of A.S. Ensworth for $415.[51]

Racism in San Diego

Rose was a witness to the shooting of Juan Mendoza by one of his colleagues on the Board of Supervisors on February 6, 1865. He told a coroner's inquest that between 7 o'clock and 8 o'clock that morning: "I saw Cave J. Couts leveling or aiming with a gun at Mendoza who was running across the Plaza. When Mendoza was about 20 or 35 yards from Couts, the first shot was fired. I heard Mendoza uttering some words. I do not know what. When about 5 or 6 yards farther, I heard the second shot fire, but did not see him fall, and saw him running around Lyons' corner. When Couts shot he was about 6 or 8 yards in front of Tebetts' butcher shop."[52]

Couts subsequently testified that Mendoza had threatened him. A jury decided that the shooting had been in self-defense. Latter-day historians have cited this case as evidence of the racism against Mexicans that permeated nineteenth century San Diego society.[53]

As a school board trustee, Rose was among those who supervised Mary Chase Walker, whose written memories of San Diego gave us a picture of the city in middle 1865. She was the first teacher at the Mason Street School, which in modern times has been maintained as a learning museum at Old Town San Diego State Park. In a remembrance, written in 1898, she recalled:

> I arrived on the Bay of San Diego on the morning of July 5, 1865, having been sent to San Diego by the state superintendent of schools in San Francisco. It was a most desolate looking landscape. The hills were brown and barren; not a tree or green thing was to be seen. Of all the dilapidated miserable looking places I had ever seen, this was the worst. The buildings were nearly all of adobe, one story in height, with no chimneys. Some of the roofs were covered with tile and some with earth. I was driven to the hotel which was to be my future boarding place. This was a frame structure of two stories, since burned. The first night at the hotel a donkey came under my window and saluted me with an unearthly bray. I wondered if some wild animal had escaped from a menagerie, and was prowling

around Old Town. The fleas were plentiful and hungry. Mosquitoes were also in attendance. ...[54]

Her narrative possibly described the Franklin House. She eventually rented from Sarah Robinson, for $2 per month, two upstairs rooms in the home the late James W. Robinson had built on the Plaza.

"There were no furniture or stove shops in Old Town at that time, but the people were kind. One lent me a lounge, another a rocking chair. The bed came with the room. An old stove that smoked badly was procured somewhere," the teacher recollected. "Thus I commenced housekeeping. Each room was about 10 x 12 feet. Two large glass doors opened on a veranda, from which I witnessed many amusing scenes. Wild Indians, naked with the exception of a cloth around the loins, stalked majestically across the plaza, their long hair streaming in the wind, or if in mourning plastered with a paste made of grease and ashes. The lumbering Spanish cart could be seen, with the wheels made whole from a cross section of a large log of wood, and usually uttering excruciating cries for lack of grease..."

Walker's mostly Spanish-speaking pupils "were very irregular in their attendance at school, on account of so many fiestas and amusements of various kinds. For a week before a bull fight boys were more or less absent, watching preparations, such as fencing up the streets leading to the plaza," she recalled. The children's families showed the teacher great hospitality, often inviting her to dinners where "sheep, pig or kid were roasted whole in an outside oven..."[55]

Racist feelings were manifested in San Diego nearly a year following her arrival. Walker spotted in J.S. Mannasse's general store a woman whom she recognized as the stewardess who had paid her kindnesses while aboard the steamer between San Francisco and San Diego. She invited the woman to join her for lunch at the nearby Franklin House. When the school marm and the stewardess—who was African American—came in together, there was a murmur of protest. Some patrons actually got up from their seats and left, while others glared at the two women.

California may have been a "free" state, but San Diego was a place where Southern sympathizers abounded and where, in the 1864 presidential election, Abraham Lincoln came in second to General George B. McClellan by a vote of 51-180. Socializing between the races was quite distinctly frowned upon. The uproar was so great that many parents kept their children away from the school and Mary Chase Walker decided to resign as school teacher. One of the trustees, the widower E.W. Morse, obviously didn't join other San Diego residents in condemning Miss Walker. Enchanted by her independent mind, he soon proposed and was married to her. Later in the century, she would become one of San Diego's leading campaigners for granting the vote to women.[56]

Businessman and Civic Leader

Rose, meanwhile, had opened a new general store on Juan Street, causing the San Francisco mercantile firm of Breed & Chase to write worriedly on Nov. 30, 1866, to San Diego merchant E.W. Morse: "...Notice that Rose has opened a new store. How is he doing? Does he cut into your trade?"[57] And when another general store operator closed down his business in San Diego, the San Francisco wholesaler cautioned Morse: "You must not let Rose get too much of the trade."[58]

Rose received good news about his holdings on the Point Loma peninsula. A federal court decreed that the City of San Diego, not the government of the United States, was the successor-in-interest to lands within the municipal boundaries that prior to the Mexican-American War had been owned by Mexico. A July 18, 1867, letter from the U.S. Engineers headquarters in Washington instructed officers in the San Francisco field office to "therefore apply to the city authorities of San Diego for a grant of the land required for defensive purposes, including the peninsula from Point Loma north to a line running east and west at a distance of 1½ miles north of Ballast Point and such other land as you may regard as necessary." The military in no way considered the judge's ruling the end of the matter.

After this letter was forwarded to San Diego City Clerk George Pendleton, the San Diego Board of Trustees—aware that "benefits accruing from such conveyance are incalculable"[59]—was prompt to recommend to the state legislature that it be authorized to cede most of the land to the military. But it noted that Joseph Reiner, O.S. Witherby, and the late N.J. Alexander—the nephew who had come to San Diego to help Louis Rose establish his tannery—each had purchased a tract of land within the designated area. Alexander's holding, purchased at auction on January 25, 1854 for $291, covered 160 acres, including the present-day Fort Rosecrans National Cemetery.[60] As Rose was Alexander's successor in interest, those acres legally belonged to him.

As chairman of the San Diego County Board of Supervisors, Rose helped to determine the local property tax rate. In 1865, the board voted to add $1.20 in local levies to the $1.15 already set by the state, bringing the total tax burden to $2.35 per assessed $100 valuation. The county tax rate included 60 cents for the general fund, 35 cents to offset interest on debts, 10 cents for schools, 10 cents for roads, and 5 cents for contingencies. By the following year, interest payments temporarily had been satisfied, so the local tax rate was lowered to 90 cents per $100 assessed valuation. In 1867, the last year during which Rose served on the board, the local tax rate climbed back to $1.35, reflecting new assessments for interest payments and school spending.[61]

Other duties of the Board of Supervisors included creating new districts for road construction in the county, appointing justices of the peace and members of the Grand Jury, supervising elections within the county, and filling vacancies in public offices. On August 7, 1865, the supervisors were petitioned to appoint a new district attorney, which Couts opposed on the grounds that the September 6 election was too close at hand. Nevertheless, Rose and Smith decided to appoint D.A. Hollister to the position, thereby giving him the advantage of incumbency over G.A. Berezen in the approaching election.[62] However, the stratagem went for naught; Hollister withdrew from the race and Berezen was elected.

The race for state assembly meanwhile was hotly contested between George A. Johnson, a Republican, and D.B. Kurtz, a Democrat. Shortly after the election, both candidates attended a September 18 meeting of the Board of Supervisors. First, Kurtz asked for a recount of the ballots in the Temecula precinct. The board ordered that the ballots be brought forward, but found that there were no ballots accompanying the statement of returns. Smith and Rose thereupon ordered that the vote from the Temecula precinct be thrown out. Next, Johnson asked that more time be allowed for returns to arrive from the far-off Colorado River precinct. In another instance of what today is called "hardball" politics, Smith and Rose denied this request. With two precincts accordingly unrepresented, Kurtz was declared elected to the Assembly on the basis of returns from the other precincts. The vote was 94-23.[63]

Almost overlooked in the controversies regarding the district attorney and state assembly races was the fact that Smith and Rose had won reelection to the county Board of Supervisors with 93 and 86 votes respectively. This was a respectable showing for the two incumbents, but their totals were far out-stripped by that of John Minter who received 114 votes. When the new Board met on November 6, 1865, the members decided that inasmuch as Berezen had been elected, he, rather than Hollister, should be appointed to fill the remainder of the predecessor's term. Kurtz, meanwhile, resigned as a justice of the peace to take his position as an assemblyman in the state capital. Marcus Schiller then was appointed as Kurtz's replacement as a justice of the peace.[64]

Responding to calls for stepped-up road construction, Rose and his colleagues on the Board of Supervisors levied a $2 tax on each able-bodied man in the county, which they could either pay in cash or work off as labor on the roads.[65] Another notable action in 1866 was to appoint former Judge Benjamin Hayes to the office of district attorney to fill a vacancy caused by Berezen's resignation.[66]

In 1867, the Board of Supervisors appointed D.A. Hollister to the position of public administrator[67] and certified the election of District Attorney Hayes to the state assembly. Hayes defeated G.A. Johnson in the latter's second bid for the office by a margin of 148 to 109. In the race for district attorney, there was a near repetition of the Board of Supervisors' controversial meeting to decide the 1865 Kurtz-Johnson contest for state assembly. One candidate, David Hoffman, demanded a recount of the votes cast in the Colorado precinct. When it turned out that no ballots had accompanied the returns, Hoffman urged the Board to throw out the results from the Colorado precinct, just as it had thrown out the returns from Temecula in 1865. But the supervisors reversed their policy, and declined to do so, with the result that Hoffman was defeated by another Johnson—Cullen A. Johnson—by the slenderest of all vote margins, 106-105. Minter thereafter moved that this Johnson be appointed to the vacancy left by Hayes in the district attorney's office. To Rose's later regret, this motion was adopted.[68]

Like Rose, Cullen Johnson knew how to play political hardball. Less than a month after taking office, he decided to seek a felony indictment against Rose, persuading the Grand Jury that Rose on the preceding April 5 and June 26 had violated an ordinance prohibiting county officers from "purchasing, selling, dealing in or any manner receiving for his own use any county warrants, scrip, or other evidence of indebtedness against said County of San Diego." According to the indictment, Rose in April had purchased a warrant for $48 from John Compton, and in June another warrant for $474 from Thomas Lusk.[69] As no records can be found indicating that the case went to trial, and given the fact that Rose some years later would occupy another position of public trust, as a U.S. Postmaster, it is likely that this case was dismissed. Although the indictment obviously was a blow to Rose's ego, economic opportunity in post-war San Diego was far too exciting to permit the entrepreneur to dwell on the insult.

Alonzo Horton Comes to San Diego

Ever since Louis Rose and his friend James W. Robinson began assembling land along the bay front between Old Town and La Playa, Rose had thought and dreamed about creating a new city on the bay, one that would spread its arms in welcome to deep-draught ships from around the world. When Robinson died in 1857, Rose not only was deprived of a friend and mentor, he lost a partner in this vision. Rose's mining speculations thereafter temporarily derailed his dream, and the economic slow down attendant to the Civil War caused its implementation to be pushed back further to some undetermined future date. Ten years after Robinson's death, Rose received another big shock. A developer with equally big dreams, but with more cash reserves, more energy, and a greater ability to stay focused on his objective, came to town. His name was Alonzo Erasmus Horton.

Horton, a native of Connecticut who had started the town of Hortonville, Wisconsin, and later moved to San Francisco, was six years younger than Rose. After arriving in San Diego by steamship, he decided that, with proper salesmanship and verve, some location alongside the bay could become the place of San Diego's future. As most available land was publicly owned, Horton needed

to purchase it at public auction. Only the city Board of Trustees could schedule such an auction, but at the time no such board was legally constituted. How
Horton reacted to this challenge illustrates the man's energy and character.

There no longer was a newspaper in town to chronicle these events, but as
Horton told the story later, he approached George Pendleton, who then was
city clerk, and asked how much it would cost to schedule an election for a new
board of trustees. Told it would be at least five dollars, Horton gave Pendleton
ten. That night they put up notices in three conspicuous places about an election to be held ten days hence. Horton thereafter went with Ephraim Morse
in search of some suitable land.

On the Sunday after his arrival, although he was not Catholic, Horton
attended church services conducted by Father Antonio Ubach in Old Town.
Whereas others put perhaps ten cents apiece into the collection plate, he
deposited $5 in silver, drawing the attention of the congregation and of Father
Ubach. Afterwards the priest asked what Horton's business was in town, and
when he told of his desire that a board of trustees be elected, Ubach asked who
he'd like to see run.

Horton mentioned three whose acquaintance he already had made—
Morse, Joseph S. Mannasse, and Thomas Bush—and Ubach responded, "You
can have them." As Horton told the story, the men subsequently were elected
with 32 votes apiece.[70]

The newly elected trustees agreed to schedule an auction of city lands on
May 10, 1867. Horton purchased 960 acres for $2,165, which figured to 27½
cents per acre. He set about surveying and staking "Horton's Addition." Later
in the year, the land developer suggested to the city trustees that a large amount
of land to the north of his holdings should be set aside for a public park. First
given the prosaic name "City Park," the set-aside acreage nearly a half century
later would become San Diego's cultural pride and joy, Balboa Park.[71]

Horton's ambitious vision for San Diego was based on the same idea that
had fired the imaginations of Robinson and Rose when they had formed the
San Diego and Gila Southern Pacific and Atlantic Railroad Company back in
1854. As the only natural deepwater port between San Francisco and Mexico,
San Diego seemed an ideal terminus for a transcontinental railroad. With the
horrible Civil War over and the issue of slavery all but settled, thoughts turned
to construction of a transcontinental railroad along the 32nd Parallel from
California through Arizona, New Mexico to Texas, where it could be linked to
already existing track running from Texas east to the Atlantic through Louisiana,
Mississippi, Alabama, and Georgia.

New Railroad Stirrings

John C. Fremont was the California trailblazer who had accepted the surrender of Mexican forces at Cahuenga Pass in 1846, had served as the presidential nominee of the newly formed Republican party ten years later, and had become in 1859 a U.S. Senator from California. After serving the Union as an Army general during the Civil War, he became president of the Memphis and El Paso Railroad in 1867.

This news of their fellow Californian potentially playing a major role in the future of a transcontinental railroad system impressed San Diego and Gila Railroad trustees who included Rose, Horton, William Cleveland, George Hyde, George Lyons, Joseph Mannasse, Ephraim Morse, James Pascoe, William Robinson (the son of James), Thomas Whaley and O.S. Witherby.[72] The trustees voted in 1868 to send the president of their board, San Diego attorney William Jeff Gatewood, to Memphis to persuade Fremont to bring his railroad to San Diego. Fremont promised to dispatch General Morton C. Hunter to San Diego to look into the matter.[73]

Spurred by the proposed railroad merger of the San Diego and Gila with the Memphis and El Paso, land speculation became more frenzied in San Diego. While Horton supervised construction and sold lots in New Town, Rose met with the son and widow of James W. Robinson. Wanting to move to ranch land in Jamul (east of San Diego), Sarah and William Robinson were willing to sell to their longtime family friend some seventy landholdings in the western portion of the county, ranging in size from one-eighth of a lot in New Town to a 160-acre spread in Mission Valley. They settled with Rose on an aggregate price of $10,000, recording the sale on May 20, 1868.[74]

Of the seventy parcels purchased from the Robinsons, including their home on the Plaza, none was more important to Rose than a 73½-acre tract along the northwestern shore of San Diego Bay bearing the legal description "South half lot 17."[75] Combined with Rose's own holdings, this Robinson land was the missing part Rose needed to lay out a new town on the bay.

Although Rose did not have the kind of money Horton had accumulated as a merchant in booming San Francisco, he could and did obtain funds from his successful nephew, Ludwig S. Rose. Since his arrival in San Francisco, Ludwig had been consolidating his financial and social standing. On June 15, 1867, the younger Rose became one of the incorporators of the San Francisco Verein, a club for both Jews and Gentiles that was formed for "the promotion of social intercourse and of literary pursuits." The forerunner of San Francisco's Argonaut Club, the verein warned in its bylaws against any conduct "unbecoming a gentleman, or in any way calculated to disturb the harmony or impair the good name or prosperity of the club..." Membership was limited to 275 people who could afford dues of $100 a year. As the club approached its twentieth anniversary, the *San Francisco Morning Call* observed, "Whereas the normal purpose of English clubs was to drink and be merry and the normal purpose of the French clubmen was to gamble, and the purpose of New York clubs was to furnish a place where they may gossip, the essential aim of the San Francisco club appears to be to provide the members with lunch and a place where, at night, homeless outcasts may play a rubber of bridge."[76]

With Horton so active, Rose gearing up, and railroad talk making life in San Diego exciting, Gatewood decided the time was right to start a new publication in San Diego, which hadn't seen a local newspaper since the demise of the *San Diego Herald* in 1860. An attorney and a fellow member of the board of directors with Rose and Horton of the San Diego and Gila Railroad, Gatewood published the inaugural issue of the *San Diego Union* on October 10, 1868.

A letter to the editor in the weekly newspaper's second issue on Oct. 17, 1868, questioned whether the San Diego and Gila Railroad should continue to lay claims to 2 leagues of public land that had been entrusted to it before the Civil War for the purpose of building a railroad. The letter writer, under the pseudonym of "A Voter," asked "What is to be done with those two leagues of Pueblo Land that were donated over 15 years ago for a railroad under quite different auspices by a confiding people in their first impulse to promote the interest of the community? Things were in their infancy then; we knew no ring that would descend to anything for self as we see and hear too much of nowadays."

Someone favoring the railroad's interest, signing himself, "Also a Taxpayer," responded in the following issue of the *Union*: "It is true that the authorities did make a donation of two leagues of land to the company. But, our friend, mystified from some cause, be it what it may, was unable, or not generous enough to admit that the donation as made was not to be fulfilled until after the completion of the road."[77]

Union General William Rosecrans was among the agents on the East Coast speaking in behalf of San Diego's interests. Writing to Morse, Rosecrans enunciated eight points he planned to utilize in urging Congress to subsidize a transcontinental railroad route through the southern states that would extend west to the port of San Diego. He said such a railroad would:

> (1) accommodate all the roads from Kansas to the Pacific border...(2) conciliate the commercial and railroad interests of the entire sections lying east of them from New Orleans to St. Louis...(3) give development of the entire body of the country we acquired from Mexico, called the Gadsden Purchase, which must otherwise remain unsettled...(4) enable us to support the frontier troops, on our southern border much more cheaply than at present, and by giving us the power to concentrate troops on that border at pleasure by rail, would diminish the number required in any contingency...(5) attract the trade and friendship, while it would greatly promote the pros-

perity, of the neighboring states of Mexico, as well as our own...(6) offer the railroads which may be constructed in Mexico northern connections...(7) avoid the snowline of the more northerly routes and pass the backbone of the continent at a lower elevation than any route...(8) give an auxiliary depot on the Pacific at San Diego, one of the finest harbors on the Pacific Coast, within 36 hours of San Francisco by water, and only 160 miles distant by land from Fort Yuma, a point for transshipment of goods to the interior of Arizona, Nevada and Southern Utah, which it now requires our San Francisco goods from 45 to 55 days to reach and, at a freight of from $40 to $60 per ton...[78]

Another advocate for San Diego was Union General Thomas S. Sedgwick, whose letter to General W.J. Palmer, treasurer of the Union Pacific Railroad, offered financial and engineering arguments for locating the Pacific terminal of that line at San Diego rather than at San Francisco. He argued:

First, to go to San Francisco will require the construction of 300 miles more of road than to go to San Diego, at a proba- ble cost of say, twenty millions of dollars, which is an enter- prise of great moment... Nor will any greater benefits accrue therefrom in regard to local freights than by going to San Diego, if considered proportional to the cost of construction. ...Tehachape (sic) pass section of the proposed line to San Francisco will be a formidable item of cost in construction, and will entail the operation of a maximum gradient, say twenty miles long, up which a locomotive could draw but about one-fourth of its load on a level; or at least three loco- motives would be required to draw thereon the average load of one locomotive on a grade level. Now the annual cost of operating said gradient would be equal to the cost of operat- ing nearly 120 miles of level road... The cost of the necessary land, in a desirable locality, on which to erect necessary repair and machine shops, and passenger and freight depots, for the Pacific terminus of your road, will be very great at San Francisco, perhaps one million of dollars. Real estate is now relatively higher in San Francisco than elsewhere in the United States, and so soon it shall become known that you want lands for the above purposes, they will be held to fabu- lous prices and you will have to pay accordingly... The propri- etor of New San Diego (Horton) will donate lots for depot purposes and street room for tracks and switches... for car wharfs, etc. I have his proposition to that effect.[79]

These seemingly technical letters from Rosecrans and Sedgwick were not simply dry engineering reports to San Diegans; numerous speculators read these reports with as much attention others might devote to poetry or to a fine novel. These words helped were the keys to unlocking San Diego's dream of becoming an important commercial city. Moreover, if the efforts were successful, land developers Horton and Rose could graduate from the ranks of the simply rich to those of the fabulously wealthy.

Although Sedgwick wrote of San Francisco, it was not the only potential competitor San Diego had to worry about. Engineer A.B. Gray, examining possible routes for an Atlantic and Pacific Railway, reported that building a railroad to the port of San Diego might not be any easier than building one to the port of San Pedro, which served Los Angeles. In order to keep the railroad line inside U.S. territory, and not dip into Mexico, he reported, it might be wisest to cross the San Gorgonio Mountains at a point located about 160 miles northwest of Fort Yuma. "From San Gorgonia (sic) Pass it is 100 miles by the valley of Los Angeles to the Port of San Pedro, and from the same pass likewise to the harbor of San Diego through Temecula."[80] More expensive tunneling might be required to go to San Diego than to San Pedro, but in Gray's opinion, "to reach the fine harbor of San Diego... would be so immeasurably superior."[81]

Roseville Takes Shape

In the January 9 issue of the *Union*, editor Gatewood provided a description of another kind of road—the one that passed through Rose's proposed bayside settlement. After stopping to pay respects to the memory of James W. Robinson, whose grave was "upon a little eminence on the eastern slope of the Loma mountains, and looks complacently upon the busy denizens of Old Town," Gatewood, Morse, and their wives paused a little farther along the La Playa Trail "where the green hillside slopes gently down to the waters of the bay." They found that "innumerable stakes denote the streets and blocks of an embryo city." Gatewood mistakenly called the area under development "Rose City." His description, however, is one of the first we have of the area that in fact became "Roseville."

> The horses cantered gaily over the greensward along the water's verge and our friend took particular pains to inform us that we were passing through the principal street of Rose City, while the lady passengers amused themselves by building airy

castles upon innumerable blocks and filling the streets with industrious citizens. A few minutes more and we were among the ruins of the Playa. At the end of a little wooden walk, not far from the shore, stands a small cabin on stilts in which is kept the tide gauge. Back, some distance from the Bay, stands an old dilapidated building, once occupied by the government as the Custom House, but the only building in which a live soul could be found was the residence of Mrs. Brown. The place is five miles from Old Town and in years 'lang syne' was the place of landing for vessels entering this port to trade for hides...Here we turned around the old Custom House and began the ascent of the mountain. The road, though bad, is not all that difficult...[82]

In need of cash to develop his town site, Rose on February 19, 1869, sold for $1,369.20 to George Cofer 136 acres he had acquired in Mission Valley from James W. Robinson's family.[83] This appeared quite a favorable price to fetch for the land, considering the fact that only three days later Rose purchased 80 undeveloped acres northeast of Old Town from city trustees for only $20, or 25 cents an acre.[84]

Roseville was laid out in grid fashion, with all streets being 75 feet wide except Main Street, which, replacing La Playa Trail, became the major southwest-to-northeast thoroughfare. Main Street, which many years later came to be called Rosecrans Street after the Civil War general and railroad promoter, was 100 feet wide and stretched from 1st Street on the southwest side of the development to 30th Street on the northeast side, closest to Old Town. The courses of four streets below, or southeast, of Main Street were interrupted by the curvature of San Diego Bay. From southeast to northwest they were: Water Street, Front Street, Tide Street, and Short Street. Above, or northwest of Main Street, were five streets named for trees: Locust, Elm, Willow, Pine and Chestnut. The development had two full blocks set aside for public squares. Buena Vista Square, or Block 150, was bounded by Locust, Elm, 19th and 20th Streets. Washington Square, or Block 175, was delineated by Pine, Chestnut, 21st and 22nd Streets.[85] Except for the blocks along the northwest side of Main Street, which had a different configuration intended for commercial use, in each block those lots designated as Lots 1-6 were on the northeastern side of a street, while those designated 7-12 were on the southwestern side. Each of these residential lots had a street frontage of 50 feet and a depth of 100 feet.

When William Lynch paid Rose $450 on March 12 for lots 7-12 of Block 25, at a per-lot cost of $90, he was purchasing a parcel on 3rd Street that stretched from the southeast or bay side of Main Street to the northwest side of Water Street. On the same day, for the same amount, Joel Harland, purchased lots 1–6 of the same block. His land backed up against Lynch's property, while facing 2nd Street.[86]

The commercial lots on Main Street also measured 50 by 100 feet. In this case, however, the lots designated as 5, 6, 7 and 8 were rotated 90 degrees so as to face Main Street rather than the residential streets. This enabled each block on the northwest side of Main Street to have four commercial lots.

Although Rose's sales were but a fraction of Horton's, the entrepreneur could exult that his investment in San Diego and his belief in its future at last were beginning to pay off. On March 13, he sold three residential lots near Front and 2nd streets to David Glass.[87] Four weeks later four local businessmen each purchased some lots on Main Street. Julius Rachfeleke bought a pair at 2nd Street; Max Lowenstein took three lots at 3rd Street; William Cleveland another three at 4th Street; and Gustavus Witfeld three more at 5th Street. Rose received $2,700 for those sales alone.[88] On that date, it became clear to Rose that—given how inexpensively he had purchased the land many years before—he could not lose money on the Roseville development. He would make a profit. The only question was how much.

The *San Diego Union* took note of Rose's development in its April 14, 1869, edition:

> Roseville—The lovely spot of land is beginning to assume an importance and attention worthy of the citizens of San Diego. Over two hundred and thirty thousand feet of lumber have been landed there; fences have been built and are being built; the streets will soon be cleared of the brush, and houses will be started in a few days. The vessel discharging the lumber, anchored but a short distance from the beach, and during the low tide, had over fifteen feet of water beneath her. Mr. Rose, the proprietor of the place, has found water of a good quality, and in sufficient quantity, a short distance from the bay, to justify the belief that no fears need to be entertained for the success of the place on account of good water. The site is one of the finest on the bay and though nothing like so extensive a plateau as at New Town and Horton's Addition, it is beautiful in the extreme, and when built upon will make a more imposing appearance from the bay than any other point upon it. It is situated upon the northern curve of the bay, about half way between Old Town and Ballast Point, or the entrance of the Bay. We predict that within one year from this date it will be as large a place as New Town is today.[89]

Although the newspaper's prediction was far too optimistic, it was predicated upon an undeniable sense of momentum. Max Pollock purchased a lot for $200 on April 9[90] and William Wiley Davis bought two lots on April 12.[91] About this time, Rose purchased from J.S. Mannasse & Co. a consignment of pine lumber that was brought to San Diego aboard the cargo ship *A.P. Jordan*. As there was then no wharf in Roseville, the 230,000 board feet had to be floated on a raft to the shore. The *San Diego Union* advised its readership that "many of our enterprising (sic) citizens are asking permission to build upon and improve their lots." It predicted that the "sound of the hammer will soon break the silence and bustle and activity disturb the repose of our years. Such indications of enterprise and energy on the part of our citizens are extremely gratifying."[92]

The Gallant Rose

Although Rose made lasting friendships with people of all backgrounds and both genders, apparently he hewed to the belief that Jews should marry other Jews, certainly no easy task for one who rarely left the confines of nine-teenth century San Diego. Had he been marriage-minded, Rose might have taken a steamboat up to San Francisco, where the Jewish community was better established and sought introductions. Or, he could have returned to Germany to visit his family, perhaps finding a wife in Hamburg. Occupied as he was with so many business activities, Rose remained a bachelor many years, gratefully accepting invitations to dinners and social events from friendly married couples.

There is reason to suspect that the German-born merchant Jacob Newman and his wife Mathilde (Matilda) were friends of Rose and that they may have had some comparable experiences as German-Jewish immigrants who made their way to the West Coast. When Newman left Matilda a widow, it was natural in a small town like San Diego that the two would be thrown together notwithstanding the fact that Rose was 29 years older than she.

April 24, 1869, was one of the most important days in Louis Rose's life. According to records on file at the county recorder's office, not only did he have considerable real estate activity in Roseville that day; he also took out a license to marry Matilda. Edward Burr, a deputy to County Clerk George Pendleton, filled out a document stating: "I do hereby authorize any judge, jus-tice of the peace, clergyman or preacher of the gospel, to celebrate and certify the marriage of Louis Rose with Mrs. Matilda Newman. In witness whereof I have hereunto set my hand and official seal this twenty fourth day of April AD 1869."[93]

As if to celebrate this marital engagement, which came more than twenty-two years after his first marriage to Caroline Marks, Rose gave away or sold for a pittance a number of lots in Roseville: To José Estudillo, a member of the family that had greeted him on his arrival in San Diego in 1850, Rose sold one lot for $5,[94] and to John Chauncy Hayes, he sold another for the same amount.[95] Additionally, he gifted to Mary Chase Morse—the former school-teacher who married E.W. Morse—two 50-by-100-foot lots as tokens of his "esteem and regard" and for her "better maintenance and support."[96] The gift to Mrs. Morse was the first of many outright grants of land Rose would make to women. Such deeds specified that the property was to be held exclusively in their names, independent of their husbands. As property of wives then was assumed to belong to their husbands, Rose may be considered one of the first males in San Diego County to advocate for women's rights.

Illustrating the value of these gifts, Rose also sold a lot in Roseville on April 24 to James McCoy for $250[97] and another to Thomas Fox for the same amount.[98] Another was sold April 26 to James Giffin[99] and one more on April 26 to Max Pollock for $200,[100] Pollock's second purchase. Rose made another gift of land on April 29, this time to Emma Solomon. Again he cited in the deed of sale his "esteem and regard" for the recipient.[101]

The beginning of May also was busy for the entrepreneur. In rapid succession, he sold 19 lots to 9 buyers for a total of $2,100, while giving 2 other lots away, one of them for a token $1 payment. Among recipients of his gifts on this occasion were Polly Ann Nottage, who paid $1 for her lot and Ellen Bush,[102] who received hers for free. Word of Rose's gallantry spread quickly among his female acquaintances, many of whom probably had set an extra place at their family's table for him on more than one occasion during his long period as a bachelor. Bertha Bernard[103] received a lot on May 4; Pauline Mannasse[104] got one on May 7 and Henrietta Hueck[105] received another on May 14. Other recipients of one lot each were Nellie Pascoe[106] on May 15; Sarah Jane Burr, Mary Taggart and Henrietta Schiller[107], all on May 17; and Mary Gatewood on May 18.[108] Almost as quickly as he was giving away lots, Rose also was selling them. Thomas Judd[109] purchased one for $200 on May 5 and James Hinds and Rufus Porter[110] purchased lots for $250 and $200 respectively on May 6.

May 8 was another big day. To his nephew, L.S. Rose, "in consideration of service heretofore rendered," Rose sold three full blocks of Roseville for $100.[111] Judging by other sales recorded that day, the property at that point was worth close to $6,000. On that same day, R.C. McConnick purchased six lots constituting a half block for $1,000, while Cornelius Cole likewise purchased a half block for $1,000. George Pendleton, meanwhile, bought a single lot for $250.[112]

The brisk pace continued on May 15 with William Weider paying $200 for one lot and Alice Dentler $200 for another.[113] On May 18, the same day Mary Gatewood received a gift from Rose, her husband, W. Jeff Gatewood, also purchased a lot for $200.[114] The attorney had divested himself of the *San Diego Union* two weeks previously by selling it to the partnership of Bushyhead and Taggart.[115]

The Second Mrs. Rose

The Gatewoods took title to their land on May 18, 1869, the same day that Louis Rose and Matilda Newman were married by Judge Thomas H. Bush, whose wife, Ellen, had received a gift of a lot earlier in the month from Rose. Historians have speculated that there may have been a Jewish wedding performed by M. Cohn in addition to the civil ceremony at which Bush officiated.[116]

"Married—At San Diego, May 18, by Hon. T.H. Bush, Mr. Louis Rose to Ms. Mathilda (sic) Newman," read an announcement in the *San Diego Union* published one day later.[117]   No mention was made of a separate Jewish ceremony, nor did the newspaper consider it unusual enough to remark upon the fact that at the time of his wedding Rose was 62 years old, while at 33, Matilda was a little more than half his age. Bavarian-born, Matilda could speak German at home with her new husband, although her dialect differed considerably from Rose's Plattdeutsch.

Thereafter, the second Mrs. Rose maintained a fairly low profile life, she came to public attention for her domestic achievements when *The Hebrew*, a San Francisco newspaper, reported that Mrs. Rose and the wives of Marcus Schiller and Heyman Solomon were all fine cooks who often tried to outdo each other. [118]

Perhaps to spend more time with his bride, Rose decided to engage the services of a real estate firm to help him sell the lots in Roseville. The week following the wedding, Culverwell & Taggart advertised "the very desirable property adjoining La Playa, at the entrance to the Bay of San Diego, known as Roseville, will be sold by us. A limited amount of property is now offered for sale. Here is a rare opportunity for persons who wish to invest."[119] The firm also advertised properties owned by other clients in other parts of the city, which may be why the pace of sales in Roseville slowed down considerably. There were no sales recorded for the rest of May, nor through all of June, and only one sale in July: Louis Dobson purchased a pair of lots for $200.[120] One can assume that by this point or soon afterwards, Rose decided to end his relationship with the real estate firm.

Rose's Investments

Rose did not limit his land speculation exclusively to Roseville. On March 23, 1869, he combined with E.W. Nottage, E.W. Morse, Marcus Schiller, Thomas Whaley, Edward Hueck and William H. Cleveland to form the Crystal Lake Water Company. Notwithstanding the company's romantic name, it was formed "to furnish and supply the County of San Diego and the City of San Diego, and the inhabitants thereof with pure fresh water by conducting, conveying and distributing water of the *San Diego River* (emphasis added) by means of aqueducts, ditches, pipes or otherwise." Corporate papers also said the company would endeavor to provide water for "mining, irrigating, agricultural, manufacturing, domestic and other purposes" in the county. The venture never progressed beyond the conceptualization stage.[121]

Rose also purchased a 10-acre parcel from Jesus Marrino for $200 and another 80 acres of unimproved land from the city trustees. He sold to Heyman Solomon for $1,000 the building on Old Town Plaza that was known as the Barker-Soto Building (which Solomon converted to a restaurant.)[122]

A long-simmering dispute over the ownership of land in Middletown that originally had been subdivided by a group led by Juan Bandini came to a legal head on August 3, 1869, with the filing of a lawsuit by a large group of San Diegans, including Judge Benjamin Hayes, against another group of San Diegans, including Rose. The suit asked the court to determine titles and to partition property within Middletown.[123] That this was "friendly" rather than "hostile" litigation was indicated nine days later when Rose disposed of a small portion of the Middletown land holdings. He gave six lots to his friend Benjamin Hayes for $5, while selling another eight lots for $500 to A. Brunson.[124]

The year 1869 marked the first time in U.S. history that passengers could board trains on the East Coast and make their way by rail to the West Coast, or vice versa. The golden spike for the last link in the transcontinental system was driven May 10 at Promontory Point, Utah, when the tracks of the Union Pacific, 1,086 miles from its terminus in Omaha, Nebraska, were joined with those of the Central Pacific, 689 miles from its terminus in Sacramento.

Early in July, General Hunter, representing the Memphis and El Paso Railroad, made his long-awaited visit to San Diego to promote a more southerly transcontinental rail link. At a town meeting, he was so encouraging about the likelihood of San Diego becoming the western terminus of a second transcontinental railroad that a committee of ten people was selected to solicit contributions of San Diego land to achieve that purpose. Rose and four others were chosen to represent the Old Town area, while five others were selected to represent "South San Diego" as New Town and Horton's Addition were known collectively.[125]

To stimulate interest in his side of San Diego Bay, Rose engaged the firm of D.B. Kurtz in July to construct a "good size building" in the La Playa area, which later became known as the Roseville Hotel.[126] One assumes that Kurtz had more impressive construction jobs on his resume than the old jail, which he had built so many years before in Old Town. Roseville sales resumed in August, with surveyor James Pascoe and Myron Wheeler purchasing lots for $1,200 each.[127] Next, Rose petitioned the Board of Supervisors for permission to build a wharf in La Playa stretching from his bayside property to a point less than 350 feet from the shore. Rose said that the wharf would be 75 feet wide and that an additional 50 feet on either side of the wharf should be dedicated to its use "for the purpose of loading and unloading of ships." He contended in the petition that the "public good will be greatly promoted and it will be of especial benefit to the people of said city."[128] The board agreed to Rose's request, "granting to him, his heirs, executors, administrators and assigns, for the period of ten years from the date thereto, the right to erect a wharf and to use the same upon the tract of lands in said county..."[129] John Blecker, a San Franciscan commented in a letter to E.W. Morse: 'old Rose has a town to himself...I should not be surprised if it became valuable."[130]

The Pear Garden

If latter-day business executives could fault Rose, it would be for failing to exhibit the single-mindedness about developing his bayside property that Alonzo Horton demonstrated. He seemed to have what psychologists today are fond of calling "Attention Deficit Disorder," spending too little time on any project to give it sufficient attention. Given the blessing of finally having a wife, the 62-year-old groom now acted with considerable sentimentality. With $2,000 that he might otherwise have invested in his Roseville project, Rose purchased from D.A. Hollister the romantic Pear Garden in Old Town. This was no doubt a special wedding gift for Matilda.[131]

Captain Francisco María Ruiz, the commandant of the Presidio, planted the garden in 1806—years before soldiers were permitted to build houses in the area that became Old Town. Ruiz's garden was surrounded by an adobe wall and boasted 26 pear trees, 3 olive trees, 2—or possibly 3—fig trees, and an unspecified number of pomegranate trees.[132] Located close to the San Diego River, it also had 2 on-site wells. The garden was beloved by San Diegans who associated it with the elopement in 1829 of Josefa Carrillo and Henry Delano Fitch.

Josefa was said to have caught the eye of Mexican Governor José María Echeandia. However, she was smitten with Fitch, master of the *María Ester*, an American sailing vessel that called frequently in San Diego. To marry her, he converted to Catholicism. Josefa's uncle served as a godfather. The wedding was to occur the next day, but Echeandia forbade the uncle, who worked for him, to serve as a witness in the wedding. The ceremony was called off, and Josefa, heartsick, was said to have whispered, "Why don't you carry me off, Don Enrique?"

The next night, Josefa waited in the pear garden. Pio Pico (who later would become the last Mexican governor of California) rode one horse while leading another for Josefa. She sped to the *Vulture*, a ship owned by a friend of Fitch's, and, with the lovers aboard, the ship promptly put out towards sea. Before it could reach the open waters of the Pacific Ocean, it had to sail beneath the guns of Fort Guijarros. One can imagine how tightly Henry and Josefa might have held each other as the scary passage was made—without incident.

The couple was married in a Catholic church ceremony in Chile, and eventually they were forgiven by Josefa's parents.[133]   Finally married after a long, lonely bachelorhood, Rose may have felt as giddy about Matilda as Fitch felt about Josefa. Owning the Pear Garden also may have invoked happy memories of Rose's boyhood in Neuhaus-an-der-Oste. Although smaller, the Pear Garden—which later became known as Rose's Garden—could not fail to remind him of pleasant excursions to Graf Bremer Park in the neighboring village of Cadenberge.

Visit of William Seward

Tempting as it might have been to spend lazy days with Matilda in the shade of a pear tree, railroad developments soon lured Rose from his garden. On September 22, 1869, the *San Diego Union* reported on one of the most famous Americans to visit San Diego to date: former Secretary of State William Seward, the man who two years earlier, as part of the Cabinet of the seventeenth U.S. President, Andrew Johnson, had arranged the American purchase of Alaska from Imperial Russia.

Seward arrived in San Diego for a visit accompanied by a pair of congressmen and several former Civil War generals, including William Rosecrans, Morton Hunter and Thomas Sedgwick. While Seward stayed in New Town at the home of G.W. B. McDonald, many others in the traveling party went to Old Town to attend a function hosted by Joseph S. Mannasse and Marcus Schiller. Louis Rose was among the notable citizens who offered a toast to the men who might secure San Diego's future by bringing a railroad. Later, back in New Town, 500 people crowded into Gregg's Hall to meet Seward, while another 1,000 waited outside to catch a glimpse of him.[134]

Sedgwick, chief engineer of the Memphis and El Paso, said he expected to be able to start quickly upon construction of the railroad from San Diego. Citizens assured him of their support for trading for Memphis and El Paso stock the land rights once enjoyed by the San Diego and Gila, Atlantic and Pacific Railroad. With such assurances, surveying soon began.[135]

Excitement generated by Seward's visit—and its portent for San Diego's future—was reflected in Rose's land sales. On September 23, he received $800 from George Ligare for another six lots in Middletown, $600 from Andrew Shaw for two lots in Roseville and $300 from James McCoy for another Roseville lot—for a single day total of $1,700.[136] Five days later, he sold three lots in Roseville to Samuel Lambert for a total of $2,500.[137]

The Gallant Rose, Part II

Having by this time made gifts of lots in Roseville to eleven other women for their "better support and maintenance" and in consideration of his "esteem and respect" for them, what kind of land grant did Rose plan for his own wife? He answered that question on September 28, formally conveying to her for her own use, three full blocks of Roseville, the equivalent of thirty-six lots.[138]

On October 5, 1869, Rose presented one Roseville lot to Melinda Burkhart and another to Hattie Wallace, charging each of them the nominal sum of $1 for the property. He made gifts of adjoining lots in Roseville to Rebecca Schiller, and her sister-in-law, Hannah Mannasse, on November 3.[139] He required men, on the other hand, to pay dearly for Roseville lots. Thomas Sedgwick, the railroad representative, paid $500 for two lots; Howard Volney paid $450 on October 23 for two others, and Simon Jackson paid $500 on December 6 for two more.[140] Always in need of cash, Rose disposed of holdings in other parts of the city and county, raising $510 during the balance of 1869 through five transactions.[141]

The tightness of money may have been one factor leading members of the Jewish community of San Diego, including Rose, to gather on June 2, 1870, at the home of Marcus Schiller, where they adopted the following resolution: "Whereas the population of Israelites in Old and South San Diego has been and is increasing rapidly, it become necessary that we establish a society strictly in accordance with our faith, for the purpose of assisting the needy, attending the sick and burying the dead."[142]

About the same time, David Glass, Joel Harland and William Lynch, who were among the original investors in Roseville, came to Rose asking permission to sell him back their lots. He refunded their money, a total of $1,050.[143]

Promoting San Diego

Possibly at the instigation of the newly formed San Diego Chamber of Commerce, which held its inaugural meeting January 22, 1869, at the 6th and F Street store owned by David Felsenheld,[144] the *San Diego Union* published in March a special edition telling about San Diego's history, climate, and geography. The tone of the article suggests that the special edition was underwritten principally by Alonzo Horton, whose interests the article served well.

Ostensibly, the idea behind the edition was for local residents and businessmen to send copies of the newspaper to potential investors and settlers around the country. While the overall mood was one of optimism, a close reader can detect that even in the promotional article, growing tension between "Old Town" and "New Town" could not be papered over. Within the article, we glimpse the rivalry then growing among businessmen whose interests lay in the promotion of one section of the city over the other. These indicators of below-the-surface conflict are more valuable to a historian than some of the "facts" presented in the article. For example, although the article estimated the city's population to be 4,000, census records for 1870 set the actual figure at 2,300—only slightly more than half that number.[145]

It told how Horton had his land surveyed, and a town site laid out, adding that "through the indefatigable energy of this gentleman a town speedily arose upon the Addition; people flocked in from far and near, and today there are more than 1,000 buildings and nearly 3,000 people, where in 1867 there was but two or three houses, and some dozen inhabitants." Old Town was given comparatively short shrift. The article reported it:

> …has a population of perhaps 1,000. The county buildings are *at present*(emphasis added) located there, and several mercantile houses carry on a profitable business, supplying the farmers of the interior with provisions, etc. There are two good hotels, which are well supported. The people have faith that this will yet be a place of importance, their belief based upon the fact that the deepest water is found off 'La Playa' on the peninsula which divides the true harbor from the ocean and False Bay, and at the base of which the town is situated. It is contended that upon the completion of the railroads to this port heavy freights will be shipped from wharves running out from La Playa and Roseville, on the same peninsula…[146]

Whether because of this article, or in spite of it, four days after it appeared, Rose sold three Roseville lots to Roger Thornburgh for $500.[147] On April 1, he sold three more lots to W.D. Whipple for $1,000 and also sold a 40-acre parcel for $1,000 to Sister Scholastica Lagdson.[148]

The feeling was contagious that San Diego's eventual success was inevitable. In Spring, Western Union proposed building telegraph lines between Los Angeles and San Diego, provided that San Diego would guarantee that the company would receive at least $8,000 worth of business within three years of construction. Subscriptions were sought, payable once the lines were erected. San Diegans promptly pledged $4,710, with the biggest subscribers being A.E. Horton for $1,000; the *San Diego Union* for $1,000; J.S. Mannasse & Co $750 and Louis Rose $200.[149] Rose's confidence in the future of Roseville proved prescient, at least in the short term. The block for which he had refunded $900 to Harland and Lynch he sold again on May 21, for $1,700, to David Robinson.[150] Eight days later, the entrepreneur all but gave away another lot to Thomas Slade for $25.[151]

Except for Rose himself, who had erected the large building intended as a hotel, all the landowners in Roseville essentially had been mere speculators, holding their raw land against the day when it would become valuable. Rose recognized that if his settlement were to become anything but a town on paper, he needed to make something happen. On June 9, the *San Diego Union* reported: "We are informed that Mr. Louis Rose has commenced building a wharf at Roseville and will push the work of construction with his characteristic energy."[152]

Rose also was dabbling in real estate in other areas of the city. On April 21, he and the heirs of William Leamy reached agreement on how to split the large tract of land in Middletown that Rose and Leamy had acquired from Bandini. Rose and the group of heirs each retained approximately forty-two lots for their exclusive use.[153] In June, Rose affected another trade of his land with the Serrano family in Old Town in an effort to straighten the property line between their neighboring residence and his[154]

On June 14, Rose sold three lots in Roseville to Benjamin Truman for $400.[155] Sales now were long in coming, and the lots were selling for considerably less than they had the previous year.

The Memphis and El Paso Failure

Rose was not the only one whose plans were frustrated by a tight money supply. The Memphis and El Paso Railroad, born amid such bright hopes, was hamstrung even more severely. The great pathfinder, John C. Fremont, had sought financing in France for his railroad. He was able to persuade investors in Paris to purchase $116,430 worth of bonds, but hoped-for financial backing from the U.S. government did not materialize. Investors scrambled to get their money back.

Among those concerned by the Memphis and El Paso failure were San Diego investors, who dispatched General Sedgwick to cancel various contracts between the San Diego and Gila Railroad and the Memphis and El Paso. To the city's great relief, he was successful.[156]

Notwithstanding investors' skepticism, railroaders considered the Memphis and El Paso's failure to be just a temporary setback. On July 27, a successor corporation, the Southern Transcontinental Railroad Company, was chartered. New York financiers organized a subsidiary company to administer the business on October 31.[157]

Money in desperately short supply, Rose petitioned the county Board of Supervisors on July 5, 1870, stating that he was:

the holder and owner of large amounts of county warrants
drawn by the auditor of said county on the treasury thereof
which warrants have been presented to the said treasurer for
payment and have not been paid for want of funds, which
warrants be at interest at the rate of ten percent per annum,
from the date thereof and amounting in principal and interest
to more than the sum of eight thousand dollars; that there are
in the treasury of said county, moneys of the funds set aside by
law for the payment of the said and like warrants, amounting
to the sum of eight thousand dollars, which are lying idle in
the said treasury, at no interest...[158]

Rose went on to argue in his petition that it made more sense to retire the
interest-bearing debt, and thereby prevent it from growing in size than to leave
the funds in the non-interest bearing account. He then made an offer he hoped
the county Board of Supervisors would not refuse: "If your honorable board
will apply to the payment of his said warrants the money now in the treasury
of said county, properly applicable by law, to the payment thereof, he will
charge and demand no interest thereon." Furthermore, said Rose, he would
forego all interest due since April 7, 1868, a potential savings to the county of
22½ percent.[159] Apparently the request fell on deaf ears; the county Board of
Supervisors took no action on his request.

Old Town vs. New Town

On July 9, Rose became a buyer—rather than a seller—of real estate, purchasing from E. W. Nottage a portion of a block in Old Town and a 25 x 50 foot
lot on 5th Street in New Town.[160] It may have been coincidental, but on the
same day, a majority of the County Board of Supervisors, faced with agitation
from New Town residents to move the seat of the county government to their
more populous portion of the city, voted to remove county records from
Thomas Whaley's brick building in Old Town to a building in Horton's
Addition. Furthermore, they decided that the courts should also be relocated
from Old Town to New Town.[161]

Notwithstanding the recent promotional piece in the *San Diego Union*, in
which potential investors were assured "there is no occasion for rivalry
between the two sections of the municipality," there was rivalry aplenty. Judges
took umbrage at the Board of Supervisors telling them where their courts
should meet. Judge Thomas Bush, a longtime Old Town resident, ordered that
the business of the county court continue to be conducted at Old Town.
District Court Judge Murray Morrison from Los Angeles similarly ordered that

the business of his court's San Diego branch continue at Old Town. When it appeared that the Board of Supervisors planned to move the records to New Town anyway, Judge Bush on July 17 ordered the sheriff to enlist a posse to guard the records. [162]

One of the factors keeping the political skirmishing from escalating into a Hatfield-McCoy-like feud between Old Town and New Town was that the citizens of both areas recognized that they needed to work together to attract a railroad to the city. Both sections of the municipality would benefit if the San Diego dream were to be realized. Accordingly, the factions united to send representatives to Washington to join other cities and states along the 32nd parallel in pressing for passage of legislation by Congress to subsidize a new railroad. Ephraim Morse was put in charge of a campaign to seek donations of land from private individuals to help persuade railroad officials that San Diego was serious about becoming the site of the West Coast terminal.[163]

On September 15, the *San Diego Union* reported:

> We are pleased to learn that the wharf at Roseville will be completed Saturday next. It is built in the most substantial manner and is one of the permanent improvements of our growing town. Mr. Rose is entitled to a great credit for his efforts in this behalf, and we trust the day is not far distant when he may reap a rich reward. Soon as the times will warrant he intends constructing a regular wharf front some sixty or eighty feet in width by about three hundred in length. The deepest sea going steamers can here anchor in safety. We hail the work for the good times coming.[164]

Ironically, a woman who two decades later would become the fifth wife of Rose's rival entrepreneur, Alonzo E. Horton, was among the first to live in the building that Rose had intended for a hotel. Lydia Knapp had arrived in San Diego with her first husband, retired naval officer William Knapp, who had taken the job as the tidal gauge keeper. She never forgot Rose's wharf, which measured 30 feet wide and 472 feet long.

> When we landed here, we had to walk up the long and rather narrow wharf. My husband taking the baby in his arms, left me to follow slowly with our small boy. As we neared the middle of the wharf, we met a formidable looking man of great size, roughly dressed with dark skin and long black hair. I was quite sure he must be one of the wild natives of this unknown region and trembled with fear as he approached as there was no one else near. But he passed by without even training his eyes toward us. When I reached the shore, I met Mr. W.W.

Stewart who laughingly told me that the man was a quite civilized Gay Head Indian from Cape Cod, Mass., who belonged
to the whaling camp at Ballast Point.[165]

The hotel was sat virtually alone. According to historian Elizabeth C.
MacPhail, "the entire area was nothing but a brush-covered desert with only
one dirt road leading from Old Town to the lighthouse at the tip of Point
Loma...The Knapps' closest neighbors were whalers on Ballast Point, a few
Chinese fishermen along the shores of the bay and a Mexican family in La
Playa."[166] Knapp had succeeded Andrew Cassidy as the keeper of the tidal gauge
at La Playa, which he visited twice a day. His wife later recalled that "there were
floats put down in the water and attached to an upright and as the tide rose
there was a sheet of paper on a roll—and as the tide rose, the pencil traveled
across the sheet and would give the rise and fall of the tide."[167]

The tension between Old Town and New Town came to a legal head in
September when Judge Morrison dismissed the three most adamant New
Town advocates on the five-member county Board of Supervisors: Joseph C.
Riley, E.D. French and G.W. B. McDonald. Judge Bush then took it upon himself to appoint three supervisors to complete their terms: Charles Thomas,
Joseph S. Mannasse, and William Flynn.[168] Arguing that Bush had no such
authority, Riley, French and McDonald continued to meet while appealing his
ruling to the state Supreme Court. For a while, San Diego had two rival Boards
of Supervisors. If James W. Robinson still were alive, he might have drawn a
comparison with pre-Independence Texas, when he and Henry Smith debated
which of them was the real governor.

Helene Rose

While the Board of Supervisors' battle was the talk of the town, Rose may
have been forgiven for not paying as much attention as other people. At the age
of 63, he finally became a father. Matilda delivered a baby daughter on October
1, 1870.[169] They named the girl Helene.

Perhaps the girl's birth prompted Rose to refocus his energies on trying to
develop his side of the bay. On October 22, he and Solomon Abels decided to
trade tracts of land, which for the record they each valued at $1,000. Rose gave
up the balance of his holdings in Middletown—some 51 lots. In return, he
received from Abels just five lots in the La Playa area, closer to his Roseville
development.[170] Then on November 1, Rose paid $1,000 to the Pacific Mail
Steamship Co. for Blocks 93 and 94 in La Playa.[171]

Although proposed railroad legislation failed to win approval from
Congress before its adjournment at the end of 1870, San Diegans maintained

a sense of optimism. They told themselves that the failure of the Memphis and El Paso had been just a temporary setback, and that the lack of action by Congress surely would be rectified the following year. San Diego's unique resource, the bay, would be a guarantor of its future. Surveying this important asset, The *San Diego Union* noted in its November 24, 1870, edition:

> New Town, in the center, has long had two fine wharves, and a splendid and durable one has recently been completed at the Playa, on the west, by Mr. Rose. We have now to notice still the wharf in the course of construction on the east (in modern-day National City). The Kimball brothers are certainly not lacking in the spirit of enterprise and energy which is so prominent a characteristic of our people. Their faith seems not to have been shaken in the least by the discouraging failure of the railroad bill in the last session of Congress, and they have been making improvements on their property during the past few months at no small outlay of capital and labor... The wharf is being constructed in the most substantial manner and of the very best material. It is 24 feet wide, and will be 1,800 feet long. A railing will run along each side the entire length.[172]

Three townsites with wharves on the bay meant three rivals for the terminus of any railroad line. Although they worked together to advance San Diego's interests over those of rival Los Angeles, Rose, Horton and the Kimball brothers behind the scenes would become rivals.

Enticing a Railroad

At the end of November, a large number of citizens met in Horton's Hall in New Town to plot railroad strategy. Horton, Rose, and 11 other people were appointed to work together as an executive committee on San Diego's behalf. Significantly, the membership included representatives of both Old Town and New Town, most notably former county Supervisor G.W. B. McDonald of New Town and Judge Thomas Bush, the Old Town judge who appointed McDonald's successor. Other members of this committee included H. H. Dougherty, who was designated president; Morse, Felsenheld, Levi Chase; Joseph Mannasse; D. Choate; W.H. Cleveland; W. B. Leavitt and D.W. Briant.[173]

Ever hopeful, Rose on January 17, 1871, again submitted to the county Board of Supervisors a request that it pay its debts to him. He stated in a petition:

> Your petitioner would respectfully show to your honorable
> board that he is one of the principal owners and holders of
> certain county bonds. That the said bonds are drawing interest at
> the rate of ten percent per annum. That there is a large amount
> of money lying in the fund known as the interest fund over
> and above the amount necessary to pay the interest on the pres-
> ent indebtedness. That said amount is needed in the redemp-
> tion fund to redeem the aforesaid bonds. Therefore your
> petitioner asks that an order be made, directed to the county
> treasurer, ordering him to transfer such portion of the interest
> fund to the redemption fund as is not absolutely necessary to
> pay the interest on the indebtedness of this said county.[174]

The Board, however, was too distracted to pay much attention. The state
Supreme Court soon would determine whether the Board with a majority
appointed by County Judge Bush was even legal. In a rebuke to Judge
Morrison, the court ruled on January 27 that the old Board of Supervisors had
been within its rights to transfer the court records to New Town. Further, it
opined that Morrison had no right to dismiss the old Board. Chastened,
Morrison subsequently ordered the sheriff's office to provide courtroom facilities
in New Town.[175]

Morse, meanwhile, wrote a letter to Matthew Sherman, who was among
the city's railroad advocates in Washington, D.C., about his efforts to obtain
pledges of land to show San Diego's seriousness:

> Today I telegraphed you that deeds will be made for fifteen
> blocks in Horton's Addition, and two hundred acres worth
> seventy five thousand dollars (and) probably two hundred
> acres more...I urged Mannasse & Schiller to canvass Old
> Town...I then went to Old Town and talked with them
> plainly...I asked them what the devil (I had to swear some)
> these lands were worth without a railroad...There was a possibil-
> ity these lands were necessary to pass the bill, and if so we had
> better throw away half what we have than to feel our parsi-
> mony had caused a failure of the bill.[176]

Rose eventually donated 153 blocks of Roseville and 80 acres elsewhere,
while Horton donated 20 blocks in the much more valuable New Town area.
Deeds for the land were held in the vault of the San Diego Bank, located in
New Town.[177] Trying to interest the Southern Transcontinental Railroad
Company to come to San Diego, Rose sold it some land late in January. He
made out one deed to the railroad for $2,000 and another deed to Marshall
Roberts, one of its officers, for $1. The $2,000 sale was for the 80-acre tract

that Rose had purchased two years before from the city trustees for 25 cents an acre, or $20-earning on paper 100 times his investment.[178] But at the same time, for only $1 he deeded to Roberts, who briefly would serve as president of the Southern Transcontinental Railroad Company's successor—the Texas and Pacific Railroad Company—nearly three full blocks of Roseville, the equivalent of 35 lots.[179]

Before the collapse of the Memphis and El Paso, Roseville lots had sold for approximately $250 apiece, and Roberts must have known if he brought a railroad to San Diego they would again command high prices. While paying out $2,000 of railroad money for $20 worth of land, Roberts paid $1 in personal money for at least $8,750 worth of land. Rose, admired by his fellow San Diegans for his honesty, probably did not feel very good about being extorted for what may have been a bribe. On the other hand, he may have considered this the standard cost of doing business. San Diego historian Richard Pourade later suggested there was an "honored practice of the day of assuring directors and promoters of the proposed railroads of gifts of lands that would certainly turn up small fortunes for themselves."[180]

The debate in Congress pitted the interests of the Central Pacific and Union Pacific railroads—which had linked up at Promontory Point in Utah in 1869—against the hopes of those who wanted to build a new railroad. The Central Pacific, led by California businessmen Charles Crocker, Mark Hopkins, Collis Huntington, and Leland Stanford, was not about to give up its monopoly without a fight. Central Pacific poured resources into convincing members of Congress that there was no need to spend the public's money on yet another railroad. Just as they had built a railroad across the Sierra Nevada to Promontory Point, the Californians said they could build a railroad down to Fort Yuma, located on the Colorado River at the Arizona-California border. Further complicating the national debate were various bills to create local north-south railroads that could tie into a new east-west transcontinental railroad. These bills created other competitions, with resultant conflicting political alliances.

As the debate dragged in Congress, not all investors could stand the suspense. Max Lowenstein sold back to Rose two lots he had purchased in Roseville two years before. He had paid $550 for them; Rose refunded $500.[181]

So closely did San Diegans follow national railroad developments that in February 1871, the local newspaper was able to recount the latest actions in Congress almost in shorthand fashion:

> The good time coming for which we have all waited, hoped and prayed is very near at hand. The Senate bill, as we predicted last week, has been amended by striking off all branch roads and providing only for one through road from Marshall (Texas) to San Diego. By this action, the scheme of the Central Pacific monopolies to tap the main trunk road at the

Colorado River and give San Diego the go by, has been frustrated. The western terminus is fixed at our magnificent harbor beyond controversy. We have little fear that the Senate will hesitate over the passage of the amended bill. The very large majority given in the House will have a powerful influence upon the actions of the senators, who cannot refuse a transcontinental road to the south on the grounds that the land grant asked for is less than provided in the original bill. Indeed we think that the friends of the measure are pretty sure of their strength.[182]

The news seemed to augur so well that the *San Diego Union* suggested that major landowners "Horton and Rose are the happiest men in San Diego as well they might be."[183] On March 3, 1871, Congress finally passed the railroad bill, chartering the Texas and Pacific Railroad and authorizing the line to build a continuous railroad from Marshall, Texas, "by the most direct and eligible route to San Diego." Work was to commence simultaneously in Marshall and San Diego, and a ten-year time frame was established for completion of the railroad.

Local officials had read each dispatch concerning the congressional debate to an anxious gathering of citizens. In a subsequent edition, the *San Diego Union* recounted the drama:

All day, Friday, our citizens waited, in anxious suspense, for tidings from Washington. At four o'clock in the afternoon a rumor was in circulation that the bill had passed both houses, but no direct dispatch to that effect had been received in the city. At 7½ o'clock, the joyful news first reached our people as follows: 'Washington, March 3—The Southern Pacific Railroad bill has passed both houses./s/ Thomas S. Sedgwick.' The dispatch was read aloud to the people who thronged around the telegraph office and was immediately printed and issued from this office as an Extra. A few moments later was received the following: 'Washington, March 3, to Douglas Gunn, editor of the *San Diego Union*—The Southern Pacific bill has finally passed both houses. The San Diego and Los Angeles Railroad is the next necessity. /s/ L.C. Gunn.' Next came the following telegram to the agent of the telegraph company: 'San Francisco, March 3—A dispatch dated at Washington, 6 p.m., says the bill assures the western terminus of the road at San Diego. The bill has gone to the President (U.S. Grant) and will be signed in a few hours.'... These dispatches were given to the public as fast as received, in successive extras, and a scene of the wildest excitement ensued. The

city was ablaze with bonfires, houses were illuminated; fire-
works set the sky aglow and the booming of twenty anvils in
part of the city, the heavy roar of the cannon at Old Town, an
incessant fusillade of crackers and Chinese bombs, and the
unearthly sound of half a dozen steam whistles, created such a
din as San Diego has never heard before. From the time the
first dispatch was received, until nearly midnight, our press was
constantly running, throwing off in all 2,200 extras; in the
morning the demand was renewed and we were obliged to
print several hundred more. [184]

Aware that residents were wary that secret machinations in Congress might
have frustrated the city's designs to become the western terminus, the *San
Diego Union* also printed in its March 9 issue the text of the Railroad Bill,
drawing special attention to Section 17, which stated: "Be it further enacted
that the Texas Pacific Railway Company shall commence the construction of
its road simultaneously at San Diego in the state of California and from a point
at or near Marshall, Texas... and to prosecute the same as to have fifty consec-
utive miles of railway from each of said points complete and in running order
within two years after the passage of this action, and to continue to construct
each year thereafter a sufficient number of miles to secure the completion of
the whole line from the aforesaid point in the state of Texas to the Bay of San
Diego in the state of California... within ten years after the passage of this act;
and upon failure to so complete it, Congress may adopt such measures it may
deem necessary to secure its speedy completion."[185]

Although the newspaper had anticipated that both Horton and Rose
would soon be rolling in more money, Horton, by far, was the chief beneficiary
of the subsequent land sales that in a two-month period reached $100,000.
"Horton has sold about $80,000," Morse commented in correspondence during
this period. "He is erecting several buildings near his hotel. Buildings are going
up all over town, but business is not as brisk as we all had expected, and I think
I was very moderate in my expectations too... Old Rose is being cursed by Old
Town folks for not showing a little of Horton's energy in building up Roseville
and La Playa. Old Town is nearly deserted."[186]

A day after the historic vote, Rose gave another Roseville lot away, for a
nominal $1 fee, to Johanna Audlum, repeating the process two weeks later with
a gift to John Minter, his former colleague on the county Board of Supervisors.
During the intervening week, he purchased two other Roseville lots from
Heyman Solomon for $400. One can appreciate how much land prices fluctu-
ated when one notes that Rose originally had sold the same two lots to
William Wiley Davis for $550, who in turn had sold them to Solomon.[187]

Marketing Roseville

"The general activity in real estate circles is not confined to this part of the city," the New Town-based *San Diego Union* reported on March 24. "At National City (owned by the Kimball brothers) considerable movement is visible and property is advancing rapidly. A stage line has been put on and makes regular trips between the two places. The old Playa site is agitated by the breeze of prosperity and real estate about the site of the ancient customhouse is in some inquiry, if not active demand. Our respected and venerable friend, Louis Rose, feels richer day by day, and anticipates marked changes for the better in the neighborhood of the town site that bears his odorous name."[188] To modern-day readers, "odorous" sounds like an insult, but the newspaper probably was using the word then as we would use "aromatic" today in reference to the sweet smell of roses.

With Horton doing so well, and the Kimball Brothers offering lots ranging from 10 acres to 160 acres in National City, near their new wharf,[189] Rose was under pressure to get people not only to purchase land, but to make improvements on it. Otherwise, how would Roseville and La Playa ever achieve sufficient population to spur further development and gain in value? Accordingly, Rose and others created the San Diego Mutual Land Association. Rose, who became president of the association, earmarked 221 lots that the association could use to attract settlers to Roseville, while he retained the deeds in his own hands. Similarly, Thomas Whaley, secretary, pledged 15 lots; James McCoy designated an unspecified number of lots, described as a quarter of his La Playa property, and O.S. Witherby donated 100 acres near Roseville. N. H. Dodson was appointed agent for the association, and given the charge to recruit settlers to Roseville. The association offered generous terms: "A lot of 50 x 100 will be given to any person who will erect thereon a house worth not less than $250."[190] An advertisement in the *San Diego Union* expanded upon the offer:

FREE LANDS! FREE LANDS!

"The San Diego Mutual Land Association having fully organized with over 300 lots at Roseville and La Playa, are now prepared to give land away to settlers who will improve the same. With a first-class wharf almost completed, the advantages of this part of the Bay as a shipping point cannot be overestimated. Good fresh water is readily obtained, while the climate far exceeds that of any other point on the Bay, and is especially inviting to invalids. A lot 50 x 100 feet in size will be given to any person erecting a house thereon, worth at least $250, while extra inducements will be held out to those wishing to start an extensive business or make more valuable improvements. Titles perfect to all lands of the association. For further particulars, apply to N.H. Dodson, Esq., Old San Diego, agent of the association. Louis Rose, Thomas Whaley, James McCoy, trustees. Thos P. Slade, Esq., attorney for the association.[191]

The first to take up the offer was the tidal gauge keeper William Knapp, who already was living with his wife Lydia in rented quarters in Roseville. Rose deeded a lot to Knapp for $1 on April 3[192], with the *San Diego Union* reporting ten days later that the Knapp building was expected "to be a credit to that part of the bay. The main house is 34 by 32 feet in size, one story high, 11 feet in the clear, with an L for kitchen purposes. The frame is already erected and the cupola roof now going on will soon give it a finished appearance. The outside is to be covered with rustic, while the inside will be hard finished throughout. We hope to chronicle the erection of many more residences in that delightful part of the pueblo."[193] One can almost hear Louis Rose responding to this report with an old Jewish folk saying: "From your lips to God's ear!"

On April 4, Rose deeded two adjoining lots for $1 each to Kay Love and to Johanna Audlum.[194] *The Voice of Israel*, published in San Francisco, spread word of Rose's proposal. It reported that San Diego was "encouraging immigration" by offering free land to settlers.[195] On April 17, Colonel E.J.C. Kewen took Rose up on his offer, paying $1 for the lot.[196] D.A. Hollister, a long time acquaintance of Rose's, obtained two lots for $1 the following day.[197]

All this prompted the *San Diego Union* to report in its weekly edition on April 10 that "The San Diego Mutual Land Association are meeting with success in their efforts to develop the interests of La Playa. We feel sure that the delightful slopes of Roseville and Mannasse's Addition between Roseville and Old Town will at no distant day be dotted over with dwellings."[198] A week later the daily version of the *San Diego Union* said: "We are glad to learn that the efforts of the San Diego Mutual Land Association in advancing the property interests at La Playa and Roseville are meeting much success. Several new buildings will be commenced on that side of the bay in short time. The terms offered by the association are exceedingly liberal and cannot fail to induce the settlement and consequent development of the delightful portion of the Pueblo which it represents."[199]

The Texas and Pacific Railroad

Meanwhile, having gained its charter from Congress, the Texas and Pacific Railroad was organizing itself. Marshall Roberts, to whom Rose had made a gift of several blocks of Roseville land, was elected by shareholders as president at an April 15 meeting. Other officers were Henry G. Stebbins, vice president; Edward Pierrepont, treasurer; E.B. Hart, secretary; and directors John W. Foreny,

John S. Harris, George W. Kass, John McManus, H.D. McComb, Henry S. McComb, George W. Quintard, E. W. Rice, Thomas A. Scott, Moses Taylor, J. W. Throckmorton, Samuel Tilden, W. R. Travers, and W.T. Walters.[200]

It is a matter of incidental interest that later in his career Tilden narrowly would miss becoming president of the United States. Although he would receive more popular votes than Rutherford B. Hayes in the 1876 election, he would lose when a disputed electoral college vote was sent to the House of Representatives for a decision.

Of greater importance to San Diego was the presence on the board of Tom Scott who, upon the resignation of Roberts, would become president of the Texas and Pacific on February 2, 1872.[201] The *San Diego Union* was impressed with the makeup of the railroad's board, commenting optimistically: "The names are those of the leading capitalists of the nation, and the company as represented in its directory, is the strongest combination ever formed in the United States. New York capital is prominently represented by Marshall O. Roberts, Moses Taylor, Samuel J. Tilden, Wm. R. Travers, and Henry Stebbins. Thos. A. Scott and John McManus represent the Pennsylvania Central Railroad Company. The other names are those of men of highest standing. There is no doubt that operations on the road will be at once commenced. We predict the beginning of work at Marshall and San Diego within the next sixty days and the completion of one hundred miles of road from San Diego, east, before this day next year."[202]

Slow Sales in Roseville

The pace of sales in Roseville must have seemed glacial to Rose, who naturally wanted to secure the economic future of his wife and daughter. Not until June 1 did the weekly *San Diego Union* report: "We learn another person has taken advantage of the liberal offer of the Mutual Land Association and will at once erect a home 20 x 20 feet at the Playa."[203] It is not clear whether the item may have referred to Kewen, Love, Audlum or some other party who may have purchased land from other members of the San Diego Mutual Land Association. What is clear is that a 20 x 20 house was too small to cause much stir among investors.

Rose not only was active in Roseville. On April 10, he sold to A. Brunson 150 feet of frontage on Taylor Street in Old Town for $10.[204] This, of course, was not very much money, but Rose may have taken grim satisfaction that at least he actually received money, not promises. In contrast, Rose was twice frustrated in his efforts to improve his cash flow. Through E. W. Morse, he continued to push in Washington, D.C., for payment of the loan he had made some two decades before to Lieutenant George Derby and the Army Engineers for work on a dike for the San Diego River. Morse wrote to Rose on May 3: "My agents at Washington say if they can get the total amount of claims and list of claimants for amount due by the Engineers of the San Diego River appropriation, they will be able to get an appropriation at the next Congress to pay them. The chief engineer will recommend it, which will be sufficient they think..."[205]

Rose also continued his quest to persuade the county Board of Supervisors to pay some of the money it owed to him. But Morse again had disappointing news, writing to Rose on June 7, 1871, that he had intended to appear in his behalf that Tuesday before the Board of Supervisors, having been assured the Board would meet then. However, the Board decided on Monday not to meet again for six months.[206]

On June 6, Rose sold to Samuel Barkley 11 lots spread over seven blocks of New Town for $200.[207] A week later, he finally was able to dispose of another Roseville lot through the San Diego Mutual Land Association to John Francis Eccles, who paid $2.[208] "Mr. Echols (sic) has nearly completed his house at Roseville," the *Union* reported on June 22.[209] "Dan Clark (who purchased a lot from another Association member) will commence the erection of a good-sized building next week."

Various items appearing in the *San Diego Union* around this time illustrate the sense of distance and separation between the Old Town-Roseville-La Playa area and New Town. On June 4, the newspaper reported: "The steamer *Vaquero* will make an excursion trip to La Playa today, leaving Culverwell's Wharf at 10 o'clock. Fare 50 cents."[210] On June 28, the newspaper noted: "Mr. Louis Rose, of Old Town, was in town yesterday seeing the sights!"[211] On July 19, it said "Captain Knapp of Roseville called yesterday. He reports all serene on that side of the bay."[212]

In an illustration of the rivalry among National City, Roseville and New Town, Frank Kimball approached Charles Crocker of the Central Pacific Railroad in August about the possibility of building a terminus in National City—a development that would have undercut the Texas and Pacific Railroad. Crocker indicated he might be interested, provided that Kimball would sell six miles of waterfront in National City to the railroad. Kimball later reported that when he refused, Crocker told him "that I should never live to see a railroad laid to the Bay of San Diego nor in the states east of California, which they did not lay and that no competition should come into the state. Further, he said, we have our foot on the neck of San Diego and we shall keep it there."[213] The die was cast. If San Diego were to have a railroad at all, it would have to be in an alliance with the Texas and Pacific Railroad.

N.H. Dodson, the agent for the San Diego Mutual Land Association, purchased another Roseville lot on August 25, 1871, committing to live in the area he was representing. The lot cost him $2.[214] Eccles, another resident, demonstrated that the area had attraction for hunters—although it may have made conservationists of the period wince. The *San Diego Union* reported: "Mr. John Eccles at La Playa on Tuesday shot a large bald eagle measuring eight feet from tip to tip of his wings. These birds are, we understand, quite numerous in our vicinity and are as great marauders on hen roosts as the hawks. The destruction of the fellow will undoubtedly save many poor chickens from a premature death."[215]

Members of the Jewish community paused on September 11, 1871, to observe Rosh Hashanah. Rose, who now owned Robinson's old home and office building on the plaza, provided the space for the services where Masonic Lodge #35 once held its meetings.[216] On the second day of Rosh Hashanah, it was proposed to strengthen the thus far dormant Hebrew Benevolent Society. In response, another meeting was held at Rose's house on September 24. Marcus Schiller became the society's president, and other officers included his brother, Rudolph, as well as Joseph S. Mannasse and Charles Wolfsheimer. The Benevolent Society decided to adopt as a model the constitution and bylaws of Congregation B'nai B'rith of Los Angeles. It also retained H. Meyer to serve as a "reader and teacher" of the congregation.[217]

"The idea of forming an association of this kind in San Diego originated about a year since," the *San Diego Union* stated in its September 28, 1871, edition. "A society composed nearly of all the Israelites in this city has been silently engaged in the work of benevolence since that time, and the object of organizing at present is to secure perfect harmony in working." [218]

With the board of the Texas and Pacific Railroad now in place, the shareholders of the San Diego and Gila Railroad met to elect their own board—men whom they charged with the responsibility of negotiating the local concern's land rights with the larger railroad. Early in October, W. Jeff Gatewood was elected president; E. W. Morse, vice president; Joseph S. Mannasse, treasurer and C.L Carr, secretary. Rose was elected to the board of directors as were Horton, Thomas Whaley, Gustave Witfeld, Thomas Sedgwick, James McCoy, José G. Estudillo, Marcus Schiller, Bryant Howard, and Wm. N. Robinson.[219]

Rose recorded one more land transaction before 1871 ended. He sold 3 82/100 acres of tideland property, near Roseville, to Isaac Hartman for $5.[220] The buyer would prove controversial.

While 1871 had been a difficult year for Rose financially, he still was one of San Diego's biggest property owners, according to an article published February 29, 1872, in the *San Diego Union*. A list of the "principal property holders and the assessed valuation of their property" showed Horton first with $124,971, followed by John Forster with $87,681; the Kimball brothers $52,840; Sable Felsenheld & Co $42,156; San Diego and Gila Railroad $41,899; J.S. Mannasse & Co. $38,566; the heirs of Miguel de Pedrorena $36,766; and Louis Rose, in eighth position, with $36,330. Rounding out the top ten were D.W. Smith with $35,700 and Cave J. Couts with $28,122. [221]

However, there was no question that Rose's hopes for greater fortune had been dimmed by the lackluster response to the San Diego Mutual Land Association's offer of a free lot to any homebuilder in Roseville. Even N. H. Dodson, the attorney who worked as the association's agent, decided in January 1872 to remove his law offices from Old Town to New Town, choosing rented space in a building across the street from the Horton House. He told the *San Diego Union* that he planned to keep his residence in the Old Town vicinity, which at least kept open the possibility of following through on constructing a home in Roseville.[222]

Whether by accident or design, news coverage of Roseville and environs in the Horton-friendly *San Diego Union* continued to reinforce the image of the area being a nature reserve. On February 2, the daily newspaper reported that a surveying party of the U.S. Engineer Corps had captured near the head of the bay three large turtles that together weighed 550 pounds.[223] On February 11, it said that Old Town resident and saloonkeeper Dan Clark recently fished up a bottle encrusted with oysters at La Playa.[224] On March 13, the newspaper advised residents that Spanish Bayonets, members of the cactus family, were in the process of blooming in the hills overlooking La Playa and Roseville.[225]

Towards the end of the year, the weekly *San Diego Union* reported: "Captain Knapp informs us that on Monday night ice was formed at Roseville three-eighths of an inch thick. This will seem almost incredible to many of our readers but it is nevertheless a fact. Singular as it may seem, the thermometer at 1:55 p.m. on the same day, in this city, marked 69 degrees. As the inhabitants of this city will know frost very rarely makes its appearance here, and ice is a still more rare sight than frost. Therefore the appearance of ice at Roseville may be set down (as) something very singular." [226]

Demise of Old Town

San Diego was intending to have one of its normal elections in March for the three-member Board of Trustees when the state legislature adopted a bill providing for a five-member City Council for San Diego. Henceforth, it would be a "general law city"; a step up from trusteeship, but not nearly so autonomous as a "charter law city." As part of the legislation, the city was divided into roughly equally populated districts. Old San Diego was entitled to only one of the five seats. In order to permit a transition, the legislation directed that the then-sitting Board of Trustees should remain in office until May, by which time the results of a full-scale election for the new City Council would be known. High-spirited citizens in Old Town decided to conduct a mock election for the three new trustees anyway, with "voting" taking place at Dan Clark's saloon on the south side of the Plaza. "We learned that 50 votes were cast, Judge Slade being the favorite and receiving all but one of them," the *San Diego Union* reported on March 6. "Mr. Begole had 29 votes, and Colonel Bradt 26. Louis Rose and Thomas Bush received 11 votes each. W. Jeff Gatewood had 2 votes and J.A.C. Lee and N.H. Dodson 1 each. There was considerable fun in the vicinity of the poll." [227]

That was one of the last times for such gaiety on the south side of the Plaza. On April 20, a disastrous fire erupted between the ceiling and the roof of the old courthouse building, which had been built in the 1840s by members of the Mormon Battalion and which presently was occupied by Rudolph Schiller's general store.

Apparently caused by a spark from the stovepipe, the fire spread to adjoining stores on the south side of the Plaza. "Schiller's, Asher's and Wallach's stores, the Franklin House (hotel) and Dan Clarke's saloon were in ruins," the *San Diego Union* later reported. The flames were prevented from leaping to the wooden structures on the north side of the plaza by the tile roof on the Estudillo house located at the plaza's southeastern end. [228] Estimates of losses totaled approximately $20,000, the equivalent of $295,000. [229] Historians mark the fire as ending the Old Town era; thereafter, San Diego's history largely would be enacted in New Town. [230]

Henrietta Rose

Rose, who had moved his residence from Juan Street to the old Robinson house on the west side of the plaza, had a good reason for remaining at Old Town, fire or no fire. His wife Matilda was then in the final trimester of her second pregnancy. On May 22, 1872, she gave birth to a second daughter, whom they named Henrietta. The baby was born two months after Rose's 65th birthday and 19 months after the birth of his first child, Helene. [231]

The Great Railroad Fight

After Tom Scott replaced Marshall Roberts as president of the Texas and Pacific Railroad, he sought legislation that struck San Diego like a thunderclap. Scott proposed that he be permitted to construct the railroad from the eastern terminus only, instead of simultaneously building from Marshall, Tex., and San Diego.

Rose and other residents of San Diego naturally were fearful that the western terminus might be switched in the future to another location on the California coast. San Diego with the help of its congressman, S.O. Houghton, who served on the House Committee on Pacific Railroads, organized its resistance. [232] "Congress has pledged its faith to the people of Southern California, Arizona and New Mexico, that this road shall be built speedily, and that to this end construction shall commence at San Diego at the same time as the eastern terminus," editorialized the *San Diego Union.* "Thousands of dollars have been invested at this point because of the assurances given in the Act of the completion of fifty miles of railway east from San Diego within two years from its passage. Capital has been invested in enterprises not only here but throughout this section of the state upon the faith that Congress would require the fulfillment of the terms of the law." [233]

On March 18, Horton left San Diego for Washington, D.C., to join the city's lobbying effort in Congress. A few days later, Congressman Houghton sent a telegram to David Felsenheld, president of the San Diego Chamber of Commerce, reporting that Scott wanted a two-year moratorium on building from San Diego. If it were granted, he would build 25 miles per year afterwards until the junction with the line from the east. Congressman Houghton pushed instead for having Scott build 25 miles per year, starting immediately. "Will San Diego assent to Scott's proposal?" he asked in a telegram? "Answer immediately."[234]

A mass meeting of citizens directed that Houghton's telegram be answered as follows: "Scott's proposition not acceptable. Yours is. Otherwise have franchise transferred to a company that will comply with charter. Do the best you can for us. We place entire confidence in you." [235]

As the drama continued, the Jewish community paused to celebrate Rose's birthday holiday of Purim.[236] With emotions running high, one can imagine Tom Scott being substituted in Rose's mind for the evil villain Haman. On April 17, the *San Diego Union* told of a *Los Angeles News* article that seemed to confirm San Diego's worst fears: "it is probable that Scott contemplates the abandonment of San Diego as a terminus and seeks to substitute San Pedro!"[237]

There was considerable bargaining between Scott and the San Diego representatives in Washington, D.C., including Horton. Eventually, Houghton wired "The Texas Pacific Supplemental Bill passed in the Senate requires work to be commenced within one year and the completion of twenty-five miles in three years. It will now be amended in the House so as to require work to begin in one year and not less than ten miles to be completed in the second year, and twenty five miles every year thereafter...."[238]

At another mass meeting of San Diego citizenry, a committee of 30 prominent citizens, including Rose and Horton, was created to look after San Diego's railroad interests. T.L. Nesmith was elected as president and W.W. McLellan as secretary.[239] On April 29, Houghton again telegraphed. "The Texas Pacific Railroad bill has passed the House with my amendment." [240] The Senate concurred in the amendments on May 1.

Tidelands Controversy

With the railroad business apparently settled, San Diego turned its attention to the election of its new City Council. In four of the five districts, the results were clear. José A. Estudillo was elected to represent the Old Town area, while E.G. Haigh, W.J. McCormick and D.W. Briant were chosen to represent the newer parts of the city. However, in the fifth ward, J.M. Boyd and Matthew Sherman were forced into a runoff. [241] The contest quickly became bitter.

The *San Diego Union*, backing Sherman, headlined an article in its May 21 edition: "The City Waterfront–Going, Going, Gone!" It noted that there recently had been a brisk trade in tideland properties, with Tabb Mitchell and Isaac Hartman buying up local property and selling it to speculators named Philip Smith and J.W. Tyson. Rose sold one of the properties in question for $5 to Hartman the previous November. "The waterfront of San Diego is being gobbled up," the *Union* averred. Locked in a rivalry with an upstart newspaper called the *Bulletin*, the *San Diego Union* promptly lost focus: "When we warn the people of their danger, the organ of the ring (that is, the *Bulletin*) calls it a threadbare question." The *Union* went on to raise many questions, without answering them, about who owns the most valuable lands on the bay, who owned interest in a proposed coastal railroad between San Diego and Los Angeles, whose claims regarding Ballast Point were hampering plans for a U.S. military base on Point Loma and who was backing the *Bulletin*.[242] In its May 23 edition, the *Union* made its suspicions more explicit: "The *Bulletin* lies flatly when it says it is opposed to State Tide Landers"—as it referred to the people who were purchasing the tidelands. "Men do not oppose their own interests. Morse, Briant, Nash, Cleveland, Klauber and the other leading stockholders in the *Bulletin* are state tidelanders. There can be no doubt about its position." [243]

The ferocity of the *San Diego Union* attack did not stir a great voter turnout. Eventually, John M. Boyd defeated Sherman by a vote of 32 to 22, but the *San Diego Union* claimed a victory in bringing the issue of private ownership of the waterfront to the fore.[244] Although the newspaper had focused on Morse's property at Ballast Point, Rose had inherited from his nephew Nisan Alexander a large tract of land in the hills above Ballast Point, today the site of Fort Rosecrans. Like Morse, he too hoped that he would receive compensation from the military. However, the military still believed that the land—won in the Mexican-American War—belonged to the U.S. government and had not been the property of the City of San Diego to sell to Alexander in the first place. Development in nearby Roseville, meanwhile, remained at a standstill. On May 27, Benjamin Truman sold three lots in Roseville back to Rose for $60. Originally, Truman had paid $400 for them.[245]

The *Bulletin* was sold to W. Jeff Gatewood, who renamed it the *Daily World*. Its mission was to support the Democratic presidential candidacy of Horace Greeley against the reelection bid of the nation's eighteenth president, Ulysses

S. Grant. In an early issue, Gatewood noted how little activity there was at Roseville: "Seagulls have taken possession of old Rose's Wharf. Possession is nine points of the law. The old gentleman takes his tithe contentedly and mutters, "Shoost vait avile' when we will bring ejectment. Horton is ahead just now."[246] However Gatewood may have intended his parody of Rose's German accent, the quotation, "Just wait awhile" typified the faith Rose had that someday his project would come to fruition.

Tom Scott Comes to San Diego

"Avile" came within three days, when Tom Scott arrived in San Diego with a delegation of Texas and Pacific officials, prompting Rose to stay in New Town for the duration of the Scott visit so as not to miss any of the discussions.[247] In the party were Grenville M. Dodge, the chief engineer, and J. W. Throckmorton, a railroad director and former governor of Texas. Excited, forgiving San Diegans cheered Scott and party as they disembarked from a steamer. Scott's message was music to their ears: San Diego's location "south of San Francisco and in a direct line of the Great Orient gives you unrivaled advantages."[248] Horton, Morse, Gatewood and C. L. Carr had hoped to sell the franchise rights of the San Diego and Gila Railroad to the Texas and Pacific, and thereby realize a profit on the local corporation's longstanding efforts to earmark public lands for railroad development. But the cagey Scott understood better than they how property values would soar once the railroad came to town. He insisted that all the lands controlled by the San Diego and Gila franchise should be purchased back by the City of San Diego and then donated to the Texas and Pacific. Furthermore, Scott asked for a 100-foot-wide right of way through the city and county of San Diego, and also asked for substantial tracts of land for a depot, for repair shops, and for contingency purposes. He also played San Diego landowners against each other, conferring not only with the group led by Horton, but also separately with Rose and the Kimball brothers respectively.[249]

One wonders if during the "small talk" prior to the negotiations, Rose might have quizzed Throckmorton if he ever had met Rose's old partner James W. Robinson, the former acting governor of Texas. Once the conversation got down to business, Rose offered Scott "as much land at Roseville as would be required for the construction of the machine shops of the San Diego terminus of the Texas and Pacific Railroad," the *World* reported. Scott "promised to entertain the proposition but would not give any definite offer to Rose."[250] Kimball offered a large amount of acreage, with later reports differing over whether the offer was for 11,000 acres or 20,000.[251]

The San Diego and Gila board of directors, having both Horton and Rose among its members, decided to follow Scott's directive and sell its holdings back to the City of San Diego, which, in turn, could then make lands available to the Texas and Pacific Railroad. While the city and the local railroad negotiated over the price, land values in downtown San Diego began to increase. Although speculators also had some renewed interest in Roseville—with John Murry[252] purchasing a lot for $125 on September 5, 1872—Horton's development continued to enjoy the overwhelming preponderance of interest. A gossip item in the *Daily World* that "Roseville lots are rising like a cork in water" had no basis in fact.[253]

Business in Old Town for all practical purposes ceased October 4 for the observance of the Jewish High Holy Days.[254] A writer for the *San Diego Union* evidently thought that the Jewish New Year was like the secular New Year, rather than a day of reflection and repentance. The newspaper reported: "The Hebrew residents of the city commenced the celebration of their New Year yesterday. Several stores were closed and most of the proprietors were enjoying themselves."[255] Whether proprietors "enjoyed" themselves or not, they apparently believed on the basis of the Tom Scott boom that the outlook for the community was positive enough to give serious consideration to building a permanent synagogue.[256]

By mid-December, the negotiations between the city and the San Diego and Gila were completed. The city agreed to pay $58,000 in city bonds, and forgive the San Diego and Gila its outstanding taxes, in return for the corporation's holdings. As a shareholder, Rose received a pro rata portion of that $58,000.[257]

Rose and E. W. Nottage consolidated their holdings on January 4, 1873, then sold to Robert Kelly for $1,100 a portion of a pueblo lot lying east of the Middletown area. Rose also sold to Nottage for $100 a quarter of a lot in New Town.[258]

As sweet as Rose may have considered those deals, they were bitter in comparison to the honey-coated bargain gathered up by James A. Evans, in his capacity as an engineer for the Texas and Pacific Railroad. As the only bidder at a public auction of lands formerly held by the San Diego and Gila Railroad, he purchased 160 parcels of land, totaling 8,606 acres, for $1 per parcel. Scott estimated the aggregate value at $5 million.[259] In another point of comparison, E. W. Bushyhead paid $5 to Rose for one of the small San Diego Mutual Land Association lots on February 13.[260]

Death in the Family

As railroad excitement gripped the town, Rose found himself with far more serious matters to worry about. His oldest daughter, Helene, began suffering from fever, sore throat and vomiting. Within a couple of days of the onset of this malady, small red spots began appearing on the little girl's neck and chest and under her arms. The inside of her mouth also became inflamed, her tongue swelled and the glands of her body enlarged. Doctor D.B. Hoffman was powerless to help her.

Helene died of scarlet fever on March 13, 1873, just two years and five months after she was born.[261] She probably was buried in the Jewish cemetery that her father had donated to the community a decade previously. The mortality rate for children was high in San Diego, where the medical arts were comparatively primitive.

In the same March 20 issue in which it reported the death of Helene Rose, the *San Diego Union* also reported that a neighbor in the Old Town area, two-year-old Emily Minter, also had died.[262] Children of former colleagues on the county Board of Supervisors, they perhaps had played together.

Texas and Pacific Groundbreaking

Rose, 66, was plunged into deep mourning for his first-born child. It was not recorded whether he was in attendance on April 21 when the Texas and Pacific held a groundbreaking ceremony for the beginning of construction on its line. His victorious rival, Alonzo Horton, was given the honor of turning the first shovel full of dirt at the site, located approximately a quarter of a mile southeast of Mannasse's Addition (located between Old Town and Roseville). As Congress had required only 10 miles on the San Diego side of the route to be completed within the first two years, most of the railroad's efforts were concentrated near the other terminus at Marshall, Tex. But eleven men were employed in San Diego to grade 10 miles including a stretch through the Old Town area.[263] After weighing three possible routes from San Diego to Fort Yuma, the railroad decided in May to head northeast through the San Gorgonio Pass rather than build along either of the two more southerly routes.[264]

Rhythms of Life

It is likely that the Roses attended the circumcision party for Elias Klauber, son of Mr. and Mrs. Abraham Klauber. Performed by H. Meyer, it was the first known *brit milah* ceremony in San Diego. As an active member of the Hebrew

Benevolent Association, Rose probably would have been invited to this very special June event, which was followed by a Sunday brunch at the Klauber residence.[265]

Rose probably was considered a "patriarch" of San Diego's small Jewish community, not only because he had been in the city the longest but also because he was among San Diego's oldest residents. The *San Diego Union* reported on May 22 that of 1,756 voters in the county, Rose, at 66, was among the oldest three dozen. The oldest was Horton's father, Erastus, who was 85. The newspaper found that 1,392 voters, or 79 percent, were native Americans. Of the 21 percent who came from other countries, 21 like Rose had listed the Kingdom of Hanover as their place of origin.[266]

The Jewish pioneer accompanied a number of families on a picnic to Roseville[267] where no doubt he enjoyed sharing with his coreligionists his vision of a new settlement on the bay.

Rose gave evidence of renewed optimism about the future of San Diego in general and his Roseville project in particular. The *San Diego Union*, in brief items, charted his favorable mood swing. June 19: "Our friend Louis Rose is full of the spirit of the time. He informs us that the hotel at Roseville is to be opened ere long, and that two new houses are shortly to be erected on that side of the bay."[268] June 26: 'Mr. J. F. Eccles intends digging a well on his lot in Roseville. Mr. Rose's lot was dug four years ago. The water was analyzed by Dr. Witfeld and found to contain less alkali than the river water."[269] July 6: "Mr. Rose, many years ago, prophesied we might see what is now taking place. His 'Just vait a little vile and you'll see' is becoming a reality. The deep water at La Playa and the pleasing situation at Roseville will carry out before many years the cherished wish of hopeful Mr. Rose."[270]

The promotional drumbeat continued, probably at Rose's instigation. July 10: "The (U.S. military) fortifications are progressing rapidly. There are about twenty men at work. This will benefit San Diego greatly, and more particularly La Playa, Roseville, and, in fact, Old Town. It is actually the making of these places... Old Town is centrally situated and is bound to be a place of some note. Its superiority of climate and sweet water alone will demand this for it. The river will soon be changed and the flat will then be a perfect Eden as it was of yore."[271] Another July 10 item: "Mr. Rose's wharf, at La Playa, is 472 feet in length by 30 feet wide, having 16½ feet at low tide. He contemplates adding 60 feet and then (will) have 24 feet of water at low tide. The 'T' will be 100 x 200 feet."[272] Sept. 11: "Mr. Louis Rose, one of the patriarchs of Old Town, and the proprietor of Roseville-on-the-Bay, is 66 years of age. He came to San Diego May 30, 1850. Since then he has never been 40 miles out of Old Town but once. In 1858, he had remained for a while at Milpitas, where he had been working a copper mine, and from there he went to San Luis Rey."[273]

The Panic of 1873

The "happy news" items did not last. San Diego, which had seemed so economically secure with the employment of a Texas and Pacific construction crew, once again, and through no fault of its own, suddenly was facing an uncertain and possibly bleak economic future. In New York City on September 18, the large banking house of Jay Cooke and Company, unable to sell the securities of its Northern Pacific Railroad Company, unexpectedly announced its bankruptcy. The bank's collapse sent stock prices on Wall Street into a deep dive. U.S. President Ulysses S. Grant hurried from Washington, D.C., to New York City to confer with the wise men of the financial world, but their advice was so conflicting, he was paralyzed into inaction.[274] A Depression spread across the country, shutting down 10,000 businesses over its duration of approximately five years.

While it took a while for the full effect of the "Panic of 1873" to be felt directly in San Diego, other sad news had an immediate impact on Rose. William N. Robinson, the son of his late friend James W. Robinson, had, in spectacular fashion, like the economy, gone insane.

The Sad Tale of William Robinson

Two years after he and his mother sold his father's San Diego properties to Rose, William was elected to the state assembly. Just a year later, in 1871, he came under criticism after he and Miguel de Pedrorena applied for a franchise to build a toll bridge across the Colorado River on the border of Arizona and California. The *San Diego Union* said the bridge could interfere with a railroad crossing over the river, thereby frustrating San Diego's cherished plans.[275] The toll bridge idea was dropped.

After a term out of office, William was nominated once again by the Democrats for the Assembly, but he was defeated by Republican W. W. Bowers, who managed the Horton House Hotel. After the election, the exhausted candidate came on horseback from his home in Jamul to San Diego. "Gradually, he became worse, and frequently he was very violent," the *Union* reported. "At an interview with Dr. Gregg and while talking rationally, he struck the doctor in the face. After that he assaulted City Attorney Phillips on the sidewalk and after dealing him a stunning blow on the head, Mr. Robinson fell headlong on the sidewalk in a spasm."

After recovering temporarily from the spell's effects, "he escaped from the parties who were with him and procuring his own horse from a livery stable...rode away."[276] He subsequently was captured while wandering in the Chollas Valley, and was committed by Judge Bush to the asylum at Stockton.

Rose had known poor William since he was a child traveling with his parents on the wagon trail from El Paso to San Diego. First Rose's own daughter Helene, had succumbed to smallpox. Now madness had claimed the son of his dear old friend and political partner James W. Robinson. Rose suffered another blow in October with the death of "Mother" María Victoria Dominguez Estudillo at 72 years old.[277] She was the woman who had welcomed the exhausted Rose at the Cajon ranch in 1850, given him a good solid meal and provisions, and directed him to Old Town.

Notwithstanding Rose's personal grief and the economic depression resulting from the failure of Jay Cooke's enterprises, Rose continued to push for the development of his beloved Roseville. On October 17, he sold two lots to Mark M. Shaffer for $475.[278]

Letter to Brigham Young

Mindful of the longstanding interest on the part of the Mormons in Utah to have a railroad connect to a trading outlet on the Pacific Ocean, Rose on December 24 penned a letter to the religious group's spiritual leader, Brigham Young, that "our citizens will be prompt and cordial" in cooperating with him, should he choose San Diego for a port.

Rose went on to say that he owned a mile and a half of lands along San Diego Bay, with between 8,000 and 9,000 feet right at the water's edge. He mentioned that he owned a wharf at La Playa, and added that he had "2,300 lots unsold," all well situated for a community. Notwithstanding the national economic depression, he expressed a belief that the Texas and Pacific Railroad ultimately would locate its operations at Roseville, "it being the best place on the bay." He told Young in that letter that he was willing to offer "ample" resources to further the Mormon community's goals, and asked Young to favor him with an early reply for publication.[279] No record could be found that Young responded to Rose's overtures. But the letter illustrates Rose's entrepreneurial spirit.

The problem for the Texas and Pacific Railroad after the stock market crash was to find funds to permit the continuation of construction. Businesses in San Diego, which joyously had provided goods and services to the construction arm of the railroad, suddenly found that this valued customer had accumulated $13,000 in local debts. Feeling the pressure of creditors, the local engineer, James Evans, suggested to his superiors that the line's lumber be sold to pay off the debt. The railroad management rejected this solution.

Wanting to keep prospects for a railroad alive, San Diegans agreed to provide wages and provisions for a dozen workmen who had been grading the San Diego section of the road. But by January, 1874, construction on the line ceased in San Diego.[280]

Troubles Multiply

While Scott sought funds from investors and from Congress to finish construction of the Texas and Pacific, San Diegans, at least temporarily, had to lay their dreams aside. No more graphic example of this was the fact that Rose occasionally donned an apron to resume his old profession of butchering.[281]

Nature conspired to add to San Diego's problems. In February 1874, rain-swollen waters of the San Diego River sliced a bank in Old Town, pulling two large fig trees and two sycamore trees down into its current. The rain created lakes around some homes and crumbled several adobe walls, including one near the Commercial House, sometimes referred to as "Rose's Hall." There also was a fire that year, damaging the roof of the Robinson-Rose House on the northwest end of the Plaza.[282]

Under the circumstances, the City of San Diego was in its customarily difficult financial situation, prompting Morse on April 9 to appeal to Rose to seek help from his nephew Ludwig in selling San Diego city bonds in San Francisco.[283]

On April 10, Rose suffered an important loss when President Grant reserved for the military all the lands in Point Loma, including the lot that Rose had obtained from the estate of his nephew, N.J. Alexander.[284] Had Rose been able to keep the land, he would have been the owner of the breathtakingly beautiful parcel that later became the Fort Rosecrans National Cemetery—with views of both San Diego Bay and the Pacific Ocean.

While Rose fretted over his land being confiscated by the government, others simply abandoned their real estate holdings rather than pay the taxes. In October, Rose successfully bid $5 at a sheriff's auction for a Roseville parcel that the tax collector had seized because of D.C. Robinson's failure to pay a $1 school tax levy.[285]

The Central Pacific, meanwhile, had decided to construct the subsidiary Southern Pacific from San Francisco to Los Angeles. San Diegans, especially Rose, hoped that the railroad would continue its main line all the way down the coast to San Diego. Perhaps naively, Rose offered the railroad a large block of land in Roseville to accomplish this very purpose.[286] Owners of the line had flirted with San Diego in an effort to lessen the community's rock solid political support for the Texas and Pacific, but it was only political coquetry. Central Pacific's real desires were to keep the Texas and Pacific out of California and to make Los Angeles—rather than San Diego—the center of its Southern California operations.

A five-year-long suit to establish property boundaries in Middletown at last came to an end in October, with Referees James M. Pierce, Chalmers Scott and W.A. Winder giving to Rose clear title to two regulation-sized blocks and to 11 lots spread over another two blocks. Additionally, the referees said Rose owned two lots that had been designated for railroad right of way through Middletown. The $7,052.06 cost of the "friendly" litigation was apportioned among the various property owners.[287] Rose probably was unenthusiastic about paying his $59.45 share given the financial hard times that he and everyone in San Diego had been experiencing since the onset of the Panic of 1873. It had been a challenge for Rose in 1874 just to hang on. What Rose couldn't know was that 1875 would be far worse—perhaps the worst year of his life.

Louis Rose, circa 1870
©San Diego Historical Society

CHAPTER 5

The Rose Wilts

Rose's Worst Year

The year began inauspiciously. An Indian known simply by the name of "José" was found January 13, 1875, lying face down in the dirt near the Cosmopolitan Hotel, an empty liquor bottle in his hand. Louis Rose and four other Old Town residents were summoned by Coroner Charles Merwin Fenn to serve as a jury in the inquest. There was little for the jury to decide: José had died from gunshot wounds.[1]

A few days later, some "strangers" called on Rose and offered him $20 a lot for some of his Roseville property. Rose told them the asking price for each lot was $250 and he was sticking to it. "He has faith in the future," applauded the *San Diego Union*.[2] The newspaper knew more than it reported, but had been asked by Rose to keep mum about the subject of a possible sale. However on April 29, 1875, following publication in the *Los Angeles Star* of an item about the Southern Pacific Railroad Company reportedly being interested in Roseville, the *San Diego Union* felt it was freed from the pledge of confidentiality it had made to Rose. "Some two months ago we were informed by Rose that he had a standing offer of $65,000 for that magnificent waterfront property... It was not stated that the railroad people were the parties proposing the buy, but that was the surmise of Mr. Rose and others."[3]

Rose apparently enjoyed brief respite from such financial news when members of the Teutonia Verein, a German-speaking social club, took a ferry to his "handsomely decorated" hotel in Roseville for a picnic. In June, he sold to Elias M. Robinson for $20 the Roseville lot he had purchased from the tax collector eight months before for $5.[4] This was not really a significant enough profit to take much pleasure in, but at least it was not a loss.

The most devastating blow of the year came on August 4, after six years and four months of his marriage to Matilda. Rose was 68, nearly 30 years older than his wife. But it was she, not he, who took sick during the summer. Suddenly she was experiencing high fever, terrible headaches and vomiting. Dr. Fenn, who five years earlier had been one of the seven founding members of the San Diego Medical Society, said sadly that there was little that could be done to help her in her fight against meningitis. She was only 39 when she died.[5] It is assumed that she also was buried at the old Jewish cemetery, next to her little daughter Helene.

Their other daughter, Henrietta, then 3 years and 3 months old, mitigated Rose's grief. But how could a 68-year-old man, even one as energetic as Rose, take care of a toddler? Obviously he needed help, not only from servants but also from neighbors. The Robinson-Rose home and the Casa de Wrightington nearly joined at the southwest corner of Old Town Plaza. The widow Juana Machado de Wrightington was known throughout the city for her kind heart, and she showered attention and affection on the motherless Henrietta.

"There was a patio behind the house," Henrietta told an interviewer more than a half-century after her mother's death. "I remember old roses, acacia, old century plant. Twilight in that old garden—a rambling garden, it almost touched the Wrightington place... Mrs. Wrightington made the best tortillas. She cared for my mother when I was born." Henrietta also recalled childhood walks with her father to the old Pear Garden, which had become known as "Rose's Garden." "I remember the pomegranates from the Rose Garden place and the figs and the pears," she said. [6]

The family tragedy was coupled with continued hard financial times resulting from the effects of the Panic of 1873 and San Diego's lack of progress in attracting a railroad. Rose, land rich and cash poor, again was experiencing cash flow problems. He sold an entire block of Roseville—12 lots—to Charles Yassen on September 24, 1875, for $1,200. Instead of $250 per lot, he had settled for $100 per lot.[7]

In a letter to Rose on October 19, 1875, Morse commiserated. "Friend Rose," he wrote. "I saw an acquaintance who often has money but at this time he has none and I do not know where any can be had. Money is really very scarce. In looking over the delinquent advertisement published this week in the *Union* I notice that several lots of yours are among the number (unless you have sold them)."[8] As the county recorder's records do not indicate any properties seized from Rose for taxes, it was possible that Morse was mistaken or that Rose scraped up enough money to pay the tax bill.

Writing for the *San Diego Union* a little more than fifty years later, Daniel Cleveland reported about Rose: 'In later years from unfavorable conditions, he suffered heavy losses and was unable to, as had been his wont, to pay his obligations promptly and in full. A few years later he again prospered in business. He then paid all his old obligations in full—principal and interest—though they were then barred by the statute of limitations."[9] Cleveland's account was repeated in one form or another many times and became part of the legend of Louis Rose. One reporter suggested that the debts in question were incurred in the 1860s and paid in the 1870s.[10] Another account suggested Rose incurred the debts in question in the period following the end of the Tom Scott boom.[11] As Rose did not keep records of his transactions, and no other first-person account has been cited, we only can take this story on faith. However, the tale provides a sense of Rose's values and determination during hard times. No year ever had been harder for him than 1875.

Sale of the Pear Garden

To meet financial obligations, Rose made two sales on May 23, 1876. He received $800 from Joseph Allison for 55 undeveloped acres near Roseville[12] and another $800 from G. Ligare for five lots in Middletown.[13] On June 22, he made what must have been one of the most painful land sales in his life. For $500, he sold to attorney Norman H. Conklin[14], attorney for the San Diego Mutual Land Association, some lots in Old Town. Among them was what was known in the cold language of real estate transactions as a portion of Block 410 on the Poole Map. It was the beloved Pear Garden, the spot from which Josefa Carrillo had dashed on horseback to her lover Henry Fitch. The romantic Rose had paid $2,000 to present it for Matilda, now gone from him.[15]

As stretched financially as Rose was, he still was personally quite generous. Morse did not hesitate to write to him, for example, to look after the interests and health of Joshua Sloane, a fellow Mason residing in Old Town, who had fallen on hard times.[16]

Abandonment by the Railroad

Meanwhile, Texas and Pacific President Tom Scott tried to overcome the effects of the Panic of 1873 by asking Congress to subsidize construction of his line. But Collis Huntington told Congress that his new Southern Pacific could construct a railroad from California to the southern tier of states at far less cost to the federal government. As the rival railroad men each had powerful supporters in Congress, they eventually were forced to conclude that a compromise was essential.

At the end of 1876, Huntington agreed to stop opposing a subsidy for the Texas and Pacific east of California. For his part, Scott agreed to cede the Texas and Pacific's rights in California to the Southern Pacific. Further the two men agreed that each company could operate trains on the other's tracks. Scott also agreed to support a congressional subsidy for the Southern Pacific.[17]

The compromise eliminated San Diego as the western terminus in favor of San Francisco. The outraged citizenry of San Diego sent a telegram to Scott contending that he had failed to honor his contractual obligations to the city. "Have used my utmost efforts to secure San Diego a railroad line on such route as can best affect the object and if can affect it in any better shape that I can, I should be very glad to have you take it up and adjust it with any party or on any terms that you may think best, but in taking these steps I shall expect you to relieve me of all possible obligations," he telegraphed back.[18]

San Diegans decided they should try to reclaim from the Texas and Pacific Railroad the lands in the city and the county that had been donated for its right of way, terminal and shops. They wanted to be able to offer the same lands to any other railroad willing to lay a line between Fort Yuma and San Diego.

However, the effort did little to alleviate the sense of economic disaster that settled over many speculators who had pinned their hopes on San Diego someday becoming an important land-sea transportation center. Rose's dream for Roseville had been predicated on the economic success of the greater San Diego region. While he certainly was unwilling to abandon his dream, Rose had to conclude reluctantly that the plans for a bayside city that he once had laid with James W. Robinson were at very best a long shot—at least during his lifetime. Unlike Horton's Addition, which for nearly a decade could boast a permanent population, Roseville remained a town with only a few dwellings.

Postmaster

On September 19, 1877, during the administration of the nineteenth U.S. President, Rutherford B. Hayes, Rose was appointed as postmaster for the North San Diego Post Office, otherwise known as the Old Town San Diego Post Office.[19] As Rose had been a long-time Democrat, it was a considerable honor for his application to be accepted during a Republican's administration. He continued to serve under the twentieth and twenty-first U.S. presidents, James Garfield and Chester Arthur, also Republicans. Rose remained in the post through 1883.

Postmaster for North San Diego was by no means a high-paying position. Official Registers of the United States showed that in 1879 Rose received only $121.08 in compensation—less than half of what he had received in payment for a single lot during the real estate boom in Roseville. In 1881, he was compensated $135.81, and in 1883, $93.61.

At age 70, the widower Rose was entering a new, more passive, phase of his life. His Roseville dreams were on hold; he no longer was active in any policy-making positions either in local government or on a railroad board of directors. His daughter, now old enough to begin elementary school, needed less attention. What was he to do with his life? Not for the money, but the opportunity it gave him to spend his time constructively, the postmaster position was well suited for the old entrepreneur. Always one who enjoyed talking over public affairs with his fellow townsmen, the new postmaster was assured of hearing lots of news while it still was fresh.

Coincidentally, Rose's friend James W. Robinson had applied for the same job twenty years before, but his appointment from the fifteenth U.S. President, James Buchanan, did not come through until November 18, 1857—about three weeks after Robinson's death.[20]

Renewed Railroad Hopes

Rivalry again flared between the Southern Pacific and the Texas and Pacific Railroad, notwithstanding their previous agreement. In May 1877, the Southern Pacific had completed its track to Fort Yuma and began to eye Arizona—a territory that the T&P considered its exclusive turf. To counter this move, the T&P made overtures to San Diego about building a railroad from the Colorado River to the port. Once again, San Diego decided to back that line's efforts in Congress to obtain funding.

"Friend Rose, Please bring me 200 1-cent stamps when you come down and oblige your humble servant," New Town-based Morse wrote April 11, 1878, to the postmaster of Old Town. He added: "I was pleased to see the large majority with which the railroad-funding bill passed, 40-19. I think it is good augury for our bill. It shows that the railroads do not own the Senate yet. But yet many who voted to bring them to terms will vote against the Texas and Pacific for fear of creating another great monopoly..."[21]

Quoting Matthew Sherman, who had been in Washington to represent San Diego's railroad interests, Morse again wrote Rose on June 17:

> The general opinion at Washington among our friends (is) that the bill... is continually gaining friends throughout the country. He says he feels quite cheerful over the prospect. Sherman had a talk with Huntington (of the Southern Pacific) and says he is satisfied that we can never hope for anything from them, that they never intend to come here and will prevent if possible anyone else from coming. Huntington told him they were going to build 100 miles immediately into Arizona and would never allow Scott to get here. The T&P people don't believe they will build a mile; they say they don't have the financial ability to do so, that they are now paying 1 percent interest per month on the millions borrowed to build the Southern Pacific upon their individual notes.[22]

Rose in Semi-Retirement

The next day Rose turned his attention to far more pleasant local matters. As he had in 1863 for the wedding of Heyman Mannasse and Hannah Schiller, Rose conducted a Jewish marriage ceremony for Rosa Meyer and Daniel Cave, one of the town's dentists. The couple also was united in a civil rite officiated by the Justice of the Peace Joseph Leonard. The Jewish wedding was held in the home of Simon Levi, who served as official witness to the proceedings along with Isaac Meyer.[23]

As railroad matters continued to drag on in Congress, San Diegans sought ways to stimulate the local economy. Morse, promoting the cause of a local apiary, suggested to a correspondent that Rose might be persuaded to contact his brother, Simon, in Germany, to see if he'd be interested in introducing San Diego honey to the European market.[24] There is no evidence anything ever came of the inquiry.

Rose again was experiencing cash flow problems when Morse wrote on February 22, 1879, "Friend Rose: I had a talk with Dr. Cave. He spoke of you with very good feeling and was surprised that the amount was so small that you needed to save so much property. He thought you wanted $10,000. He thinks your nephew would unquestionably assist you if he was here (in San Diego), but not to the amount of the thousands that you expect, for they have no confidence in the value of San Diego lands. He wrote to them very favorably, that you had been offered $100,000 at one time for a portion of your property, but he don't think they would make much on the value of the lands." Morse then encouraged Rose to ask old friends like Oliver Witherby and James McCoy to help him raise money, and added: 'If you let this property be sold, your nephew will not be half as likely to help you. Don't give up as long as there is any show of help...'[25]

We may surmise that Rose followed Morse's advice or found some other source of money, because no sales of his land were recorded at any time proximate to this communication.

The delicacy of Rose's financial situation was illustrated by frequent references by Morse to some matter involving jewelry for which Rose apparently owed Morse money. "I want that jewelry matter settled," Morse wrote with irritation on April 23, 1879:

> They have called on me for a settlement and I can't put it off any longer. I shall expect you to come down next Tuesday and settle it up. You have treated me badly in this matter you had no right to compromise me, whatever you might do for yourself, especially when you knew I did it as an act of kindness to you. Please bring me 100 postal cards when you come next Tuesday.[26]

Morse followed up on May 27:

> Friend Rose, it is over a month since I wrote to you about the
> jewelry matter; that was not an ordinary debt and I want it set-
> tled or there will be trouble.[27]

Again on June 22, 1879, he wrote to Rose, dropping the usual "Friend" from
the salutation:

> Mr. Rose. I do dislike to keep continually reminding you of
> that jewelry matter. I must have an account from you in some
> shape immediately or it will be unpleasant for both of us.[28]

Yet, in that same letter, Morse turned to the possibility of a new railroad
having some interest in San Diego. "I have very little hope but an effort can do
no harm if it does us good," he said.

On July 10, matters between the two old friends had thawed somewhat:
"Friend Rose," Morse wrote. "I wish you would bring me 300 1-cent stamps
for 5s and 10s first time you come down. No special RR news but there is a
rumor in town that the A.T. & Santa Fe people will yet come here to look at
our place before they return east."[29] Morse's reference apparently was to the
fact that Frank Kimball was attempting to stimulate other railroads to take an
interest in San Diego, and particularly in his extensive property in National City.

When Kimball approached the financier Jay Gould the year before about
constructing a railroad to the San Diego area, he was rebuffed with the memorable line: "I don't build railroads; I buy them!"[30] Thomas Nickerson, president
of the Atchison, Topeka & Santa Fe Railroad, gave Kimball a more sympathetic
hearing.

Morse wrote to Rose in better humor on September 2, 1879: "Friend
Rose, I want that jewelry matter fixed up so that I can settle with the banks. I
won't send you a bit of good railroad news till you fix this up, mind ye now!"[31]

Three representatives of the railroad came to San Diego to conduct a survey,
but although they seemed positive, the Santa Fe contact suddenly went cold.
Nickerson's company decided to join forces with a railroad known as the
Atlantic and Pacific and cross into California at Needles, well north of San
Diego.[32]

Frank Kimball nevertheless continued to pursue the Santa Fe, eventually
persuading the railroad to build a line from National City through San Diego
to a point 80 miles east of San Bernardino where the railroad could join with
the line of the Atlantic and Pacific. San Diego city lands previously deeded to
the Texas and Pacific were needed to bring this deal to fruition, prompting the
Board of Trustees to send Tom Scott a telegram on December 18, 1879, offering

to drop the city's lawsuit against the Texas & Pacific provided that the contested land were split between the city and the railroad.[33]

Scott responded by telegram the following day: "We will do what you desire, provided all pending suits are settled in such a way that no future annoyance or litigation can arise out of the lands that were deeded to our company..."[34] The agreement was accepted by the courts in February 1880, and the land not retained by the Texas and Pacific Railroad was deeded by the city to the Santa Fe Railroad.

On July 17, 1880, Morse wrote to Rose: "Of we can only hold on for a few years, we must see busy times here. God grant we may see it this year but things do move terribly slow."[35]

Kimball's long-sought train route between National City and San Diego was inaugurated on July 27, 1881. The line that became known as the California Southern was extended to Colton in 1882 and to San Bernardino on September 13, 1883. [36]

In 1881, when Rose was 74, the postmaster drew an admiring few lines from a *San Diego Union* editor who came upon him in New Town: "Mr. Rose thinks this is a healthy climate. He walks in and back from Old Town."[37]

Rose answered an appeal from Abraham Klauber in July 1882 to contribute funds for the renovation of the Jewish cemetery that Rose had donated to the community approximately two decades earlier. Thirty-one members of the cemetery organization refenced and replanted the property, laying out little streets and boundaries. Other members of the organization included Abraham Blochman, the vice president, and Simon Levi, the treasurer.[38]

At age 76, Rose gave up his position as postmaster.[39] He was succeeded by Percy W. Goodwin on July 11, 1883. That same year, the *San Diego Union* reported that Rose had decided to give up chewing tobacco "after 67 years of indulgence." This was probably an exaggeration. If Rose had been at it that long, it meant he had been chewing since the age of nine.[40] Morse continued to update Rose with railroad news in 1884, also warning him that several parcels of his land were being advertised in the *San Diego Union* for delinquent taxes.[41] Not long after Rose received that letter, he decided that it was time for him to retire once and for all.

The Final Years

In 1884, Rose moved from his beloved Old Town to New Town, where chronic health problems could be carefully monitored. There were reports that Rose was going blind and that he suffered from a bad hernia. He placed his fiscal affairs on November 3, 1884, in the hands of five trustees: Dr. Daniel Cave, Simon Levi, George Dannals, Charles P. Noell and John A. Love, stipulating that once taxes and necessary expenses were paid, all his assets should vest in his daughter Henrietta. As she then was a minor, Rose said the trustees should continue to act in her behalf "until she married becomes of lawful age, when this trust shall terminate."[42]

Noell, who had resigned the Common Council in 1850 in protest of its profligacy, ironically would die two months before Rose.[43] A member of Love's family, Lizzie, was appointed to serve as guardian for Henrietta, who turned 12 years old in 1884. Trustees of Rose's estate sold six lots in Roseville for $100 in August of 1885.[44]

Always interested in the railroad, Rose probably was told by his friends that on November 15, 1885, the first train left San Diego on a trip over Atchison, Topeka and Santa Fe tracks that would connect with eastbound trunk railroad lines, and that on November 21 the first westbound through-train brought 60 passengers to a San Diego celebration that wasn't at all dampened by pouring rain.[45] We do not know if the ailing Rose was able to attend either ceremony, or if he subsequently learned that following a washout of the Santa Fe's tracks in the Temecula area, the railroad decided to abandon the through route to San Diego. Henceforth, what little rail service to or from San Diego would have to be via a branch line from Los Angeles[46]

Promotional writers filled national magazines with paeans of praise for San Diego and its various venues. In approximately 1886, a writer for *The Golden Era* magazine likened the vista from Roseville to one seen in Italy—and if anyone read the description to Rose, he no doubt would have enjoyed it:

> From the townsite of Roseville the gaze goes beyond the three inlets or reaches from the bay, and we rest our eyes on the city that already hugs the hill in so compact a way, with a certain newness about it, to be sure, and a deal of character on its own, and yet betraying a form and a suggestion of the Bay and City of Naples, with table Mountain, far away in Mexico, and San Miguel, a little to the left, the two standing instead of Vesuvius, the dust in lieu of smoke from the crater, and the adjacent mountains lying back in sullen grandeur like those frowning over Naples... Is this the busy nineteenth century in America, or the seventeenth in Italy? is the reality a dream, or the dream a reality?[47]

On December 18, 1887, Dr. M.E. Munger was called to Rose's bedside at 742 Third Street in New Town. The 80-year-old pioneer was suffering from what appeared to be a bad case of asthma.[48]

Two weeks after Rose's asthma attack, efforts to once again interest investors in Roseville property were made at the behest of Frank Jennings and George Crippen, a pair of developers who understood Rose's vision and decided to build upon it. The partners formed Point Loma Land, Loan and Town Co. and purchased property in the hills just west of Roseville. They named their new development "Roseville Heights." Additionally they built a new wharf and arranged to purchase a steamboat, which became the *Roseville*, to provide service between its namesake townsite and San Diego.[49]

An advertisement placed by Bancroft & Company, a real estate concern, appearing New Year's Day, 1888, told *San Diego Union* readers:

> Roseville is close to deep water. Roseville property is in good demand. Roseville has got a new and substantial wharf. Roseville will be connected with the California Southern Railroad at Old Town by a broad gauge heavy steel track. Roseville will have lumber yards for the transshipment of lumber to the interior. Roseville will soon be connected with Ocean Beach by steam motor. Roseville will have a ferry running to San Diego soon. Ties have already been delivered at Roseville for the Ocean Beach motor road. Roseville will be supplied with water from Mission Valley. All passengers to and from Ocean Beach will pass through Roseville. Roseville is a good business property. Roseville is a fine residence property. Roseville is attracting the attention of investors. Roseville offers special advantage to speculators. Roseville is all we claim for it. For a reliable list of Roseville property call at our office.[50]

It is regrettable that Rose's eyesight was not keen enough to permit him to read the advertisement personally. Had his daughter Henrietta read the notice to him aloud, the repeated refrain of Roseville might have calmed him as surely as David's songs comforted King Saul. Also soothing to Rose would have been the news that investors had decided to build Roseville's first factory, San Diego Nail and Iron Works.[51]

Death of Louis Rose

Rose died February 12, 1888—exactly 80 years, ten months and ten days after his birth in Neuhaus-an-der-Oste. He was buried two days later at the Hebrew Cemetery that he had donated to the community. The death certificate listed Rose's profession as a capitalist, and noted that he had resided for thirty-eight years in the city that he had helped to shape. The actual cause of death was given as "old age and asthma which was contracted at San Diego, Calif."[52]

In an obituary the following morning, the *San Diego Sun* suggested that Rose did more "to advance the interest of the county than any of his followers." The newspaper continued: "His death occurred at the house of a friend on Third Street and was due to a complication of diseases. His career was an eventful one...The remains of Lewis Rose will be interred in the Jewish cemetery at Old Town, deceased having deeded the land for a cemetery at that place. The funeral which will be conducted by the Masonic Lodge of San Diego, will take place tomorrow afternoon at 2 o'clock from the Masonic Temple. Mr. Rose was, perhaps, the oldest Mason in San Diego County, having advanced to a high degree in the order. There will be a short service at his late residence on Third Street conducted by the rabbi of the Israelite Synagogue, after which the body will lie in state in the Masonic Temple."[53]

On February 14, 1888, the *San Diego Union* recalled that Rose had "laid out the townsite of Roseville, built a hotel and constructed a wharf to the deep water of La Playa. His object was to found the present city of San Diego at that point. At one point, he was the possessor of about 4,000 acres. About four years ago, he disposed of nearly all his property except a portion of Roseville... It is estimated he was worth $75,000, which is bequeathed to his daughter Henrietta."[54]

Many years later, Henrietta said her "father made and lost several fortunes here in San Diego. He was a man of great honor. He was always talking about the future of San Diego."[55]

San Diego historians refer to Alonzo Horton as "Father Horton" for the key role he played in developing San Diego's downtown. It is equally fair to describe Louis Rose as San Diego's "Uncle Rose." Parents are the primary influences on a child, and such was true of Horton's relationship to modern San Diego. Yet many children cherish the memories of their aunts and uncles as people who helped them to develop and who occasionally offered them new perspectives. Such was Rose's role.

Louis Rose brand

EPILOGUE

The Robinson Family Fight

*L*ouis Rose and James W. Robinson would have been deeply disappointed to learn that the friendship they forged would result in their descendants being pitted against each other in a protracted court suit over who had rightful claim to Robinson's estate.

In his will, Robinson had left all his property to his second wife, Sarah, and to their son, William. The document made no mention of Robinson's first wife, Mary, nor of their surviving children, Albina and Martha.

William died a few years after being committed to an insane asylum. Sarah's assumption that her husband's estate therefore belonged exclusively to her was challenged in 1890 in a lawsuit brought by Robinson's married daughter, Albina Whitworth. She was joined in a court suit by her late sister Martha's four children, who claimed a share of the inheritance was due them as the grandchildren of James W. Robinson. They were Martha R. Barker, Lucy F. Barker, Cora E. Fizz, and Albina Humphrey.

They contended that they, not Sarah, were entitled to Robinson's estate because they were the product of a legitimate union whereas Sarah had committed adultery with their father. Not only did they lay claim to whatever property Sarah still controlled, but to all the property that had been in Robinson's possession at the time of his death, about thirty years previously. As Sarah and William Robinson had sold most of that property to Rose, and that which Rose retained had been passed on to his daughter, Henrietta Rose became one of the many defendants in the Robinson family suit.

Robinson's properties had been located in Old Town, Middletown, and along that portion of the bay that Rose had fashioned into Roseville. While Rose had retained many of the parcels, others, especially in Roseville, had been sold to a variety of buyers. By the time the case came to court in 1891, the interests of more than 160 people and corporations were involved.

Why had the heirs of Robinson's first marriage waited so long to bring their case? They explained that they had seen various letters that Robinson had written to his brother, William, back home, and as he was always pleading for money, they had concluded that Robinson had been a poor man. But after they became aware that Sarah was about to cash government bonds worth $10,000 in a Cincinnati bank, they learned the truth: that although Robinson may have at one time been cash poor, he had left many assets. Sarah, who had run away

with the man who was the plaintiff's father or grandfather, had become a relatively rich woman—rewarded, in their view, for her sin.[1]

Henrietta Rose turned 18 years old on May 22, 1890. As this meant
Henrietta had reached the "age of majority," Lizzie Love's guardianship over
her duly was terminated July 17. At the same time, under the provisions of the
trust set up by her father, Henrietta stood to inherit the properties that had
been managed since 1884 by trustees.

Before she could make any use of the portion of her father's estate that previously had been owned by Robinson, Henrietta had to await the outcome of
the court case. Superior Court Judge George Puterbaugh ruled on December
22, 1891, that Martha's children and Albina indeed were rightful heirs.
However, he said that various properties that already had been sold by Sarah
Robinson could not be included in their inheritance.

To Henrietta, Judge Puterbaugh specifically awarded 21 blocks of
Roseville (each with a potential of being divided into 12 lots) as well as
another 20 lots scattered over three other Roseville blocks. He also awarded to
her 9 blocks in Old Town, each divisible into approximately 4 lots, as well as 9
other lots dispersed over 4 Old Town blocks. Additionally he ruled that
Henrietta was the owner of a large, undeveloped irregularly-shaped Pueblo
Lot, No. 22, which required 15 lines in his opinion to describe.[2]

Apparently anticipating such a decision from the judge, the plaintiffs on
March 1, 1891, deeded the properties in question over to Henrietta, charging
her only $10 to cover various recording fees.[3] Other litigants were not so for-
tunate; for some of them, the case dragged on through 1913.[4]

Henrietta Rose, School Teacher

Known as "Hattie" to her friends, Henrietta Rose decided to pursue a
career as a schoolteacher. She studied at both the University of California and
at San Diego State College.[5] The June 4, 1894, minutes of the San Diego Board
of Education reveal that she was among more than a score of applicants for a
job as a teacher. However, she was not among those who were recommended
for positions on June 18.[6]

After the board received notification on December 3, 1894, that construction had been completed on a new elementary school in the Roseville area,
the board decided to appoint Henrietta as a teacher there at the salary of $70
per month. Appointing the 22-year-old daughter of the man who founded
Roseville to the area's first school may have been the board's way of acknowl-
edging the memory of Louis Rose, who himself once had been a school board
trustee. The decision was not made for lack of other candidates. Roseville residents, in fact, had petitioned for the appointment of Lina Stone to the posi-

tion. Carrie A. House, the school board member who headed the board's committee on teachers, recommended Hattie.[7]

When school assignments were made in June for the following term, Hattie Rose was transferred to the Middletown School, where she was assigned as a fourth-grade teacher. Lina Stone was given Hattie's former job as a beginning teacher at Roseville School. At the board meeting at which this was approved, there was an interesting side discussion over the board's policy to routinely dismiss women teachers upon their marriages. Mr. Arndt objected to the policy and told his fellow board members he wanted his protest entered in the record. All that teachers should be judged upon, he said, was whether they did good work—married or not.[8]

Hattie taught fourth grade in Middletown school from 1896 through 1908, except or a brief stint in 1907 in the lower grades. The year that she accepted the assignment in a lower grade, it took a 12-1 vote by the school board for her to continue receiving the $80 a month earned by fourth grade teachers. Without the school board's endorsement, her salary would have gone down to the $70 paid to teachers in the lower grades.[9]

When not teaching, Hattie filled her life with Masonic activities. Because her father had been a Mason, she was eligible to join the Eastern Star organization, a women's affiliate. In 1901, she became worthy matron of Southern Star, Chapter 96, of the Eastern Star. No doubt her father, who rose only to the level of Junior Warden of Masonic Lodge No. 35, would have been pleased that his daughter made it to the very top of her lodge.

She was recommended for transfer to Sherman Elementary School, located at 22nd and J Streets, in June 1908. The school had been named for an acquaintance of her father's, Matthew Sherman, who had represented the San Diego's railroad interests and later had been a candidate in a hotly contested city council election. By the time of Hattie's transfer, she was a veteran fourth grade teacher. Pay scales varied according to how many years experience the teacher had, with five years teaching experience (or higher) being the top pay grade. A pay scale adopted on June 8 indicated Hattie's yearly salary as well as those of other teachers.[10]

Grades	1st	2nd	3rd	4th	5th
5–8	650	680	710	750	800
3–4	610	640	670	710	760
2	600	630	660	700	760
1	650	680	710	750	800

A committee of the school board reported in 1912 that other school districts throughout the state were paying their teachers on a year-round basis rather than just for the school term. A new schedule would have advanced Hattie's salary by perhaps a couple hundred dollars. As it turned out, however, she did even better because at the same time the new schedule went into effect, Hattie was promoted from fourth-grade teacher to a departmental teacher specializing in literature and geography. Accordingly her yearly salary for the 1912-1913 school year increased to $1,092. [11]

Residing at 1148 8th Street, Hattie's circle of friends most likely included the teachers who were listed year after year on the roster with her at Sherman Elementary School. Among them were Alice Bradley, who was a departmental teacher for history; Ruth MacLenathan, who became a vice principal and special education teacher; 6th grade teacher Kate Wright; 5th grade teacher Helena Krause and 2nd grade teacher Sara Leisenring. Should any of them want to confer with Hattie after hours, they could telephone her at the Main exchange 1227-J.[12]

Destined to remain unmarried, Hattie's life was regulated by the rhythms of the school year. Changes in her life were marked by slight differences in the way her assignments were listed in the school directory. Instead of literature and geography, her departmental specialties in the 1914–15 school year were listed as literature and drawing. In 1916–17, they were literature and Spanish; in 1918–19, the specialty was just literature, but the following year, Spanish again was added to her responsibilities. In the 1921–22 year, she continued to be departmental teacher of literature and Spanish, but added the 8A grade to her portfolio.[13] This proved to be important experience, because after 28 years of teaching at the elementary and middle school levels she was transferred in the 1922–23 school year to Theodore Roosevelt Junior High School. The junior high had been named for the nation's 26th president, whose death had come only a few years before on January 6, 1919.

Hattie is Crippled

The Thanksgiving 1924 issue of *Rough Rider*, a student magazine at the junior high school, reported: "Señorita Rose is greatly missed by her classes. They sincerely hope she will recover quickly and be back with them soon. In the meantime, Señora Sterne from the senior high is doing a great deal for them and is leading them right along keeping them up to standard and preparing them for the Latin work which will confront them as soon as they reach high school." [14]

Apparently Hattie had been hit by a car, or had suffered a major fall. In its Christmas issue, the student magazine addressed this wish to Miss Rose: "There is probably no student in Roosevelt who does not know that through accident Miss Rose has been in the hospital for several weeks. Everyone thinks she has been remarkably cheerful and wish her speedy recovery. Her Spanish pupils would say *Felices Pascuas* but we want to deliver a message for a Merry Xmas and a Happy New Year." [15]

The fact that Miss Rose was born of two Jewish parents either was unknown to the students or not an issue. There is no evidence that Hattie was particularly involved in the Jewish community, nor is there any suggestion that she had converted. On the back page of the student magazine, where students listed their wishes, one said: "I wish Santa would bring…Miss Rose a new hip so she could get back to us." [16]

The teacher was back helping her students by the 1925-26 school year. A student editor picked Hattie's name for use that year in a *Rough Rider* humor column:

> Miss Rose: "I would like an apron to slip on around the house."
> Fresh young clerk: "How large is your house?" [17]

Hattie taught both English and Spanish the following two years, and also was assigned in the 1929–30 school year to a one-year stint supervising study hall.

At the end of 1929, a humor columnist for the *Rough Rider* informed students that "we have been looking into the past lives of our various instructors and you would be surprised at the dire things we have found there." Among the unlikely "discoveries," the fanciful writer found that "Miss Rose wrote scenarios for custard pie comedies." [18]

Hattie moved from 8th Street to 3630 Indiana Street in time for the 1930-31 school year. Her new telephone number was Hillcrest 0433W. In *Roosevelt Roundups,* as students named their publication that year, writer Marilyn Brenner devised "Phamous Phrases Phrom Teachers" as a humorous offering. For Miss Rose it was "I'm Right Here." [19] In the 1931–32 school year, Hattie taught English exclusively. [20]

Elizabeth LaBorde attended Roosevelt Junior High School from 1932 through 1934. She was then known by her maiden name of Elizabeth Cook and nickname "Cookie." "I can remember Miss Rose standing by the door of her classroom, with a pencil at her side, wearing a high-shirt waist, and a bell-shaped skirt longer than the other teachers', perhaps to cover her awkwardness," she recalled in an interview 65 years later. The former Roosevelt Junior High School student also remembered that Hattie "walked with a limp," no doubt as a result of the accident that had injured her hip. [21]

San Diego History Revival

In 1934, there was a revival of interest in San Diego history, perhaps attendant to the buildup for the 1935 California-Pacific Exhibition in Balboa Park.

Hyman Wolf, representing various Jewish organizations as well as the San Diego Historical Society, affixed a small bronze plaque to a giant eucalyptus tree on Rosecrans Street between Byron and Addison Streets, which read: "Here Louis Rose founded Roseville, 1869."

The tree was cut down in a road-widening project, and the plaque found its way to the Point Loma Real Estate offices at 1050 Rosecrans Avenue, where realtor Robert Leanders and his wife Gail hung it on a wall for approximately 15 years, with one interruption. For approximately three years, Leanders recalled, the plaque was displayed in the lobby of San Diego Federal Savings & Loan at 1004 Rosecrans, where it remained until the financial institution went out of business. In March 2003, Leanders placed the plaque in the offices of the San Diego County Credit Union, where San Diego Federal previously had its offices, because "more people would see it there." When this author visited the credit union building at the corner of Rosecrans and Talbot on February 9, 2004, the plaque was being kept in the office of Assistant Vice President Annette Balelo.[22]

Hattie participated in a ceremony that was held May 30, 1934, on the median divider along Highway 101 in the area of the city still known as Rose Canyon. The ceremony was sponsored by members of the Cuyamaca Club, a luncheon group of San Diego business leaders. In particular, Leroy A. Wright, the club's president, wanted to take notice of Rose for having the vision to start the first tannery in Southern California. Apparently believing that the entre-preneurial Rose also was responsible for a major brick making operation in Rose Canyon, club members gave him undeserved attention during the cere-mony for being a brickmaker.

The Rose Canyon Brick Company[23] was not started by Thomas Hill until 1888, the year Rose died and more than a quarter century after Rose's indebt-edness had forced him to sell Rose Canyon. Hill's operation was the one that inspired the Atchison, Topeka and Santa Fe Railroad to name one of its sidings in Rose Canyon the "Ladrillo Station"—"ladrillo" being Spanish for brick.

San Diego Mayor John F. Forward, featured speaker at the Rose Canyon ceremony, pointed out that Rose had come to San Diego in 1850, was a mem-ber of the first grand jury and had helped to found the San Diego and Gila Railroad as well as Masonic Lodge Number 35. Forward also told the gather-ing of about 100 people that Rose had founded Roseville and that "at one time he was offered $100,000 for the town site, but refused it, believing it would be the future city… He was a most enterprising citizen, and, at times, had consid-erable means."

When Hattie's turn came to speak, she said, "my father was a modest man and I know he never dreamed of the honor you are bestowing upon him." Among those organizations and individuals who donated funds for the monu-ment were Tifereth Israel Synagogue, $15; Lasker Lodge, B'nai B'rith, $5; San

Diego Masonic Lodge No. 35, $12; Hattie herself, $10; Samuel I Fox, $5; Mayor Forward, $5 and Dan Rossi, $5 for a total of $57.[24] The plaque said:

HONORING
Louis Rose
1807–1888
Founder of Roseville
Pioneer of Rose Canyon
Brickmaker-Tanner
Outstanding Citizen
Congregations
Beth Israel
and
Tifereth Israel
and
San Diego Lodge F. & A.M.
May 30, 1934

Hattie Retires

Students editing Roosevelt Junior High School's publication *Twentieth Century Progress*, a name that reflected the theme of the 1935 California-Pacific Exhibition that had been held next door in Balboa Park, decided to draw a composite of the ideal female teacher. She would have the patience, luck, sweetness, sewing ability, cooking ability, clothes, personality, fairness, kindness, artistic ability, smile, and musical ability of various named teachers on the faculty, as well as "the handwriting of Miss Rose."[25]

In the 1938–39 year, Hattie's teaching hours were reduced to half-time. She taught not only English but social science as well. The student publication, renamed that year as *The Scarlet and the Grey*, again lauded Miss Rose's handwriting as a component in the assembly of a perfect teacher.[26]

Hattie's last year teaching was in the 1939–40 school year. After 45 years, she was ready to retire. But the teaching profession still was her love. In the 1941–42 school year, she became treasurer of the retired teachers' club. She also moved to a new residence at 4031½ Highland Avenue. Her phone number was Talbot 6874.[27]

Relocation of the Jewish Cemetery

Meanwhile, the Jewish Cemetery that had been deeded by Louis Rose to the community had fallen into disuse. Jewish families preferred to bury their loved ones in consecrated ground adjacent to the city's Mount Hope Cemetery in Southeast San Diego. This separate land became known as the Home of Peace Cemetery.

In 1939, with the approval of the board of directors of Congregation Beth Israel, the bodies of Louis Rose and other pioneer Jews were exhumed from their graves near Roseville and re-interred at the Home of Peace Cemetery. As the successor in interest to both Congregation Adath Yeshurun and the Hebrew Benevolent Society, Congregation Beth Israel was the owner of the old 5-acre Jewish cemetery land, which it subsequently sold to developers. Eventually, Doctor's Hospital was built upon the land; that institution later became Sharp Cabrillo Hospital.

Hattie gave permission for four members of her family to be re-interred— her father Louis, mother Matilda, sister Helene, and an unidentified "uncle" whom she said she never knew.[28] Beth Israel's Rabbi Moise Bergman conducted the re-interment ceremony in which Rose was placed in a wooden casket donated by the City of San Diego. A weather-beaten marker that had designated his grave at the old cemetery was reinstalled above him at his new resting place. It's an unresolved question whether the family was buried together. There are no grave markers nearby for Matilda Rose or Helene Rose. Although all the family members reportedly were re-interred at the Home of Peace Cemetery, by 1995 only Louis Rose's name was listed in that cemetery's records, according to Roberta Wagner Berman of the San Diego Jewish Genealogical Society.[29]

Death of Hattie Rose

Besides in the retired teachers' club, Hattie remained active in the Southern Star chapter, today known simply as the San Diego chapter of Eastern Star. However, on February 11, 1957, Hattie was taken by ambulance to the county hospital, where she was treated for nine days for pneumonia. She died on February 20 at the age of 85.

Ethel Lyman, a friend who knew that Hattie's father had been named Louis Rose, could provide only scant details about Hattie's family to the County Recorder's Office. She was unaware that Hattie's father had been born at Neuhaus-an-der-Oste. She knew even less about Hattie's mother, not even that her name had been Matilda Rose.[30]

Ethel apparently was quite fond of Hattie, perhaps considering her an older sister. Instead of having Hattie buried near her own family at the Home of Peace Cemetery, she arranged for her to be buried in the only unused grave in a four-grave family plot, specifically in Grave 2, Lot 26, Section 1, Division 4 of Mount Hope Cemetery.

When Hattie was buried on Feb. 26, 1957, she was placed in a grave between those of Ada Farley (buried May 1, 1895) and Catherine Farley (buried Aug. 29, 1939). Adjacent to Catherine was Joseph Farley, who had purchased all four plots and who was buried June 24, 1926. The inclusion of Hattie's remains in the Farley family plot created something of a logistics problem. Later, all these graves, except Hattie's, eventually became double-occupied. Ethel Lyman's body was placed on November 12, 1971, in the same grave as Catherine Farley. Ethel's husband, Roy H. Lyman, previously had been buried in the same grave as Joseph Farley.[31]

Visitors to Mount Hope Cemetery on Nov. 29, 2000, learned that there was no marker above the members of the Farley and Lyman families or above Hattie Rose. Instead a patch of unmarked lawn stretched between gravestones dedicated to members of the Cantlin family and to James Stewart.[32] There was no indication in cemetery records that a monument ever had been at the location.

Where's Louis?

The lack of a stone for Hattie Rose is reminiscent of the search for Louis Rose's grave that was the subject of newspaper articles in the 1960s.

Orion Zink, as a historian for Masonic Lodge No. 35, wondered in an article for the *The Master Mason* what had happened to Rose's body, once buried in the Hebrew Cemetery near Roseville. The mystery was resolved in 1968 when Samuel Druskin, a member of the lodge, told of Rose's reburial at the Home of Peace. In the intervening 29 years, the deteriorating wooden marker must have been removed or perhaps it disintegrated. That may also have been the fate of the markers for Rose's family members.

Druskin remembered that some of the others who attended the reburial had included Isadore Jacobsen, Paul Nestor, M.S. Berlin and Sol Stone. "It is brother Druskin's belief that he is the only one living who was present at the services that day," Zink wrote in December 1969. "Brother Rose's grave is located on Lot 1, Section B, Plot 1, Row D" of the Home of Peace Cemetery.[33]

Following Druskin's revelations, a new headstone for Rose was placed at the Home of Peace Cemetery on July 13, 1969, compliments of Masonic Lodge No. 35 F. & A.M.[34] The stone, lying flat against the ground, features a stylized Magen David on the left side and the Masonic compass and T-square on the right. Between these two symbols is the legend:

In Memory of
LOUIS ROSE
1807–1888
Pioneer Builder
Member of SD Lodge
No. 35, F.& A.M.

This did not end the Rose plaque saga, however. A few months later, the plaque that had been set in 1934 on the boulder in the median of Highway 101 was reported missing. In the interim, the highway had been realigned to make room for the University of California San Diego campus in La Jolla and the plaque either was stolen or lost during the confusion of construction. Subsequently, a replica of the plaque was made by UCSD and now may be seen on the lawn in front of the university's applied physics and mathematics building.

There is a delicious irony in Rose being remembered at that location. During the first two-thirds of the 20th Century, La Jolla realtors had observed the practice of "covenants and restrictions" to discourage Jews, African Americans, Mexican Americans and other minorities from purchasing property in the high-tone suburb. So well known was La Jolla's discriminatory practices, that Jews nicknamed the area "La Goy-a," a play on the Hebrew word, "Goyim," which means "nations" but is used to indicate non-Jewish peoples.

When San Diego sought construction of a campus of the University of California in its environs, university officials bluntly told the city that the property restrictions in La Jolla would have to be removed so that Jewish faculty, staff, and students could live near the campus. Rather than forego the prestige and economic stimulus of having a University of California branch in San Diego, the realtors complied. Attracted by the university, and the lovely village overlooking the Pacific Ocean, Jews thereafter flocked to La Jolla. Rose, the very first Jew of San Diego, whose Rose Canyon stretches to the campus, also was among the first Jews to leave his mark in latter day La Jolla.[35]

The Memory Endures

Dating its start from Louis Rose's arrival in San Diego in 1850, San Diego's Jewish community marked its 150th anniversary in ceremonies held October 29, 2000, on the San Diego State University campus. As part of the occasion, the archives of the Jewish Historical Society of San Diego were opened in a room of the Malcolm Love Library in cooperation with SDSU's Lipinsky Institute for Judaic Studies. A sightseeing bus, operated by Old Town Trolley Tours of San Diego, was brought onto the campus, and officially named the "Louis Rose." [36]

In another tribute, the San Diego Archaeological Center developed story boards for "Rose Canyon—A Walk Through San Diego History," which included information on Louis Rose. It was exhibited in the west terminal of San Diego International Airport from Oct. 1, 2002 to Jan. 31, 2003 before being placed in the center's permanent collection. [37]

As a result of the Base Reduction and Consolidation (BRAC) process undertaken by the United States military, San Diego's Naval Training Center had been declared surplus and turned back to the City of San Diego, which in cooperation with Corky McMillin Companies decided to redevelop it as a combination residential, historical and office complex. A 49-acre park along the Navy's old boat channel was designated for incorporation into San Diego's park system.

Norman Greene, co-publisher with the author of the *San Diego Jewish Press-Heritage* and a member of the San Diego City Park and Recreation Board, persuaded fellow commission members November 21, 2002, to endorse the concept of creating a memorial to Rose within that public park. [38]

On June 17, 2004, the (Pt. Loma) Peninsula Community Planning Board, at the author's request, adopted a resolution "to support honoring Louis Rose's contributions to Pt. Loma with an appropriate plaque in the Roseville area." [39]

On July 16, 2004, San Diego Mayor Dick Murphy voiced support for honoring Rose as part of the nationwide celebration in 2004 of the 350th anniversary of Jewish life in North America. [40] On August 12, an ad hoc committee representing various city offices, private parties, and the United Jewish Federation identified a parcel overlooking the boat channel and commanding a view of Roseville, to be named "Louis Rose Point." [41]

Mayor Murphy, City Councilman Michael Zucchet, city Park and Recreation Director Ellie Oppenheim, and Steve Solomon, president of the United Jewish Federation of San Diego, on September 22 officially announced plans to memorialize the pioneer. They made their announcement at the proposed site at the foot of Womble Street in Liberty Station, known formerly as Naval Training Center.

At the ceremony, Murphy said that Rose "believed that the city had the potential to grow near its magnificent San Diego Bay waterfront... Periodically the city struggled economically, causing many to doubt the city's potential, but Mr. Rose never lost faith in what he believed San Diego could become. His famous quote certainly resonates today: 'Just wait awhile and you will see.' If Louis Rose could see what San Diego has become, he would believe it was well worth the wait."

The San Diego mayor added: "How better to participate in this celebration than to announce the honoring of a great Jewish San Diegan, who helped make San Diego a city worthy of our affection!" [42]

Zucchet, whose council district included the Roseville area, defined a "visionary" as someone "who sees what other people maybe don't see at the time. I think Louis Rose fits that characterization perfectly."

How "visionary" Rose was as a real estate speculator was measured in July 2004, at the request of the author. Malin Burnham, principal of Burnham Real Estate, authorized Stath Karras and Christopher D. Reutz of his staff to run a computer program comparing the prices that Rose had paid in the 1850s for land in Roseville and Rose Canyon with the prices that the same parcels, stripped of the houses built upon them, fetched in 2004. Reutz found that the parcels for which Rose had paid an average $1.33 per acre in the Roseville/ La Playa area commanded an average per acre price in 2004 of $1.14 million. The $1.22 he paid for land in Rose Canyon compared to an average per acre price in 2004 of $936,142.

Even allowing that $1 in 1850 was worth over $22 in 2004 dollars, Rose's investments had increased "astronomically," Reutz noted. [43]

The 350th anniversary of Jewish settlement in North America—harkening back to the September 1654 arrival in Nieuw Amsterdam of the French privateer *St. Catherine* with 23 Jewish refugees from Portuguese-controlled Recife, Brazil—triggered plans across the United States for Jewish history observances.

Besides the City of San Diego's plans for a memorial to Rose, this biography, published by San Diego's Agency for Jewish Education in cooperation with Sunbelt Publications, was one such observance. Rose's legacy was scheduled to be the subject of lectures, seminars, and panel discussions in 2004 and 2005.

Major financial contributors to the AJE's Louis Rose Project were two San Diego families who, in their own right, continued a San Diego tradition typified by Louis Rose. As Rose did in his day, the Jacobs and the Lipinskys play an active role both in Jewish communal life and in the civic improvement of San Diego. Brief sketches of these two families follow in the *Afterword*.

The Lipinsky Family

A decade after Louis Rose's death, a family that would follow in his tradition of philanthropy and San Diego civic involvement immigrated to the United States from a little village on the frequently changing Russian-Polish border.

Harris and Ida Lipinsky passed through Ellis Island en route to Brooklyn, where Harris hitched up a horse and wagon to drive to nearby dairies to purchase milk for churning. He sold the butter products from a small store while, meanwhile, the couple had five children: Kitty (Katherine), Betty, Lou, Bill and Bernard.

Kitty moved to San Diego where Ida's sister, Bess Breitbard, already was settled. After one of several family visits to the West Coast, Ida informed Harris: "We're moving to California and you're welcome to come too." Harris obligingly turned his successful dairy business over to a brother. In 1924, the Lipinskys took a ship to New Orleans where they boarded a train for San Diego—coincidentally following Rose's overland route to San Diego.

Sisters Ida and Bess, joined by Ida's daughters Kitty Wolff and Betty Barkin, were four members of a group of sixteen women—known as the "Jolly Sixteen"—who became concerned that no nursing home catered to Jewish seniors, particularly kosher-observing and Yiddish-speaking immigrants. Meeting often in Ida's dining room, the Jolly Sixteen decided in 1944 to pool resources to fund the first San Diego Hebrew Home, a 10-bed facility on Fourth Avenue. Over the years, as San Diego's Jewish population expanded, so did the Home, which today, as Seacrest Village Retirement Communities, occupies campuses in Encinitas and the Rancho Bernardo-Poway area.

Bernard Lipinsky celebrated his bar mitzvah at Congregation Beth Israel, was active as a leader in the Western Region of the B'nai B'rith Youth Movement, and graduated from San Diego High School in 1931. After a year at San Diego State and a year at Los Angeles Junior College, Bernard joined his brother Bill Lipin in operating the Roxy Jewelry and Loan located in the shadow of the Balboa Theatre downtown. The brothers obtained pinball games and other concessions at nearby military bases, and also owned coin-operated horses and other kiddy rides located just outside supermarkets.

Bernard married Jane Goldberg, and they had two children during the World War II years: Jeffrey and Elaine. Jane developed Hodgkins Disease, which medical research centers across the country were unable to cure. She died in

1952. After six months, Jane's mother, Bess Goldberg, a matchmaker by avocation, began urging Bernard to start dating again. A friend had a widowed
daughter in Los Angeles, she said. Bernard and that widow, Dorris Fagelson
Levine, initially were reluctant to go on the blind date, but Bess never took
"no" for a permanent answer. On their first date, Bernard and Dorris spoke
about their late spouses and about his children, and that date led to others. After
the couple married, Dorris adopted Jeffrey and Elaine.

Brothers Bill and Bernard meanwhile had formed the North Park
Mortgage Company, buying properties throughout the county, particularly
apartment units. At one time, they owned as many as 2,000 rental units in addition to commercial properties. The brothers were so successful that an account-
ant advised them to seek a new business that might provide them a tax loss.
Hearing that, banker C. Arnholt Smith offered to sell them the Kona Kai Club
on Shelter Island, saying he was otherwise involved with his Westgate Hotel.
The deal was sealed in 1968 with a handshake. Bernard said he and Bill concluded most of their deals on a handshake. If they felt they couldn't trust someone with whom they were negotiating, they walked away from the deal. After
making the Kona Kai Club a success, the Lipinskys sold it in 1984 during a
period when San Diego real estate was booming.

In their retirement, Bernard and Dorris financed the Lipinsky Institute for
Judaic Studies at San Diego State University, donated in excess of seven hundred scholarships based on students' financial need, and funded the Thomas B.
Day Freshman Success Start Program, named for an SDSU president. The
grateful university named a bell tower after the Lipinskys and in 1996 conferred an Honorary Doctor of Humane letters degree on Bernard. He was the
second person to be so honored. The first was U.S. President John F. Kennedy.
The third was Israel's former Prime Minister, Shimon Peres.

Over the years, Bernard and Dorris donated in excess of $10 million to
charitable causes in the area of education, senior citizens, health and the arts,
according to his children. Dorris, who believed in "women's liberation" long
before the subject was on everyone's lips, made certain that SDSU's Women's
Studies Department was a recipient of their philanthropy. Other major benefi-
ciaries, in addition to San Diego State, were the UCSD Cancer Center, San
Diego Hospice, Seacrest Village Retirement Communities, Temple Emanu-El,
the San Diego Agency for Jewish Education, Soille San Diego Hebrew Day
School, Jewish Historical Society of San Diego, Jewish Film Festival, KPBS,
Old Globe Theatre, Malashock Dance Co., Young Playwrights Project, and the
San Diego Repertory Theatre.

Dorris died in 1998, and Bernard followed three years later, leaving the
Lipinksy Family Foundation to be administered by his children. Philanthropy
also is important to Jeff's and Sheila's sons, Daren and Steven, and their wives,
Gina and Christy respectively, as well as to Elaine's children, Jane Murphy,
Diane Zeps, and Nathan Segal and their respective spouses, Brad, Robert and

Cara. In turn, they expect that the great-great grandchildren of Ida and Harris Lipinsky—who in 2004 included Yardyn Shraga, Grant Zeps, and Noah, Dylan, and Kyle Segal—will continue the family's philanthropic tradition.

"Life is not easy, but it can become easy in your later years if you work hard in the beginning," Bernard Lipinsky once advised family members. "Work hard and be honest in all your dealings... It all comes back to you."

Lipinsky Bell Tower, San Diego State University

Gary and Jerri-Ann Jacobs High Tech High School

The Jacobs Family

*F*rom Hungary, Poland and Russia, ancestors of Gary and Jerri-Ann Jacobs made their way to New York and Massachusetts—intermediate steps on a journey to successful, contributing lives in San Diego.

Jerri-Ann's parents, Dave and Doris Yorysh, left Brooklyn for David's job in California's burgeoning aerospace industry. Working as an electrical engineer for Grumman Aircraft, he was involved in such projects as the Lunar Module (LM), which was borne to the moon by the Apollo space missions, before taking a job in San Diego with General Dynamics to work on the Tomahawk Cruise Missile.

The Yoryshes also became inveterate volunteers, the kind of people who "would make peanut butter sandwiches for walkathons," Jerri-Ann said. Their wide-ranging activities included membership in Parents of North American Israelis (PNAI), prompted by the fact that one of Jerri-Ann's sisters, Terry Shlomo, lived in Israel. Her other sister, Eilleen, resided in Canada and her brother, Jerome, in San Diego.

Dave and Doris were active volunteer ushers for many arts and theater groups as well as members of the San Diego Police Department's Retired Volunteer Service Patrol (RSVP).

From New York and Massachusetts, where several generations of their families had resided, Gary's parents, Joan and Irwin Jacobs, set down roots in San Diego in 1966. UCSD Professor Irwin Jacobs later co-founded Linkabit with UCLA Professors Andrew Viterbi and Len Kleinrock. After merging it with M/A-Com, he left and co-founded Qualcomm, steering it into a multi-million dollar corporation specializing in digital communications including cellular telephone technology.

Joan and Irwin Jacobs underwrote the UCSD Jacobs School of Engineering, donated a record $120 million to the San Diego Symphony, and made major contributions to the La Jolla Playhouse, Congregation Beth El, Lawrence Family JCC and the San Diego Food Bank among numerous other charitable institutions.

Reared in La Jolla, before any synagogue was built in the once-restricted community, Gary, the oldest of four sons, attended religious school in his and other people's homes. His bar mitzvah was at the Jacobs' home in a service led by a UCSD graduate student. Like Gary, his brothers, Hal, Paul, and Jeff, remained in San Diego.

The Jacobs enjoyed volunteering, particularly in Democratic party politics. Gary met Jerri-Ann in 1982 after he volunteered to start up a singles program for young adult members of Congregation Beth El. In 1983, they became the first couple to be married in the Conservative congregation's new facility in La Jolla. The couple remained active at the synagogue, with Jerri-Ann serving on the Torah School's education committee and the rabbinic search committee that brought Rabbi Philip Graubart to the area.

Gary obtained a degree from UCSD in management science and worked for his father both at Linkabit and Qualcomm. In between, he consulted with the district attorney's office on systems to track thefts from parking meters and to organize cases and court dates for attorneys prosecuting "special circumstances" crimes.

Gary later formed an investment company specializing in real estate development. He purchased the Lake Elsinore Storm, the Class-A farm team of the San Diego Padres, and served on the executive committee of the California Baseball League and as member of the San Diego Padres Baseball Club's Board of Directors.

For four years, Gary served as president of the Lawrence Family JCC, raising money for the modernization and expansion of the facility at its Jacobs Family Campus in La Jolla. He later served a two-year term as president of the United Jewish Federation of San Diego County.

Gary and Jerri-Ann focused their philanthropy on education, in particular on the Gary and Jerri-Ann Jacobs High Tech High school in the Roseville area of Point Loma.

High Tech High featured project-based learning in which students applied their academic skills to such enterprises as constructing a human-powered submarine, or building trenches to study World War I. Some students demonstrated such creativity that they actually developed inventions eligible for patents. Impressed, the Bill and Melinda Gates Foundation donated $10.5 million to help create 15 other schools like it. Officials in China and Israel also expressed interest in importing the concept. The couple also helped start San Diego's High Tech International High school, focusing on international relations, and High Tech Middle School.

Jerri-Ann, decrying that public schools no longer teach students how to play musical instruments, served on the board of the Foundation for the Advancement of Music Education (FAME) in the San Dieguito School District. Additionally, she was founding president of the Parents Association for High Tech Middle School and served on the Torrey Pines High School major gifts committee.

Another of the couple's projects was the Jacobs International Teen Leadership Institute (JITLI) bringing Arabs and Jews together from San Diego, Israel and the Palestinian Authority to travel, learn about each other and to break down stereotypes. In 2004, the year of this writing, JITLI brought Bedouin Arabs from the Israeli community of Segev Shalom, Israeli Jews from the area of Sha'ar Hanegev, and Palestinian Arabs from several communities in the Gaza Strip to San Diego where they met Jewish teenagers from San Diego. After several days of getting to know each other, the group traveled together to Spain and to Israel on a three-week journey.

The couple's four children—Adam, Sara, Beth and Mara—participated in various Jacobs family enterprises and were taught about philanthropy. Adam, for example, went on the JITLI trip one year, and Sara planned to participate in JITLI when she reached the 11th grade. Beth was a student at the High Tech Middle School, where Mara expected to go.

Their ancestors' stories are those of "immigrant families coming to the United States looking for a better life and through a lot of hard work—and the support of their communities when they got here—of really being able to create that better life for their descendants," Gary said. "Now it is our opportunity to give back to that community who helped us get there."

E N D N O T E S

Chapter 1

The Purim Baby

[1] Olaf Rennebeck to Donald H. Harrison, Jan. 3, 1996. Rennebeck, an archivist for Emmaus Church of Neuhaus-an-der-Oste, amplified on Rose's genealogy in an interview with the author on March 7, 2000. As the archivist, Rennebeck was intimately acquainted with both the civil and religious records of Neuhaus a.d. Oste. Rose would have been familiar with the Lutheran church of Neuhaus because its chapel was built in 1621 and the modern church structure was completed in 1738, according to Peter Rondthaler, who was serving as its pastor in the year 2000. In Rose's time, the congregation was known simply as the church of Neuhaus. Inspired by a painting inside the church, it was renamed about 1970 as the Emmaus Church. The painting depicts the scene in Christian Scriptures (Luke 24:35) in which, following the crucifixion, Jesus revealed himself to two disciples in the village of Emmaus.

Background on The Great Nordic War, from Antti Lahelma and Johan Olofsson, Swedish History, 1521-1718, http://www.lysator.liu.se/nordic/scn/faq734.html.

Information on Stade from the city's website at http://www.stade.de/

[2] Ketuba (Marriage Certificate), June 20, 1847, Copies of Marriage Contracts Which Have Taken Place in the Hebrew Congregation of Shanarai Chased of New Orleans, Tulane University Library, Louisiana Collection.

[3] Prof. Zvi Har'El, Dec. 31, 2003, to Donald H. Harrison via email. Har'El, a mathematics professor at the Technion/Israel Institute of Technology, maintains the website http://www.math.technion.ac.il/~rl/, permitting instantaneous conversions between dates of the Hebrew calendar and the Julian calendar.

Napoleonic Reforms

[4] Rennebeck, March 7, 2000, interview with Harrison.

[5] H. I. Bach, *The German Jew: A Synthesis of Judaism and Western Civilization*, the Littman Library of Jewish Civilization by Oxford University Press, New York: 1984, p. 75.

[6] *Intelligenz Blatt* (of the Herzogtuerner Bremen and Verden), 47th edition, Stade, June 12, 1811.

[7] "Names," Encyclopaedia Judaica, CD-ROM Edition, Keter Publishing House Ltd., Jerusalem: 1997.

Childhood in Neuhaus

[8] Bach, *The German Jew*, page 79

[9] Population estimate made by Rev. Peter Rondthaler of Emmaus Church of Neuhaus during an interview with the author on March 8, 2000, interpreted by Avi Masori and Hollister Mathis.

[10] History of Ulex Liqueur Factory provided by Olaf Schlicting, its owner, in an interview with the author on March 8, 2000.

[11] Rennebeck, who escorted author on an area tour on March 8, 2000.

[12] Rennebeck, citing Book of Mortgages from 1815 in Neuhaus a.d. Oste archives.

[13] Steven E. Aschheim, *Brothers and Strangers: the East European Jew in German and German Jewish Consciousness, 1800 – 1923*, University of Wisconsin Press, Madison: 1982, pp. 7-8.

[14] Jacob R. Marcus, *The Rise and Destiny of the German Jew*, Department of Synagogues and School Extension of the Union of American Hebrew Congregations, Cincinnati: 1934, p. 25.

[15] Bach, *The German Jew*, pp. 79, 81.

[16] Har'El to Harrison, Dec. 31, 2003. For method of calculation, see note 3.

[17] Ibid.

Louis Rose Immigrates to America

[18] Rennebeck to Harrison, Jan. 3, 1996

[19] *Intelligenz Blatt* (of the Herzogtuemer Bremen and Verden), 97th edition, Dec. 5, 1838.

[20] Works Progress Administration of Louisiana, Survey of Federal Archives in Louisiana: Passenger Lists Taken from Manifests of the Customs Service, Port of New Orleans, 1839 – 1849, Including Names of Sloops, Brigs, Schooners, Sailing Ships and Steamboats as well as Passenger Embarkation Points and Destinations, Survey of Federal Archives in Louisiana, 1941; Tulane University Louisiana Collection, L976 31 (656.4) U58p Vol. 3.

[21] Rennebeck, tour of Neuhaus, March 8, 2000

[22] Cargo Manifest, Ship *Wales*, New Orleans inward, National Archives RB41 Stack 15E4/18/23/4 Box 145.

[23] Ship's Register, Bath, Maine, Ship *Wales*, Dec. 21, 1839, National Archives RG 41 Stack: 15E2/21/12/1 Vol. 166; also New York, RG 41 Stack 15E3/9/7/1 Vol. 12020, and RG41 Stack 15E3/8/7/1 Vol. 12010.

[24] *Daily Picayune* (New Orleans), Dec. 25, 1840, p. 2. Rigging accounted for the differences in classification among ships, barks and brigs. Ships had all three sails square-rigged, whereas barques or barks had their foremast and mainmast square-rigged, but their mizzenmast rigged fore and aft. Brigs have only two masts.

[25] Works Project Administration, Survey of Federal Archives in Louisiana. Listed passengers, rearranged in alphabetical order by this author, included: G. Alberdeny; H.A. Baumgarten; Anton Berbosue; F.W. Bohite; H. Bohite; R. Buhner; H. Cohen; W. Freye; C. Gilbert and family; A. Gotte; B.H. Hakert and family; H. Henke; Aug. Jewels; H. Kaiser; G. Kemper; Aug. Kinnpart and family; Casper Knese and family; Aug. Koch; A. Kreby; D. Lange; C. Lanekminn; C. Mage; Anton Mais; Meta Meyers; G. Mundes; M. Natheman; E. Neilhard; G. Nestern; G. Pluy; Eliza Pooks; G. Reissneider; Carl Ritter; G.G. Rolfes; Aug. Romueber; Louis Rose; G.E. Steinling and family; H. Thuridt; Mayer Trammer; John Uhrlich; F. Witting; and C. Ylotho.

New Orleans

[26] *History of the Jews of Louisiana: Their Religious, Civic, Charitable and Patriotic Life*, New Orleans: Jewish Historical Publishing Co. of Louisiana, no date, Louisiana collection of Tulane University. Also, Ellen C. Merrill, "History of the German Americans on the Lower Mississippi Delta," Louisiana German-American Resources (LAGAR), Vol. 2, "Cultural Resources," Jean Lafitte National Historic Park and Preserve, German American Cultural Center, United States Department of Interior National Park Service, Gretna, Louisiana: 2000, page 136. (On file at German American Cultural Center as Contract #1443CX509098048; Ref S72 (SERO) c. 2000 Ellen C. Merrell)

[27] Elliott Ashkenazi, "Creoles of Jerusalem: Businessmen of Louisiana, 1840-1875," doctoral dissertation, George Washington University, 1983 (on file in Louisiana collection of Tulane University), p.18.

[28] Rose obituary, *San Diego Sun*, February 14, 1888.

[29] Klaus J. Kueck, past master of Germania Lodge No. 46, to Donald H. Harrison, July 25, 2000.

[30] "Organization of Germania Lodge, No. 46, F. & A.M.," a booklet published by the lodge about its founding, pages 3 – 4. Besides Rose, other founders were Gustave Martel, worshipful master; U. Haussmer, senior warden; Charles Dannaples, secretary; James D. Kamper, treasurer; John Freidrich, master expert; Theobald H. Koenig, master of ceremonies; Nicholas Fiedler, chaplain; J.S. Hirschbuel, orator; Chris H. Wiedman, tyler; K. Theurer, almoner; J.H. Hildebrand, care-taker; B.L. Wolf; William Ganglof; E.H. Haverman; Stanislaus Weber; John Gerlach; and B.H. Stehr.

[31] Criminal Court of the First District (Orleans Parish), Minute Book, Vol. 6 (March 3, 1845 – April 18, 1846).

[32] Organization of Germania Lodge, op. cit.

An Ill-Fated Marriage

[33] "Copies of Contracts Which Have Taken Place in the Hebrew Congregation of Shanarai Chased of New Orleans," Louisiana collection 224, Vol. 8, Tulane University. The translation to English is a composite of separate interpretations, rendered in the year 2000 by Rabbi Chaim Hollander, spiritual leader of Young Israel of San Diego and head of the Judaic Studies Department at the Soille San Diego Hebrew Day School, and Hebrew speakers I. Gerry Burstain and Shahar Masori, both of San Diego and respectively the friend and son-in-law of the author.

[34] A plaque placed by Orleans Parish Landmark Commission provides the history. Mary Lou Eichhorn, a research assistant at the Williams Research Center of the Historic New Orleans Collection, said tiny Jefferson Street had been renamed as Wilkinson Street. James Wilkinson was the U.S. Army brigadier general who accepted Louisiana from France on behalf of the United States in 1803, and served as the territory's military governor.

[35] Jo Ann Carrigan, "Impact of Epidemic Yellow Fever on Life in Louisiana," *Louisiana History*, Vol. 4, 1963, p. 25.

[36] Bertram Wallace Korn, *The Early Jews of New Orleans*, American Jewish Historical Society, Waltham, Mass: 1969, p. 126.

[37] *Phillip Willman, assignee of S. Weber vs. Louis Rose*, Case #1500, Second District Court of New Orleans, Petition of Stanislaus Weber, Sept. 19, 1848 (records on file in Louisiana and City Archives, New Orleans Public Library).

[38] *L. Rose vs. Adam Reuth*, Case #1450, Second District Court of New Orleans, Petition of Liebman Rose, June 2, 1848 (records on file in Louisiana and City Archives, New Orleans Public Library).

[39] *Eckel vs. Rose*, Case #1632, Second District Court of New Orleans, Ouesiphoese Drouet, notary public, statement of service of a demand note to Caroline Rose (records on file in Louisiana and City Archives, New Orleans Public Library).

[40] *Voigts & Teauremand vs. Rose*, Case #1251, Fifth District Court of New Orleans, petition of Voigts & Teauremand (partners in Voigts Teauremand), May 9, 1848 (records on file in Louisiana and City Archives, New Orleans Public Library).

[41] *Brichta vs. Rose*, Case #1632, Second District Court of New Orleans. Petition of Francis Brichta, Aug. 1, 1848 (records on file in Louisiana and City Archives, New Orleans Public Library).

[42] *Eckel vs. Rose*, promissory note of L. Rose, April 5, 1848, location cited.

[43] *Voigts & Teauremand vs. Rose*, Case #1251, location cited.

[44] *L. Rose vs. Adam Reuth*, location cited.

[45] Organization of Germania Lodge, No. 46, F. & A.M., p. 3.

[46] *Eckel vs. Rose*, location cited.

[47] *Rose vs. Rose*, District Court Records, June 21, 1854, San Diego Historical Society Archives, R3.38.

[48] Daniel Cleveland, "What the City has Done With Its Pueblo Lands," *San Diego Union*, April 18, 1926, p. 18.

[49] Ashkenazi, *Creoles of Jerusalem*, page 28.

San Antonio

[50] "Alamo" and "Bexar County," *The Handbook of Texas Online*, http://www.tsha.utexas.edu/handbook/online/artilces//articles/view/AA/uqa1.html and... /BB/hcb7.html

[51] *Rose vs. Rose*, Deposition of Henry H. Thal, June 21, 1854, location cited.

Jewish Land Barons

[52] "De Cordova, Jacob Raphael," *The Handbook of Texas Online*, location cited.

[53] Julia Nott Waugh, *Castro-ville and Henry Castro, Empresario*, Castro Colonies Heritage Association: 1986 reprint of the 1934 edition, p. 58 (copy on file in the Castroville, Tex., public library).

[54] "Castro, Henri," *The Handbook of Texas Online*, location cited.

[55] Waugh, *Castro-ville and Henry Castro, Empresario*, p. 59.

[56] Ibid.

[57] Henrietta Rose interview with Winifred Davidson, San Diego Historical Society archives, Louis Rose vertical file.

[58] *Galveston Weekly News*, May 28, 1849, p.1.

The Van Horne Expedition

[59] Maj. Gen. Worth (by Geo Deas, Asst. Adjutant General), Orders No. 8, Feb. 3, 1849 (on file in the Fort Bliss, Tex., Museum Archives).

[60] Jefferson Van Horne to Asst. Adjutant General, 9th Military Department, Santa Fe, N.M., Sept. 10, 1849 (on file in the Fort Bliss, Tex., Museum Archives).

[61] *Galveston Weekly News*, June 18, 1849, page 1. Unaccompanied officers included Brevet Maj. Horne, the commander; Brevet Majors Shepherd and Richardson; Capt. William H. Johns; Brevet Captains A.W. Bowman and William G. French; Lieutenants Thomas J. Mason; W.J. Mecling; L.W. O'Banion; John Trevitt and William H. Wood; and Assistant Surgeons P.G.S. Ten Broeck and Lyman H. Stone.

[62] J.E. Johnston, "Report to the Secretary of War with Reconnaissances of Routes from San Antonio to El Paso," Sen. Ex Doc. No 64, 31 Cong, 1 Sess, July 24, 1850, page 64.

[63] T.B. Eastland to Josephine Eastland, June 3, 1849, footnote 8, page 132, in Thomas B. Eastland and Joseph G. Eastland, "To California Through Texas and Mexico," foreword by Douglas S. Watson and footnotes by Dorothy H. Huggins, *California Historical Quarterly*, Vol. 18, No. 2, June 1939. Hereafter referred to as "Eastland."

Castroville

[64] S.G French, "Reconnaissance of Route from San Antonio to El Paso," Dec. 31, 1849, in Senate Ex Doc, 31 Cong, 1 Sess, No. 64, pages 41–42. Hereafter referred to as "French."

[65] Eastland, June 8, 1849.

[66] Castroville Visitor Guide, Castroville Chamber of Commerce, 1998, p. 45.

[67] French, p. 42.

Life on the Wagon Trail

[68] Eastland, p.103

[69] Ibid, June 15, p 103.

[70] Ibid, June 24, p. 104.

[71] French, p.44.

[72] Eastland, June 29, p.105.

[73] José Policarpo Rodríguez: "The Old Guide: His Life in His Own Words," originally published in 1897, reprinted Nov. 1, 1968 in *Old West Magazine*.

[74] Eastland, p.106.

[75] French, p. 44.

[76] Eastland, July 3, pp. 106 – 107.

[77] Ibid, July 4, p. 107.

[78] Ibid, July 6, pp. 106—107.

[79] Ibid, July 4, p. 107.

[80] Ibid, July 9—12, pp. 108—109.

Rose is Banished

[81] Ibid, July 13—19, pp. 109—110.

[82] Ibid, July 22—24, p. 111.

[83] Ibid, July 25, p. 111.

[84] Ibid, July 26, pp. 111—112.

Coward of the Alamo

[85] "Rose, Louis (Moses)," The Handbook of Texas Online, location cited.

[86] W.P. Zuber, "The Escape of Rose from the Alamo," *The Quarterly of the Texas State Historical Association*, Vol. 5, No. 1, July 1901.

[87] Susan Lindee, "Why Did One Man Flee the Alamo?" *San Antonio Express-News*, July 11, 1987, p. 158.

[88] Kevin R. Young, "Rose Escapes Daily," *San Antonio Express-News*, letter, July 21, 1987, p. 7b. Young, site historian at the "Remember the Alamo Theater and Museum," also pointed out in this letter to the editor that a film showing Moses Rose's escape from the Alamo is shown eighteen times a day at the site.

[89] The debate is similar to one about the Jews who committed suicide atop Masada rather than surrender to the Roman legions. As with the Alamo some 18 centuries later, the bravery of Masada's defenders inspired later generations. At the same time, those Jews who quietly lived in Judea under Roman rule, studying Torah at an academy in Yavne, preserved a religion that might otherwise have disappeared. One wonders whether either Rose knew of the analogy.

Wagon Train Religion

[90] Eastland, July 28, p.112.

[91] Robert Eccleston, *Overland to California on the Southwestern Trail, 1849*, edited by George P. Hammond and Edward H. Howes, University of California Press, Berkeley: 1950, page 78. Hereafter referred to as Eccleston. The sermon was based on Matthew 10:37.

[92] Ibid.

[93] Eastland, July 29, pp 112-113.

[94] Ibid, Aug. 1, p. 114.

[95] Ibid, Aug. 4—7, pp. 113 – 115.

[96] Ibid, Aug.10, p.115.

Nearing El Paso

[97] Eccleston, Aug. 11, p. 95.

[98] Ibid, Aug. 24, p. 115.

[99] Eastland, Aug. 25, p. 118.

[100] Eccleston, Aug. 27, p.118.

[101] Eastland, Aug. 29, pp. 118 – 119.

[102] Eccleston, Aug. 30, pp. 121 – 122.

[103] Eastland, Aug. 31, p.119

[104] Eastland, Sept. 3 –5, p. 120.

[105] Ibid, Sept. 11.

[106] Eccleston, p, 137.

[107] Richard K. McMaster, "Major Jefferson Van Horne," *Password*, Vol. 12, No. 2, El Paso County Historical Society, Summer 1967, p. 35.

[108] "Juarez, Benito," *Encyclopaedia Brittanica*, CD edition. After the French invaded Mexico and established Maximilian as an emperor, President Juarez retreated to El Paso del Norte to continue his fight to liberate his country.

[109] Eastland, Sept 3 – 5, p. 120.

Rose and His Mentor

[110] San Diego County Probate Case No. 670, Box 6, San Diego County Law Library. The details of Robinson's early life were revealed more than 30 years after his death when members of his first family sued to recover properties they believed they should have inherited. Depositions were given in 1890 by Robinson's daughter, Albina Whitworth; Sarah's sister, Euphemia Buckingham; and various friends and relatives including Harret Bonnell, , John Elliott, William Humphrey, James Snyder, Nicholas Todd and Samuel Weller.

[111] John Henry Brown, *Life and Times of Henry Smith, the First American Governor of Texas* A.D. Aldridge & Co, Dallas: 1880, p. 80. W. Roy Smith, "The Quarrel Between Governor Smith and the Council of the Provisional Government of the Republic," *The Quarterly of the Texas State Historical Association*, Vol. 5, No. 4, April 1902, p. 279. Rupert N. Richardson, "Framing the Constitution of the Republic of Texas," *The Southwestern Historical Quarterly*, Vol. 31, No. 3, January 1928, p. 203.

[112] Ralph W. Steen, "Analysis of the Work of the General Council, Provisional Government of Texas, 1835-1836," *The Southwestern Historical Quarterly*, Vol. 40, No. 4, April 1937, p. 332; Vol. 41, No. 3, January 1938, p. 228; Vol. 42, No. 1, July 1938, pp 32, 34, 41, 44. Brown, op. cit., p. 194. Stanley Siegel, *A Political History of the Texas Republic, 1836-1845*, University of Texas Press, Austin: 1956, p. 20. Sam Houston, *The Writings of Sam Houston*, 1813-1863, Amelia W. Williams and Eugene Barker, editors, University of Texas Press, Austin: 1938, p. 332.

[113] "Robinson, James W.," The Handbook of Texas Online, location cited. *Daily Commercial Advertiser*, Buffalo, New York, June 15, 1836, cited in Walter McCausland, "Charles Drake Ferris: Unknown Veteran of San Jacinto," *The Southwestern Historical Quarterly*, Vol. 62, No. 2, October 1959. James W. Robinson to Thomas J. Rusk, May 9, 1836 (MS, Thomas J. Rusk Papers, Archives, University of Texas Library) cited in McCausland.

[114] "Robinson, James W.," *Biographical Encylopedia of Texas*, Southern Publishing Co., New York: 1880, p. 272. Paul C. Boethel, *Colonel Amasa Turner: The Gentleman from Lavaca and other Captains at San Jacinto*, Von Boeckmann-Jones, Austin: 1963, p. 24.

[115] "Council House Fight," *The Handbook of Texas Online*, location cited. Rena Maverick Green, editor, *Samuel Maverick: Texan*, privately printed, San Antonio: 1952, p. 106. There were many confused reports following the melee, among them the notion that Robinson had been among those slain by Comanche arrows. The mistaken report found its way into a footnote in *Recollections of Early Texas*, a memoir of settler John Holland Jenkins, edited by his great-great grandson, John H. Jenkins III, and published in 1958 by the University of Texas Press.

[116] Adrian Woll, "Report of Expedition into Texas in 1842," translated and edited by Joseph Milton Nance, *The Southwestern Historical Quarterly*, Vol. 58, No. 4, April 1955, pp. 528, 532. Anderson Hutchinson, "Diary," reprinted in E. W. Winkler, "The Bexar and Dawson Prisoners," *The Quarterly of the Texas State Historical Association*, Vol. 12, No. 4, April 1919, pp. 312—313.

[117] James W. Robinson to Santa Anna, April 10, 1843, in Houston, op. cit., Vol. III, p. 351; Sam Houston to Joseph Eve, April 22, 1843 in Houston, op. cit., Vol. IV, pp. 184—186, fn. 2. Ephraim Douglas Adams, editor, "Correspondence from the British Archives Concerning Texas, 1837-1846," *The Southwestern Historical Quarterly*, Vol. 16, No. 2, October 1912, pp. 204, 207; Vol. 16, No. 4, January 1913, p. 307; Vol. 17, No. 1, July 1913, p. 67. John Quincy Adams, *Memoirs of John Quincy Adams, Comprising Portions of His Diary from 1795 to 1848*. Edited by Charles Francis Adams, Vol. XII, p. 49, cited in Samuel Flagg Bemis, *John Quincy Adams and the Union*, Library of the Presidents, The Easton Press, Norwalk, Conn.: 1987 (reprint of previous edition by Alfred A. Knopf, Inc.). John Niven, *Martin Van Buren: the Romantic Age of Amnerican Politics*, Library of the Presidents, Easton Press, Norwalk, Conn.: 1986, (reprint of 1983 edition by Oxford University Press) pp. 526—527. Charles Sellers, *James K. Polk, Continentalist*, Library of the Presidents, Easton Press, Norwalk, Conn.: 1987 (reprint of 1966 edition by Princeton University Press), p. 61.

[118] L.U. Spellman, "Letters of the Dawson Men from Perote Prison, Mexico, 1842-1843," *The Southwestern Historical Quarterly*, Vol. 38, No. 4, April 1935. Sam Houston speech, Aug. 1, 1854, in Houston, op. cit., Vol. 6, p. 83. Siegel, op. cit., p. 218.

[119] Robinson to Turner, April 1, June 18, July 5, 1849; Sarah Robinson to Turner, June 29, 1849; Manuscript Collection, Turner (Amasa) Papers, Robinson and Bowers folder, 2.325/K23 Center for American History, the University of Texas at Austin. Alfred N. Robinson, deposition, San Diego Probate Case No. 670, location cited.

[120] Ronald Quinn, "James W. Robinson and the Development of Old Town San Diego," *The Journal of San Diego History*, Vol. 31, Summer 1985, p. 155.

[121] Brian Frederick Smith, "The San Diego of Judge Benjamin I. Hayes: Excerpts from the Emigrant Notes, 1850-1875," master's thesis, University of San Diego, Helen K. & James S. Copley Library, 979.498 S643s, page 229, entry for September 1856.

[122] James W. Robinson to Amasa Turner, March 2, 1851, Turner (Amasa) papers, location cited.

[123] Winifred Davidson, notes on Louis Rose, Louis Rose vertical file, San Diego Historical Society.

[124] Brown, *Life and Times of Henry Smith*, p. 76.

Trouble at the Colorado River Crossing

[125] Douglas B. Martin, *Yuma Crossing*, University of New Mexico Press, Albuquerque: 1954, p. 140.

[126] Ibid, p. 144.

[127] Frank Love, *Hell's Outpost: A History of Old Fort Yuma*, Yuma Crossing Publications Series, Yuma, Ariz.: 1992, pp. 6-7.

[128] Ibid.

The Last Leg

[129] *California Historical Landmarks*, Office of Historic Preservation, California State Parks, Sacramento: 1996, p. 62.

[130] Brian Frederick Smith, "The San Diego of Judge Benjamin I. Hayes," p. 217.

[131] Thomas W. Sweeny, *Journal, 1849-3*, edited by Arthur Woodward, Westernlore Press, Los Angeles: 1956, p. 239 footnote.

[132] *San Diego Union* (weekly), July 10, 1873, p. 3, col. 5. It seems logical that this precise bit of imformation was provided to the newspaper by Rose himself.

Chapter 2

The Family Estudillo

[1] Cecil B. Moyer, *Historic Ranchos of San Diego,* Copley Books, Union-Tribune Publishing Company, San Diego: 1969, pp. 82-86.

[2] "José Antonio Estudillo" and "José María Estudillo," San Diego Historical Society, Online Biographies, http://sandiegohistory.org/bio

[3] "Legends of Lakeside," The Lakeside Historical Society, Lakeside, Calif.: 1995, p. 4.

[4] Mary H. Hagland, "Don José Antonio Aguirre: Spanish Merchant and Ranchero," *The Journal of San Diego History,* Vol. 29, No. 1, p. 54.

[5] In noting Louis Rose as the first permanent Jewish settler in San Diego, we should be cognizant of the fact that previous settlers possibly could trace their roots to Conversos—Jews who converted to Catholicism to avoid being expelled from Spain in 1492. Whatever their roots, such settlers were, in their own generation, practicing Christians.

[6] William Kramer, "Lewis Polock Reluctantly Goes to San Diego," *Old Town, New Town: An Enjoyment of San Diego History,* William M. Kramer, editor; Stanley and Laurel Schwartz, associate editors, Western States Jewish History Association, Los Angeles: 1994, p. 4.

[7] William Heath Davis, *Seventy-Five years in California,* J. Howell, San Francisco: 1929, p. 334. The incident at Punta de los Muertos was in 1782.

Historic San Diego

[8] "No. 52: Mission Dam and Flume," *California Historical Landmarks,* p. 201. A plaque at the site says: "The aqueduct system continued in existence until 1831 when constant flooding caused the dam and flume to fall into disrepair. They were not repaired due to the secularization of the mission."

[9] Donald C. Cutter, "Sources of the Name California," *Arizona and the West,* Vol. 3, No. 3, Autumn 1961, pp. 223-235.

[10] Edgar J. Kendall, "San Diego County Ordinances," *San Diego Historical Society Quarterly,* Vol. 1, No. 1, January 1955, p. 4.

[11] Richard F. Pourade, *The Silver Dons,* Union-Tribune Publishing Co., San Diego: 1966, p. 160.

[12] Iris Engstrand, *San Diego: California Cornerstone,* Continental Heritage Press, Tulsa, Okla.: 1980, p. 38. Pamela Tamplain, "Philip Crosthwaite, San Diego Pioneer and Public Servant," *The Journal of San Diego History,* Vol. 21, No. 3, Summer 1975, p. 44.

A New City and County Take Shape

[13] *California Statutes*, 1850, Chapter 134, p. 410.

[14] E.W Morse, "Reminiscences of Early San Diego," *San Diego Union,* June 1, 1900, p. 6.

[15] San Diego Common Council, Minutes, June 17, 1850 (on file at the San Diego Historical Society). Pourade, op. cit., p. 162.

Rose Settles In

[16] Mary A. Helmich and Richard D. Clark, Interpretive Program: "Old Town San Diego State Historic Park, Vol. II: Site Recommendations," California Department of Parks and Recreation, 1991, GDP No. 26, no page listing.

[17] Ben Dixon, "First Taxpayers of San Diego County," typescript, San Diego Historical Society.

[18] Iris Engstrand and Ray Brandes, *Old Town San Diego 1821-1874,* Alcala Press, San Diego: 1976 (see "Louis Rose Building.")

[19] James W. Robinson to Amasa Turner, March 2, 1851, Manuscript Collection, Turner (Amasa) papers, 2.325/K23 Center for American History, the University of Texas at Austin.

Plundering the City

[20] San Diego Common Council, Minutes, July 7, 1850.

[21] San Diego Common Council, Minutes, Aug. 12, 1850.

[22] San Diego Common Council, Minutes, Aug. 26, 1850.

The Jail Debacle

[23] San Diego Common Council, Minutes, June 29, 1850.

[24] San Diego Common Council, Minutes, July 6, 1850.

[25] San Diego Common Council, Minutes, July 13, 1850.

[26] San Diego Common Council, Minutes, July 29, 1850.

[27] "Charles P. Noell," San Diego Biographies Online, location cited.

[28] San Diego Common Council, Minutes, Aug. 5, 1850.

[29] San Diego Common Council, Minutes, Aug. 21, 1850.

[30] James R. Mills, "San Diego...Where California Began: A Brief History of the Events of Four Centuries," *San Diego Historical Society Quarterly*, Vol. 6, No. 1, January 1960, p. 22.

[31] "Agoston Haraszthy," biographical sketch prepared by the House of Hungary, cited in San Diego Biographies Online, location cited.

[32] "Charles P. Noell," op. cit.

[33] San Diego Common Council, Minutes, Nov. 7, 1850.

[34] San Diego Common Council, Minutes, Nov. 8, 1850.

[35] Ibid.

[36] San Diego Common Council, Minutes, Dec. 26, 1850.

[37] San Diego Common Council, Minutes, Dec. 30, 1850.

Robinson and Rose in Civic Affairs

[38] Lyle C. Annable, "The Life and Times of Cave Johnson Couts, San Diego Pioneer," manuscript, 1965, San Diego State University library, F868 S15C6, p 52. Couts, whose uncle Cave Johnson had been postmaster in President John Tyler's Cabinet, also named streets for President Andrew Jackson and Gen. Winfield Scott, his two military heroes. "Not forgetting the Mexican War, Couts honored additional leading military men of both nations. Mexican Generals Ampadia, Arista, Conde and Trias, as well as Generals Taylor and Twiggs, and Colonel Harney of the United States received tribute," Annable wrote. "Two military governors of California, Col. Richard B. Mason and General Bennett Riley, and Persifor F. Smith, one-time commander of the Pacific, were likewise remembered." Also receiving recognition was Captain Moore, a dragoon who fell at the Battle of San Pasqual. Rounding out the variety of subjects selected to grace the street signs of San Diego were Marcus Whitman, the evangelist killed by Indians in Oregon, and Commodore Robert F. Stockton's flagship, *Congress*.

[39] Joshua Bean to Common Council, Sept. 8, 1850, San Diego Historical Society, Document File, Common Council.

[40] San Diego Common Council Minutes, Aug. 31, Sept. 23, Sept. 30, Oct 18, 1850. San Diego Historical Society's typescript of the minutes says Robinson received $175, but logic indicates this was a misprint.

[41] Engstrand, *California's Cornerstone*, p. 39.

[42] "Grand Jury" document file, San Diego Historical Society.

[43] Ibid.

Roseville Genesis

[44] Louis Rose to City Lands Commission, Oct. 17, 1850 (San Diego Historical Society, Land Commission Document Files).

[45] Engstrand, *California's Cornerstone*, p. 39.

[46] Morse, "Reminiscences of Early San Diego."

[47] Sarah Robinson to Charles Haraszthy, Oct. 21, 1850 (Robinson family document file, San Diego Historical Society).

[48] San Diego County Recorder, Deed Book, C, pages 111, 122: Control of the City Treasurer's Receipts for lots and land commencing with the 10th of December 1850," San Diego Historical Society.

[49] San Diego County Recorder, Deed Book C, p. 199

[50] Morse, "Reminiscences of Early San Diego."

[51] Federal Reserve Bank of Minneapolis, Consumer Price Index (Estimate) 1800-2004, online http://min-neapolisfed.org/research/data/us/calc/hist1800.cfm (Accessed Aug.4, 2004).

[52] San Diego City Treasurer Book No. 1, the Town of San Diego in Account with Louis Rose, treasurer of the Board of Trustees, San Diego Historical Society. Register of Grants Made Since the 12th of December, 1850, San Diego City Clerk's archives, Box A-001-CC.

[53] Harold Guy Hevener Jr., "The Pueblo Lands of the City of San Diego, 1769-1950," master's thesis, San Diego State College, June 1950, p. 107.

[54] San Diego Common Council Minutes, June 17-18, 1850.

[55] Hevener, "The Pueblo Lands of the City of San Diego, 1769-1950," p. 107.

New Council, Same Troubles

[56] Mills, "San Diego…Where California Began," p. 22.

[57] San Diego Common Council, Minutes, Jan. 21, 1851.

[58] San Diego Common Council, Minutes, Feb. 28, 1852.

[59] San Diego Common Council, Minutes, Jan. 23, 1851.

[60] San Diego Common Council, Minutes, Jan. 30, 1851.

[61] Ibid.

[62] San Diego Common Council, Minutes, March 25, 1851.

[63] Morse, "Reminiscences of Early San Diego."

[64] The Haraszthy profile prepared by San Diego's House of Hungary, previously cited, identifies him as the "father of the California Wine Industry," as the man who "introduced the Zinfandel red wine grape and the Muscat of Alexandria raising grape" and as the founder of the Buena Vista Winery in Sonoma. According to the state publication, *California Historical Landmarks*, previously cited, two state-designated historical sites in Sonoma County are associated directly with Haraszthy. The Buena Vista Winery and Vineyards bears an official state plaque, which reads: "Founded in 1857, this is the birthplace of California wine. Its founder, Colonel Agoston Haraszthy, called the father of the state's wine industry, toured Europe in 1861 to gather grape vine cuttings; he also oversaw planting the vineyards and digging wine storage tunnels into the limestock rock of the hillsides." Nearby, a plaque at the site of Haraszthy Villa reads: "Here Count Agoston Haraszthy, "Father of California Viticulture," built an imposing villa in 1857-58, as his home. California's first formal Vintage Celebration, a masked ball, was held at this site on October 23, 1864. General and Mrs. Mariano Guadalupe Vallejo were guests of honor. While living here, Haraszthy oversaw operations of the Winery and Buena Vista Vinicultural Society."

[65] San Diego Common Council, Minutes, March 25, 1851.

More City Financial Woes

[66] San Diego Common Council, Minutes, April 19, 1851.

[67] San Diego Common Council, Minutes, April 24, 1851.

[68] California Statutes, 1851, Chapter 3, p. 37.

[69] San Diego Common Council, Minutes, May 15, 1851.

[70] San Diego Common Council, Minutes, July 8, 1851.

San Diego's Jewish Population Grows

[71] United States Census for San Diego, 1850 (copy on file at San Diego Historical Society).

[72] San Diego Common Council, Minutes, June 5, 1851.

[73] *San Diego Herald*, May 29, 1851.

Secessionist Sentiment in San Diego

[74] *San Diego Herald*, Aug. 29, 1851, p. 2. Other signers included Joaquin Ortega, W. H. Moon, R. M. Hobson, Thomas K. Hort, Enoch Coffin, José Antonio Aguilla, John Cook, Juan Merone, and R.M. Winants.

[75] *San Diego Herald*, Sept. 4, 1851, p. 2.

[76] San Diego Common Council, Minutes, Sept. 1, 1851.

[77] *San Diego Herald*, Sept. 4, 1851, p. 2. Robert Seager II, *and Tyler too: A Biography of John & Juliia Gardiner Tyler*, Easton Press, Norwalk, Conn: 1963, pp. 382-386. John Bleeker had been a partner in the La Playa firm of Gardiner and Bleeker with David Lyon Gardiner, brother-in-law of the tenth U.S. President John Tyler. Gardiner returned to the East from San Diego earlier in 1851, leaving Bleeker in charge of their joint investments. It is possible that Bleeker and Blecker are the same person.

[78] *San Diego County vs. Russel Sacket and others*, June 16, 1851, "James W. Robinson" Document File, San Diego Historical Society.

[79] *San Diego Herald*, Sept. 11, 1851, p. 2. San Diego Common Council, Minutes, Sept. 15, 1851.

[80] *San Diego Herald*, Sept. 18, 1851, p. 3.

[81] San Diego Common Council, Minutes, Nov. 15, 1851.

[82] San Diego Common Council, Minutes, Nov. 22, 1851.

Masons and Jews

[83] Orion Zink and Irvin Shimmin, "The Story of San Diego Lodge No. 35, F. & A.M.," The Master Mason, 125th anniversary edition, private publisher, San Diego: 1976, p. 3.

[84] *Journal of the Proceedings of the Grand Lodge of the State of California, 1850-1854*, San Francisco: 1857, p. 97.

[85] Zink and Shimmin, "The Story of San Diego Lodge No. 35, F. & A.M.," p. 3

[86] *Journal of the Proceedings of the Grand Lodge of California, 1850-1854*, op. cit., p. 113.

[87] Arthur R. Anderson and Leon O. Whitsell, *California's First Century of Scottish Rite Masonry, Supreme Council, Oakland: 1962*, p. 107. Samuel F. Black, *San Diego County, Calif.: A Record of Settlement, Organization, Progress and Achievement*, S.J. Clarke Publishing Co., Chicago: 1913, p. 296. Zink and Shimmin, op. cit., p. 4, supplemented on June 7, 2000, by author's interview of Jim Leach, treasuer and past master of San Diego Lodge No. 35, Free & Accepted Masons.

[88] *San Diego Herald*, Sept. 25, 1851, p. 2.

[89] *San Diego Herald*, Oct. 9, 1851, p. 2

[90] Ronald D. Gerson, "Jewish Religious Life in San Diego, CA, 1851-1918," typed manuscript for master's thesis, Hebrew Union College-Jewish Institute of Religon, Cincinnati, Ohio: 1974, footnote citing *Occident* Vol. X, No. 1, p. 60, April 1852 (manuscript filed as RCC 296 Gerson at California Room, San Diego Public Library), p. 8.

[91] Samuel H. Levey, introduction to "The First Jewish Sermon in the West: Yom Kippur, 1850, San Francisco," *Western States Jewish Historical Quarterly*, Vol. 10, No. 1, October 1977, p. 4.

[92] Ibid. The assessment was according to Levey, who wrote a commentary on the speech in 1977. Levey was Professor of Rabbinics and Jewish Religious Thought at the Edgar F. Magnin School of Graduate Studies at Hebrew Union College-Jewish Institute of Religion.

[93] Lewis A. Franklin, sermon, cited in Samson H. Levey, "The First Jewish Sermon in the West," p. 12.

[94] Kendall, "San Diego County Ordinances," p. 4

[95] Richard L. Carrico, *Strangers in a Stolen Land: American Indians in San Diego, 1850-1880*, Sierra Oaks Publishing Co., Sacramento: 1987, p. 46.

The Garra Uprising

[96] William E. Smythe, *History of San Diego, 1542-1908*, Vol. 1-Old Town, The History Company, San Diego: 1908, p. 187. William Edward Evans, "The Garra Uprising: Conflict Between San Diego Indians and Settlers in 1851," pp. 2-3 (typed manuscript on file in the California Room, San Diego Public Library). San Diego Herald, Nov. 27, 1851.

[97] Smythe, op. cit., p. 189. *San Diego Herald*, Nov. 28, 1851. Lorrin L. Morrison, *Warner: The Man and the Ranch*, Lorrin Morrison Publisher, Los Angeles: 1962, p. 47. Pourade, *The Silver Dons*, p. 177. Thomas Joseph Adema, "San Diego's Oldest Pioneer, Philip Crosthwaite, 1825-1903," master's thesis, 1988, University of San Diego, Helen K. and James S. Copley Library (979 498 c951a), p. 86.

The San Diego Historical Society has on file a list of the Fitzgerald Volunteers later compiled by authorities in connection with small land grants made as a reward to each of the volunteers. Their ranks somewhat at variance with other reports, the fifteen men included under the categories of commissioned and non-commissioned officers were Henry Adams, corporal; I.E. Arguello, corporal; Henry Clayton, sergeant; Andrew Cotton, sergeant; Cave Couts, adjutant and captain; Philip Crosthwaite, corporal; John Dillon, sergeant; Lewis Franklin, quartermaster; Agoston Haraszthy, 1st lieutenant; G.T. Hooper, lieutenant; R.D. Israel, corporal; D.B. Kurtz, lieutenant; G.P. Tebbetts, lieutenant; Thomas Tilghman, lieutenant; and Irving Lewis, assistant surgeon. Forty-five "enlisted men," or privates, were Ramon Ahodara, Julian Ames, R. Atkinson, L. Bartlett, _____ Brady, Chas. Brinley, John Brown, Darius Bustamente, D. Cade, Bernardino Cota, Martin Escajadillo, José María Estudillo, Salvador Estudillo, Willliam Evans, Pedro Faude, George Fisher, Felipe Garcia, George Gaskill, H. Goodlander, Francis Hinton, Charles Johnson, Willliam Leamy, Francisco Lopez, Jesus Markada, José Marroso, A.E. Maxey, William H. Moon, Joaquin Moreno, Charles P. Noell, J.J. Painter, Pedro Pedrorena, Joseph Reiner, Bernardino Rochoa, Franco Rodríguez, Louis Rose, José Tirado, M.P. Tolero, V. Torre, J. Varler, George Wasson, Axel Watkinson, Thomas Whaley, Charles Williams, J. Wood, and Thomas Wrightington.

[98] *San Diego Herald*, Dec. 5, 1851, p. 2.

[99] Thomas Whaley to Anna Lannay cited in Pourade, *The Silver Dons*, p. 180.

[100] Pourade, *The Silver Dons,* p. 181. Adema, *San Diego's Oldest Pioneer: Phillip Crosthwaite*, p. 86.

[101] *San Diego Herald,* Dec. 18, 1851, p. 2.

[102] Thomas Whaley to Anna Lannay, Dec. 17, 1851 (microfilmed letter file, Whaley House Archives, San Diego).

[103] Thomas W. Sweeney, *Journal, 1849-53*, edited by Arthur Woodward, Westernlore Press, Los Angeles: 1956, p. 142.

[104] Adema, *San Diego's Oldest Pioneer: Phillip Crosthwaite*, pp. 96 - 97.

[105] Evans, *The Garra Uprising*, p. 8.

[106] Pourade, *The Silver Dons*, p. 184. Sweeney, Journal, p. 146.

[107] Ibid. Patricia F. Klenner, "Robert Decatur Israel, San Diego Pioneer and Keeper of the Light, 1826-1908," master's thesis, University of San Diego, Helen K. and James S. Copley Library (979.498 185zk), p. 20. Robert Wells Haven, "Thomas Whaley," master's thesis, San Diego State College, San Diego: 1963, p. 87. Thomas Whaley to Anna Lannay, Jan. 12, 1852 (microfilmed letter file, Whaley House Archives, San Diego). *San Diego Herald*, Jan. 17, 1852.

Last Days of the Common Council

[108] San Diego Common Council, Minutes, Jan. 10, 1852.

[109] "Chapter CXXXIX: An Act to Repeal the Charter of the City of San Diego and to Create a Board of Trustees," *Statutes of California passed at the Third Session of the Legislature*, G.K. Fitch & Co. and V.E. Geiger & Co., State Printers, San Francisco: 1852, pp. 223 - 225.

[110] Winifred Davidson, "Early History," *History of San Diego County*, San Diego Press Club, San Diego: 1936, p. 89.

[111] San Diego Common Council, Minutes, Feb. 17, 1852. San Diego City Clerk's Office, Document 20485 regarding cave-in, Box. No. A-0018CC, Folder No. 11.

[112] *San Diego Herald*, Feb. 21, 1852, p. 2

[113] *San Diego Herald*, Feb. 28, 1852, p. 3, col. 1

[114] Paul Michael Callaghan, "Fort Rosecrans, California," master's thesis, University of San Diego: 1980, Helen K. and James S. Copley Library (974.404 C156f), p. 4.

[115] *San Diego Herald*, Feb. 28, 1852, p. 2.

[116] James W. Robinson to Amasa Turner, March 2, 1851, Manuscript Collection, Turner (Amasa) papers, 2.325/K23 Center for American History, the University of Texas at Austin.

[117] *San Diego Herald*, March 6, 1852, p. 2, col. 3.

[118] *San Diego Herald*, March 13, 1852, p. 2, col. 3.

[119] *San Diego Herald*, March 13, 1852, p. 2.

First Board of Trustees

[120] San Diego Board of Trustees, Minutes, March 25, 1852.

[121] San Diego Board of Trustees, Minutes, March 26, 1852.

[122] San Diego Board of Trustees, Minutes, March 26, 1852.

[123] San Diego Board of Trustees, Minutes, April 2, 1852.

Franklin's Grand Jury

[124] *San Diego Herald,* April 17, 1852, p.2.

[125] Jack Skiles, *Judge Roy Bean Country,* Texas Tech University Press, Lubbock: 1996, pp. x–xi, 2–3.

[126] *San Diego Herald,* April 17, 1852, pp. 2–3.

[127] Ibid.

[128] *San Diego Herald,* May 8, 1852, p. 2

[129] *Journal of the Proceedings of the Grand Lodge of the State of California, 1850-1854,* op. cit., p. 192.

Demise of the First Board of Trustees

[130] "Chapter CXl: An Act Respecting the Trustees of the City of San Diego," *Statutes of California passed at the Third Session of the Legislature,* op. cit., p. 225.

[131] San Diego Board of Trustees, Minutes, May 20, 1852.

[132] San Diego Board of Trustees, Minutes, June 9, 1852.

[133] San Diego Board of Trustees, Minutes, June 10, 1852.

[134] San Diego Board of Trustees, Minutes, July 31, 1852.

[135] Adema, *San Diego's Oldest Pioneer: Phillip Crosthwaite,* p. 113. Puorade, *The Silver Dons,* p. 199.

Chapter 3

An Instant Majority

[1] San Diego Board of Trustees, Minutes, July 31, 1852.

[2] San Diego Board of Trustees, Minutes, Aug. 25, 1852.

[3] San Diego Board of Trustees, Minutes, Aug. 26, 1852.

The Sad Saga of Yankee Jim

[4] "Hanging Yankee Jim, " *San Diego Union,* Oct. 9, 1873.

Rose Sets Down Roots

[5] *San Diego Herald,* Aug. 27, 1852.

[6] San Diego County Recorder I, Deed Book D, p. 17. The property was located in Block 42 of the map drawn by Cave Couts. It fronted 36 1/2 feet on Fitch Street and ran back to a depth of 36 feet, 3 inches.

[7] *Rose v. Rose,* Deposition of Henry H. Thal, June 21, 1854, San Diego Historical Society, "District Court Records," R3.38, Box. 17.

[8] Ibid.

[9] San Diego Board of Trustees, Minutes, November 29, 1852.

[10] San Diego Board of Trustees, Minutes, Dec. 7, 1852.

[11] San Diego Board of Trustees, Minutes, Dec. 10, 1852.

[12] San Diego Board of Trustees, Minutes, Jan. 6, 1853. Rose's purchases included, in the Playa: Block 40, Lot 3, $37; Block 45, Lot 2, $5; Block 45, Lot 3, $13; Block 46, Lot 1, $5; Block 46, Lot 2, $11; Block 46, Lot 3, $22; and Block 46, Lot 4, $2. In Old Town, they included: Block 1, Lot 2, $20; Block 1, Lot 3, $21; Block 2, Lot 2, $10; Block 2, Lot 3, $11; Block 3, Lot 2, $20; Block 21, Lot 3, $29; Block 23, Lot 2, $15; Block 23, Lot 3, $20; Block 23, Lot 4, $16; Block 58, Lot 1, $17; Block 58, Lot 2, $19; Block 58, Lot 3, $21; Block 58, Lot 4, $21; Block 59, Lot 1, $20; Block 59, Lot 2, $20; Block 59, Lot 3, $22; Block 59, Lot 4, $27; Block 60, Lot 3, $7.

[13] San Diego Board of Trustees, Minutes, Dec. 28, 1852.

[14] San Diego Board of Trustees, Minutes, Dec. 30, 1852.

[15] San Diego Board of Trustees, Jan. 6, 1853.

[16] San Diego County Recorder, Deed Book D, page 229: These included: Block 17, Lots 4, 5, 6, 10, 11, 12; Block 29, Lots 1, 2, 3, 8; Blcok 48, Lots 4, 5, 6; Block 66, Lots 1, 2, 3 7, 8, 9; Block 80, Lots 4, 5, 6, 10, 11, 12; Block 83, Lots 1, 2, 3, 7, 8, 9; Block 98, Lots 1, 2, 3; Block 104, Lots 4, 5, 6, 10, 11, 12; Block 117, Lots, 1, 2, 3, 7, 8, 9; Block 125, Lots 1, 2, 3, 7, 8, 9; Block 134, Lots, 1, 2, 3, 7, 8, 9; Block 140, Lots 4, 5, 6, 10, 11, 12; Block 142, Lots 1, 2, 3, 7, 8, 9 and Block 152, Lots 1, 2, 3, 7, 8, 9.

[17] San Diego County Recorder, Deed Book D, pp. 81, 82. These were Block 56, Lot 4 and Block 62, Lots 1, 2, 3, 4.

[18] San Diego Board of Trustees, Minutes, Jan. 8, 1853.

[19] San Diego County Board of Supervisors, Minutes, February 3, 1853 (microfiche records; Clerk of the County Board of Supervisors).

[20] San Diego County Board of Supervisors, Minutes, March 14, 1853.

[21] San Diego County Board of Supervisors, Minutes, March 28, 1853.

[22] San Diego Countyh Board of Supervisors, Minutes, April 4, 1853.

[23] Richard F. Pourade, *The Silver Dons*, Union-Tribune Publishing Co., San Diego: 1966, p. 205.

[24] San Diego County Board of Supervisors, Minutes, April 4, 1853.

[25] San Diego County Board of Supervisors, Minutes, April 13, 1853.

[26] Robert Wells Haven, "Thomas Whaley," p. 111. Carl Heilbron, editor, *History of San Diego County*, 1936, p. 424. Quinn, *op. cit.*, page 58. *San Diego Herald*, May 21, 1853, p. 2.

The Making of Rose Canyon

[27] San Diego Board of Trustees, Minutes, June 3, 1853.

[28] San Diego Board of Trustees, Minutes, July 12, 1853. San Diego County Recorder, Deed Book D, p. 132. Rose purchased Lots 1, 2, 3, 4, and 8, of 160 acres each, in La Cañada de las Lleguas.

[29] San Diego Board of Trustees, Minutes, July 12, 1853. San Diego County Recorder, Deed Book D, pp. 134, 136.

[30] San Diego Board of Trustees, Minutes, July 13, 1853. San Diego County Recorder, Deed Book C, p. 199, renumbered in Deed Book D as page 136. The parcels were Block 94, Lots 1-4; Lot 9 of 10 acres and Lot 15 of 5 acres. When the trustees decided to create a continuous numbering system to avoid confusion, these parcels were renumbered respectively as Block 340, Lot 310 and Lot 277.

[31] San Diego Board of Trustees, Minutes, July 13, 1853. San Diego County Recorder, Deed Book D, p. 138. Lot No. 5 was sold to Sophia Fisher, Lot 6 to Gustave Fisher, and Lot 7 to their daughter Louisa Fisher.

[32] San Diego Board of Trustees, Minutes, July 13, 1853. Lands acquired by Robinson included Old Town Block 12; Lot 1 in Mission Valley; Lot 16 containing 172 and 6 rods; half of Lot 17 (73 1/2 acres); Lot 4 in the 40-acre range; Lot 4 in the 20-acre range; Lot 5 in the 10-acre range; Lot 10 in the 5-acre range and Lot 96, a 100-vara lot.

[33] San Diego County Recorder, July 21, 1853, Deed Book D, p. 323.

[34] San Diego County Board of Supervisors, Minutes, July 28, 1853.

[35] San Diego Historical Society, "Taxable Property of Louis Rose, 1852 - 1853" (File R2.102, Box 1, Folder 2).

[36] Leo Rosten, *The Joys of Yiddish*, Simon & Shuster Pocket Books, New York: 1968, p. 313.

[37] San Diego County Recorder, Deed Book I, p. 268.

[38] *Rose v. Rose*, location cited, deposition by Henry Thal.

[39] Davidson, Winifred, Notes on Louis Rose, vertical file, San Diego Historical Society. *San Diego Union*, Nov. 2, 1873, cited in Norton B. Stern and William M. Kramer, "The Rose of San Diego," *Old Town, New Town: An Enjoyment of San Diego History*, William M. Kramer, editor; Stanley and Laurel Schwartz, associate editors, Western States History Association, Los Angeles: 1994.

San Diego County Bookkeeping Woes

[40] San Diego County Board of Supervisors, Minutes, July 30, 1853.

Attitudes Toward Jews in San Diego

[41] *San Diego Herald*, Aug. 6, 1853, p. 2.

[42] Henry Schwartz, "The Uneasy Alliance-Jewish-Anglo Relations in San Diego, 1850-1860," *The Journal of San Diego History,* Vol. 20, No. 3, Summer 1974, p. 55.

[43] Norton B. Stern, "The Franklin Brothers of San Diego," *The Journal of San Diego History,* Vol. 21, No. 3, Summer 1975, p. 34.

[44] San Diego Board of Trustees, Minutes, Sept. 10, 1853.

[45] Orion Zink and Irvin Shimmin, "The Story of San Diego Lodge No. 35, F. & A.M.," *The Master Mason,* 125th Anniversary Edition: 1976, p. 5.

[46] *Journal of the Proceedings of the Grand Lodge of the State of California,* 1850-1854, San Francisco: 1857, p. 266.

[47] "Squibobiana," typescript, George Derby document file, San Diego Historical Society archives.

[48] Grover M. Dickman, "San Diego Lodge No. 35 Celebrates Eighty-Fifth Anniversary," Document File, "Masons," San Diego Historical Society.

[49] *San Diego Herald,* Aug. 24, 1853, p. 2

[50] Ibid. Others endorsed on the Phoenix slate were: for governor, William Waldo; for lieutenant governor, Samuel Purdy; for state treasurer, Richard Roman; comptroller, Sam Bell of Mariposa; justice of the Supreme Court, Todd Robinson; attorney general J.R. McConnell; surveyor-general Selim E. Woodworth; superintendent of public instruction, Sherman Day; state senator, J.P. McFarland; member of Assembly, W.C. Ferrell; clerk of the county court, Phiip Crosthwaite; sheriff, Francis Hinton; county surveyor, Charles H. Poole; public administrator, W.H. Moon; coroner, L. Strauss; assessor, George Lyons; constables, C. Morris and R. Israel.

[51] *San Diego Herald,* Sept. 3, 1853, p. 3.

[52] *San Diego Herald,* Sept. 17, 1853, p. 3.

[53] San Diego Board of Trustees, Minutes, Sept. 10, 1853.

[54] *San Diego Herald,* Sept. 17, 1853, p. 4.

[55] *San Diego Herald,* Oct. 1, 1853, p. 3.

[56] *San Diego Herald,* Oct. 29, 1853, p. 3.

Another Jail Escape

[57] *San Diego Herald,* Sept. 3, 1853, p. 2.

[58] *San Diego Herald,* Sept. 10, 1853, p. 2; Sept. 17, 1853, p. 2.

The Entrepreneurial Rose

[59] *San Diego Herald,* Oct. 29, 1853, p. 3

[60] Ibid. Lucille C. Duvall, "Louis Rose," manuscript, archives of the San Diego Historical Society.

[61] Benjamin Hayes, Scrapbooks, 103 Southern California-San Diego County 1, Local History, 1850-1867 (The Bancroft Library, University of California, Berkeley, F 851.H4 R103x).

[62] *Rose v. Rose,* Thal deposition, location cited.

[63] San Diego Board of Trustees, Minutes, Oct. 28, 1853. San Diego County Board of Supervisors, Minutes, Nov. 9, 1853.

[64] San Diego County Board of Supervisors, Minutes, Nov. 7, 1853.

[65] San Diego County Recorder, Deed Book D, p. 263. *San Diego Herald,* Feb. 18, 1854, p. 2.

[66] *San Diego Herald,* Dec. 24, 1853, p. 2.

[67] *San Diego Herald,* Jan. 28, 1854, p. 2.

[68] Ibid.

[69] *San Diego Herald,* Jan. 28, 1854, p. 2.

Settlement of the Jail Controversy

[70] *San Diego Herald,* Oct. 29, 1853, p. 3.

[71] San Diego Board of Trustees, Minutes, Nov. 2, 4, 5, 10, 12, 1853.

[72] *San Diego Herald,* Dec. 31, 1853, p. 2.

[73] San Diego Board of Trustees, Minutes, Aug. 28, 1854.

[74] San Diego Board of Trustees, Minutes, Feb. 1, 1853. Alexander purchased at auction in the area adjoining La Cañada de las Lleguas: Blocks A, 10, 12, and 14. In the Playa area, he acquired Blocks 6, Lot 1; Block 15, Lot 2; Block 30, Lot 1; Block 47, Lot 2; Block 54, Lot 2; and Block 56, Lot 3. Although the lattermost purchase was auctioned to Alexander, it was recorded by the San Diego County Recorder as being granted to Rose, Book I, p. 149.

Unshackling San Diego

[75] Samuel F. Black, *San Diego County, Calif.: A Record of Settlement, Organization, Progress and Achievement*, S.J. Clarke Publishing Co., Chicago: 1913, p. 139. Winifred Davidson, "Early History" in *History of San Diego County*, San Diego Press Club, San Diego: 1936, p. 146.

[76] *San Diego Herald*, April 1, 1854, p. 2.

[77] *San Diego Herald*, April 8, 1854, p. 2.

[78] San Diego County Board of Supervisors, Minutes, June 19, July 18, 1854.

[79] E. W. Morse, "Reminiscences of Early San Diego," *San Diego Union*, June 1, 1900, p. 6.

[80] Dickman, "San Diego Lodge No. 35 Celebrates Eighty-Fifth Anniversary."

[81] San Diego Board of Trustees, Minutes, Aug. 24, 1854.

Attitudes Toward Jews in San Diego, Part II

[82] *San Diego Herald*, May 27, 1854, p. 3.

[83] *San Diego Herald*, June 17, 1854. Henry Schwartz, "The Uneasy Alliance," p. 56.

[84] *San Diego Herald*, June 24, 1854.

[85] *San Diego Herald*, Nov. 11, 1854, p. 2.

[86] The receipt was included in a letter, A.S. Ensworth to Chas Tucker, Aug. 19, 1857, San Diego Historical Society, "Claims-Land Bounty File."

[87] Elizabeth C. MacPhail, *The Story of New San Diego and Its Founder Alonzo E. Horton*, Pioneer Printers, San Diego: 1969, p. 21.

Plenty of Tsuris

[88] *Rose v. Rose*, District Court Records, San Diego Historical Society, R2.38, Box 17.

[89] Norton B. Stern and William M. Kramer, "The Rose of San Diego," footnote 6, p. 85.

[90] Lucille C. Duvall, "Louis Rose," manuscript, archives of the San Diego Historical Society, in which she quotes Leland Gent Stanford.

[91] San Diego Genealogical Society, Deed Book 1, July 23, 1854. Brian F. Smith and Associates, "A Cultural Resources Study for the Rose Canyon Trunk Sewer Project," San Diego: June 24, 1992 (City of San Diego, DEP #89-0976), p. 300.

Law and Order

[92] *San Diego Herald*, Sept. 2, 1854, p. 2.

[93] *San Diego Herald*, Aug. 26, 1854, p. 2.

[94] *San Diego Herald*, Sept. 9, 1854, p. 2.

[95] *San Diego Herald*, Sept. 16, 1854, p. 2.

[96] *San Diego Herald*, Dec. 23, 1854, p. 2.

[97] San Diego County Board of Supervisors, Minutes, Oct. 21, 1854.

[98] San Diego County Board of Supervisors, Minutes, Nov. 15, Dec. 4, Dec. 30, 1854; Jan. 4, 1855.

[99] San Diego County Board of Supervisors, Minutes, June 15, 1855.

The San Diego & Gila Southern Pacific and Atlantic Railroad Company

[100] Earl Samuel McGhee, "E.W. Morse, Pioneer Merchant and Co-Founder of San Diego," master's thesis, San Diego State College, June 5, 1950, p. 87.

[101] Anson Sutton to Thomas Whaley, Oct. 23, 1854, cited in Robert Wells Haven, "Thomas Whaley," "Railroads" File, San Diego Historical Society, Box 59, File 20.

[102] San Diego and Gila Southern Pacific and Atlantic Railroad Co., Articles of Association, Nov. 1, 1854. San Diego Historical Society, "Railroads," Box 59, File 20. Other investors and the number of shares they purchased were Lewis Franklin 50, Maurice Franklin 50, Lyons 50, Pendleton 50, Crosthwaite 40, Moon 30, Sexton 30, Witherby 30, Tebbetts 25, Joseph A. Anderson 20, J.C. Bogart 20, Thomas R. Darnall 20, Fisher 20, Gitchell 20, James Keating 20, Kurtz 20, Morse 20, J. Judson Ames 15, Julian Ames 10, Sam Aspell 10, R.D. Israel 10, H. Jacobs 10, H.C. Ladd 10, Mannasse 10, Charles Poole 10, K. Rauschenbach 10, L. Strauss 10, Wall 10, W.W. Ware 10 and G.B. Tolman 5.

[103] Iris Engstrand and Roy Brandes, *Old Town San Diego 1821-1874*, Alcala Press, San Diego: 1976, p. 20.

[104] William Uberti, "Oliver S. Witherby: First State District Judge in San Diego," *Journal of San Diego History*, Vol. 24, No. 2; Spring 1978, p. 221.

[105] San Diego Herald, Nov. 18, 1854, p. 2; Jan. 6, 1855, p. 2; April 28, 1855, p. 2.

The Entrepreneurial Rose, Part II

[106] *San Diego Herald*, Feb. 3, 1855, p. 2.

[107] *San Diego Herald*, Feb. 10, 1855, p. 2.

[108] *San Diego Herald*, April 28, 1855, p. 2.

[109] Ibid.

[110] Mary A. Helmich, "The Old Town San Diego Retailer's Reference and Historic Account Book, or Advice for Merchants Recreating a (circa) 1835–1872 Period Store," California Department of Parks and Recreation: 1993, p. 43.

[111] San Diego Board of Trustees, Minutes, April 24, 1855.

[112] *San Diego Herald*, April 28, 1855, p. 2. Also Stern and Kramer, "The Rose of San Diego."

[113] *San Diego Herald*, June 16, 1855, p. 2.

[114] *San Diego Herald*, Sept. 15, 1855, p. 2.

[115] *San Diego Herald*, Oct. 13, 1855, p. 2.

[116] *San Diego Herald*, Nov. 3, 1855, p. 2.

[117] *People vs. Robinson*, Oct. 1, 1855, San Diego Historical Society.

[118] "School District No. 1, Operating Expenses, 1855," San Diego Historical Society, 2.68, Box 21, Folder 3

[119] San Diego County Tax Assessment file, Box 1, File 4, 1855; San Diego Historical Society.

[120] *San Diego Herald*, Sept. 8, 1855, p. 2.

[121] *L. Strauss & Co. vs. Louis Rose*, May 5, 1858, District Court Case 01030015, "District Court Records," San Diego Historical Society.

Indians and Mormons

[122] Cyrus Field Willard, "Freemasonry in San Diego," *The San Diego Times*, no date, "Masons" document file, San Diego Historical Society.

[123] *San Diego Herald*, Feb. 17, 1855, p.2.

[124] *San Diego Herald*, May 12, 1855, p. 2.

[125] Harold Guy Hevener Jr., "The Pueblo Lands of the City of San Diego 1769-1950," master's thesis, San Diego State College, June 1950, p. 93.

[126] James W. Robinson to William Robinson, Oct. 9, 1855, San Diego County Probate Case 670, Box 6, San Diego County Law Library.

Attitudes Toward Jews in San Diego, Part III

[127] *San Diego Herald*, Sept. 28, 1855, p. 1.

[128] *San Diego Herald*, Nov.17, 1855, p. 1.

[129] *San Diego Herald*, Jan. 19, 1856, p. 1.

[131] Davidson, "Early History," op. cit., p. 146.

Tight Economic Times

[132] *San Diego Herald*, Feb. 9, 1856, p. 2.

[133] *San Diego Herald*, May 17, 1856, p. 2.

[134] Ibid.

[135] Brian F. Smith, "The San Diego of Judge Benjamin I. Hayes."

[136] Plaza School Report, March 20, 1856, San Diego Historical Society, 2.68, Box. 21, San Diego School District, 1851.

[137] *San Diego Herald*, May 31, 1856, p. 2.

[138] *L. Strauss & Co. vs. Louis Rose*, op. cit.

[139] *O.S. Witherby vs. Louis Rose,* May 5, 1858. District Court Case 01030016, "District Court Records," San Diego Historical Society.

Know-Nothing Movement

[140] *San Diego Herald*, June 7, 1856, p. 2.

[141] *San Diego Herald*, June 28, 1856, p. 2.

[142] *San Diego Herald*, July 26, 1856, p. 2.

[143] Audrey R. Karsh, "Mannasse Chico: Enlightened Merchant of San Diego," *Western States Jewish Historical Quarterly*, Vol. 8, No. 1: Oct. 1975, pp 45-54.

[144] *San Diego Herald*, July 5, 1856, p. 2. Victoria Jacobs, *Diary of a San Diego Girl, 1856*, edited by Sylvia Arden, Norton B. Stern, publisher. Santa Monica, Calif.:1974, p. 23.

[145] *San Diego Herald*, July 5, 1856, p. 2.

[146] Ibid, p 2. *San Diego Herald*, July 12, 1855, p. 2. Pourade, *The Silver Dons*, p. 207.

[147] *San Diego Herald*, Nov. 15, 29, Dec. 6, 1856. Stern and Kramer, "The Rose of San Diego."

Trade with San Bernardino

[148] *San Diego Herald*, July 19, 1856, p. 2.

Robinson Takes Ill

[149] Robinson, James W., "Will," July 31, 1856, "James Robinson" document file, San Diego Historical Society.

[150] Sarah R. Robinson, Declaration to District Court, Aug. 30, 1856, and Jonathan R. Scott, Declaration to District Court, Aug. 30, 1856, in *Maurice A. Franklin v. Joseph Reiner*, District Court files, San Diego Historical Society.

The Entrepreneurial Rose, Part II

[151] "Assessments," Personal Property of Louis Rose, San Diego Historical Society, File 56-98, Box 1, File 5, 1856 Assessments, R.1.102.

[152] Benjamin Hayes, *Pioneer Notes from the Diaries of Judge Benjamin Hayes, 1849-1875*, edited by Marjorie Tisdale Wolcott, private printing, Los Angeles: 1929, p. 120 (San Diego Public Library, California Room collection). Hereafter *Pioneer Notes*.

[153] Ibid, pp. 120-121.

[154] Benjamin Hayes, *Emigrant Notes,* Vol. 1, p. 188, handwritten diaries of Judge Benjamin Hayes, Bancroft Library, University of California at Berkeley.

[155] Ibid, Vol. 2, pp. 191-192.

[156] Ibid, Vol. 2, pp. 193-194.

[157] Ibid, Vol. 2, pp. 106-197.

[158] Ibid, Vol. 2, p. 197.

[159] Ibid.

[160] Ibid, Vol. 1, p. 191.

[161] Smith, Brian Frederick, "The San Diego of Judge Benjamin I. Hayes.

[162] Hayes, *Emigrant Notes*, Vol. 2, p. 150.

[163] Hayes, *Pioneer Notes*, p. 133. Stern and Kramer, "The Rose of San Diego," p. 21.

[164] Victoria Jacobs, *op. cit.*, p. 57.

[165] Hayes, *Pioneer Notes*," p. 143.

[166] Thomas Savage, *Documentos para Historia de California; Papeles Originales Sacados de Varios Archivos Particulares*, Tom IV, University of California, Bancroft Library: 1874, p. 5 (C-96, pt. 1 photo).

[167] Victoria Jacobs, *Diary of a San Diego Girl*, pp. 62, 64.

[168] *Frank Ames vs. Louis Rose*, San Diego District Court, Case 01010004, Dec. 11, 1857; San Diego Historical Society archives, "District Court Records."

[169] *San Diego Herald*, Dec. 14, 1856, p. 2; Dec. 27, 1856, p. 2.

[170] *San Diego Herald*, Dec. 20, 1856, p. 2.

[171] Victoria Jacobs, *Diary of a San Diego Girl*.

[172] *San Diego Herald*, Dec. 27, 18556, p. 2.

Attitudes Toward Jews in San Diego, Part IV

[173] *San Diego Herald*, Jan. 3, 1857, p. 2.

[174] *San Diego Herald*, Jan. 10, 1857, p. 2.

[175] *San Diego Herald*, Jan. 24, 1857, p. 3.

[176] *San Diego Herald*, March 7, 1857, p. 2.

[177] *San Diego Herald*, July 25, 1857, p. 2.

[178] *San Diego Herald*, Sept. 12, 1857, p. 2.

[179] *San Diego Herald*, April 4, 1857, p. 2.

Boom and Bust

[180] *San Diego Herald*, Feb. 21, 1857, p. 2; Feb. 28, 1857, p. 2.

[181] *San Diego Herald*, March 28, 1857, p. 2.

[182] San Diego County Coroner, Inquest into Death of Judge John Hays, May 25, 1857, File F1-5, Collection R.2.69, San Diego Historical Society.

[183] *San Diego Herald*, June 13, 1857, p. 1.

[184] Hayes, *Pioneer Notes*, p. 163.

[185] Bertram B. Moore, "Road Development in San Diego County" in *History of San Diego County*, Carl Heilbron, editor, 1936, p. 383. Pourade, *The Silver Dons*, pp. 220-221. Stuart N. Lake, "Birch's Overland Mail in San Diego County," *The Journal of San Diego History*, Vol. 3, No. 2, p. 15. San Diego Herald, Sept. 19, 1857, p. 2; Nov. 21, 1857.

[186] *San Diego Herald*, Oct. 17, 1857, p. 2.

[187] *San Diego Herald*, Oct. 10, 1857, p. 2; Oct. 17, 1857, p. 2; Oct. 24, 1857, p. 2; Oct. 31, 1857, p. 2.

Mine Speculations

[188] *San Diego Herald*, Feb. 21, 1857, p. 2; Feb. 28, 1857, p. 3.

[189] *San Diego Herald*, May 2, 1857, p. 2. *Solomon Goldman and James Donohoe vs. Louis Rose,* May 5, 1858, District Court Case 01030013, and *Daniel N. Breed vs. Louis Rose*, May 5, 1858, District Court Case 01020017, "District Court Records," San Diego Historical Society.

[190] *San Diego Herald*, May 2, 1857, p. 1.

[191] *San Diego Herald*, June 20, 1857, p. 2.

[192] San Diego County Recorder, May 28, 1857, Miscellaneous Book 1, p. 24.

[193] *Daniel N. Breed vs. Louis Rose*, op. cit., and *Andrew Casidy vs. Louis Rose and E. W. Morse*, District Court Case 01030014, "District Court Records," San Diego Historical Society.

[194] *San Diego Herald*, Sept. 12, 1857, p. 2

[195] *L. Strauss & Co. vs. Louis Rose,* op. cit.

[196] *San Diego Herald*, Nov. 14, 1857, p. 2.

[197] *San Diego Herald*, Dec. 5, 1857, p. 2.

[198] *Solomon Goldman and James Donohoe vs. Louis Rose*, op. cit.

[199] *Frank Ames vs. Louis Rose*, District Court Case 0100004, "District Court Records," San Diego Historical Society.

[200] "Assessments," File 57-11, Box 1, File 6, 1857; Assessments "Property of Louis Rose," San Diego Historical Society.

[201] A.S. Ensworth to Tucker & Lloyd, Aug. 19, 1857, "Claims–Land Bounty" file, San Diego Historical Society.

Death of Robinson

[202] Hayes, *Pioneer Notes*, p. 159.

[203] *San Diego Herald*, Oct. 31, 1857, p. 2.

[204] Orion Zink (Lodge No. 35 historian) to George Robinson Jr., July 9, 1948, San Diego Lodge No. 35, F. & A. M., "James Robinson" file. Orion M. Zink, "Places in Old Town," *The Journal of San Diego History*, Vol. 15, No. 1, Winter 1969, in which Zink locates the site as Pueblo Lot 32, Map of City of San Diego by Clayton & Hesse.

[205] "James Robinson" document file, payment order, San Diego Historical Society.

Chapter 4

Beset by Creditors

[1] *San Diego Herald*, Jan. 3, 1858, p. 2.

[2] *San Diego Herald*, Feb. 13, 1858, p.2.

[3] A.J. Chase to E.W. Morse, Feb. 17, 1858, San Diego Historical Society, E.W. Morse Collection, MSS 341, Box 1 of 6, File 2, Document 17.

[4] A.J. Chase to E.W. Morse, May 1, 1858, San Diego Historical Society, E.W. Morse Collection, MSS 341, Box 1 of 6, File 2, Document 19.

[5] San Diego County Recorder, March 8, 1858, Miscellaneous Book 1, p. 28.

[6] D. N. Breed to E.W. Morse, May 17, 1858, San Diego Historical Society, E.W. Morse Collection, Box1 of 6, File 3, Document 1.

[7] D.N. Breed to E.W. Morse, June 2, 1858, San Diego Historical Society, E.W. Morse Collection, Box 1 of 6, File 3, Document 1.

[8] A.J. Chase to E.W. Morse, June 3, 1858, San Diego Historical Society, E.W. Morse Collection, Box 1 of 6, File 3. Document 2.

[9] A.J. Chase to E.W. Morse, June 17, 1858, San Diego Historical Society, E.W. Morse Collection, Box 1 of 6, File 3, Document 3.

[10] *Lorenzo Soto vs. Louis Rose,* District Court Case 02070037, 1860, San Diego Historical Society Archives.

[11] D.N. Breed to E.W. Morse, June 18, 1858, San Diego Historical Society, E.W. Morse Collection, Box 1 of 6, File 3, Document 5.

[12] Tucker & Lloyd to A.S. Ensworth, July 13, 1858, San Diego Historical Society, A.S. Ensworth file.

[13] Tucker & Lloyd to A.S. Ensworth, Oct. 19, 1858, San Diego Historical Society, A.S. Ensworth file.

Franklin vs. Franklin

[14] *San Diego Herald*, Feb. 6, 1858, p. 2.

[15] *San Diego Herald*, Feb. 20, 1858, p. 2.

[16] *San Diego Herald*, March 13, 1858, p. 2.

[17] *San Diego Herald*, March 20, 1858, p. 2.

[18] *San Diego Herald*, April 2, 1858, p. 2.

[19] *Lewis Franklin vs. Maurice Franklin*, testimony of Jesus Gonzales, Hyman Mannasse, "District Court Records," San Diego Historical Society, Collection R3.38, Box 1, File 2.

[20] Benjamin Hayes, decision, Feb. 1, 1859, *Lewis Franklin vs. Maurice Franklin*, location cited.

[21] *San Diego Herald*, Nov. 13, 1856, p. 2.

The Great Seaweed Adventure

[22] *San Diego Herald*, Jan. 29, 1859, p. 2.

[23] Pourade, *The Silver Dons*, p. 245.

The 'San Diego Incident'

[24] *San Diego Herald*, Oct. 15, 1859, p. 2.

[25] *Weekly Gleaner*, Nov. 11, 1859, cited in Ronald D. Gerson, "Jewish Religious Life in San Diego, CA, 1851–1918," master's thesis, Hebrew Union College-Jewish Institute of Religion, Cincinnati, Ohio: 1974, p. 16 (filed as RCC 296 Gerson at California Room, San Diego Public Library).

[26] *Occident*, Dec. 22, 1859, cited in Gerson, *op. cit.*

[27] *San Diego Herald*, Oct. 22, 1859, p. 2.

Rose Loses His Canyon

[28] *Lorenzo Soto vs. Louis Rose,* op. cit.

[29] Louis Rose deed to Lorenzo Soto, April 15, 1861, San Diego County Recorder's Office, Deed Book 2, pp. 38–41.

[30] Judith Gribetz, Edward L. Greenstein, and Regina Stein, *The Timetables of Jewish History: A Chronology of the Most Important People and Events in Jewish History*, Simon and Schuster, A Touchstone Book, New York: 1993, pp. 281–282.

[31] *San Diego Herald*, March 17, 1860, p. 2.

[32] *San Diego Herald*, Jan. 23, 1860, p. 2.

[33] Stern and Kramer, "The Rose of San Diego."

[34] Gerson, "Jewish Religious Life in San Diego, CA," citation of *Weekly Gleaner*, June 20, 1861.

[35] Samuel I. Fox, "Looking Backward," *The San Diego Jewish Community News*, Vol. IV, No. 20, Sept. 20, 1922, p. 6.

[36] Laurie Bissell, "San Diego Cemeteries: A Brief Guide," *The Journal of San Diego History*, Vol. 28, No. 4, Fall 1982, p. 272.

[37] Stanley Schwartz, "A Brief History of Congregation Beth Israel," Congregation Beth Israel, 135th Birthday 1861-1996, San Diego: 1996.

[38] Ronald J. Quinn, editor, "If Only You Could Send Me a Strong and Sound Leg: Letters of A.S. Ensworth to Thomas Whaley, 1862-1865," *The Journal of San Diego History*, Vol. 43, No. 1, Winter 1997.

[39] D.N. Breed to E.W. Morse, July 2, 1863, San Diego Historical Society, E.W. Morse Collection, MS 341, Box 1 of 6, File 9, Document 1.

[40] Audrey R. Karsh, "Mothers and Daughters of Old San Diego," *Western States Jewish Historical Quarterly*, Vol. XIX.

[41] Audrey R. Karsh, "Mannasse Chico: Enlightened Merchant of San Diego," *Western States Jewish Historical Quarterly*, Vol. VIII, No. 1: Oct, 1975, p. 52.

[42] The 1868 San Francisco directory lists an Abraham Galland as a money and stock broker doing business in the same building as L.S. Rose, the nephew of Louis Rose. Many rabbis also had businesses.

Rose Recovers Financially

[43] San Diego County Recorder, January 10, 1864, Miscellaneous Book I, p. 57.

[44] Lorenzo and María Soto deed to Louis Rose, Feb. 4, 1864, San Diego County Recorder, Deed Book 2, p. 125.

[45] George Pendleton, appointment of Louis Rose, Feb. 4, 1864, "Louis Rose" vertical file, San Diego Historical Society.

[46] San Diego County Board of Supervisors, Minutes, Sept. 18, 1864, San Diego Historical Society, Document files.

[47] Andrew Cassidy to A.S. Ensworth, Sept. 18, 1864, San Diego Historical Society, Document files.

[48] Henrietta Rose interview with Winifred Davidson, San Diego Historical Society archives, Louis Rose vertical file. "Father... never kept books-that is why there is so little of his personal transactions on record anywhere."

[49] Henry O. Langley, *The San Francisco Directory for the Year Commencing December, 1865*, Towne & Bacon, printers, San Francisco: 1865, p. 674.

[50] San Diego County Recorder, Jan. 9, 1866, Deed Book 2, p. 250.

[51] San Diego County Recorder, Feb. 9, 1866, Deed Book 2, p. 233.

Racism in San Diego

[52] Clare V. McKanna, Jr., "An Old Town Gunfight: The Homicide Trial of Cave Johnson Couts, 1866," *The Journal of San Diego History*, Vol. 44, No. 4, Fall 1998, p. 261.

[53] Beatrice Frichette Knott, "Reading Between the Lines: Social History of San Diego During the Early American Period as Derived From Public and Business Records," master's thesis, University of San Diego, 1991, p. 142 (Helen K. and James S. Copley Library, University of San Diego, 979 498 K72r).

[55] Ibid.

[56] Henry Schwartz, "The Mary Walker Incident: Black Prejudice in San Diego, 1866," *The Journal of San Diego History*, Vol. XIX, No. 2, Spring 1973, pp. 15–16. Also Pourade, op. cit., p. 254.

Businessman and Civic Leader

[57] Breed and Chase to E.W. Morse, Nov. 30, 1866, San Diego Historical Society, MSS 341, Box 1, File 18, Document 14.

[58] Ibid.

[59] Thomas Savage, *Documentos para la Historia de California, Papeles originales sacados de varios archivos particulares*, Tom. IV, Part 2, University of California, Bancroft Library 1874 (C-B 96 pt 2 phot), circa 1867-68.

[60] H.C. Hopkins, *History of San Diego: Its Pueblo Lands & Water*, City Printing Co., San Diego: 1929, p. 248.

[61] San Diego County Board of Supervisors, Minutes, Feb. 6, 1865; May 9, 1866; Feb. 5, 1867.

[62] San Diego County Board of Supervisors, Minutes, Aug. 7, 1865.

[63] San Diego County Board of Supervisors, Minutes, Sept. 18, 1865.

[64] San Diego County Board of Supervisors, Minutes, Nov. 6, 1865.

[65] San Diego County Board of Supervisors, Minutes, May 9, 1866.

[66] San Diego County Board of Supervisors, Minutes, Aug. 13, 1866.

[67] San Diego County Board of Supervisors, Minutes, May 9, 1867.

[68] San Diego County Board of Supervisors, Minutes, Sept. 16, 1867.

[69] *People vs. Rose*, 1867, San Diego County Law Library, Pioneer Room collection.

Alonzo Horton Comes to San Diego

[70] Robert Mayer, *San Diego: A Chronological and Documentary History 1535-1876*, Oceana Publications Inc., Dobbs Ferry, N.Y. 1978, p. 102.

[71] Elizabeth C. MacPhail, *The Story of New San Diego and its Founder Alonzo E. Horton*, Pioneer Printers, San Diego: 1969, pp. 9, 26.

New Railroad Stirrings

[72] *San Diego Union*, Oct. 10, 1868, p. 2.

[73] Carl Heilbron, editor, *History of San Diego County*, San Diego Press Club, San Diego: 1936, p. 425.

[74] San Diego County Recorder, May 20, 1858, Deed Book 3, p. 156.

[75] "Robinson-Rose house," vertical files, San Diego Historical Society. The bay land also was identified as "Block 199" on a more recent map that had consolidated various holdings in the Pueblo of San Diego under a new numbering system.

[76] *San Francisco Morning Call,* Jan. 16, 1887, cited in Bernice Sharlach, *House of Harmony: Concordia Argounaut's First 130 Years,* Judah L. Magnes Memorial Museum, Berkeley: 1983, p. 12.

[77] *San Diego Union,* Oct. 10, 1868, p. 2. *San Diego Union,* Oct. 17, 1868, p. 2.

[78] *San Diego Union,* Oct. 24, 1868, p. 2.

[79] *San Diego Union,* Nov. 14, 1868, p. 2.

[80] *San Diego Union,* Nov. 28, 1868, p. 2.

[81] *San Diego Union,* Dec. 5, 1868, p. 1; Dec. 12, 1868, p. 1.

Roseville Takes Shape

[82] *San Diego Union,* Jan. 9, 1869, p. 2.

[83] San Diego County Recorder, Feb. 19, 1869, Deed Book 4, p. 260.

[84] San Diego County Recorder, Feb. 22, 1869, Deed Book 4, p. 366. Also Savage, op. cit., p. 227.

[85] James Pascoe, Map of Roseville, January 1869, San Diego County Assessor's Office. Comparison to street maps of 2004 indicates that 1st Street became Avenida de Portugal (and, before that, Addison Street). In an alphabetical salute to authors, 2nd became Bryon; 3rd Carlton; 4th Dickens; 5th Emerson; 6th Fenelon; 7th Garrison; 8th Hugo; 9th Ingelow; 10th Jarvis; 11th Keats; 112th Lowell; 13th McAulay; 14th Newell; 15th Oliphant; 16th Poe; 17th Quimby; 18th Russell; 19th Sterne; 20th Tennyson; 21st Udall; 22nd Voltaire; 23rd Whittier; 24th Xenophon; 25th Yonge; 26th Zola; 27th Abbott; 28th Browning, 29th Curtis; and 30th Dumas.

[86] San Diego County Recorder, March 12, 1869, Deed Book 5, pp. 228-229.

[87] San Diego County Recorder, March 13, 1869, Deed Book 5, p. 243.

[88] San Diego County Recorder, March 27, 1869, Deed Book 5, pp. 182, 188, 234, 236.

[89] *San Diego Union,* April 14, 1869.

[90] San Diego County Recorder, April 9, 1869, Deed Book 5, p. 345.

[91] San Diego County Recorder, April 12, 1869, Deed Book 5, p. 273.

[92] *San Diego Union,* April 21, 1869, p. 3, col. 1.

The Gallant Rose

[93] San Diego County Recorder, Marriage Licenses, p. 116.

[94] San Diego County Recorder, April 24, 1869, Deed Book 5, p. 291.

[95] San Diego County Recorder, April 24, 1869, Deed Book 5.

[96] San Diego County Recorder, April 24, Deed Book 7, p. 84.

[97] San Diego County Recorder, April 24, 1869, Deed Book 5, p. 305.

[98] Ibid.

[99] San Diego County Recorder, April 26, 1869, Deed Book 5, p. 305.

[100] San Diego County Recorder, April 26, 1869, Deed Book 5, p. 346.

[101] San Diego County Recorder, April 29, 1869, Deed Book 5, p. 367.

[102] San Diego County Recorder, Deed Book 5, p. 343. Purchases of lots on this date also were recorded for Hannah Bernard (Deed Book 5, p. 349); Moses Mannasse (Deed Book 5, p. 350), William Bryson (Deed Book 5, p. 355); John C. Caprow (Deed Book 5, p. 386); Henry R. Johnson (Deed Book 5, p. 445); Charles Morgan (Deed Book 5, p. 452); Ellis Abner (Deed Book 6, p. 330); Philip Crosthwaite (Deed Book 7, p. 9); and Walter Walsh (Deed Book 23, pp. 250, 324).

[103] San Diego County Recorder, May 4, 1869, Deed Book 5, p. 348.

[104] San Diego County Recorder, May 7, 1869, Deed Book 5, p. 383.

[105] San Diego County Recorder, May 14, 1869, Deed Book 5, p. 383.

[106] San Diego County Recorder, May 15, 1860, Deed Book 5, p. 384.

[107] San Diego County Recorder, May 17, 1869; Deed Book 5, p. 408; Deed Book 6, p. 64; Deed Book 6, p. 288.

[108] San Diego County Recorder, May 18, 1860, Deed Book 6, p. 83.

[109] San Diego County Recorder, May 5, 1869, Deed Book 5, p. 348.

[110] San Diego County Recorder, May 6, 1869, Deed Book 5, p. 397; Deed Book 7, p. 53.

[111] San Diego County Recorder, May 8, 1869, Deed Book 5, p. 362.

[112] San Diego County Recorder, May 8, 1869, Deed Book 6, pp. 285-286; Deed Book 5, p. 363.

[113] San Diego County Recorder, May 15, 1869, Deed Book 65, pp. 59, 424.

[114] San Diego County Recorder, May 18, 1869, Deed Book 6, p. 85.

[115] *San Diego Union*, May 5, 1869, p. 2. col. 1.

The Second Mrs. Rose

[116] Stern and Kramer, "The Rose of San Diego," p. 24.

[117] *San Diego Union*, May 19, 1869, p. 3, col. 2.

[118] *The Hebrew*, San Francisco, Oct. 13, 1871, p. 4, cited in Stern and Kramer, "The Rose of San Diego."

[119] *San Diego Union*, May 26, 1869, p. 3, col. 3.

[120] San Diego County Recorder, July 7, 1869, Deed Book 6, p. 76.

Rose's Investments

[121] San Diego County Recorder, March 23, 1869, Miscellaneous Book 2, pp. 42-44.

[122] San Diego County Recorder, July 9, 1869, Deed Book 6, pp. 80, 140; Deed Book 4, p. 356.

[123] San Diego County Recorder, Aug. 3, 1869, Miscellaneous Book 2, p. 68.

[124] San Diego County Recorder, Aug. 12, 1869, Deed Book 7, pp. 20-21.

[125] *San Diego Union*, July 7, 1869, p. 2, col. 2.

[126] *San Diego Union*, July 28, 1869, p. 3, col. 2.

[127] San Diego County Recorder, Aug. 20, 1869, Deed Book 6, pp. 266-267.

[128] Louis Rose, Petition to the San Diego County Board of Supervisors, Sept. 8., 1869, San Diego Historical Society, Collection R 2.93, Petitions to Board of Supervisors, Box 1, File 1869, Document 69-13.

[129] Ibid.

[130] John R. Bleeker to E.W. Morse, Sept. 11, 1869, San Diego Historical Society, E.W. Morse Collection, MSS 341, Box 1 of 6, File 26, Document 12.

The Pear Garden

[131] San Diego County Recorder, Sept. 8, 1869, Deed Book 6, p. 339.

[132] *El Pueblo de San Diego*, Junior League of San Diego, San Diego: 1968, p. 339.

[133] Eugene B. Chamberlin, "Casa de Carrillo, Old Town, San Diego," Squibob Chapter of E Clampus Vitus (pamphlet accompanying dedication of Casa de Carillo as California Registered Landmark No. 74), August 6, 1994.

Visit of William Seward

[134] *San Diego Union*, Sept. 22, 1869.

[135] Richard F. Pourade, *The Glory Years*, Union-Tribune Publishing Co., San Diego: 1964, p. 41.

[136] San Diego County Recorder, September 23, 1869, Deed Book 6, p. 449; Deed Book 7, pp. 8, 74.

[137] San Diego County Recorder, Sept. 28, 1869, Deed Book 7, p. 50.

The Gallant Rose, Part II

[138] San Diego County Recorder, Sept. 28, 1869, Deed Book 7, p. 52.

[139] San Diego County Recorder, Oct. 5, 1869, Deed Book 17, p. 339; Nov. 3, 1869, Deed Book 7, pp. 157, 276, 283.

[140] San Diego County Recorder, Oct. 21, 1869, Deed Book 7, p. 187; Oct. 23, 1869, Deed Book 7, p. 345; Dec. 6, 1869, Deed Book 7, p. 440.

[141] San Diego County Recorder, Rose to C.C. Hunter, Oct. 20, 1869, Deed Book 7, p. 196. Rose to Gustave Witfeld, Oct. 23, 1869, Deed Book 7, p. 177. Rose to Ezekial Wilson, Nov. 2, 1869, Deed Book 7, p. 345. Rose to William Norris, Dec. 9, 1869, Deed Book 7, p. 452. Rose to N.D. Broughton, Dec. 21, 1869, Deed Book 11, p. 449.

[142] *San Diego Union*, Jan. 13, 1870, p. 2, col. 4. Norton B. Stern, notes on file at Magnes Museum of Berkeley regarding Myron Lustig, "Louis Rose, First Jew of San Diego, Patriarch of Old Town," typescript.

[143] San Diego Recorder, Feb. 9, 1870, Deed Book 8, p. 223; March 2, 1870, Deed Book 9, p. 239.

Promoting San Diego

[144] MacPhail, *The Story of New San Diego and Its Founder Alonzo E. Horton*, p. 28.

[145] Robert Mayer, *San Diego: A Chronoligical and Documentary History, 1535-1836.*

[146] *San Diego Union*, March 24, 1870, p. 2, col. 2.

[147] San Diego County Recorder, March 28, 1870, Deed Book 9, p. 273.

[148] San Diego County Recorder, April 1, 1870, Deed Book 8, p. 320; Deed Book 9, p. 303.

[149] *San Diego Union*, clipping, undetermined date between March 31 and May 12, 1870.

[150] San Diego County Recorder, May 21, 1870, Deed Book 9, p. 439.

[151] San Diego County Recorder, May 29, 1870, Deed Book 26, p. 1.

[152] *San Diego Union*, June 9, 1870, p. 3, col. 1.

[153] San Diego County Recorder, April 21, 1870, Deed Book 9, p. 339.

[154] San Diego County Recorder, June 18, June 18, 1870, Deed Book 14, p. 551.

[155] San Diego County Recorder, June 14, 1870, Deed Book 13, p. 281.

The Memphis and El Paso Failure

[156] Heilbron, *History of San Diego County*, p. 42

[157] "From Ox Trails to Eagles: A History of the Texas and Pacific Railway,"nd, archives of the Harrison County, Texas, Historical Museum Library, p. 11.

[158] Louis Rose to San Diego County Board of Supervisors, July 5, 1870; San Diego Historical Society, Collection R 2.93, Box 1, 1870 file. Document 70-14.

[159] Ibid.

Old Town vs. New Town

[160] San Diego County Recorder, July 9, 1870, "Deed Book 10, p. 474.

[161] Pourade, *Glory Years*, p. 74.

[162] Ibid, p. 77.

[163] Ibid, p. 79.

[164] *San Diego Union*, Sept. 15, 1870, p. 3, col. 3.

[165] Clarence Alan McGrew, *City of San Diego and the County of San Diego: The Birthplace of California*, Vol. 1, American Historical Society, Chicago and New York: 1922, p. 316.

[166] MacPhail, *The Story of New San Diego and Its Founder Alonzo E. Horton,* p. 21.

[167] Ibid.

[168] Pourade, *Glory Years*, p. 74.

Helene Rose

[169] *San Diego Union*, Oct. 6, 1870, p. 3, col. 4.

[170] San Diego County Recorder, Oct. 22, 1870, Deed Book 10, pp. 474, 576.

[171] San Diego County Recorder, Nov. 1, 1870, Deed Book 11, p. 105.

[172] *San Diego Union*, Nov. 24, 1870, p. 3, col. 2.

Enticing a Railroad

[173] *San Diego Union*, Dec. 1, 1870, p. 3, col. 2.

[174] Louis Rose to County Board of Supervisors, Jan. 17, 1871, San Diego Historical Society, Collection R. 2.93, Box 1, File 1, Document 71-3.

[175] Pourade, *Glory Years*, p. 79.

[176] Rickey D. Best, "San Diego and the Gilded Age: The Efforts to Bring the Texas and Pacific Railroad to San Diego," *The Journal of San Diego History*, Vol. 34, No. 4, Fall 1988, p. 260, citation of Ephraim Morse to Matthew Sherman, Jan. 19, 1871, Morse Letterpress Books, San Diego Historical Society.

[177] Pourade, *Glory Years*, p. 79.

[178] San Diego County Recorder, Jan. 30, 1871, Deed Book 12, p. 104.

[179] San Diego County Recorder, Jan. 30, 1871, Deed Book 12, p. 145.

[180] Pourade, *Glory Years*, p. 79.

[181] San Diego County Recorder, Feb. 14, 1871, Deed Book 13, Page 6.

[182] *San Diego Union*, Jan. 30, 1871, Deed Book 12, p. 145.

[183] *San Diego Union*, Feb. 23, 1871, p. 3, col. 2.

[184] *San Diego Union*, March 9, 1871, p. 2, col. 1.

[185] Ibid.

[186] Pourade, *Glory Years*, p. 85.

[187] San Diego County Recorder, March 4, 1871, Deed Book 15, p. 200; March 8, 1871, Deed Book 13, p. 3; March 16, 1871, Deed Book 12, p. 173.

Marketing Roseville

[188] *San Diego Union*, March 24, 1871, p. 2, col. 1.

[189] *San Diego Union*, March 30, 1871, p. 1, col. 2.

[190] *San Diego Union*, March 30, 1871, p. 3, col. 2. *San Diego Union (Weekly)*, April 6, 1871, p. 3, col. 1.

[191] *San Diego Union*, April 3, 1871, p. 2, col. 3.

[192] San Diego County Recorder, April 3, 1871, Deed Book 12, p. 328.

[193] *San Diego Union (Weekly)*, April 13, 1871, p. 3, col. 2.

[194] San Diego County Recorder, April 4, 1871, Deed Book 13, p. 192; "Deed Book 15, p. 200.

[195] Stern and Kramer, "The Rose of San Diego," p. 8 and footnote, p. 86.

[196] San Diego County Recorder, April 17, 1871, Deed Book 13, p. 225.

[197] San Diego County Recorder, April 18, 1871, Deed Book 13, p. 212.

[198] *San Diego Union (Weekly)*, April 10, 1871, p. 4, col. 1.

[199] *San Diego Union*, April 17, 1871, p. 3.

The Texas and Pacific Railroad

[200] *San Diego Union*, April 27, 1821, p. 4, col. 1.

[201] "From Ox Trails to Eagles: A History of the Texas and Pacific Railway," location cited.

[202] San Diego Union, May 24, 1871, p. 2, col. 1.

Slow Sales in Roseville

[203] *San Diego Union (Weekly)*, June 1, 1871, p. 4, col. 3.

204 San Diego County Recorder, April 10, 1871, Deed Book 12, p. 323.

205 E.W. Morse to Louis Rose, May 3, 1871, San Diego Historical Society, Morse Letterbook, MSS 341, E.W. Morse Collection, Box 5 of 6.

206 Ibid, June 7, 1871.

207 San Diego County Recorder, June 6, 1871, Deed Book 12, p. 592.

208 San Diego County Recorder, June 13, 1871, Deed Book 13, p. 286.

209 *San Diego Union (Weekly)*, June 22, 1871, p. 3, col. 1.

210 *San Diego Union*, June 4, 1871, p. 3, col. 2.

211 *San Diego Union*, June 28, 1871, p. 3, col. 2.

212 *San Diego Union*, July 19, 1871, p. 3, col. 2.

213 Irene Phillips, *The Railroad Story of San Diego County,* South Bay Press, National City, Calif.: 1956, pp. 12-13. Quoted in Best, "San Diego and the Gilded Age, p. 268.

214 San Diego County Recorder, Aug. 25, 1871, Deed Book" 14, p. 202.

215 *San Diego Union (Weekly)*, Aug. 31, 1871, p. 4, col. 3.

216 *San Diego Union (Weekly)*, Sept. 21, 1871, p. 4.

217 Gerson, "Jewish Religious Life in San Diego, CA," pp. 28, 31.

218 *San Diego Union (Weekly)*, Sept. 28, 1871, p. 4.

219 *San Diego Union*, Oct. 3, 1871, p. 3, col. 3; Oct. 5, 1871, p. 3, col. 2.

220 San Diego County Recorder, Nov. 27, 1871, Deed Book 16, p. 372.

221 *San Diego Union, (Weekly)*, Feb. 29, 1872, p. 4, col. 1.

222 *San Diego Union*, Jan. 16, 1872, p. 3, col. 1.

223 *San Diego Union*, Feb. 2, 1872, p. 3.

224 *San Diego Union*, Feb. 11, 1872, p. 3, col. 1.

225 *San Diego Union*, March 13, 1872, p. 3, col. 2.

Demise of Old Town

226 *San Diego Union*, Nov. 28, 1872, p. 3, col. 5.

227 *San Diego Union*, March 6, 1872, p. 3., col. 1.

228 *San Diego Union*, April 25, 1872, p. 3, col. 1.

229 Federal Reserve Bank of Minneapolis, Consumer Price Index (Estimate) 1800-2004.

230 Pourade, *Glory Years*, p. 101.

231 *San Diego Union*, May 30, 1872, p. 4, col. 5.

The Great Railroad Fight

232 *San Diego Union*, March 13, 1872, p. 2. col. 1.

233 *San Diego Union*, March 13, 1872, p. 2, col. 1.

234 *San Diego Union*, March 23, 1872, p. 2, col. 1.

235 *San Diego Union*, March 24, 1873, p. 3, col. 1.

236 *San Diego Union*, March 28, 1872, p. 3, col. 2.

237 *San Diego Union*, April 17, 1872, p. 2, col. 1.

238 *San Diego Union*, April 26, 1872, p. 2, col. 2.

239 *San Diego Union*, April 27, 1872, p. 3, cols 1 and 2. Other committee members were listed as W.B. Burns, John D. Capron, C. Choate, Sydney S. Clark, S.W. Craigue, Ed Daugherty, A. DeFrees, H.H. Dougherty, C.Dunham, A.P. Frery, A.H. Gilbert, Douglas Gunn, J.S. Harvey, H.M. Higgins, A.F Hinchman, D.A. Hollister, Bryant Howard, Charles Hubbell, George Hyde, Warren Kimball, A. Landes, Joseph S. Mannasse, George P. Marston, I. Matthias, G.W.B. McDonald, A.B. McKean, M.S. Patrick, A. Pauly, D.T. Phillips, Matthew Sherman, W.W. Stewart, Joseph Tasker, P.L. Webb, John N. Young, and a Mr. Brooks of Chicago.

[240] *San Diego Union*, May 1, 1872, p. 2, col. 1.

Tidelands Controversy

[241] *San Diego Union*, May 10, 1872, p. 2, col. 1

[242] *San Diego Union*, May 21, 1872, p.2, col. 3.

[243] *San Diego Union*, May 23, 1872, p. 3, col. 2.

[244] *San Diego Union*, May 28, 1872, p. 3, col. 2.

[245] San Diego County Recorder, May 27, 1872, Deed Book 16, p. 483.

[246] *The (San Diego) Daily World*, Aug. 23, 1872, p. 3, col. 3.

Tom Scott Comes to San Diego

[247] *The (San Diego) Daily World*, Aug. 28, 1872, p. 3, col. 3.

[248] Best, "San Diego and the Gilded Age," p. 262.

[249] Ibid.

[250] *The (San Diego) Daily World*, Aug. 29, 1872, p. 3, col. 6.

[251] Best, "San Diego and the Gilded Age."

[252] San Diego County Recorder, Sept. 5, 1872, Deed Book 18, p. 1.

[253] *The (San Diego) Daily World*, Sept. 5, 1872, p. 3, col. 2.

[254] *The (San Diego) Daily World*, Oct. 5, 1872, p. 3, col. 1.

[255] *San Diego Union (Weekly)*, Oct. 10, 1872, p. 4, col. 2.

[256] *The (San Diego) Daily World*, Oct. 9, 1872, p. 3, col. 2.

[257] *San Diego Union (Weekly)*, Dec. 12, 1872, p. 3, col. 1.

[258] San Diego County Recorder, Jan. 4, 1873, Deed Book 18, p. 535.

[259] Harold Guy Hevener Jr., "The Pueblo Lands of the City of San Diego, 1769–1950, master's thesis, San Diego State College, June 1950, p. 96.

[260] San Diego County Recorder, Feb. 13, 1873, Deed Book 21, p. 45.

Death in the Family

[261] San Diego County Recorder, Register of Deaths, March 13, 1873. The register miscalculated Helene's age at 3 years, 7 months, 12 days. She was born Oct. 1, 1870.

[262] *San Diego Union*, March 30, 1873, p. 3, col. 8.

Texas and Pacific Groundbreaking

[263] Best, "San Diego and the Gilded Age," p. 269.

[264] Heilbron, *History of San Diego County,* p. 427.

[265] *San Diego Union (Weekly)*, June 5, 1873, p. 3, col. 4.

[266] *San Diego Union (Weekly),* May 22, 1873, p. 3, col. 3.

Rhythms of Life

[267] *San Diego Union (Weekly)*, July 12, 1873, p. 3, col. 4.

[268] *San Diego Union (Weekly)*, June 19, 1873, P. 4, col. 2.

[269] *San Diego Union (Weekly)*, June 26, 1872.

[270] *San Diego Union*, July 6, 1873, cited in Stern and Kramer, "The Rose of San Diego."

[271] *San Diego Union (Weekly)*, May 22, 1873, p. 3, col. 3.

[272] Ibid.

[273] *San Diego Union (Weekly)*, Sept. 11, 1873, p. 3, col. 1.

The Panic of 1873

[274] William S. McFeely, *Grant: A Biography*, The Easton Press, Library of the Presidents, reprinted with permission of W.W. Norton & Co, Inc., Norwalk, Conn.: 1987, p. 392.

The Sad Tale of William Robinson

[275] *San Diego Union*, April 28, 1871, p. 2, col. 1.

[276] *San Diego Union (Weekly)*, Sept. 25, 1873, p. 4, col. 3.

[277] *San Diego Union (Weekly)*, Oct. 23, 1873, p. 3, col. 5.

[278] San Diego County Recorder, Oct. 17, 1873, Deed Book 22, p. 193.

Letter to Brigham Young

[279] Brian Frederick Smith, "The San Diego of Judge Benjamin I. Hayes: Excerpts from Emigrant Notes, 1850-1875," master's thesis, University of San Diego, Helen K. & James S. Copley Library, 979 498 S643s.

[280] Best, "San Diego and the Gilded Age."

Troubles Multiply

[281] *San Diego Union (Weekly)*, Jan. 9, 1874.

[282] *San Diego Union (Weekly)*, Feb. 19, 1874, p. 3, col. 5. State of California, Old Town San Diego State Historic Park online brochure, www.parks.ca.gov.

[283] E.W. Morse to Louis Rose, April 9, 1874, San Diego Historical Society archives, Morse letterbook, MSS.

[341] E.W. Morse Collection, Box 5 of 6.

[284] Hevener, "The Pueblo Lands of the City of San Diego, 1769-1950," p. 114.

[285] San Diego County Recorder, Oct. 15, 1874, Deed Book 25, p. 50; June 1, 1875, Deed Book 25, p. 430.

[286] *San Diego Union (Weekly)*, Oct. 28, 1874, p. 3, col. 1.

[287] San Diego County Recorder, Oct. 12, 1874, Miscellaneous Book 4, p. 57 (re-recorded in Deed Book 598, p. 22.)

Chapter 5

Rose's Worst Year

[1] *San Diego Union (Weekly)*, Jan. 14, 1875, p. 4, col. 1.

[2] *San Diego Union (Weekly)*, Jan. 28, 1875, p. 3, col. 6.

[3] *San Diego Union (Weekly)*, May 30, 1875, p. 3, col. 1.

[4] San Diego County Recorder, June 1, 1875, Deed Book 25, p. 430.

[5] San Diego County Recorder, Register of Deaths, Aug. 21, 1875.

[6] Henrietta Rose interview with Winfred Davidson, April 9, 1932, San Diego Historical Society, Louis Rose vertical file.

[7] San Diego County Recorder, Sept. 24, Deed Book 26, p. 274.

[8] E.W. Morse to Louis Rose, Oct. 19, 1975, San Diego Historical Society, location cited.

[9] Daniel Cleveland, "What the City Has Done With Its Pueblo Lands," *San Diego Union*, April 18, 1926, p. 18.

[10] R.V. Paine Jr., "Monument Will Honor Pioneer Louis Rose," *San Diego Sun*, March 23, 1934, clipping, San Diego Historical Society.

[11] Henry Schwartz, "Our San Diego History: Louis Rose," *Israel Today*, San Diego, March 3, 1983.

Sale of the Pear Garden

[12] San Diego County Recorder, Mary 23, 1876, Deed Book 28, p. 250.

[13] San Diego County Recorder, May 23, 1876, Deed Book 28, p. 151.

[14] According to Claude Reddy Conklin's oral history interview with the San Diego Historical Society Norman Conklin later became an investor in a nail works factory that became one of Roseville's first industries.

[15] San Diego County Recorder, June 22, 1876, Deed Book 28, p. 326.

[16] E.W. Morse to Louis Rose, March 6, 1876, location cited.

Abandonment by the Railroad

[17] Best, "San Diego and the Gilded Age," pp. 274–276.

[18] Ibid.

Postmaster

[19] Melody Savage (Research Associate, Postal History, United States Postal Service) to Donald H. Harrison, Sept. 26, 1994.

[20] Melody Savage to Donald H. Harrison, Sept. 26, 1994.

Renewed Railroad Hopes ·

[21] E.W. Morse to Louis Rose, April 11, 1878, location cited.

[22] E.W. Morse to Louis Rose, June 17, 1878, location cited.

Rose in Semi-Retirement

[23] William M. Kramer, "Daniel Cave: Southern California Pioneer, Dentist, Civic Leader and Masonic Dignitary," *Western States Jewish Historical Quarterly*, Vol. IX, No. 2, January 1977, p. 100.

[24] E.W. Morse to illegible recipient, Morse letterbooks, March 1878 to July 1879, p. 163, San Diego Historical Society.

[25] E.W. Morse to Louis Rose, Feb. 22, 1879, location cited.

[26] E.W. Morse to Louis Rose, April 23, 1879, location cited.

[27] E.W. Morse to Louis Rose, May 27, 1879, location cited.

[28] E.W. Morse to Louis Rose, June 22, 1879, location cited.

[29] E.W. Morse to Louis Rose, July 10, 1879, location cited.

[30] William E. Smythe, *History of San Diego, 1542-1908*, Chapter 4, San Diego Historical Society Online, sandiegohistory.org/books/smythe

[31] E.W. Morse to Louis Rose, Sept. 2, 1879, location cited.

[32] Heilbron, *History of San Diego County,* p. 429

[33] Hevener, "The Pueblo Lands of the City of San Diego, 1769-1950," p. 99.

[34] Ibid.

[35] E.W. Morse to Louis Rose, July 17, 1880, location cited.

[36] Smythe, *History of San Diego: 1542-1908.*

[37] Heilbron, *History of San Diego County.*

[38] Gerson, "Jewish Religious Life in San Diego, CA, 1851-1918," p. 37.

[39] Melody Savage to Donald H. Harrison, Sept. 26, 1994.

[40] Stern and Kramer, "The Rose of San Diego," p.25, citation of *San Diego Union*, Oct. 18, 1883.

[41] E.W. Morse to Louis Rose, circa February 1884, location cited.

The Final Years

[42] San Diego County Recorder, Nov. 3, 1884, Miscellaneous Book 48, p. 133.

[43] *San Diego Sun*, Dec. 30, 1887, p. 5, col. 3.

[44] *San Diego Sun*, Aug. 14, 1885, news clipping, San Diego Historical Society.

[45] Heilbron, *History of San Diego County*, p. 429.

[46] Ibid.

[47] Pourade, *Glory Years*, p. 195.

[48] San Diego County Recorder, Feb. 12, 1888. Death certificate for Louis Rose.

[49] Gary Fink, "A Brief History of Roseville," paper submitted for the Institute of the San Diego Historical Society, 1985-1986, p. 5.

[50] *San Diego Union*, Jan. 1, 1888.

[51] Fink, "A Brief History of Roseville," p. 5.

Death of Louis Rose

[52] San Diego County Recorder, Feb. 12. 1888. Death certificate for Louis Rose.

[53] *San Diego Sun*, Feb. 13, 1888, p. 5. San Diego Historical Society clipping. Stanley Schwartz, "A Brief History of Congregation Beth Israel of San Diego, 135th Birthday Celebration, 1861-1996," private printing, San Diego, library of Congregation Beth Israel. Samuel Freuder, *A Missionary's Return to Judaism: The Truth About the Christian Mission to the Jews*, Sinai Publishing Company, New York: 1915.

Based on Schwartz's research, it is possible that the rabbi who conducted Rose's funeral was Samuel Freuder, who was hired "sometime between February and June 1888" by the Jewish community as it pondered construction of its first synagogue building. Once named Adath Yeshurun, the congregation decided upon the name Beth Israel as more suitable for a congregation with a permanent meeting place. The small synagogue, located at 2nd and Beech Streets, was dedicated at the High Holy Day services of 1889. Freuder, ironically, did not remain at his post to celebrate the synagogue's inauguration. The rabbi subsequently converted to Christianity and became an evangelist to his former co-religionists. After another change of heart, he converted back to Judaism and wrote the above-cited book about his experience.

[54] *San Diego Union*, Feb. 14, 1888, San Diego Historical Society clipping.

[55] Fink, "A Brief History of Roseville," p. 5.

Epilogue

[1] Albina Whitworth, deposition, Dec. 12, 1890, San Diego County Probate Case 670, Box 6, San Diego County Law Library. Ronald Quinn, "James W. Robinson and the Development of Old Town San Diego," *The Journal of San Diego History*, Vol. 31, No. 3, Fall 1985, p. 154.

[2] Decree, Superior Court Judge George Puterbaugh, Dec. 22, 1891, San Diego County Probate Case, Box 6, San Diego County Law Library. Defendant's name mentioned twice so indicated: Joseph Allison, Robert Allison, E.S. Babcock, Jr., Joanna Rosa Baker; Samuel Barkley; H.T. Beauregard; William Beven; Bishop of Monterey; Minerva J. Blackman; Mrs. I.D. Broderick; Frank A. Brown; Euphemia B. Buckingham; J.G. Bunnell; Mary C. Burgess; E.W. Bushyhead; California Southern Railway Company; Caroline G. Carter; John H. Carter; D. Cave; City of San Diego; N.H. Conklin; Ella G. Connor; Arthur Cosgrove; Albina E. Covell; T.J. Daley; S.S. Dann; George M. Dannals; C.A. Dievendorf; A.F. Dill; E. Dougherty; Mary Elsasser; J.S. Escher; Emma Everhart; Daniel Fairbanks; F.E. Farmer; J.F. Farrell; First National Bank of San Diego; Ira Floyd; M.N. Foss; Lizzie France; Mary E. Frederick; A.G. Gassen; Alice Gassen; Anna Gerichten; Ella Gerichten; Emily Gerichten; Florentine Gerichten; Katie Gerichten; Lida Gerichten; Isaac Gleason; A. Grannan; Emma Gregg; R.J. Gregg; Jemima W. Hall; Delia E. Hammack; Anna O. Haney; E.W. Hendrick; J.W. Hendrick; Mary Herlihy; H.R. Higgins; W. Hollington; F.A. Holtzhier; E.S. Houston; Allen B. Howard; Bryant Howard; Medora H. Howard; Fred J. Huse; Frances J. Johnson; G.W. Jorres; William Jorres; George Journeay; Attilia Kaatz; Joseph Kelley; G. L. Kenney; Mrs. G. L. Kenney; Cora E. Kinney; Jacob Kunner; R.H. Lacy; Simon Levi; I.M. Lider; Louis E. Little; W.S. Little; Emma L. Loomis; John A. Love; Lizze Love; T.G. Lyster; F.G. Mack; Benjamin Macready; J.S. Mannasse; Charles Martin; John Mason; Mrs. John Mason; Vernon G. Matthews; G.B. McConnelly; Rebecca McKay; Julia McMichail; Delia McWilliams; Charles E. Merrill; Albert Meyer; Emanuel Meyer; Anna Miller; Robert Miner; Annie Momand; D. Momand; D.R. Moore; Francis Mora; Rosa Moran; E.W. Morse; J. K. Mulkey; A.W. Naylor; Ed O'Donnell; W.F. Osborn; E.F. Parmalee; Charles H. Pascoe; Edwin Pascoe; William J. Pascoe; Emma Peery; Amos Pettingill; R.F. Phillips; Emily M. Pierce; F.P. Rand; J.J. Rauer; P.L. Rider; Sarah Robinson; William Roe; Henrietta Rose; San Diego and Coronado Water Co.; Harry M. Schiller, Marcus Schiller; A.W. Schilling; Charles E. Schmitt; A. Schneider; G.W. Schnelbacher; Dashwood Skyring; Anna M. Smith; Frances Snyder; Frank Snyder; W.W. Stewart; H.C. Stone; Melvin Stone; R.A. Thomas; Peter Tillman; A.D. Ubach; Caroline Vander Reis; J.E. Wadham; Mary E. Walker (2); D. Wallach; H.

Warner; Wellborn, Parker and Stevens; Thomas Whaley; Arvilla A. White; Eva Della White; Sam T. Wills; Mary E. Woodmansee and J.M. Woods.

³ San Diego County Recorder, March 1, 1891, Deed Book 178, p. 318.

⁴ Herbert Lockwood, "The Skeleton's Closet," *San Diego Independent*, March 10, 1968, San Diego Historical Society clipping.

Henrietta Rose, School Teacher

⁵ *The Cactus*, Theodore Roosevelt Junior High School, February 1933.

⁶ San Diego Board of Education, Minutes, June 4, June 18, 1894.

⁷ San Diego Board of Education, Minutes, Dec. 3, 1894.

⁸ San Diego Board of Education, Minutes, June 28, 1895.

⁹ San Diego Board of Education, Minutes, March 11, 1907.

¹⁰ San Diego Board of Education, Minutes, June 8, 1908.

¹¹ San Diego Board of Education, Minutes, June 10, 1912.

¹² San Diego City School Directory, 1912-1913.

¹³ San Diego City School Directories, 1912-1922.

Hattie is Crippled

¹⁴ *Rough Rider*, Theodore Roosevelt Junior High School, San Diego, Thanksgiving 1924.

¹⁵ *Rough Rider*, Christmas 1924.

¹⁶ Ibid.

¹⁷ *Rough Rider*, Fall 1925, Vol. 7, No. 1.

¹⁸ *Rough Rider*, June 21, 1929.

¹⁹ *Roosevelt Roundups*, June 1931, p. 14.

²⁰ San Diego City Schools Directory, 1932-33.

²¹ Elizabeth LaBorde interview with Donald H. Harrison, March 30, 2000.

San Diego History Revival

²² Winifred Davidson, "City Pioneer, Prominent in Many Fields, To Be Honored, " *San Diego Union*, March 4, 1934. Donald H. Harrison interview with Robert Leanders, Feb. 7, 2004; interview with Annette Balelo, Feb. 9, 2004.

²³ Naomi Baker, "'S.D. Leaning Tower' Stands for 48 Years: Rose Canyon Rival of Old World Wonder. Will It Topple?" *San Diego Union*, June 21, 1936, San Diego Historical Society clipping file.

²⁴ "Boulder Marker Honoring Memory of Roseville Founder Unveiled at Canyon Junction on Coast Highway," *San Diego Union*, May 31, 1934, San Diego Historical Society clipping file. N.B. Stern, research notes, Manges Museum, Berkeley.

Hattie Retires

²⁵ *Twentieth Century Progress*, Roosevelt Junior High School, San Diego, June 1937.

²⁶ *Scarlet and Gray*, Roosevelt Junior High School, June 1939, p. 9.

²⁷ San Diego City Schools Directory, 1941-42.

Relocation of the Jewish Cemetery

²⁸ Stern and Kramer, "The Rose of San Diego," p. 28, citation of Congregation Beth Israel correspondence quoted by Myron Lustig, "The History of the San Diego Jewish Community," *Southwestern Jewish Press*, San Diego, April, 1952, p. 12.

²⁹ Roberta Wagner Berman, "San Diego's First Jewish Cemetery," Newsletter of San Diego Jewish Historical Society, Vol. 4, No. 2, May 1995. Reprinted in *Discovery*, newsletter of San Diego Jewish Genealogical Society, Vol. 10, No. 1, Winter 1995. Besides Louis Rose, Ellen (Helene) Rose, and Matilda Rose, Berman's

article listed "names I have been able to find of those who were reinterred. The sources I used are the records of Mount Hope cemetery (which kept records for the Home of Peace during its early years), mortuary records extracted by the San Diego Genealogical Society, and records of the *San Diego Union*." Others listed with their years of death were S.E. Ables (1885); Mrs. Barnett (1871); Mrs. Celia L. Carr (1882); infant Cline (1886); Arthur Lincoln Klauber (1884); infant Klauber (1875); Proff Segemund Le Batt (1881); Ike Newberger (1883); and Bernard Shaffer (1884).

Death of Hattie Rose

[30] San Diego County Recorder, Henrietta Rose death certificate, Feb. 20, 1957.

[31] Mt. Hope Cemetery Records, Lot 26, Graves 1 through 4, Sec. 1, Division 4.

[32] Donald H. Harrison, the author, and Shahar Masori, his son-in-law, visited on Nov. 29, 2000, and several times searched the exact area indicated by Mt.Hope's Cemetery map for the gravesites. Cemetery workers later confirmed the location as correct.

Where's Louis?

[33] Orion Zink, "Louis Rose Grave Found," *The Master Mason*, San Diego Lodge No. 35, F. & A.M., December 1969.

[34] "Pioneer San Diego: Louis Rose Left His Name, Heritage," *San Diego Union*, July 14, 1969, p. B-1.

[35] Mary Ellen Stratthaus, "Flaw in the Jewel: Housing Discrimination Against Jews in La Jolla, California," *American Jewish History*, Vol. 84, No. 3, September 1994, pp. 189-219.

The Memory Endures

[36] Aaron J. Hoskins, "Celebrating Our First 150 Years," San Diego Jewish Press-Heritage, Nov. 3, 2000, p. 10.

[37] Cindy Stankowski, director, San Diego Archaelogical Center, to Donald H. Harrison, Sept. 16, 2002.

[38] San Diego City Parks and Recreation Board, Minutes, Nov. 21, 2002.

[39] Peninsula Community Planning Board, Minutes, June 17, 2004.

[40] Murphy met at his offices with the author, Park and Recreation Board Member Norman Greene; Murray Galinson and Alan Ziter, respectively chairman and executive director of the NTC Foundation; Hank Cunningham and Maureen Ostrye of the city's Community Economic Development department; Kimberly Elliott of the Corky McMillin Companies; Ellie Oppenheim, San Diego City Park & Recreation Department; Adam Wexler representing District 2 Council Member Michael Zucchet, and Seth Litchney, Colleen Rudy and Rachel Shira of the mayor's staff.

[41] Some attendees of the July 16 meeting also participated in the Aug. 12 site inspection including the author, Greene, Litchney and Ostrye. Others on hand Aug. 12 were Drew Ector, representing District 2 Councilman Michael Zucchet; Kevin Oliver of the city's Park and Recreation Department; Victoria Hamilton and Lynda Forsha of the city Commission for Arts and Culture; Walter Heiberg and Kathi Riser of the Corky McMillin Companies; Libby Day of the Community Economic Development Company, Job York of the NTC Foundation, and Elliot Wolf of the United Jewish Federation.

[42] The proceedings were tape recorded and transcribed by the author.

[43] Christopher D. Reutz to Stath Karras, July 14, 2004, and Stath Karras to Malin Burnham, July 16, 2004. Reutz, in a conversation with the author, noted that the land was vacant when Rose purchased it; whereas, in 2004, its value was determined by how the city later developed. Comparing raw land costs in 1850 to property values in 2004, Reutz said, is somewhat similar to comparing the price of a canvas in Leonardo da Vinci's day with the value of his Mona Lisa. According to the Federal Reserve Bank of Minneapolis, the value of a dollar in 1850 was $22.42 in 2004, whereas the value of Rose's property had increased by many thousand fold. It's fair to say that Rose's old friend, Judge Benjamin Hayes, would have been pleasantly surprised.

BIBLIOGRAPHY

Author Interviews

Annette Balelo, assistant vice president, San Diego County Credit Union, Point Loma branch, Feb. 9, 2004.

Elizabeth LaBorde, former Roosevelt Junior High School student, March 30, 2000.

Robert Leanders, real estate agent in Point Loma, Feb. 7, 2004

Jim Leach, treasurer and past master of San Diego Lodge 35, Free & Accepted Masons, June 7, 2000.

Olaf Rennebeck, archivist of Emmaus Church, Neuhaus-an-der-Oste, March 7, 2000.

Rev. Peter Rondthaler, pastor of Emmaus Church, Neuhaus-an-der-Oste, March 7, 2000.

Olaf Schlichting, owner of Ulex Liqueur Factory, Neuhaus-an-der-Oste, March 8, 2000.

Primary Sources

"Control of the City Treasurer's Receipts for lots and lands commencing with the 10th of December 1850," San Diego Historical Society.

Ephraim Douglas Adams, editor, "Correspondence from the British Archives Concerning Texas, 1837-1846," *The Southwestern Historical Quarterly*, Vol. 16, No. 2, October 1912; Vol. 16, No. 4, January 1913; Vol. 17, No. 1, July 1913; Correspondence included: Charles Elliot to the Earl of Aberdeen, March 29, 1843; Elliot to Richard Pakenham, April 14, 1843; Percy Doyle to Elliot, May 27, 1843; Lord Aberdeen to Elliot, June 3, 1843; Elliot to Doyle, June 21, 1853.

Andrew Cassidy vs. Louis Rose and E. W. Morse, District Court Case 00130014, "District Court Records," San Diego Historical Society.

"Assessments," Personal Property of Louis Rose, San Diego Historical Society, File 56-98, Box 1, File 5, 1856 Assessments, R.1.102

Joshua Bean to Common Council, Sept. 8, 1850, San Diego Historical Society, Document File, Common Council.

John R. Blecker to E.W. Morse, Sept. 11, 1869, San Diego Historical Soceity, E.W. Morse Collection, MSS 341, Box 1 of 6, File 26, Document 12.

D.N. Breed to E.W. Morse, 1858: May 17, June 2, 18; 1863: July 2 (San Diego Historical Society, E.W. Morse Collection, Box 1 of 6, File 2, Document 24; File 3, Documents 1, 5; File 9, Document 1.

Breed & Chase to E.W. Morse, Nov. 30, 1966, San Diego Historical Society Collection, MSS 341, Box 1, File 18, Documents 14, 18.

Brichta vs. Rose, Case 1632, Second District Court of New Orleans, Petition of

Francis Brichta, Aug. 1, 1848 (Records on file in Louisiana and City Archives, New Orleans Public Library)

Cargo Manifest, Ship *Wales*, New Orleans inward, National Archives RG41 Stack 15E4/18/23/4 bx 145.

Andrew Cassidy to A.S. Ensworth, Sept. 18, 1864, San Diego Historical Society, Document Files.

A.J. Chase to E.W. Morse, 1858: Feb. 17, May 1, June 3, June 17 (San Diego Historical Society, E.W. Morse Collection, MSS 341, Box 1 of 6, File 2, Documents 17, 19; File 3, Documents 2, 3).

Criminal Court of the First District (Orleans Parish), Minute Book, V. 6 (March 3, 1845–April 18, 1846).

Daniel N. Breed vs. Louis Rose, May 5, 1858, District Court Case 01020017, "District Court Records," San Diego Historical Society.

William Heath Davis, Seventy-Five Years in California, J. Howell, San Francisco: 1929

Thomas B. Eastland and Joseph G. Eastland, "To California Through Texas and Mexico," forward by Douglas S. Watson and footnotes by Dorothy H. Huggins, *California Historical Quarterly*, Vol. 18, No. 2, June 1939. Includes Thomas B. Eastland to Josephine Eastland, Sept. 11, 1849.

Robert Eccleston, *Overland to California on the Southwestern Trail, 1849*, edited by George P. Hammond and Edward H. Howes, University of California Press, Berkeley: 1950.

Eckel vs. Rose, Case 1632, Second District Court of New Orleans, Ouseiphoese Drouet, notary public, statement of service of a demand note to Caroline Rose (Records on file in Louisiana and City Archives, new Orleans Public Library).

A.S. Ensworth to Chas. Tucker, Tucker & Lloyd, Aug. 19, 1857 (San Diego Historical Society, Claims–Land Bounty File).

Frank Ames vs. Louis Rose, San Diego District Court, Case Number 01010004, Dec. 11, 1857, San Diego Historical Society archives, "District Court Records."

Lewis A. Franklin, sermon, cited in Samson H. Levey, introduction to "The First Jewish Sermon in the West: Yom Kippur, 1850, San Francisco," *Western States Jewish Historical Quarterly*, Vol. 10, No. 1, October 1977.

S.G. French, "Reconnaisance of Route from San Antonio to El Paso," Dec. 31, 1849, in Senate Ex Doc, 31 Cong, 1 Sess, No. 64.

Rena Marverick Green, ed., *Samuel Maverick: Texan*, privately printed, San Antonio: 1952.

Benjamin Hayes, *Emigrant Notes*, Volumes 1 and 2, handwritten diaries of Judge Benjamin Hayes, Bancroft Library, University of California, Berkeley.

Benjamin Hayes, Scrapbooks, 103 Southern California–San Diego County 1, local history, 1850–1867 (The Bancroft Library, University of California, Berkeley F 851.H4 R103x).

Sam Houston, *The Writings of Sam Houston, 1813-1863,* Amelia W. Williams and Eugne Barker, editors, University of Texas Press, Austin: 1938. In particular, James W. Robinson to Santa Anna, April 10, 1843; Sam Houston to Joseph Eve, April 22, 1843.

Victoria Jacobs, *Diary of a San Diego Girl, 1856,* edited by Sylvia Arden, Norton B. Stern, publisher, Santa Monica, Calif.: 1974.

J.E. Johnston "Report to the Secretary of War with Reconnaisances of Routes from San Antonio to El Paso," Sen. Ex Doc. No. 64, 31 Cong, 1 Sess, July 25, 1850.

Journal of the Proceedings of the Grand Lodge of the State of California, 1850-1854, Masonic Order, San Francisco: 1857.

Ketuba (Marriage Certificate), June 20, 1847, Copies of Marriage Contracts Which Have Taken Place in the Hebrew Congregation of Shanarai Chased of New Orleans, Tulane University Library, Louisiana Collection.

Lewis Franklin vs. Maurice Franklin, testimony of Jesus Gonzales, Hyman Mannasse, decision of Judge Benjamin Hayes ("District Court Records," San Diego Historical Society, Collection R3.38, Box 1, File 2).

Lorenzo Soto vs. Louis Rose, District Court Case 02070037, 1860, San Diego Historical Society Archives.

L. Rose vs. Adam Reuth, Case 1450, Second District Court of New Orleans, Petition of Liebman Rose, June 2, 1848. (Records on file in Louisiana and City Archives, New Orleans Public Library).

L. Strauss & Co vs. Louis Rose, May 5, 1858, District Court Case 01020015, "District Court Records," San Diego Historical Society.

E.W. Morse, "Reminiscences of Early San Diego," *San Diego Union,* June 1, 1900.

Mary Chase Walker Morse, "Recollections of Early Times in San Diego," manuscript, excerpted in San Diego Biographies on Line, www.sandiegohistory.org/bio/walker/walker.htm

James Pascoe, map of Roseville, January 1869, San Diego County Assessor's Office.

George Pendleton, appointment of Louis Rose, March 1, 1864 ("Louis Rose" vertical file, San Diego Historical Society).

Peninsula Community Planning Board, Minutes, June 17, 2004.

People v. Rose, 1867, San Diego County Law Library, Pioneer Room collection.

Philip Willman, assignee of S. Weber vs. Louis Rose, Case 1500, Second District Court of New Orleans, Petition of Stanislas Weber, Sept. 19, 1848 (Records on file in Louisiana and City Archives, New Orleans Public Library).

Plaza School Report, March 20, 1856, San Diego Historical Society, 2.68, Box 21, San Diego School District, 1851.

James W. Robinson to Amasa Turner, July 29, 1848; April 1, 1849; June 17, 1849; June 29, 1849; March 2, 1851; July 17, 1851; March 12, 1852; Manuscript Collection. Turner (Amasa) Papers, 2.325/K23 Center for American History, University of Texas at Austin.

James W. Robinson to William Robinson, Oct. 9, 1856, San Diego County Probate Case 670, Box 6, San Diego County Law Library.

Robinson, James W., "Will," July 31, 1856, "James Robinson" document file, San Diego Historical Society.

Sarah R. Robinson, Declaration to District Court, Aug. 30, 1865, in Maurice A. Franklin v. Joseph Reiner, District Court files, San Diego Historical Society.

José Policarpo Rodríguez, "The Old Guide: His Life in His Own Words," originally published in 1897, reprinted Nov. 1, 1968; in *Old West Magazine.*

Henrietta Rose interview with Winifred Davidson, San Diego Historical Society archives, "Louis Rose" vertical file.

Louis Rose to City Lands Commission, Oct. 17, 1850, San Diego Historical Society archives, "Louis Rose" vertical file.

Louis Rose to City Board of Trustees, Oct. 16, 1856, included in Thomas Savage, *Documentos para Historia de California; Papels Originales Sacados de Varios Archivos Particulares,* Tom. IV, University of California, Bancroft Library: 1874, page 5 (C-96, pt. 1 photo).

Louis Rose to San Diego County Board of Supervisors, July 5, 1870; Jan. 17, 1871; San Diego Historical Society, Collection R 2.93, Box 1, Documents 70-14; 71-3.

Rose v. Rose, Deposition of Henry H. Thal, June 21, 1854, San Diego Historical Society, "District Court Records," R3.38, Box 17.

San Diego and Gila Southern Pacific and Atlantic Railroad Co., Articles of Association, Nov. 1, 1854, San Diego Historical Society, "Railroads," Box 59, File 20.

San Diego Board of Education, Minutes, 1894: June 4, 18; Dec. 3; 1895: Jan. 7, June 28: 1907; March 11; 1908: June 8; 1912: June 10.

San Diego Board of Trustees, Minutes, 1852: March 25, 36, 27; April 3; May 20; June 9, 10; July 31; Aug. 25; Nov. 29; Dec. 7, 10, 28, 30. 1853: Jan. 6; June 3; July 12, 13; Sept. 10; Oct. 29; Nov. 2, 4, 5, 10, 12. 1854: Feb. 1, Aug. 24, 28; Sept. 30; 1855: April 24.

San Diego City Clerk, Register of the Grants Made Since the 12th of December, 1850, City Clerk archives, Box A-0001-CC.

San Diego City Clerk, Document 20485, Box #A-0017CC, Folder #11.

San Diego City Treasurer, Book No. 1, The Town of San Diego In Account with Louis Rose, Treasurer of the Board of Trustees, San Diego Historical Society.

San Diego Common Council, Minutes, 1850: June 17, 18, 29; July 6, 7, 13, 20, 29; Aug. 5, 12, 17, 21, 24, 26, 31, Sept. 23, 30; Oct. 18; Nov. 7, 8, Dec. 26, 30. 1851: Jan. 21, 23, 30; March 25, 31; April 19, 24; May 15; June 5; Sept. 1, 15; Nov. 15, 22. 1852: Jan. 10; Feb. 17. San Diego Historical Society.

San Diego County Board of Supervisors, Minutes, 1853; Feb 3; March 14, 29; April 4, 13; July 28, 30; Nov. 7, 9. 1854: June 19; July 18. 1865: Feb. 6; Sept 18; 1866:

May 9; Aug. 13; Sept. 16. 1867: Feb. 5; May 9; Aug. 7; Nov. 6. (Microfiche records, Clerk of the County Board of Supervisors).

San Diego County Coroner, Inquest into death of Judge John Hays, May 25, 1857; File F1-5, Collection R.2.69, San Diego Historical Society.

San Diego County Probate Case 670, Box 6, San Diego County Law Library; Depositions of Marcus Bodine, Eupehemia Buckingham; John Elliott, Harret Bonnell; William Humphrey; James Snyder; Nicholas Todd; Samuel Weller and Albina Whitworth; letters: James W. Robinson to William Robinson and Joseph Dana, Dec. 6, 1847; James W. Robinson to William Robinson, Oct. 9, 1855; Feb. 19, 1856.

San Diego county Recorder, Brand Book I, Brand of Louis Rose (on file with Office of San Dieo County Historian).

San Diego County Recorder, Deed Book C: pp. 111, 122, 199; Deed Book D: pp. 17, 81, 83, 132, 34, 136, 138, 229, 263, 323; Deed Book I, pp. 149, 268; Deed Book 2, pp. 38–41, 125, 233, 250; Deed Book 3, p. 156; Deed Book 4, pp. 260, 356, 366; Deed Book 5, pp. 182, 188, 228, 229, 234, 236, 243, 273, 291, 305, 343, 345, 346, 348–350, 355, 362–363, 367, 383–384, 386, 397, 408, 423, 445, 452; Deed Book 6, pp. 59, 64, 76, 89, 83, 85, 140, 285–286, 288, 330, 339, 424, 449; Deed Book 7, pp. 8–9, 20–21, 50, 52–53, 74, 84, 157, 177, 187, 196, 276, 283, 345, 440, 452; Deed Book 8, pp. 223, 320; Deed Book 9, pp. 239, 273, 303, 339, 439; Deed Book 10, pp. 114, 474, 546; Deed Book 11, pp. 105, 449; Deed Book 12, pp. 104, 145, 173, 323, 328, 592; Deed Book 13, pp. 3, 6, 192, 212, 225, 286; Deed Book 14, pp. 339; Deed Book 15, pp. 200; Deed Book 16, p. 483; Deed Book 17, p. 339; Deed Book 18, p. 535; Deed Book 19, p. 1; Deed Book 21, p. 45; Deed Book 22, p. 193; Deed Book 23, pp. 250, 324; Deed Book 25, pp. 50, 430; Deed Book 26, pp. 1, 274; Deed Book 28, pp. 151, 250, 326; Deed Book 178, p. 318; Marriage Licenses, p. 116; Miscellaneous Book 1, pp. 28, 42–43, 57; Miscellaneous Book 48, p. 133; Register of Deaths: March 13, 1873; Aug. 21, 1875; Feb. 12, 1888; Feb. 20, 1957.

San Diego County vs. Russel Sacket and others, June 16, 1851, "James W. Robinson" document file, San Diego Historical Society.

Johnathan R. Scott, Declaration to District Court, Aug. 30, 1856, in *Maurice A. Franklin vs. Joseph Reiner*, District Court files, San Diego Historical Society.

Ship's Register, Bath, Maine, Ship *Wales*, Dec. 21, 1849, National Archives RG 41 Stack: 15E2/21/12/1 Vol. #166; also New York, RG 41 Stack 15E3/9/7/1 Vol. #12020, and RG41 Stack 15E3/8/7/1 Vol. #12010.

Solomon Goldman and James Donohoe vs. Louis Rose, May 5, 1858, District Court Case 01030013, "District Court Records," San Diego Historical Society.

Statutes of California passed at the Third Session of the Legislature, "Chapter CXXXIX: An Act to Repeal the Charter of the City of San Diego and to Create a Board of Trustees," G.K. Fitch & Co. and V.E. Geiger & Co., State Printers, San Francisco: 1852, pages 223–225.

Thomas K. Sweeny, *Journal*, 1849–53, edited by Arthur Woodward, Westernlore Press, Los Angeles: 1956.

Tucker & Lloyd to A.S. Ensworth, 1858, July 13, Oct. 19, San Diego Historical Society, "A.S. Ensworth" file.

United States Census, 1850, 1860, 1870, 1880.

Voigts & Teauremand vs. Rose, Case 1251, Fifth District Court of New Orleans, petition of Voigts & Teauremand (partners in Voigts Teauremand), May 9, 1848; Louisiana and City Archives, New Orleans Public Library.

Thomas Whaley to Anna Lannay, Dec. 17, 1851; Jan. 12, 1852; Whaley House Archives, San Diego, microfilmed letter file.

Adrian Woll, "Report of Expedition into Texas in 1842," translated and edited by Joseph Milton Nance, *The Southwestern Historical Quarterly*, Vol. 58, No. 4, April 1955.

Works Progress Administration, Louisiana Historical Records Survey Division, Inventory of the Church and Synagogue Archives of Louisiana, Louisiana State University, Baton Rouge: 1941.

Works Progress Administration of Louisiana, Survey of Federal Archives in Louisiana: Passenger Lists Taken from Manifests of the Customs Service, Port of New Orleans, 1839-1849, Including Names of Sloops, Brigs, Schooners, Sailing Ships and Steamboats as well as Passenger Embarkation Points and Destinations, Survey of Federal Archives in Louisiana, 1941: Tulane University Louisiana Collection, L976 31 (656.4) U58p Vol. 3

Maj. Gen. Worth (by George Deas, Asst Adjutant General), Orders No. 8, Feb. 3, 1849 (on file in the Fort Bliss, Texas, Museum Archives).

Secondary Sources

_____ "Boulder marker honoring Memory of Roseville Founder Unveiled at Canyon Junction on Coast Highway," *San Diego Union*, May 31, 1934.

_____ California Historical Landmarks, Office of Historic Preservation, California State Parks, Sacramento: 1996: No. 52, "Mission Dam and Flume"; No. 392 "Buena Vista Winery and Vineyards"; No. 392-1 "Site of Haraszthy Villa"; No. 808, "Camp Salvation."

_____ Castroville Visitor Guide, Castroville Chamber of Commerce, 1998.

_____ *El Pueblo de San Diego*, Junior League of San Diego, San Diego: 1968.

_____ "From Ox Trails to Eagles: A History of the Texas and Pacific Railway," nd, archives of the Harrison County, Texas, Historical Museum Library.

_____ *History of the Jews of Louisiana: Their Religious, Civic, Charitable and Patriotic Life*, Jewish Historical Publishing Co. of Louisiana, nd. Louisiana collection of Tulane University.

_____ *Legends of Lakeside*, The Lakeside Historical Society, Lakeside, CA: 1985

_____ "Pioneer San Diegan: Louis Rose Left His Name, Heritage," *San Diego Union*, July 14, 1969, page B-1.

Thomas Joseph Adema, *San Diego's Oldest Pioneer, Philip Crosthwaite, 1825-1903*, master's thesis, 1988, University of San Diego, Helen K. and James S. Copley Library (979 498 c951a).

Arthur R. Anderson and Leon O. Whitsell, *California's First Century of Scottish Rite Masonry*, Supreme Council, Oakland: 1962.

Lyle C. Annable, "The Life and Times of Cave Johnson Couts, San Diego Pioneer," master's thesis, 1965, San Diego State University library, F868 S15C6.

Steven E. Aschheim, *Brothers and Strangers: The East European Jew in Germany and German Jewish Consciousness, 1800-1923*, University of Wisconsin Press: 1982.

Elliot Ashkenazi, "Creoles of Jerusalem: Businessmen of Louisiana, 1840-1875, doctoral dissertation, George Washington University, 1983 (on file in Louisiana collection of Tulane University).

H.I. Bach, *The German Jew: A Synthesis of Judaism and Western Civilization*, Littman Library of Jewish Civilization by Oxford University Press: 1984.

Naomi Baker, "'S.D. Leaning Tower' Stands for 48 Years: Rose Canyon Rival of Old World Wonder. Will it Topple?" *San Diego Union*, June 21, 1936.

Samuel Flagg Bemis, *John Quincy Adams and the Union*, Library of the Presidents, the Easton Press, Norwalk, Conn.: 1987 reprint of previous edition by Alfred A. Knopf., Inc.

A.B. Bender, "Opening Routes Across West Texas, 1848-1850," *Southwestern Historical Quarterly*, Vol. 37, Oct. 1933.

Rickey D. Best, "San Diego and the Gilded Age: The Efforts to Bring the Texas and Pacific Railroad to San Diego," *The Journal of San Diego History*, Vol. 34, No. 4, Fall 1988.

Biographical Encyclopedia of Texas, Southern Publishing Co., New York: 1880; "Robinson James. W."

Laurie Bissell, "San Diego Cemeteries: A Brief Guide," *The Journal of San Diego History*, Vol. 28, No. 4, Fall 1982.

Samuel F. Black, *San Diego County, Calif.: A Record of Settlement, Organization, Progress and Achievement*, S.J. Clarke Publishing Co., Chicago: 1913.

Paul C. Boethel, *Colonel Amasa Turner: The Gentleman from Lavaca and other Captains at San Jacinto*, Von Boeckmann-Jones, Austin, Tex.: 1963

John Henry Brown, *History of Texas, from 1368 to 1893*, Vol. 2, L.E. Daniell, Saint Louis: 1892.

John Henry Brown, *Life and Times of Henry Smith, the First American Governor of Texas*, A.D. Aldridge & Co., Dallas: 1887.

The Cactus, Theodore Roosevelt Junior High School, San Diego: February 1933

Paul Michael Callaghan, "Fort Rosecrans, California," master's thesis, 1980, Helen K. and James S. Copley Library, University of San Diego (974.404 C156f).

Richard L. Carrico, *Strangers in a Stolen Land: American Indians in San Diego, 1850-1880*, Sierra Oaks Publishing Co., 1987.

Jo Ann Carrigan, "Impact of Epidemic Yellow Fever on Life in Louisiana," *Louisiana History*, Vol. 4, 1963.

Catholic Encyclopaedia, Online Edition: "St Anthony of Padua"

Catholic Online: "St. Didacus"

Freeman Cleaves, *William Henry Harrison and His Time*, Easton Press, Library of Presidents, Norwalk, Conn., 1986.

Daniel Cleveland, "What the City Has Done With Its Pueblo Lands," *San Diego Union*, April 18, 1926.

Henry Steele Commager, editor, *Documents in American History*, Seventh Edition, Vol. I, Meredith Publishing Co., New York: 1963.

Donald C. Cutter, "Sources of the Name California," *Arizona and the West*, Vol. 3, No. 3, Autumn 1961.

The Daily World, San Diego, 1872: Aug. 23, 28, 29; Sept. 5; Oct. 5, 9.

Winifred Davidson, "City Pioneer, Prominent in Many Fields, To be Honored," *San Diego Union*, March 4, 1934.

Winifred Davidson, "Early History," *History of San Diego County*, San Diego Press Club, San Diego:1936.

Winifred Davidson, "Notes on Louis Rose," vertical file, San Diego Historical Society.

Grover M. Dickman, "San Diego Lodge No. 35 Celebrates Eighty-Fifth Anniversary," "Masons" document file, San Diego Historical Society.

Ben Dixon, "First Taxpayers of San Diego County," typescript, San Diego Historical Society.

Lucille C. Duvall, Louis Rose, manuscript, archives of the Jewish Historical Society of San Diego.

Encylopaedia Brittanica, articles on "Juarez, Benito" and "New Orleans"

Encylopaedia Judaica, article on "names."

Iris Engstrand, *San Diego: California's Cornerstone*, Continental Heritage Press, Tulsa, Okla.: 1980.

Iris Engstrand and Ray Brandes, *Old Town San Diego 1821-1874*, Alcala Press, San Diego, 1976.

William Edward Evans, "The Garra Uprising: Conflict Between San Diego Indians and Settlers in 1851," typescript on file in California Room, San Diego Public Library.

Federal Reserve Bank of Minneapolis, Consumer Price Index (Estimate), 1800–2004, online http://minneapolisfed.org/research/data/us/calc/hist1800.ctm.

Gary Fink, "A Brief History of Roseville," Institute of the San Diego Historical Society, 1985–1986.

Samuel I. Fox, "Looking Backward," *The San Diego Jewish Community News*, Vol. IV, No. 20, Sept. 20, 1922, p. 6.

Galveston Weekly News: 1849: May 28, June 18.

Ronald D. Gerson, "Jewish Religious Life in San Diego, CA, 1851-1918, master's thesis, Hebrew Union College-Jewish Institute of Religion, Cincinnati, Ohio: 1974, footnote citing *Occident*, Vol. X, No. 1, page 60, April 1852(filed as RCC 296 Gerson at California Room, San Diego Public Library).

Judah Gribetz, Edward L. Greenstein and Regina Stein, *The Timetables of Jewish History: A Chronology of the Most Important People and Events in Jewish History*, Simon and Shuster, A Touchstone Book, New York: 1993

Mary H. Haggland, "Don José Antonio Aguirre: Spanish Merchant and Ranchero," *The Journal of San Diego History*, Vol. 29, No. 1

The Handbook of Texas Online. See particularly articles on "Alamo"; "Castro, Herni"; "Council House Fight"; "De Cordova, Jacob Raphael"; "Diplomatic Relations of the Republic of Texas"; Robinson, James W.;" Rose, Louis (Moses); "Woll, Adrian"

Zvi Har'El to Donald H. Harrison, Dec. 31, 2003, via email. Har'El, a mathematics professor at the Technion/ Israel Institute of Technology, maintains a website, http://www.math.technion.ac.il/~rl/, permitting instantaneous conversions between dates of the Hebrew calendar and the Julian calendar.

Donald H. Harrison, "Marranos in America," *San Diego Jewish Press-Heritage*, Sept. 8, 1995.

Robert Wells Haven, "Thomas Whaley," master's thesis, San Diego State College, San Diego: 1963.

Carl Heilbron, editor, *History of San Diego County*, San Diego Press Club, San Diego: 1936.

Mary A. Helmich and Richard D. Clark, *Interpretive Program: Old Town San Diego State Historic Park, Volume II: Site Recommendations*, California Department of Parks and Recreation, 1991, GDP No. 26.

Harold Guy Hevener Jr., "The Pueblo Lands of the City of San Diego, 1769-1950," master's thesis, San Diego State College, June 1950.

H.C. Hopkins, *History of San Diego: Its Pueblo Lands & Water*, City Printing Co., San Diego: 1929

Aaron J. Hoskins, "Celebrating our first 150 years," *San Diego Jewish Press-Heritage*, Nov. 3, 2000

John Holland Jenkins, Recollections of Early Texas, edited by John Holmes Jenkins III, University of Texas Press, Austin: 1958.

Audrey R. Karsh, "Mannasse Chico: Enlightened Merchant of San Diego," *Western States Jewish Historical Quarterly*, Vol. VIII, No. 1, Oct. 1975.

Audrey R. Karsh, "Mothers and Daughters of old San Diego," *Western States Jewish Historical Quarterly*, Vol. XIX, No. 3, April 1987

Edgar J. Kendall, "San Diego County Ordinances," *San Diego Historical Society Quarterly*, Vol. 1, No. 1, January, 1955.

Patricia F. Klenner, "Robert Decatur Israel, San Diego Pioneer and Keeper of the Light, 1816–1908," master's thesis, University of San Diego, Helen K. and James S. Copley Library (979.498 185zk).

Beatrice Frichette Knott, "Reading Between the Lines: Social History of San Diego During the Early American Period as Derived From Public and Business Records," master's thesis, University of San Diego, Helen K. and James S. Copley Library, University of San Diego, 979. 498 K72r.

Bertram Wallace Korn, *The Early Jews of New Orleans*, American Jewish Historical Society, Waltham, Mass: 1969.

William M. Kramer, "Daniel Cave: Southern California Pioneeer, Dentist, Civic Leader and Masonic Dignitary," *Western States Jewish Historical Quarterly*, Vol. IX, No. 2, January 1977.

William Kramer, "Lewis Polock Reluctantly Goes to San Diego," *Old Town, New Town: An Enjoyment of San Diego History*, William M. Kramer, editor; Stanley and Laurel Schwartz, associate editors, Western States Jewish History Association, Los Angeles: 1994.

Klaus J. Kueck, past master of Germania Lodge No. 46, to Donald H. Harrison, July 25, 2000.

Stuart N. Lake, "Birch's Overland Mail in San Diego County," *The Journal of San Diego History*, Vol. 3, No. 2

Henry O. Langley, *The San Francisco Directory for the Year Commencing December 1865*, Towne & Bacon, printers, San Francisco: 1865.

Samson H. Levey, introduction to "The First Jewish Sermon in the West: Yom Kippur, 1850, San Francisco," *Western States Jewish Historical Quarterly*, Vol. 10, No. 1, October 1977.

Susan Linee, "Why Did One Man Flee the Alamo?" *San Antonio Express-News*, July 11, 1987.

Calvin Linton, editor, *The Bicentennial Almanac*, Regency Publishing House, Nashville, Tenn: 1975.

Herbert Lockwood, "The Skeleton's Closet," *San Diego Independent*, March 10, 1968.

Frank Love, *Hell's Outpost: A History of Old Fort Yuma,* Yuma Crossing Publication Series, Yuma, Ariz,: 1992.

Elizabeth C. MacPhail, The Story of New San Diego and Its Founder Alonzo E. Horton, Pioneer Printers, San Diego: 1969.

Jacob R. Marcus, *The Rise and Destiny of the German Jew*, Department of Synagogues and School Extension of the Union of American Hebrew Congregations, Cincinnati: 1934.

Douglas B. Martin, *Yuma Crossing*, University of New Mexico Press, Albuquerque, N.M.: 1954.

Robert Mayer, *San Diego: A Chronological and Documentary History 1535-1876*, Oceana Publications Inc., Dobbs Ferry, N.Y.: 1978.

Walter McCausland, "Charles Drake Ferris: Unknown Veteran of San Jacinto," *The Southwestern Historical Quarterly*, Vol. 62, No. 2, October 1959.

William S. McFeely, *Grant: A Biography*, The Easton Press, Library of the Presidents, Norwalk, Conn.: 1987 (reprinted with permission of W.W. Norton & Company, Inc.)

Earl Samuel McGhee, "E.W. Morse, Pioneer Merchant and Co-Founder of San Diego," master's thesis, San Diego State College, June 5, 1950.

Clarence Alan McGrew, City of San Diego and the County of San Diego: The Birthplace of California, Vol. 1, American Historical Society, Chicago and New York: 1922.

Clare V. McKanna, Jr. "An Old Town Gunfight: The Homicide Trial of Cave Johnson Couts, 1866," The Journal of San Diego History, Vol. 44, No. 4, Fall 1998.

Richard K. McMaster, "Major Jefferson Van Horne," Password, Vol. 12, No. 2, El Paso County Historical Society, Summer 1967.

Ellen C. Merrill, "History of the German Americans on the Lower Mississippi Delta," Louisiana German-American Resources (LAGAR), Vol.2, "Cultural Resources," Jean Lafitte National Historic Park and Preserve, German American Cultural Center, United States Department of Interior National Park Service, Gretna, La., 2000(on file at German American Cultural Center as Contract #1443CX509098048; Ref. S72 (SERO) c. 2000 Ellen C. Merrell).

James. R. Mills, "San Diego...Where California Began: A Brief History of the Events of Four Centuries," San Diego Historical Society Quarterly, Vol. VI, No. 1, January 1960.

Bertram B. Moore, "Road Development in San Diego County," History of San Diego County, Carl Heilbron, editor, San Diego Press Club, San Diego: 1936.

Lorin L. Morrison, Warner: The Man and the Ranch, Lorin Morrison Publisher, Los Angeles: 1962.

Cecil B. Moyer, Historic Ranchos of San Diego, Copley Books, Union-Tribune Publishing Co., San Diego: 1969.

John F. Nau, "The German People of New Orleans, 1850-1900," Deutsches Haus of new Orleans, nd.

The New Handbook of Texas, Vol. 5, Texas State Historical Association: 1996, article on "Robinson, James W."

Orleans Parish Landmark Commission, plaque at Chartres and Wilkinson Streets.

R.V. Paine Jr., "Monument Will Honor Pioneer Louis Rose," San Diego Sun, March 23, 1934.

Richard F. Pourade, The Glory Years, Union-Tribune Publishing Co., San Deigo, 1964.

Richard F. Pourade, The Silver Dons, Union-Tribune Publishing Co, San Diego: 1966

Samuel Proctor, "Jewish Life in New Orleans, 1718-1860," Louisiana Historical Quarterly, Vol. 40, No. 2, April 1957.

Ronald J. Quinn, editor, "If Only You Could Send Me a Strong and Sound Leg: Letters of A.S. Ensworth to Thomas Whaley, 1862-1865," The Journal of San Diego History, Vol. 43, No. 1, Winter 1997.

Ronald Quinn, "James W. Robinson and the Development of Old Town San Diego," *The Journal of San Diego History*, Vol. 31, No. Fall 1985.

Ethel Zivley Rather, "Recognition of the Republic of Texas by the United States," *The Quarterly of the Texas Historical Association*, Vol. 12, No. 3, January 1910.

Rupert N. Richardson, "Framing the Constitution of the Republic of Texas," The Southwestern Historical Quarterly, Vol. 31, No. 3, January 1928.

Roosevelt Roundups, Theodore Roosevelt Junior High School, San Diego: June 1931.

Leo Rosten, *The Joys of Yiddish*, Simon & Shuster Pocket Books, New York, 1968.

Rough Rider, Theodore Roosevelt Junior High School, San Diego, 1924: Thanksgiving, Christmas; 1925: Fall; 1929: June 21.

San Diego City School Directories, 1912-1942.

San Diego Genealogical Society, Deed Book 1, July 23, 1854.

San Diego Herald: 1851: May 29, Aug. 28, Sept. 4, Sept. 11, 18, 25; Oct. 9, Nov. 27, Dec. 5, 18. 1851: Jan. 17, Feb. 21, 28; March 6, 13; April 17; May 8; Aug 27. 1853: May 21, Aug. 6, 24; Sept. 3, 10, 17; Oct. 1, 29; Dec. 24. 1854: Jan. 28, Feb. 18, 25, April 1, 8; May 27; June 17, 24; Aug. 26; Sept. 2, 9, 16; Nov. 11, 18; Dec. 23. 1855: Jan. 6, Feb. 3, 10, 17; April 38; May 12; June 16; Sept 8, 15, 28; Oct. 13; Nov. 3, 17. 1856: Jan. 19; Feb. 9; May 17, 31; June 7, 28; July 5, 12, 19; Nov. 15, 29; Dec. 6, 14, 20, 27, 1857; Jan. 3, 10, 23; Feb. 21, 28; March 8, 28; April 4; June 13; July 25; Sept. 12, 19; Oct. 10, 17, 24, 31; Nov. 14, 21; Dec. 5. 1858: Jan. 3, Feb. 6, 13, 29; March 13, 20; April 3; Nov. 13. 1859: Jan. 29, Aug. 13. 1860: Jan. 23, March 17.

San Diego Historical Society, document files: "City Land Commission"; "Claims–Land Bounty File"; "Common Council"; "Grand Jury" "Masons"; "Robinson family"; "Robinson, James. W."; "Robinson-Rose House"; "San Diego County Tax Assessment"; "School District #1, Operating Expenses, 1855"; "Squibobiana".

San Diego Historical Society, Online Biographies, http://sandiegohistory.org/bio, "José Antonio Estudillo"; "José María Estudillo"; "Agoston Haraszthy"; "Charles P. Noell"

San Diego Historical Society, "Taxable Property of Louis Rose, 1852-53" (File R2.102, Box 11, Folder 2).

San Diego Sun, Aug. 14, 1885; Dec. 30, 1887; Feb. 13, 1888; March 23, 1934.

San Diego (Daily) Union, 1871: April 3, 14, 19, 27, 28; May 24, June 4, 28; July 4, 19; Aug. 18; Oct. 3, 5. 1872: Jan 16; Feb. 10, 11; March 6, 12, 13, 23, 24, 28; April 17, 18, 25-27; May 1, 2, 8, 10, 21, 26, 30. 1873: July 6, Oct. 9, Nov. 2. 1873: March 20. 1888: Jan. 1.

San Diego (Weekly) Union, 1868: Oct. 10, 17, 24; Nov. 14, 28; Dec. 5, 12. 1869: Jan. 9, 16; April 14, 21; May 5, 19, 26; July 7, 28; Sept 22. 1870: Jan. 13; March 24;

June 9; Sept. 15; Oct. 6, 22; Nov. 1, 24; Dec. 1. 1871: Feb. 23, March 9, 23, 30; April 6, 13, 20; June 1, 22; July 20; Aug 31; Sept. 21; Oct. 10; Nov. 28; Dec. 12. 1873: May 22, June 5, 12, 19, 26; July 10, 24; Aug. 7, 14; Sept 11, 25; Oct. 23. 1874; Jan. 9; Feb. 19; Oct. 29. 1875: Jan. 14, 28; May 20.

Melody Savage, Research Associate, Postal History, United States Postal Service, to Donald H. Harrison, 1994: Sept. 26, Nov. 8.

Thomas Savage, *Documentos para la Historia de California, Papeles Originales Sacados de Varios Achivos Particulares,* Tom. IV, Part 2, University of California, Bancorft Library 1874 (C-B 96 pt 2 phot), circa1867-68.

Henry Schwartz, "Our San Diego History: Louis Rose," *Israel Today*, San Diego, March 3, 1982.

Henry Schwartz, "The Mary Walker Incident: Black Prejudice in San Diego, 1866," *The Journal of San Diego History,* Vol. 19, No. 2 Spring 1973.

Henry Schwartz, "The Uneasy Alliance-Jewish-Anglo Relations in San Diego, 1850-1860," *The Journal of San Diego History,* Vol. 20, No. 3, Summer 1974.

Stanley Schwartz, "A Brief History of Congregation Beth Israel," Congregation Beth Israel, 135th Birthday 1861-1996, San Diego: 1996.

Robert Seager II, *And Tyler Too,* The Library of the Presidents, Easton Press, Norwalk, Conn: 1963.

Charles Sellers, *James K. Polk, Continentalist*, Library of the Presidents, Easton Press, Norwalk, Conn.: 1987 (reprint of 1966 edition by Princeton University Press.)

Bernice Sharlach, *House of Harmony: Concordia Argonaut's First 130 Years,* Judah L. Magnes Memorial Museum, Berkeley, Calif.: 1983

Jack Skiles, *Judge Roy Bean Country,* Texas Tech University Press, 1996.

Brian F. Smith and Associates, "The San Diego of Judge Benjamin I. Hayes: Excerpts from 'The Emigrant Notes, 1850-1875, University of San Diego, Helen K. & James S. Copley Library, 979.498 S643s.

W. Roy Smith, "The Quarrel Between Governor Smith and the Council of the Provisional Government of the Republic," *The Quarterly of the Texas State Historical Association,* Vol. 5., No. 4, April 1902.

William E. Smythe, History of San Diego 1542-1908, Vol. 1 - Old Town, The History Company, San Diego: 1908.

Norton B. Stern, notes on file at Magnes Museum of Berkeley concerning Myron Lustig, "Louis Rose, First Jew of San Diego, Patriarch of Old Town," typescript, and other Rose data.

Norton B. Stern, "The Franklin Brothers of San Diego," *The Journal of San Diego History,* Vol. 21, No. 3, Summer 1975.

Norton B. Stern and William M. Kramer, "The Rose of San Diego," *Old Town, New Town: An Enjoyment of San Diego History,* William M. Kramer, editor; Stanley and Laurel Schwartz, associate editors, Western States Jewish History Association, Los Angeles: 1994

Pamela Tamplain, "Philip Crosthwaite, San Diego Pioneer and Public Servant," *The Journal of San Diego History*, Vol. 21, No. 3: 1975.

Twentieth Century Progress, Roosevelt Junior High School, San Diego: June 1937

William Uberti, "Olilver S. Witherby: First State District Judge in San Diego," *The Journal of San Diego History*, Vol. 23, No. 2: Spring 1978.

Julia Nott Waugh, *Castro-ville and Henry Castro, Empresario*, Castro Colonies Heritage Association: 1986 reprint of the 1934 edition, page 58 (copy on file in the Castroville, Texas, public library).

Cyrus Field Willard, "Freemasonry in San Diego," The San Diego Times, no date, "Masons" document file, San Diego Historical Society.

Orion Zink, "Louis Rose Grave Found," *The Master Mason*, December 1968, Vol. VII, No. 12.

Orion Zink and Irvin Shimmin, "The Story of San Diego Lodge No. 35, F. & A.M.," *The Master Mason*, 125th anniversary edition: 1976.

Orion Zink (Lodge No. 35 historian) to George Robinson Jr., July 9, 1948, San Diego Lodge #35, F. & A.M., "James Robinson" file.

W.P. Zuber, "The Escape of Rose from the Alamo," *The Quarterly of the Texas State Historical Association*, Vol. 5, No. 1, July 1901.

INDEX

Editor's Note: Researchers desiring an MS Word document containing a more extensive index of this book are invited to contact author Donald H. Harrison at sdheritage@cox.net. Please indicate the subject of your research in your email.

Key: (af) afterword   (en) endnotes

Sunbelt Publications'
SAN DIEGO BOOKSHELF